SUEZ DECONSTRUCTED

DECONSTRUCTED

An Interactive Study
in Crisis, War, and Peacemaking

PHILIP ZELIKOW AND **ERNEST R. MAY**

AND THE HARVARD SUEZ TEAM

BROOKINGS INSTITUTION PRESS

Washington, D.C.

The Brookings Institution is a private nonprofit organization devoted to research, education, and publication on important issues of domestic and foreign policy. Its principal purpose is to bring the highest quality independent research and analysis to bear on current and emerging policy problems. Interpretations or conclusions in Brookings publications should be understood to be solely those of the authors.

Permission to use the quotation from James Salter's *All That Is* is kindly granted by Penguin Random House.

Library of Congress Cataloging-in-Publication data are available.

ISBN 978-0-8157-3572-4 (cloth: alk. paper)
ISBN 978-0-8157-3573-1 (ebook)

9 8 7 6 5 4 3 2 1

Typeset in Adobe Caslon Pro

Composition by Elliott Beard

Contents

PART ONE

What to Do about Nasser's Egypt

PART TWO

What to Do about the Crisis

PART THREE
What to Do about the War

SUEZ DECONSTRUCTED

INTRODUCTION

Three Kinds of Judgments

PHILIP ZELIKOW

One way humans evolve is that someone solves a problem, maybe learns something, and maybe tells others. In the skills of statecraft, humans have not evolved very much.

There are many studies of statecraft. But few of them help readers understand how to do it, so the skills do not necessarily advance.

Don't look to political scientists to help. They have better things to do. Policymakers are to political scientists as insects are to entomologists. Only some of the more eccentric entomologists write how-to manuals to guide the ants.

Histories, including memoirs, can be more useful. Sometimes these stories are even reasonably accurate. But knowing exactly why a bridge fell down does not make you a civil engineer.

Nor will readers get much practical help from stories that end in thin parables, in axioms that do not seem to amount to much more than a warning: Be careful. Consult with others. Don't build on a mud pile. And don't appease Hitler.

This book takes a different approach. It is historical, and it may help with understanding the history of a famous episode. But readers can treat it as a set of exercises in problem solving.

It is probably fortunate that so few people get much experience in masterminding solutions to giant international crises, especially while they are in school or early in their careers. Those who do eventually get this experience usually come by it the hard way. This book tries to convey some of that experience as a sort of simulator that can help condition readers just a little more before they step up to even a very little crisis.

Experience alone is no answer. One of the main figures in this book is the British prime minister, Anthony Eden. In 1956 it would have been hard to find any leader with more crisis experience than Eden. Before his 1955 ascent to leadership of the British government, Eden had already served three different stints as his country's foreign minister during the previous twenty years and with great distinction. He had managed tough negotiations and many crises. He could be witty, insightful, and graceful. As a young man he had served ably through some of the worst trench fighting in World War I. Articulate in his native English, Eden was fluent in French and could also get by in German, Persian, and Arabic. Yet, as the events of 1956 would show, even vast experience and all these gifts were no substitute for methodical statecraft.

When it comes to statecraft, the Suez crisis of 1956 can offer a master class. Six countries had major roles, and all had significantly different frames for seeing the situation. Two were superpowers; two were middleweight powers; and two were relatively fragile regional powers. Yet from one stage to the next, it could be hard to tell which of these powers were really driving the action. As in any good ensemble production, all the actors had pivotal parts to play.

This book has an unusual structure that may help readers join in the exercise of vicarious problem solving.

First, we cut the story up into *three distinct phases*. This is lifelike. Most large problems of statecraft are not one-act plays. People may think they have one problem at the start; then later it turns into a different problem, and then another.

To the extent anyone knows about the Suez crisis today, it is a story that gets simplified about like this: Egypt's leader took over the Suez Canal. Other countries started a war to stop him. The United States and others made *them* stop. These are three results. He did this. They went to war. Others stopped the war. Each of these results implies its own story, a story to answer this question: Why?

Each story has its own assessments, choices, and interactions. All have roads that were not taken, maybe not even adequately considered. All the players make moves. We want the readers, like the officials, to be able to reset, recalibrate, and rethink.

The second way we structure this story is to go through each episode as it was seen from the *perspective of each of the six major countries*. This compartmentation may seem awkward on the surface, because we are so used to stories being told smoothly from one narrative perspective, or perhaps by an omniscient narrator. The compartmentation here is more lifelike. The reader is forced for just a little while into seeing the world through that one country's eyes. Then, by shifting the perspective again and again, questions arise. How well do these countries, some of them friends and allies, really understand each other? Could they reasonably have done better? How?

As the book progresses, the exercises accumulate. Each part tends to focus on one basic problem. But in each part the reader, going through six countries, has six chances to reflect: What should *this* country do?

Think hard. Do not settle for instinctive reactions. Remember that in every one of these countries, and in every one of the three phases, leaders are playing the problem at three different levels:

- How does this figure in the overall global Cold War between East and West?

- How does this figure in the conflicts in a deeply divided Middle East region, with some Muslim states on one side and some Muslim states on the other?

- How does this figure in the conflict between the Arabs and the Israelis over what was then called "the Palestine question"?

That is not all. In every one of these countries, and in every one of the three phases, leaders are mindful of how their moves will play at home. And "home" does not mean just mass politics. It also means the politics of personal reputation or institutional stature among the insiders of their government. Decision-makers are not necessarily slaves to all these external and internal factors. But they do take them into account—consciously or semiconsciously.

The structure of the book may also help readers sense how difficult and uncertain are the situations that produce policy choices. Decision-makers typically have little knowledge that is sure. They usually act on the basis of shaky presumptions about what is really going on. They make choices based on even shakier guesswork about the consequences of alternative courses of action. And if, intimidated by what they don't know, they want to throw up their hands and just sit back—well, a refusal to act is also a choice, sometimes a momentous one.

As you come to better understand the uncertainty and cross-purposes, practical as well as moral, you may get at some real insights. These might be lessons about what should have happened.

More often, more usefully, they may be lessons about what questions could have been asked and what staff work could have helped. Yes, even amid the inevitable fog and pressures to make some kind of decision, more and better analysis is often possible. By studying historical episodes in this way, one can build a personal sense, even a checklist, of matters to consider. The experience also may help readers get more accustomed to the challenge of how to winnow important information from all the noise of detail.

All assessments, or appreciations, of a situation are a compound of three kinds of judgments. These are value judgments ("What do we care about? Or what difference does it make?"), reality judgments ("What is going on?"), and action judgments ("What can we do about it?").

At this stage of just sizing up the situation, the action judgments may be pretty simple. Either people think "we" can do a lot or "we" can do only a little. That sense of what "we" can do interacts instantly with the other questions about reality or value. People tend to care less about, and pay less attention to, what is going on if they think there is little they can do about it. And vice versa.

I cannot stress strongly enough that these three judgment ingredients—value, reality, and action—are an interactive compound. Ernest May and I frequently referred to this as the "Vickers triangle," because we borrowed the cognitive structure of this approach from a classic work by an extraordinary British lawyer and public official, Sir Geoffrey Vickers.[1]

Values . . . reality . . . action judgments. It seems like a simple checklist in figuring out how "we" or "they" size up a situation. As this story will reveal, making good judgments about reality or values is more complex than it seems.

For now, just note that not only do these judgments vary among people or places, even within one person the elements of assessments are not fixed. They change rapidly and sometimes unpredictably.

That this is a dynamic, not a static, image is also critically important. Both intelligence analysts and decision-makers often make the mistake of assuming that one or another set of judgments is fixed.

And then, since they interact, when one element changes (for instance, because some news arrives, a fresh reality judgment), the other elements can change, too, and with them, the whole appreciative compound. The compound keeps on evolving until, at some point, the appreciation is complete enough for someone to take some action. So, as they engage the situations, phase by phase, readers might start by reminding themselves of at least three questions.

First is the doctor's question: **What seems to be the problem?** This is the value judgment.

The answer may seem obvious, at first. For instance, in Part One of this book, all the countries except Egypt have a common problem: What to do about Nasser's Egypt?

In 1956 Egypt was ruled by a former military officer who had recently joined in overthrowing Egypt's corrupt and indolent king. Out of that group of officers, one had clearly emerged: the youthful, charismatic Gamal Abdel Nasser. He had a lot to say. He took bold actions. He drew plenty of attention.

For all the countries except Egypt, just what is their problem with Nasser's Egypt? How important do they think this problem is? Could it, maybe, be an opportunity? Are there important differences in how some of the actors assess the problem even within the same government?

Second is the reporter's question: **What's going on?** These are the reality judgments.

Third is the engineer's question: **What can we do?** Engineers are trained to practice careful and methodical ways of breaking down and analyzing possible actions, whether it is wiring a building or constructing a dam or designing an airplane engine. Engineers can work effectively in large teams because they often share approaches and a vocabulary that comes from such training.

Statecraft, unlike engineering, has no such established methods, no such standard approaches, and no such common vocabulary. One method I have advocated takes a swing at this. Combined with the judgments about reality and value, a policy design can break down the action judgment into key elements for analysis. A few principal ones are operational objectives, strategic theories of action, and blueprints/choreographies of required actions.[2]

Operational objectives are concrete statements of what is to be attained. They should be concrete enough that the doer knows if they have been accomplished. Amorphous goals like "promote peace" or "show strength" are not operational objectives.

For instance, in this case some governments wonder about military action against Egypt. Military action to accomplish what, exactly? Is it intervention just to occupy the Suez Canal? Or should the intervention overthrow and replace the Egyptian government? Should it occupy the Sinai Desert region (an Israeli option) or just a part of it? Should it scatter and degrade Egypt's military capability?

Suppose one prefers diplomacy. Again, diplomacy that, if successful, would accomplish just what?

A *strategic theory of action* is a proposition about how to connect ends and means. A diplomatic strategy might theorize, for instance, that the United States or the United Nations can bring enough nations together in concert to impose a settlement (with the desired operational objectives) on one side or another.

A *blueprint/choreography of required actions* is a plan for how to do what is to be done. But with whom? With what required instruments? It can be regarded as a blueprint or as an elaborate choreography of dance moves. Those diplomats make this move here; those ships make that move there.

The Suez crisis exhibits several such designs, some quite elaborate. Allowing for the fog and the pressures, how well considered are these designs?

By the way, once policymakers undertake the sort of analysis suggested here to flesh out their action judgments, they may find they have cycled right back to the first question: What seems to be the problem? For example, specifying an operational objective is really a concrete way of defining success. Forced to clarify just exactly what would "solve" one's problem, the problem itself is redefined.

Outsiders, both those at the time and those looking back later, will do best at understanding those judgments that are apparent to them and that remain stable over some period of time. They will do least well in grasping—or even being aware of—those judgments that are secretive and more volatile, changing from one month to the next.[3]

A rough matrix can depict the point this way:

	Apparent to outsiders?	*Stable?*
Value judgments	High	High
Reality judgments	Medium	Medium
Action judgments	Low	Low

Naturally, then, citizens at the time and the historians who come later both tend to focus more on the value judgments. They argue about what people care about, or should care about. But since they tend to see only one ingredient in the compound, only one vector of the triangle, their understanding of choices goes downhill from there.

Even the supposedly apparent and stable value judgments may be the least insightful part of the triangle to track. That is because there are so many potential values lying dormant, ready to be evoked.

In this case, for instance, the British have big concerns about the Suez Canal, about the security of their supplies of oil from the Middle East, about the stature of British power and the British Commonwealth, and more. But depending on what happens, the leaders also care about domestic public and parliamentary opinion, threats to the stability of their currency, Cold War dangers of confrontation with the Soviet Union, and the need for cooperating with Americans on other issues. One or another latent value can be lit up, activated, by the interaction with the news (reality judgments) or by encouraging or dispiriting beliefs about action options, from one day to the next.

People in positions of responsibility are besieged by constant evocations of every value. Also, rivers of information about the reality around them flow by. Thus, action judgments often are the vital ingredients that help them sort.

Yet action judgments are the hardest ones for nonspecialists to understand and follow. They can be hard for outsiders to grasp even if outsiders have access to the relevant information about the actions being considered—information they rarely have.

Going through the country stories, episode by episode, these three questions can help readers appraise the six collections of individuals and institutions we call governments. Remember these questions, too, as you also ask yourself, "What would I do if I had been a character in this story, with the reasonably available information?"

Each of the three questions calls for wearing bifocals, metaphorically, anyway. Because in each question it is best to see both "our" nearby judgments and also the quite different judgments being made by the faraway "they."

Consider, for instance, the tragic case of American judgments about Iraq in 2002 and 2003. After overrunning much of Saddam Hussein's Iraq in the spring of 2003, the Americans expected to find stocks of weapons of mass destruction the dictator had been hiding. They did not find what they were looking for. The Americans found this hard to understand.

One of their puzzles was this: If the dictator did not have all these weapons, why didn't he say so and prove so? That way he would have avoided the invasion and his eventual capture and execution.

Only in retrospect did analysts recognize that, perhaps, the dictator had not been thinking so much about how he could reassure Washington. Instead he had been thinking more about running a bluff, maybe reserving the option of a future program. He had been thinking more about how to maintain a certain

image at home and about how to discourage his long-standing enemies in Teheran. The American analysts could see their own perspective, the "we." They
had more trouble seeing the faraway "they."[4]

Ernest May and I first developed this Suez project during the mid-1990s. Back
then we both were teaching at Harvard University. For seed money, May ap-
plied funds from an unclassified Harvard research and teaching project on assessing other governments that was underwritten by the Central Intelligence
Agency. The project was built up with support from the Smith Richardson
Foundation. We recruited and supported an outstanding team of scholars to
help, the authors who helped with the country chapters in this book.

With draft studies in hand, we asked former participants in the crisis and
other leading scholars to react to the drafts our team had prepared. First they
met at a conference at Ditchley House in England. The drafts were revised.
Those drafts were then critiqued again at another, similar conference on the
other side of the Atlantic, this one hosted by the American Academy for the
Advancement of Science in Cambridge, Massachusetts.

May and I used the Suez studies in our teaching at Harvard. May expected
to finalize this book, but he and I were overtaken by other projects and duties,
some in the U.S. government, including the work both of us did with the 9/11
Commission. Then, May passed away in 2009.

I have, at last, been able to return to the project and bring it to fruition,
thanks to the invaluable aid of almost all of the original and very dedicated
country study scholars. Although the editorial prose in the current book is
mine, most of the original inspiration came from Ernest.

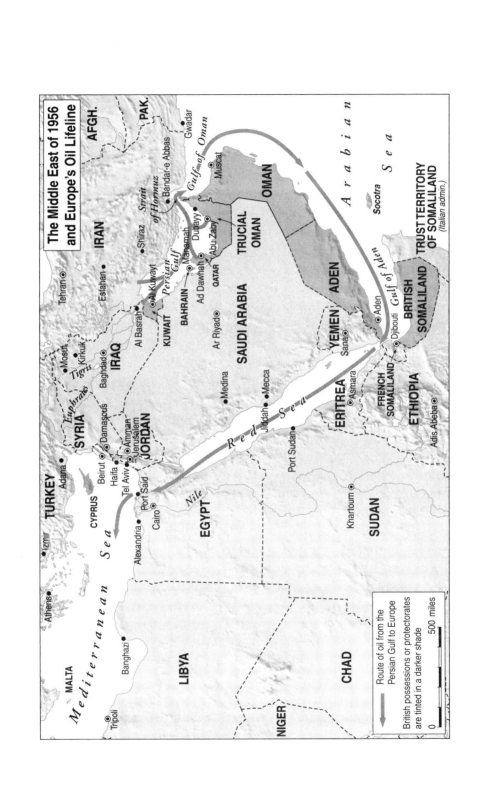

The Middle East of 1956
and Europe's Oil Lifeline

TURKEY
Izmir
Athens
MALTA
Mediterranean Sea
Tripoli
Banghazi
Alexandria
Cairo
EGYPT
Nile
LIBYA
CHAD
NIGER
CYPRUS
Adana
Beirut
Haifa
Tel Aviv
Port Said
SYRIA
Damascos
Amman
Jerusalem
JORDAN
IRAQ
Mosul
Kirkuk
Baghdad
Tigris
Euphrates
IRAN
Tehran
Esfahan
Shiraz
Bandar-e Abbas
Strait of Hormuz
Gwadar
PAK.
AFGH.
Gulf of Oman
Muscat
OMAN
TRUCIAL OMAN
Dubayy
Abu Zaby
Persian Gulf
Manamah
BAHRAIN
QATAR
Ad Dawhah
Al Kuwayt
KUWAIT
Al Basrah
Ar Riyad
SAUDI ARABIA
Medina
Mecca
Jiddah
Red Sea
Port Sudan
Khartoum
SUDAN
ERITREA
Asmara
YEMEN
Sana
ADEN
Aden
Gulf of Aden
Djibouti
FRENCH SOMALILAND
BRITISH SOMALILAND
ETHIOPIA
Adis Abeba
TRUST TERRITORY OF SOMALILAND
(Italian admin.)
A r a b i a n   S e a
Socotra

Route of oil from the
Persian Gulf to Europe

British possessions or protectorates
are tinted in a darker shade

0   500 miles

Israel and Neighboring States, 1956

Mediterranean Sea

Beirut ◉
LEBANON
Sidon ●
Damascus ◉
Tyre ●
SYRIA
Golan
Haifa ●
Tiberias ●
Sea of Galiliee
Jordan
Nablus ●
West Bank
Tel Aviv ●
◉ Amman
◉ Jerusalem
Gaza ●
Hebron ●
Gaza Strip
Beer Sheva ●
Damietta ●
● Port Said
ISRAEL
Dead Sea
Suez Canal
Ismailiya ●
Negev
J O R D A N
Great Bitter Lake
◉ Cairo
Suez ●
E G Y P T
Sinai
Nile
Eilat ● ● Al Aqbah
Gulf of Suez
Gulf of Aqaba
SAUDI ARABIA
Straits of Tiran
● Sharm el Sheikh
Red Sea

0   50   100 miles

The World of 1956

PHILIP ZELIKOW

POSTWAR

They were a wartime generation. All the adults had lived through convulsive, cataclysmic wars, some more than one. When men met, a usual question— sometimes unspoken—was "What did you do in the war?" To such men, to such a generation, war and crisis were no faraway abstraction.

Some people liked to talk about their war. Many did not. They would rather talk baseball, or rugby, or about the kidnapping that was on the front page of the morning paper, or which plant was hiring, or who was getting married or divorced. But it was a generation that knew about war.

A few people had televisions, especially in places like the United States, where you could get some news through the little, shaky black-and-white pictures. Mainly people listened to the radio or, if they were readers, they read newspapers and magazines. There were more of both back then. A worldly person might get at least a couple of newspapers every day, sometimes in both morning and evening editions, and subscribe to at least two or three magazines or newsweeklies, like Britain's *Observer* or *The Economist* or America's *Time* or *Newsweek* or, in France, the relatively new *L'Express*.

The local newspapers would put local news up front, but national and international news always had a big place. To a people wary about war, conscious of military preparations around them, there was plenty of interest in the details of world affairs and diplomacy. *Time* magazine, a mass circulation weekly, would routinely report on which new ambassadors had been assigned where, or on reshuffles of bureau chiefs in the State Department.

Meetings of statesmen were covered meticulously, their remarks and tone mused over. The new United Nations organization, meeting at its grand new headquarters in New York City, was a focus of constant interest, the great theater for the world's arguments, with much attention to its debates and votes and to the peacemaking work of its Danish secretary-general, Dag Hammarskjöld.

Not so long ago, in 1950 and 1951, for a time it had looked like the war in Korea was the opening skirmish of a new global war, World War III. That fear had since subsided a bit. But in the last few years everyone had started learning about something called a hydrogen bomb, a bomb a thousand times more powerful than the hitherto unimaginable atomic bomb. People everywhere wondered where it all might lead. The armed forces were objects of salutes and jokes but above all were familiar; back then all these countries had draft obligations for national service.

The scars of war were still fresh. Some scars were physical; veterans maimed on the outside or inside. Some were collective and psychic. Most Jews in the new state of Israel had fled from somewhere else, from the Nazi mass murders across Europe, and they mourned family members who had not made it.

Egypt's leader, a man still often called "Colonel" Nasser, had been a young major who had fought the Israelis in their 1948–49 war of creation and survival. Nasser carried his own scars from that war, the war Arabs just called "the Disaster." He had felt betrayed by his country's weak, corrupt leaders, men he had now pushed out and replaced. Hundreds of thousands of displaced Palestinians crowded refugee camps near Israel.

In France, as in the Soviet Union, much of the landscape was still marked by the ruins of shelled towns, manmade craters and dumped bridges. In 1956 there were still many, many impromptu gravesites across the countryside. There, farmers still scavenged the litter of thousands of discarded or burned-out war machines for parts to build makeshift tractors and wagons.

"England had won the war," the novelist James Salter remembered, but what a victory.

There was hardly a family, high or low, that had not been part of it—through the early disasters when the country had been unprepared, the far-off sinking of warships thought to be indestructible, symbols and pride of a nation, the absolute catastrophe of the army sent to France in 1940. . . . And still the task remained, the seemingly endless struggle, the unimaginable scale of it, the desert war . . . the reeling war in the air, great walls collapsing in darkness, entire cities on fire, calamitous news from the Far East, casualty lists, the readying for invasion, the battles without end.

And England had won. Its enemies stumbled through ruins, went hungry. What was left of their cities smelled of death and sewage, the women sold themselves for cigarettes, but it was England, like a battered fighter somehow left standing, that had paid too much. A decade later there was still food rationing and it was difficult to travel, currency could not be taken out of the country. The bells that had tolled the hour of victory were long silent. The ways of before the war were unrecoverable. Putting out a cigarette after lunch, a publisher had said calmly, "England is finished."[1]

A DIVIDED WORLD

To a woman or man of the twenty-first century, the "Cold War" is a bygone chapter of history. It was a time when there was a long confrontation between the noncommunist world, on one side, led by the United States of America, and the communist world on the other, headed by a Russian-led domain that then was called the Soviet Union (short for Union of Soviet Socialist Republics). Looking back, the Cold War may seem like a frozen standoff, enemies glowering at each other through decades of stalemate.

In the mid-1950s the Cold War did not seem frozen or stalemated. It seemed more like a sickening roller-coaster ride of maneuvers and new threats. Fears of war lurked around each turn.

Adults of 1956 were used to arguments about communism and anticommunism. That had been a staple of political back-and-forth at least since the 1920s. By the end of the 1940s, Europe was quite physically divided by what the former British prime minister Winston Churchill had memorably called an "Iron Curtain." On their side, the communists seemed to get stronger. The Chinese communists, supported by the Soviets, had won the civil war to control the world's most populous state. China and the Soviet Union were formally allied.

The shock to "the West" of the loss of China in 1949 had been followed by the further shock, later that year, that the Soviet Union had tested an atomic bomb and now had that superweapon. Then, in 1950, North Korea invaded South Korea, with Soviet and Chinese support. The United States and contingents of several European and Asian countries joined the South Koreans.

The Chinese intervened massively to turn the tide during the autumn of 1950, and World War III seemed at the doorstep. The United States declared a national emergency and tripled its defense budget practically overnight. There was much talk of possible war with China, possible use of atomic bombs, and possible global war.

The North Atlantic Alliance became an organization, called NATO, in charge of a U.S.-led multinational force deployed in the middle of divided Germany. NATO decided to include a new army made up of the formerly disarmed West Germans. The Soviets created their opposing alliance, the Warsaw Pact, to face off against NATO.

The United States and Britain also thought of creating a NATO-equivalent alliance in the Middle East. Fearing the Soviets might overrun part of Europe, and recalling the role of North Africa when Nazi Germany and its allies had dominated part of Europe, the Americans and British thought this alliance might be anchored in Egypt, using the large British base then still there. Various ideas were tried out between 1950 and 1952. Back then the Americans assumed the British would remain dominant in the region, a region where Soviet influence was weak.

During 1951 the front in Korea was stabilized. The danger of imminent global war seemed to recede momentarily. Another war flared in Asia, this one a revolutionary war—supported by the Chinese—to throw the French out of their possessions in Indochina (present-day Vietnam, Laos, and Cambodia). Despite getting money and equipment from America, the French were being defeated.

Again, in 1954, there was talk of direct U.S. military intervention, of possible use of atomic bombs. That, too, receded, but the French were ejected and two Vietnamese states were created, a communist one in the north and a non-communist one in the south.

The politics of this Cold War swung back and forth like a carnival ride. In 1953 the longtime Soviet dictator Josef Stalin died and tensions seemed to ease. A cease-fire was arranged in Korea, though no peace treaty.

Then in 1954 the open testing of a vastly more destructive kind of super-weapon, the new hydrogen bombs, introduced a whole new level of fear. Americans openly debated whether they should launch a preventive war before the

Soviets could gain the power to destroy their country. The communists were on the march in Indochina. They seemed to slowly be sweeping most of the Eurasian landmass their way, piece by piece, with no obvious way to stop them.

Yet later in 1954 there had been that diplomacy to arrange a political settlement in Indochina. In 1955 the postwar "Big Four"—the United States, the Soviet Union, Britain, and France—which had occupied Austria at the end of the war, signed another deal. They withdrew from Austria, with an agreement that it would be neutral. After loud political quarrels, Western Europe seemed to be uniting behind NATO, including the German role, all headquartered in Paris. The United States organized a Southeast Asia Treaty Organization, too.

The "H-Bomb" danger stimulated new ideas to talk about disarmament treaties. In July 1955 the Big Four—the leaders of the United States, the Soviet Union, Britain, and France—got together for a long set of summit meetings in Geneva. They seemed to be talking constructively about their differences.

The image of a Big Four was a hangover from World War II. France did not seem so big. Memories of the defeat in 1940 were still fresh, underscored by the recent loss of Indochina and new unrest in French Algeria. One government seemed to quickly succeed another in a Fourth Republic with five or six leading political parties.

Yet this image of French weakness could be deceiving. Though the Indochina task had proved impossible, the war and postwar trauma had burned off some of the older France. Elections early in 1956 brought to power a government dominated by men who had been heroes of resistance during the war, democratic socialists in a centrist coalition. There was a determined, ruthless core in the France of the 1950s, seasoned by combat, powering an astonishing economic recovery, reimagining the future of Europe, and wielding a rebuilt, modernizing, and highly competent military.

The British Empire was now a British Commonwealth. The great imperial pillar and bulwark of India was gone. But Britain still seemed big. The image and habits bred in generation after generation of global power did not fade so quickly. Sustaining that image, there was still a far-flung network of bases and influence, especially in Africa and the Middle East.

Yet that image of British power also could deceive.

By 1954 the Middle East was still considered a crucial region for the Cold War, but the old way of thinking about it had completely changed. The old plans to try to create some NATO-equivalent alliance anchored in Egypt had been junked. The Egyptians had rejected the idea out of hand. They were much more worried about British influence than about Russians.

By 1954 American attitudes about Cold War strategy had changed, too. They were no longer so worried about Soviet armies overrunning Europe. They were more interested in where they might put bases from which they could deter an attack with nuclear-armed bombers. In the mid-1950s these bombers did not have intercontinental range; they could not fly missions across oceans. And there were no intercontinental missiles yet, either. To be able to get at Russian targets, the Americans needed to put their bombers in Europe or the Middle East. By 1955 and 1956 the bombers and their refueling tankers were using bases in places like England or Morocco. The Americans were thinking more and more about anchoring their deterrent bases in countries that were closer to the Soviet Union, such as Turkey and Pakistan.[2]

Another reason the Americans cared about the Middle East was because they were worried about the security of Middle Eastern oil supplies. America was then largely self-sufficient in oil. They worried because they thought their own oil reserves were limited, and Western Europe got 90 percent of its oil from the Middle East. Europe's oil came mainly from Saudi Arabia, Kuwait (then a British protectorate), and Iraq. In 1956 American military planners wrote: "The uninterrupted supply of oil from the Middle East is so vital that nothing should be allowed to threaten its continuance."[3]

By the mid-1950s, Americans no longer assumed Britain was in charge in the Middle East. Many Arab nationalists were so hostile toward Britain that the British often seemed to be a liability—in the American view of Cold War politics. The British views of such American feelings can be imagined.

Meanwhile, as 1954 passed into 1955, the new leaders of the Soviet Union were much more interested in the Arab world. It was a region Stalin had mostly ignored. Yet it was a region that seemed ready for socialist, anti-Western revolutions.

The year 1955 was a good one for the image of the Soviet Union. The Soviet military seemed mighty. The Soviet alliance with China was still close. The Soviet socialist model of development was much admired, and the new Soviet leaders seemed less menacing, more reasonable.

At the beginning of 1956 the Soviet Communist Party leader Nikita Khrushchev went even further. The world soon knew that in February he had delivered a "secret" speech to communist leaders from around the world in which he denounced the crimes and excesses of Stalin. Khrushchev called for a different and more decentralized style of socialist leadership. By the end of 1956 the ripples from that splash would touch every communist country.

The prestige and stature of the United States of America remained immense. The president was Dwight Eisenhower, the man who had commanded the victorious Allied armies in western Europe. No country had emerged more triumphantly from the war. Long admired or mocked as a global symbol of consumerism, America had now displayed its power, prowess, and ideals on an equally global scale.

As hopes for H-bomb disarmament quickly faded, the year 1955 brought a growing sense that the Cold War had entered an entirely new stage. Global war seemed less imminent. Instead, the war was becoming a political and economic contest to win over, bribe, or coerce the still "uncommitted" countries and peoples of Asia, Africa, Latin America, and the Middle East.

Those countries were stepping forward on the world stage. In April 1955 the newly created country of Indonesia hosted, in the city of Bandung, a conference of twenty-five Afro-Asian nations, cosponsored by the new countries of Burma, Ceylon, Pakistan, and India. India and its then world-famous prime minister, Jawaharlal Nehru, played an especially important role. Egypt's new leader, Gamal Abdel Nasser, was a prominent participant.

The conference was a coming-out party. It announced there was a large group of new players in world politics. These countries called themselves neutral, with interests of their own, greatly worried about the danger of global war. They were anticolonial. They claimed—as Indonesian president Sukarno put it—that they had "no axe of power politics to grind."[4]

In the UN, too, the new members now seemed to hold the balance. By the end of 1956 the original fifty-one UN members had become eighty. The new leaders of the Soviet Union seemed to grasp this new trend and moved energetically to take advantage of it. At the end of 1955 Soviet party leader Khrushchev and the premier, Nikolai Bulganin, took a monthlong tour to India, Burma, and Afghanistan. "Therewith," experts observed, "began the struggle for the hearts and souls, and also for the more healthy material appetites, of the Asian peoples."[5]

By the first half of 1956 it seemed the neutralists were represented by a kind of triumvirate, meeting and conferring about common positions to represent the "uncommitted" balance. There was India's Nehru; there was the independent communist ruler of Yugoslavia, Josip Broz Tito; and there was Egypt's Nasser.

A DIVIDED MIDDLE EAST

In older days, while the Ottoman Empire still held at least nominal control over much of Southwest Asia, Southeast Europe, and North Africa, Europeans would refer to the problems of the Ottoman domains as "Eastern" questions. Or they would use the phrase "Near East," to distinguish its issues from those of the other side of Eurasia, out there in the "Far East."

By the 1950s, a generation after the Ottoman Empire had disintegrated, the term "Middle East" had come into vogue. It meant all of Southwest Asia south of the Soviet Union and west of Pakistan and, crossing into Africa, at least Egypt.

The Middle East has a distinct historical identity. For practically all of recorded human history it was the seat of two sets of civilizations. One of these was centered on the Nile River and the Red Sea. The other was centered on the Fertile Crescent of the Euphrates and Tigris Rivers, the eastern edge of the Mediterranean, and the Persian (or Arabian) Gulf.

The Middle East is the historical center of all three of the world's best-known religious traditions: Judaism, Christianity, and Islam. The region had always been a natural hub of the Eastern Hemisphere, a crossing point between Europe, Asia, and Africa. Even before the Suez Canal was opened in 1869, cargo and passengers landed at one end and were transported across the isthmus to the other.

No region had been more of a battleground of ancient and modern empires—Egyptians versus Assyrians, Greeks versus Persians, Romans versus Parthians, down to the more recent British versus Ottomans. In World War II it was a battlefield of British imperial allies fighting a German-Italian coalition (with the French briefly caught in the crossfire).

As 1955 turned to 1956 the Middle East was a region that was divided and insecure. The two magnetic poles were Baghdad versus Cairo. Baghdad was the seat of a conservative nationalist pro-British monarchy and its friends, on the Fertile Crescent. Cairo had the charismatic, radical military dictatorship on the Nile, calling for pan-Arab unity and suspicious of any British influence.

Study a map of the Middle East. Almost any map will do that runs from Iran to Egypt. The borders have changed in only a few places after all this time.

In 1956 this region was not so thickly populated as now—probably fewer than a hundred million people from Iran to Egypt. Most lived near water, either one of the great rivers or a seacoast. Throughout the large Arabian Peninsula, most of the people then lived within fifty miles of the coast.

In 1956 every state located between the older states of Egypt and Iran was only about one generation old or less. None felt safe. None had powerful armies, navies, or air forces. All were wary of threats, internal and external. All were looking for friends, eager for revenue or foreign aid, anxious to buy modern arms, yet wary of losing their independence.

These new states were the first big factor shaping the modern Middle East. The other big new factor, also only about a generation old, was the development of oil as a Middle Eastern resource and European dependence on it.

Oil was hugely important, but most of the Middle East did not have much of it. In 1956 the outlets for this Middle Eastern oil were, as they are today, scattered around the edges of the Persian Gulf. The older pipelines that carried oil from Iraq or the Gulf region to Mediterranean outlets in the new state of Israel or the new state of Lebanon were cut or insecure. So, to any European statesman, the oil lifeline seemed to run by sea: Persian Gulf, Arabian Sea, Red Sea, Suez Canal, then into the Mediterranean.

Again, the Suez Canal stood out. The canal had been built during the 1860s under French management in partnership with Egypt. The canal itself was Egyptian, guaranteed as an open waterway under an international treaty, the Convention of Constantinople, signed in 1888. But the canal was operated by an unusual private firm, the Universal Suez Canal Company, headquartered in Paris. The British had bought a large minority of the stock from a bankrupt Egyptian government in 1875. The company had a concession to operate the canal until 1968. Surrounding the canal, loaded with infrastructure such as railroads, harbors, and warehouses, was the Canal Zone—an elaborate British base operated under an Anglo-Egyptian treaty signed in 1936.

Britain had taken care to control or influence every part of the vital oil lifeline. A major base at Aden controlled the best natural harbor at the entrance to the Red Sea, midway between the canal and the oil terminals of the Persian Gulf or the eastern ports of India. British protectorates or partners (such as Iraq) were well placed on the southern and eastern shores of the Persian Gulf.

Except in Saudi Arabia, where the oil was being developed in a mutually profitable arrangement between the Saudis and American companies, well-connected British firms had dominated the development, transport, and marketing of Middle Eastern oil. This arrangement allowed the British to pay for the oil with their own currency and not have to use scarce dollars. Such favorable arrangements for Britain held sway in Iran, Iraq, and Kuwait, and the beginnings of oil development in the "trucial" Gulf principalities (then also British protectorates, today's United Arab Emirates).

To get a sense for the region's divisions and arguments in the mid-1950s, take a tour with that map of the Middle East and start with Iraq.

Iraq's monarch, a son of the venerable Hashemite dynasty out of the Arabian Peninsula, had been installed by the British in 1921. The country had just been created out of Ottoman imperial pieces. It had a tiny ruling elite. Under the monarch, various would-be dictators vied for power, and politics was dotted by coups and assassinations. The British usually were content to work with whoever came out on top.

The British were not so content during World War II, when the Germans made a serious play to put their man in charge and the British beat them off. After the war, a network of Soviet agents was uncovered, and that drove Iraq's rulers still closer to the British. In 1948 Iraq joined in the failed war to destroy Israel.

The British were happy with the pro-British prime minister, Nuri el-Said. Nuri worked closely with Turkish allies to organize the Middle East more strongly under a Fertile Crescent lead. During World War II Nuri had developed a plan, agreed to by the British, to create a Greater Syria incorporating Syria, Lebanon, and Palestine. This Greater Syria might then be linked in an Arab Union with his Iraq.[6]

That Arab Union plan failed, and in 1955 Nuri's strategy was different. Working with the Turks, he signed an anti-Soviet defense pact—the Baghdad Pact, which joined Iraq with Pakistan to the west and Turkey to the north. Britain joined, too, as the pact's core Western partner.

With this Baghdad Pact of 1955, Iraq seemed to stake out a position as the great opponent of Nasser and other so-called radicals in the Arab world. The pact thus "shattered the Arab system" of formal unity. There would now be "new political groupings and new patterns."[7]

The United States was ambivalent about the Baghdad Pact. It could see the advantages of access to British bases in Iraq, and the British pleaded with the Americans to join.

But the Eisenhower administration would not join. American diplomats were not entirely fetched by the Cold War arguments. The United States was willing to acknowledge the pact enough to give it some important financial support (which would further anger Nuri's rival, Egypt), but the Americans saw the Baghdad Pact maneuvers—correctly—less as a useful anti-Soviet move and more as a grand maneuver in the Baghdad-versus-Cairo struggle for Middle East dominance. The Americans also were uneasy about British purposes, seeing the pact more as a way for London to find an inexpensive way to secure British influence in Iraq and beyond.[8]

Iraq's large neighbor to the east, Iran, was not a new country. But Iran's recent political history had been even more unsettled than Iraq's.

During World War II its monarch, the shah, had flirted with the Nazis. Iran was a vital transit route for Allied aid to the Soviets, so in 1941 British and Soviet forces had easily taken over the country. They had forced the shah to abdicate in favor of his young son. The new shah, Reza Pahlavi, then managed the country as a friend of the Allies.

The Allies withdrew their occupation at the war's end. The Russians left grudgingly, under some pressure, and the British effectively controlled Iranian oil.

A populist government took power in Teheran, calling for more democracy and total Iranian control of its oil. In 1951 the populist leader Mohammad Mossadegh nationalized the Anglo-Iranian Oil Company. The next year he kicked the British out of the country.

It did not last. The British kept the Iranians from selling much of their oil, and money ran short. Meanwhile Mossadegh had antagonized elements in the clergy, the business community, and the army.

Iranian coup plotters found plenty of secret support and encouragement from the British secret service, later—especially after the British were kicked out—joined by the American CIA. The Americans feared communists would take over the country amid the chaos. The coup plotters worked through the shah and supporters in the army. In a first test of power between Shah Reza Pahlavi and Mossadegh, Mossadegh won. In August 1953 the shah's supporters tried again and barely won the day.[9]

With a friendly government back in power, the oil industry was reorganized to share the profits (and open up opportunities for the Americans to get in). Iran joined Nuri's Baghdad Pact in October 1955, bending to Turkish persuasion. This cemented the so-called "northern tier" nominally against the Soviets but was also a way to get support and stand against more radical elements in the Muslim world, such as those in Cairo.

Cairo seemed to be the base for the Arab revolution. A group of Egyptian "Free Officers" had overthrown Egypt's king in 1952. They ruled their new republic through a Revolutionary Command Council.

During 1954 Nasser emerged clearly as the top man in Egypt. He won over enough of the army to depose Egypt's initial military ruler, then he turned on Egypt's political Islamists. Bravely surviving their attempt to assassinate him, Nasser and his allies imprisoned and executed the leaders of the Muslim Brotherhood. Then Nasser suppressed the communists and labor organizers.

In 1956 Nasser turned thirty-eight years old. He was a handsome man with an easy, welcoming, popular style and a readiness to give long, lively speeches in his melodious Arabic. Nasser ran a military dictatorship, and there were no traditional political parties; there was a "Liberation Rally."

Nasser's first goal was to break British domination of Egyptian politics, a pattern that dated back to Britain's military intervention in 1882. This he did. One of his first landmark achievements was a deal with then foreign secretary Anthony Eden that renegotiated the 1936 Anglo-Egyptian treaty, and Britain agreed to evacuate the large British base (80,000 troops strong) in the Suez Canal Zone. That deal was done in 1954.

For Eden it was a sign of flexibility and adapting to the times. For Nasser, the day when the last British troops left, in June 1956, was, indeed, a day for a Liberation Rally.

At home Nasser also stood for Arab socialism. A signature initiative was land reform, breaking up and distributing large landholdings. In the summer of 1956 Egypt adopted a new constitution with a bill of rights and an elected national assembly—although only approved members of a new party, the National Union, were allowed to run for office.

Nasser stood, too, for leading a unification of the Arab nation against all colonial oppressors, like the French in Algeria, and, of course, against Israel. Nasser wrote in 1955:

> For some reason, it seems to me that within the Arab circle there is a role, wandering aimlessly in search of a hero. And I do not know why it seems to me that this role, exhausted in its wanderings, has at last settled down, tired and weary, near the borders of our country and is beckoning to us to move, to take up its lines, to put on its costume, since no else is qualified to play it.[10]

Frequently allied with Nasser was the Kingdom of Saudi Arabia. The Saudi kingdom was self-made, through the desert military campaigns of Ibn Saud after World War I. These came very much at the expense of the British-preferred Hashemite ruler (whose sons were installed in Jordan and Iraq). The Saudi king in 1956, King Saud, had been in charge since the end of 1953.

Though the Saudis had no intention of running their kingdom the way Nasser ran Egypt, the Saudi kingdom liked Nasser's approach to foreign policy. The Saudis detested Nuri's Baghdad Pact.

Also like Nasser, Saudi leaders had less and less use for the British. The Saudis chose to develop Saudi oil in partnership with Americans, a choice that became spectacularly successful for both sides. The British had taken sides against the Saudis in a sharp dispute over a little region, the Buraimi Oasis, adjoining the British protectorates on the Persian Gulf.

Caught in the middle between these two camps in the Middle East were countries in the Levant: Lebanon, Syria, and Jordan. All were pressured to join the Baghdad Pact, which became a kind of symbol of "which side are you on."

Each of these three countries was a new and unstable political creation. The Jordanians in particular were in an awkward position: they had a defensive alliance with Britain and the core of their military—the Arab Legion—was led by British officers detailed to Jordan's army, which was also led by a British officer, John Bagot Glubb, better known as Glubb Pasha.

The Arab League, created in 1945, was supposed to link the seven Arab states of the Middle East.[11] But the league itself had become a battleground between the two camps—Cairo versus Baghdad. Nasser regarded Nuri's Baghdad Pact as a betrayal of neutralism and the Arab cause. Nuri retorted that the Saudis had allowed an American air base at Dhahran.

Both sides claimed to be the great defenders against Israel. Both offered to take over the defense of Jordan. Meanwhile the Jordanian king, whose grandfather had been murdered by Palestinian assassins in 1951, might well wonder if he would survive such a friendly embrace from either side.[12]

It was in the context, then, of this divided Middle East that the world read in September 1955 that Nasser had broken out of the Western constraints on the size of his army and air force. Shocking the Western world and delighting many Arabs, Nasser had made a deal to get a massive supply of arms from the Soviet Union.

It was in this context, too, that the world read the news early in 1956 that Egypt had created a military alliance to combine its army with that of Saudi Arabia and Syria. And then the world read that Jordan's king definitely would not join Nuri's Baghdad Pact. This was followed in March 1956 by the startling news that Jordan's king had suddenly dismissed his British general, Glubb Pasha. The other British officers would soon be leaving, too.

It was against this background of a divided world and a further divided, and very insecure, Middle East that the world waited to see when the next war would start in yet another conflict. There were already two wars nearby. On Cyprus, an island near the eastern edge of the Mediterranean that had become

a British colony and military base after World War I, some of the Greek inhabitants had organized groups attacking British soldiers there, getting a sharp
British response.

In Algeria, then part of France, a much larger rebellion had been growing
since 1954, both against French rule and against the privileges of the Europe-
ans/Christians who made up about 15 percent of the population. By early 1956
France had committed nearly 200,000 troops to putting down the rebellion,
including the transfer of two divisions from its forces deployed in Germany
with NATO. France believed Nasser's Egypt was an important secret sponsor
of the rebels, in addition to the pro-rebel propaganda that could be heard on
Radio Cairo.

Yet the war the world was most worried about was the one that had not yet
started but seemed like it could blow up at any moment. That was the war that
would once again embroil the Arabs against the newly created Jewish state of
Israel.

THE DIVIDED LAND

The area known as Palestine passed from Ottoman rule to British control after
World War I. During the first half of the twentieth century the leaders of
a movement called Zionism sought to create a national home for the Jewish
people in their ancient homeland in Palestine, an area where the Jews then
numbered only about 10 percent of the population. The British tried, painfully
and unsuccessfully, to regulate Jewish immigration to Palestine and balance
Jewish and Arab aspirations for a new state. In 1947 the British, admitting their
failure, turned the problem over to the UN.

In November 1947 the UN adopted a complex plan for the partition of Palestine. The principal Zionist leaders accepted it; the principal Palestinian Arab
leaders did not. As soon as the UN adopted the plan, civil war began, which
became an international war in May 1948 when the new state of Israel declared
its creation and the neighboring Arab states declared war against it. The war
ended in July 1949 with a set of tenuous cease-fire arrangements, negotiated
with the help of UN mediators.

The armistice lines of 1949—and 1956—are similar to the present-day borders of Israel, except that the area now known as the occupied West Bank was
then controlled by Jordan, as was about half of Jerusalem, including the Old
City. On the border with Syria, Israel did not hold any of the Golan Heights,
and a thin zone on that border was demilitarized and under UN supervision,

as was an area on the Egyptian-Israeli border where a road entered the Negev desert through the village of El Auja.

A large portion of the Arab population of Palestine had fled or been driven out of Israel during the course of the 1948–49 fighting. Numbering about 700,000, these refugees congregated on Egypt's Mediterranean coast near Israel, in what is now called the Gaza Strip, and in Jordan or Lebanon. With most of the Arab Palestinian population gone, Jews now outnumbered Arabs within Israel's 1949 borders by a margin of nearly eight to one.

Although Israel joined the UN in 1949, none of the Arab states recognized the new Israeli state. All remained in a legal state of war against it. The armistice lines were overseen by, and complaints about violations submitted to, a UN Truce Supervision Organization.

To help keep this simmering conflict from again coming to a boil, in May 1950 the United States, Britain, and France had jointly issued the Tripartite Declaration. In it, they promised to regulate the sales of arms to the countries of the Middle East to prevent an arms race. They promised to prevent, even by using force, any violation of the demarcation lines.

By issuing this declaration, not only were the three powers trying to restrain those in the region, they were also trying to regulate each other. By coordinating their sales plans, for example, the United States might try to keep Britain from oversupplying its Arab friends, because that might force the United States to antagonize the Arabs by rushing offsetting arms to Israel.[13]

From 1949 to 1956, any discussion of a permanent solution to the Palestine question would focus on final borders and the fate of the Palestinian Arab refugees. On borders, Egypt and Jordan wanted some direct territorial connection, probably through the Negev desert of southern Israel, that would tie together the Arab world. On refugees, all the Arab states wanted refugees to be able to return home or be compensated for their losses.

Israeli governments opposed making any major concessions on either topic. They concentrated on building up their state within the new borders that had effectively been established by the 1949 armistice lines.

The Israelis were vexed by a problem of frequent infiltrators across the border, especially the long and twisting border with Jordan. Most infiltrators were Palestinian Arabs trying to visit relatives or their old property. Some were thieves; some were intent on revenge raids, including murder.

In addition to frequently shooting such infiltrators on sight, the Israeli government adopted a policy of deliberate military retaliation in cross-border raids. The strategy was to punish the Arab governments, show their powerlessness, by sending an elite unit into border areas of Jordan or Egypt to smash villages or military installations. The idea was that the Arab governments would, then, do a better job of stopping the infiltrators by policing their side of the border.

Despite Israeli accusations, the Jordanian forces did try to police their border, though not always successfully. The Egyptian forces also prevented most infiltrators from getting across. But Egypt changed its policy in the spring of 1955.

At the end of February 1955 the Israeli government retaliated against a raid from the Gaza Strip that had killed a cyclist inside Israel. The Israeli Defense Forces (IDF) launched a cross-border attack on the Egyptian military headquarters in Gaza, killing thrity-seven Egyptian soldiers and wounding dozens more. In March 1955 the UN Security Council passed a resolution censuring Israel.

Rather than stopping infiltration, the Egyptian government then began more actively training and sponsoring Palestinians, called *fedayeen*, to conduct raids into Israel. Nasser also redoubled his efforts to find resources to build up his army. The cycle of violence back and forth continued throughout the rest of 1955 and on into 1956. After a particularly large and apparently unprovoked Israeli raid into Syria in December 1955, the UN Security Council passed another resolution criticizing the Israeli actions.[14]

At first in secret, during the spring of 1955 the U.S. government made a major effort to defuse this time bomb. Washington reasoned that as this conflict got worse, all of Washington's Cold War or oil interests would be endangered. The cycle of violence fed Arab anger and helped the most radical elements. It deepened an already dangerous divide in the Arab world and opened up opportunities for Soviet mischief,

The U.S. peace effort of 1955 had the code name Alpha. Having already consulted with the British, who were supportive, the United States took on all the issues. Secretary of State John Foster Dulles tried to mediate and bring the sides together, working especially with Egypt and Israel. There were ideas to enhance UN truce supervision and border controls, tackle the Palestinian refugee problem with a mix of some returns and a lot of compensation, and address disputes over Jordan River water or Jerusalem. The United States put a large sweetener of foreign aid on the table.

Most important were issues of territory and security. The U.S. plan was for Israel to cede two small triangles of territory in the far south of the Negev desert. One triangle would have its base in Egypt's Sinai desert and the other would have its base in Jordan, so that the triangle points would meet at an Israeli crossroads that Israel would still control, perhaps with international supervision. Thus Israel would still have the connection to its southern port of Eilat on the Gulf of Aqaba. Egypt and Jordan could narrowly connect these two parts of the Arab world.

In exchange, the United States mentioned the possibility of a defense and security pact in which the United States might guarantee Israel's security. The United States, regarding Israel then as being clearly militarily superior to its Arab neighbors, did not go into much detail about how this security arrangement would work.

After the secret efforts to make peace along these lines did not work, Dulles went public in August 1955, hoping to bring more pressure to bear. But the U.S. initiative failed. Israel would not compromise on territory, and it demanded face-to-face meetings with Egypt's leaders, not after a deal but to negotiate one. Nasser refused, repeatedly recalling the assassination of Jordan's king in 1951.

The Israelis did muse about the U.S. offer of a security pact. But it was clear the Americans would insist as part of the deal that Israel give up on its strategy of heavy military retaliation against terrorist infiltration and would also insist on no further territorial expansion. These conditions were unacceptable to Israel, especially the issue of military retaliation.[15]

This, then, was the situation in September 1955, when Nasser announced he had concluded a landmark arms deal with the Soviet Union (nominally with the Soviet satellite, Czechoslovakia). The deal would quickly supply Egypt with hundreds of tanks and more than a hundred advanced jet aircraft.

As the cargo ships loaded with tanks and guns started moving to Egyptian harbors, the Soviet arms deal seemed, at a stroke, to destroy the West's Tripartite Declaration system of trying to regulate the Middle Eastern arms race. As British troops were completing the enormous withdrawal from Egypt as agreed in 1954, Soviet influence had jumped over the northern tier and was now right in the heart of the Middle East.

The Israeli government feared its military advantage might vanish once the Egyptians had absorbed the new arms and been trained in their use. They had no adequate counter for the Soviet jet aircraft or for deliveries of such large numbers of armored fighting vehicles and artillery. Thus, while also pleading with the United States to sell them modern arms to counter this sale, Israeli leaders immediately began very seriously considering options for launching some sort of preventive war against Egypt, and possibly other Arab states allied with Egypt.

Meanwhile the cycle of border violence continued into 1956. The United States was aware Israel was planning and preparing for a possible preventive war. All the foreign observers believed the odds of a major war were rising fast.

All sorts of options were on the table in Washington and London. Britain had a defense pact with Jordan that would oblige Britain to help defend Jordan against a major Israeli attack, and British military chiefs had contingency plans to do this.

The American government began contemplating what it might do. The Eisenhower administration considered preparing for military intervention to stop a war, but this might require a huge and costly troop commitment, diverted from NATO, and the U.S. military did not want to go there.

Harsh economic sanctions against an aggressor, perhaps even maritime or aerial blockades, were another possibility. For the Western powers, selling arms to Israel to offset the Soviet arms was another option, but that might seem to reward and encourage the Israeli policy of military retaliation and further inflame the Arab world. Or, looking at the Egyptian side, perhaps there was something that could be done that could bring Nasser's Egypt back into the pro-Western camp.[16]

After the September 1955 announcement of the Soviet arms deal with Egypt, six countries shared a sense of crisis. For five of them, the problem was what to do next about Nasser's Egypt. Nasser's Egypt, of course, had the question, What do we do next?

All six governments had to size up the situation. They had to judge what was really important, in the context of all the other problems they had to consider. All had to come up with options for doing something. Analyzing those options, they had to ask themselves: Whose support do we need to make this work? How do we get it?

Each of those six governments was made up of very particular people working in very particular institutions. Before they could persuade or coerce some other government, these people first had to persuade or coerce their own colleagues, because every one of the governments was divided. Leaders in all six capitals argued with each other about how to see the problem and what to do about it. Meanwhile, most of those arguments were really about how well these six governments understood each other.

PART ONE

What to Do about Nasser's Egypt

SEPTEMBER 1955 TO JULY 26, 1956

Part One

TIMELINE OF PUBLIC EVENTS

FEBRUARY 1955   Israeli raid on Egyptian Gaza.

MARCH 1955   Egypt, Syria, and Saudi Arabia publicly agree on military cooperation.

APRIL 1955   Anthony Eden succeeds Churchill as British prime minister.

APRIL 1955   Baghdad Pact announced: military cooperation of Britain with Iraq, Turkey, and Pakistan.

APRIL 1955   Bandung conference of "nonaligned" nations, hosted by Indonesia. Egypt, India, and China play prominent parts.

JULY 1955   Big Four Summit in Geneva of U.S., Soviet, British, and French leaders.

SEPTEMBER 1955   Soviet bloc announces massive "Czech" deal to transfer arms to Egypt.

SEPTEMBER 1955   U.S. president Eisenhower has a heart attack and is hospitalized.

OCTOBER 1955   Big Four foreign ministers meet in Geneva.

OCTOBER 1955   Iran joins Baghdad Pact.

NOVEMBER 1955   Moshe Sharett steps down and Ben-Gurion again becomes prime minister of Israel, also defense minister.

DECEMBER 1955   Israeli forces conduct a raid into Syria. UN Security Council adopts resolution criticizing Israeli action.

JANUARY 1956   Eden visits Eisenhower in Washington.

JANUARY 1956   New "Republican Front" coalition government takes power in France, led by Guy Mollet. Algerian war escalates.

MARCH 1956   After British pressure to join Baghdad Pact, Jordan expels British military advisers.

APRIL 1956   Israel-Egypt border fighting raises threat of war; UN secretary-general Dag Hammarskjöld mediates UN truce supervision.

JUNE 1956   British forces complete their withdrawal from the Suez Canal Zone, as agreed to with Egypt in 1954.

MOSCOW

CAROL R. SAIVETZ

In 1955 the Soviet Union took the strategic initiative to reset the future of the Middle East and its place in the global Cold War. But in Moscow, among those running the country, the maneuvers with Egypt were part of a much bigger and more dangerous game much closer to home. To outsiders, it might seem that the basic parameters of the Cold War—the division of Europe, German rearmament, the Korean stalemate, and the nuclear standoff between the two superpowers—were hardening. But the USSR was still undergoing a prolonged succession struggle. Following the March 5, 1953, death of Joseph Stalin, several potential rulers struggled for power.

At issue among the contenders for power were such questions as the following: Should we end the Stalinist reign of terror? Should we reorient Soviet investment from heavy industry to the consumer sector? What shape should the global competition between the United States and the USSR take in the thermonuclear age?

Where and how to wage the Cold War became an especially critical issue in the succession struggle. Within those discussions, how much assistance to provide to potential allies in the Third World assumed an increasingly prominent place.

STALIN'S DEATH AND THE SUCCESSION STRUGGLE

The earliest challenger for Stalin's mantle was Lavrenti Beria, the chief of Stalin's security services. All accounts of the period make it clear that Beria intended to use his position as head of the secret police apparatus to assure his rise to the pinnacle of power, but Beria's ascendancy was short-lived. He was arrested on June 26, 1953, and, ultimately, shot.

The second contender was Vyacheslav Molotov, the foreign minister. A doctrinaire Stalinist, he firmly believed that war between the capitalist and communist systems was inevitable. He described U.S. foreign policy as "preparations 'for a new world war—a war to restore the world domination of capitalism.'"[1] Molotov remained a significant force in the foreign policy debates until he was replaced as foreign minister in June of 1956.

The third candidate, Georgi Malenkov, had been Stalin's heir apparent, but within weeks of the leader's death he gave up the post of party secretary and retained only the premiership.[2] In his speech at Stalin's funeral, Malenkov stated: "There are not contested issues in U.S.-Soviet relations that cannot be resolved by peaceful means."[3] Approximately a year later, Malenkov elaborated. A new world war, he asserted, "given modern weapons, would mean the destruction of world civilization."[4] The then premier argued that Moscow's possession of nuclear weapons would incline the West toward cooperation out of fear of Soviet retaliation.[5] His views found little support among the other members of the Politburo at the time, and he was dismissed from the premiership in February 1955.

Nikita S. Khrushchev, the fourth contender, was indignant that Malenkov had attempted to steal the role of reformer.[6] Khrushchev initially sought to carve out a position between Molotov and Malenkov. He rejected the Stalinist line—promoted by Molotov—that war between the two world systems was inevitable at the same time that he dismissed Malenkov's assertion that the West would come to the same sober assessment of the need to cooperate in the nuclear age. Early in 1955 Khrushchev was denouncing Malenkov for not being tough enough.

Then, after Malenkov had effectively been defeated (though he was still in the ruling circle), Khrushchev and Molotov turned on each other.[7] According to Khrushchev, Moscow's primary foreign policy objective should be to "convince" the West to cooperate.

Khrushchev's reliance on the deterrent value of nuclear weapons could allow him to declare, following the 1955 Geneva summit, that the USSR had stood its ground with the West.[8] The summit had been convened to discuss Germany and disarmament. Although it was, as one scholar observed, conducted in an atmosphere of "superficial friendship and amiability,"[9] it accomplished nothing. Khrushchev's attitude toward the summit and toward the West was summed up in his memoirs:

> We returned to Moscow from Geneva knowing that we hadn't achieved any concrete results. But we were encouraged, realizing now that our enemies probably feared us as much as we feared them. They rattled their sabers and tried to pressure us into agreements which were more profitable for them than for us because they were frightened of us. As a result of our own showing in Geneva, our enemies now realized that we were able to resist their pressure, and see through their tricks.[10]

An outgrowth of Khrushchev's view of the nuclear standoff was the idea of "peaceful coexistence," which he interpreted to mean a sharp ideological struggle between the East and the West. He could emphasize a nuclear buildup while cutting back on the huge size of Soviet conventional forces. This included a July 1955 troop reduction of 640,000 men and a further cut in May 1956.[11]

Meanwhile, in the name of this ideological contest, he reached out to the newly decolonized states of Africa and Asia. In 1955, Khrushchev expanded his travels beyond Yugoslavia and the Geneva summit to include much-publicized trips to India, Indonesia, Burma, and Afghanistan. While in India, he proclaimed: "We say to the leaders of the capitalist states: Let us compete without war."[12] He meant without a war between the superpowers. The Soviet Union simultaneously approved its first arms transfer to Egypt.

When the Communist Party of the Soviet Union (CPSU) held a full congress, which did not happen every year, the occasion was always a landmark for setting out the party's new policy line. The CPSU's Twentieth Party Congress, in February 1956, was, therefore, a landmark occasion for Khrushchev to consolidate his leadership and articulate his line. In his formal speech at the congress, Khrushchev concluded that even prominent bourgeois figures must admit "there can be no victors in an atomic war." And recognizing the dangers inherent in the nuclear age, he claimed: "We want to be friends with the United States and to cooperate with it for peace and international security."[13]

Yet this enunciation of the need for "peaceful coexistence" and the noninevitability of war, in effect, shifted the locus of further conflict from Europe to the Third World. Khrushchev explained:

The forces of peace have been considerably augmented by the emergence
in the world arena of a group of peace-loving European and Asian states
which have proclaimed nonparticipation in blocs as a principle of their
foreign policy. . . . As a result a vast "peace zone," including both socialist
and nonsocialist peace-loving states in Europe and Asia, has emerged in
the world arena.[14]

During the congress Molotov did not oppose Khrushchev directly; in fact,
he admitted shortcomings in the performance of the Foreign Ministry.[15] Yet
even as he acknowledged the emerging nuclear parity between the United
States and the USSR, he urged the Soviet Union to remain vigilant about the
West. "Of course, insofar as imperialism exists, there is a danger of a new world
war, not to mention other military conflicts."[16]

Dmitry Shepilov, soon to succeed Molotov as foreign minister, more clearly
echoed Khrushchev's views. He devoted much of his speech to describing the
ideological battle between capitalism and socialism being fought in the Third
World. According to the future foreign minister:

One of the characteristic features of our epoch is the combining of socialist revolution in individual countries with a mass struggle of "all the
downtrodden and discontented. . . ."

Communists are opponents in principle of sectarian narrowness.
They advocate that the efforts of all kinds and varieties of mass movements of the present day must be merged into an anti-imperialist stream.
The great aspirations of all the downtrodden peoples, whether they be
the peoples of the Arab, Asian or Latin American countries . . . will
find their realization in the struggle against social oppression, against
colonialism, in the struggle for peace and democracy.[17]

The reference to "sectarian narrowness" was a coded attack on those within the
party who opposed Khrushchev's outreach to neutralist, noncommunist Third
World states.

CHANGING VIEWS OF THE MIDDLE EAST

The Soviet leaders were clearly having intense debates, offstage, about how to
deal with the forces of decolonization in the Third World. The central question
was this: Should the USSR value relations with local communist parties higher

than those with nationalist leaders, or should it advance ties with nationalist leaders who were noncommunist or even leaders who killed or imprisoned local communists, just because they were anti-British or anti-French?

Nowhere was this question more squarely posed for the Soviet leadership than in the Middle East. For example, when in 1952 the Egyptian Free Officers Movement overthrew the monarchy and began demanding the withdrawal of British troops, official Soviet statements seemed to see no difference between the new military leaders and the former king. In fact, the 1952 edition of the *Great Soviet Encyclopedia* described the coup as follows: "On the night of July 23, 1952, power in Cairo was seized by a reactionary officers' group connected with the USA."[18]

Two years later, Soviet statements praised those Middle East forces opposed to the British-sponsored Baghdad Pact. In this it seemed that Soviet objectives and Nasser's coincided, as the latter attempted to rally the Arabs against the proposed alliance. Indeed, in a paper prepared for Dmitry Shepilov's trip to Egypt, the USSR vowed support for Egypt as it sought to "strengthen its state sovereignty and national independence."[19]

When upheaval in Syria brought to power new leaders more sympathetic to Nasser's position, Syria and Egypt declared their joint opposition not only to the proposed Turkish-Iraqi pact but to all other defense deals in the region. The Soviet Union, which had earlier signed an arms deal with Syria (late 1954), now officially announced its readiness to assist Syria in defending its independence and sovereignty. And in Egypt, the Soviet ambassador sounded out the Cairo government on its formal stance toward the West.[20]

In a statement issued on April 16, 1955, the Soviet Foreign Ministry definitively criticized the Baghdad Pact and promised to counter it.

The situation in the Near and Middle East has recently become considerably more tense. The explanation of this is that certain Western powers have been making new attempts to draw the countries of the Near and Middle East into the military groupings which are being set up as appendages to the aggressive North Atlantic bloc. . . .

[The basis of this policy is] the desire of certain Western powers for the colonial enslavement of these countries. . . .

As has frequently happened in the past, now, too, efforts are being made to cloak the aggressive nature of the Near and Middle Eastern plans of the United States and Britain with ridiculous fabrications about a "Soviet menace" to the countries of that area. . . . Upholding the cause

of peace, the Soviet government will defend the freedom and independence of the countries of the Near and Middle East and will oppose
interference in their domestic affairs.[21]

But the USSR was concerned not only about Egypt and Syria.

If the creation of the Baghdad Pact was seen as a setback by the Kremlin,
the rise of several varieties of home-grown socialism and the vehement anti-
Westernism articulated by many Third World leaders were seen as opportunities.[22] In fact, Khrushchev urged those attending the Twentieth Party Congress
"to work untiringly to strengthen the bonds of friendship and cooperation with
the Republic of India, Burma, Afghanistan, Egypt, Syria, and other countries
which stand for peace; to support countries which refuse to be involved in military blocs."[23]

THE "CZECH" ARMS DEAL WITH EGYPT

Determined to redress the 1949 "disaster" in the war against Israel, the Free
Officers looked to purchase arms for the Egyptian military. Nasser's preference
initially was to purchase arms from the West, but the 1950 Tripartite Declaration, in which the United States, Britain, and France agreed not to sell arms to
the combatants in the Middle East, remained a major obstacle.

The Soviets and Nasser circled each other as they tried to figure out what
kind of relations they should establish. Nasser told Soviet officials of his desire
for modern weapons as early as 1953 and 1954. But Egypt's decisive moves to
create a military relationship came in February 1955, after the British helped
create the Baghdad Pact and after an Israeli raid into Gaza on February 28,
1955, in which the headquarters of an Egyptian garrison were destroyed and
thirty-eight soldiers were killed.[24] (Israeli officials claim the raid was in retaliation for Egyptian incursions into Israel through Gaza.)

At a meeting in Burma, Nasser found a chance to complain to the Chinese
foreign minister, Zhou En-Lai, about his difficulty in procuring arms because
of the Western embargo. In response, Zhou asserted he thought the Russians
would "be prepared to give a positive answer."[25]

On May 21, Nasser met the Soviet ambassador to Egypt, Daniel Solod, at a
reception. Nasser expressed his fear of another Israeli attack. Solod responded
that Moscow had already said yes. Thus negotiations began in earnest.

As the deal was being worked out, Nasser reportedly asked whether the

USSR would be willing to establish a barter arrangement—Egyptian cotton for heavy artillery. The Soviet side agreed. In July 1955 Dmitry Shepilov, then ostensibly editor of the Communist Party newspaper *Pravda*, arrived in Cairo for a long visit. He was there not as a journalist but as Khrushchev's envoy, to nail down the agreement.[26]

Nasser and Shepilov apparently got along well. "We had doubts until you visited," Nasser's defense minister later told Shepilov. Among the issues discussed at the meeting was Egypt's treatment of local communists. Shepilov's response was that the incarceration of Egyptian communists was solely an Egyptian affair, and a favorable report was sent to Moscow. Shepilov, in an interview with a Russian academic expert on the Middle East, later explained: "I received a favourable impression of Nasser during my first trip, when I first met him. He was a very honest man who was really devoted to the Arab land and the Arab people."[27]

U.S. intelligence and diplomatic reports picked up the fact that Shepilov had offered first-rate arms to Egypt, including MiG jet fighter aircraft. Although the negotiations were secret, Nasser publicly announced the arrangement on September 27. The United States already knew of the deal. John Foster Dulles had told President Eisenhower: "It seems to be authentic that they [the Soviets] are giving a massive lot of arms to the Egyptians theoretically to be paid for by cotton."[28]

Nasser's spontaneous announcement left the Soviets with no choice but to acknowledge the deal. According to Soviet press reports, Nasser, in a speech in Alexandria, both reiterated his nation's goal of creating a strong national army and acknowledged that his requests for arms had been rebuffed by Western powers. He went on: "Recently we received a proposal from Czechoslovakia to supply us with the arms needed by our army on a purely commercial basis. . . . I immediately accepted this Czechoslovak proposal with gratitude."[29] An ironclad member of the Soviet bloc, Czechoslovakia was the instrument for a choice made in Moscow.

A couple of days later the USSR added its own official statement:

For its part, the Soviet government holds the view that every state has the lawful right to provide for its defense and to buy arms for its defense needs from other states on the usual commercial terms, and no foreign state has the right to interfere in this or to present any unilateral claims that would infringe the rights or interest of other states.[30]

Privately, on September 29, Nasser requested more Soviet help in relieving unwelcome pressure from the United States to annul the arms deal. Specifically, Nasser asked Ambassador Solod what the Soviet position would be if there were more threats from the United States. Nasser asked, according to the Soviet report: "Could Egypt count on the support of the Soviet Union in this fight [against the United States]."[31]

Solod conveyed Moscow's careful reply on October 1. The Soviet Union would not offer a defense commitment. It was just offering political and moral support. But it was ready to talk about sending more arms.[32]

The Egyptian request for arms had come at a propitious time in the rethinking of Soviet foreign policy. Sergei Khrushchev, Nikita's son, recalled that the Soviet leader at first had a difficult time making up his mind about the Egyptian leadership. He writes that while Khrushchev was not indifferent to the new Third World governments, especially those proximate to the USSR, he found Nasser's nationalistic slogans "doubtful."[33]

In his own memoirs, Khrushchev attributed the positive response to Nasser's request to the influence of Yugoslav president Josip Tito, with whom the USSR had just renewed relations after an eight-year rupture. He wrote: "Soon after the coup, when the Egyptians decided to try to oust the English, Nasser's representatives came to us with a request for military aid. . . . We agreed."[34]

MOSCOW TILTS TOWARD THE ARAB CAUSE

To outsiders, the Egyptian-"Czech" arms deal opened the way for Soviet engagement on the Arab side of the ongoing Arab-Israeli dispute. Yet at the time, the Soviets still hesitated. As late as October 1955 the USSR still seemed reluctant to commit itself completely to the Arab cause. According to Dulles's account, Molotov told him "he was convinced that no aggressive purpose was in the minds of the Arabs and that if they should make an armed attack on Israel, they would be stopped by other nations through the means of the United Nations which afforded protection to Israel." When Dulles pointed out that many Arabs now seemed to believe the Soviets would veto any resolution directed against them, thereby giving them immunity, Molotov "said that the Soviet Union would abide by the principles of the United Nations."[35]

Molotov's view apparently reflected the consensus of the Foreign Ministry that the best way to become a major force in the Middle East was to mediate between the Arabs and Israel. In contrast, Khrushchev—despite earlier doubts—seems to have been tempted increasingly by the idea of aligning

Moscow with Arab nationalism. In a speech to the Supreme Soviet in December 1955, Khrushchev declared: "We understand the yearnings of the peoples of the Arab countries who are fighting for their full liberation from foreign dependence. One cannot, at the same time, fail to condemn the actions of the State of Israel which from the first days of its existence began threatening its neighbors and pursuing an unfriendly policy toward them."[36]

By January 1956 the USSR had posted ambassadors to Syria, Lebanon, and Libya. Ambassador Solod, so instrumental in the arms deal, was recalled from Cairo back to Moscow to head up the Middle East Department of the Foreign Ministry. During this same period, Moscow initialed a new trade agreement with Syria in which the USSR would build industrial installations in exchange for cotton, tobacco, and other raw materials.[37]

During the spring of 1956, as tensions between Israel and Egypt increased dramatically and news came out that the French would deliver some Mystère fighter jets to Israel, the *New York Times* reported on May 21 that at least two new Egyptian-Czech arms arrangements had been made.[38] Khrushchev—even more openly than before—abandoned any pretense of neutrality.

In an interview with the Egyptian *Al Ahram*, Khrushchev claimed Israel was "launching aggressive attacks" against its Arab neighbors. He accused Israel of seeking to maintain tensions to secure Western aid. Yet, although the Soviet leader was decidedly pro-Egyptian, he articulated the central dilemma for Soviet policymakers: Would an Arab-Israeli war lead to a world war? He urged the Arabs to be patient because the "results will be in their favor."[39]

Negotiations over the financing of Nasser's pet project, the Aswan Dam, had dragged on for months. In October 1955, shortly after the arms deal was concluded, Soviet ambassador Solod offered Egypt assistance in building the Aswan High Dam. Nasser initially rejected the Soviet offer for fear of becoming too dependent on Moscow.[40]

Yet the Soviet arms deal and Nasser's flirtation with the communist bloc were obviously complicating any effort to get aid for the dam project from the U.S. Congress. In mid-June 1956, Shepilov, recently appointed foreign minister and always an enthusiastic supporter of Khrushchev's outreach to Egypt, journeyed to Egypt himself. He was there to participate in the celebrations of the final British evacuation from its giant Suez base. The Western press speculated that Shepilov carried with him a Soviet offer to finance the dam project. The joint communiqué issued on Shepilov's departure claimed there was "full unanimity of views" on all aspects of Soviet-Egyptian relations.[41]

Shepilov was supportive, but the economic commitments were vague.

Sergei Khrushchev writes that, at the time of Shepilov's visit, Nasser secured a full range of Soviet economic assistance. Moreover, he continues, his "father considered that we with our experience in hydro-construction were in a position to build any kind of dam."[42]

But when, on July 19, the United States informed the Egyptians that the Aswan Dam financing offer was rescinded, and an Egyptian newspaper quoted the new Soviet ambassador, E. Kiselev, as remarking that the USSR would finance the dam project, Kiselev denied the report. However, Kiselev was also cited in another press report as saying the Soviet Union was ready to assist with the dam project "if Egypt asks for it." These reports were also denied by the embassy in Cairo.[43]

Two days later, in Moscow, Shepilov seemed to hedge on whether or not the Soviet Union would be interested in stepping in to replace the Western offers. The foreign minister said Egypt had many other problems that were just as vital as the dam, "particularly problems connected with industrialization." But if Egypt requested assistance for other industrialization projects, he promised that "we would find ways to meet those wishes and would consider favorably any Egyptian request without preliminary political conditions and without putting forward any enslaving economic conditions."[44]

PART ONE

JERUSALEM

PHILIP ZELIKOW

ISRAEL BESIEGED

By September 1955 the state of Israel was little more than seven years old, and its leaders wondered whether it could survive the next seven. All the neighboring Arab countries were hostile, regarding themselves as still being in the formal state of war they had declared in 1948, when the Israeli state had declared its creation. Israel's borders were unsettled, the disputed product of a UN-negotiated cease-fire in 1949.

Israel was swollen with new immigrants, many refugees displaced by the Holocaust in Europe and the wave of anti-Semitism that had swept across the Arab world during and after the Arab-Israeli war of 1948–49. The new country eagerly welcomed the immigrants yet strained to assimilate them, often fostering new settlements to populate and cultivate their new land, frequently in or near villages and farmland that had been deserted by fleeing Palestinian Arabs.

By 1955, about a million Palestinian refugees, registered as such with the UN, were gathered in or out of camps not far from Israel. They hated the Jews, who, they felt, had stolen their lands or driven them out. For years thousands of them, sometimes joined by trained soldiers from Egypt or Jordan or (less often) Syria, had infiltrated across porous borders that Israel did not have the strength to defend. Especially in the early years the Israelis had often shot such infiltrators on sight.

By 1955 the infiltrations were usually raids, to steal crops or cattle or other

41

valuables, to destroy property and infrastructure like water pipes or power lines, and, in general, to disrupt and terrorize Israeli settlements. Sometimes, in a chance encounter or deliberately, infiltrators would kill a Jewish worker or watchman or passing bicyclist. Israel was a small country; its own population was swollen by new immigrants but still only about 1.8 million in total (all but 200,000 of them Jewish). So every incident, every killing, was noticed and felt. In 1955, twenty-four Israeli civilians were killed and sixty-nine wounded; fifty soldiers were killed in border clashes.[1]

Despairing of the ability to mount a static defense everywhere, with security costs already very high and settlers wearied and fearful from constantly being on their guard (often literally in rotating watches), the Israeli government had begun trying a policy of powerful military reprisals. By 1955 the pattern was that an elite Israeli unit would target a Jordanian or Egyptian police or military post and launch a raid that would destroy the post, killing dozens of police or soldiers. The point was to coerce the Arab government to do more to stop the infiltrators.

By 1955 this reprisal policy had become a major political issue in Israel. The "activists," such as Israeli Defense Forces chief of staff Moshe Dayan, believed conflict was inevitable and Israel's only choice was to be strong and show its strength by going on the offensive, to strike back hard. Through most of that year he was supported by his longtime mentor (and former prime minister) David Ben-Gurion.

The moderates wanted to tamp down rather than escalate the cycle of violence. They believed punitive reprisals that killed scores of Arab soldiers (and often Arab civilians, too) not only fed the flames of Arab hostility but also isolated Israel in the international community. Through most of 1955 the moderates were led by Israel's prime minister and former foreign minister, Moshe Sharett.[2]

All these men were well known to Israelis. As much as anyone, Ben-Gurion was Israel's preeminent political figure. He had been the leading executive figure in the Zionist movement since 1935, throughout the years of struggle that culminated in independence in 1948. He had been the country's first prime minister. He and his party, Mapai, represented the dominant center-left of Israeli politics in the country's parliament, the Knesset.

In late 1953, after a reprisal raid to destroy a Jordanian village, a raid that turned into a massacre of Arab civilians, Ben-Gurion publicly lied about what had happened—blaming angry Israeli civilians living by the border—to deflect blame from the army. He then proceeded with his planned resignation. It would be "for two years," he told his party colleagues. He retired temporarily to a newly built little house in a collective settlement, a *kibbutz*, in southern Israel's Negev desert.[3]

Ben-Gurion turned sixty-nine in 1955. He had a kind of biblical aura—his bald head was wreathed by wispy white hair, his blunt features and stocky build were joined with a forceful, articulate speaking style. Born in Russian Poland, Ben-Gurion read deeply in classical literature, history, and philosophy and constantly put issues in a wider context. He was a strategic thinker. He could be fiery at one moment, personalizing disputes or erupting volcanically when people could not do what he thought had to be done, then become withdrawn and reflective the next.

At the beginning of 1955, after the previous defense minister had been forced to resign because of a botched terror attack launched in Egypt by a cell of Egyptian Jews working for Israel, Ben-Gurion cut short his "two years" of retirement. He joined Sharett's coalition government as the defense minister, representing the more "activist" policy. Ben-Gurion could also be tough and brutally decisive, whether in crushing right-wing Zionist paramilitary groups or in confrontations with the Arabs.

Ben-Gurion had been a mentor to Dayan, playing the part of the wise adult to the talented, impulsive youth. Dayan, forty in 1955, was no longer youthful, but he was still the informal, free-spirited combative spirit he had been all his life. Born in Palestine, he grew up in embattled settlements and was named for a friend of his father who had been killed by Arabs two years before Dayan was born. His office "looked like the headquarters of a tent camp, with makeshift tables and folding chairs. The commander acted like a field officer who may have arrived in the morning in a clean, pressed uniform but by midday looked like he had been through a series of drills: dusty shoes, trousers baggy at the knees, sleeves carelessly rolled up."[4]

Dayan was instantly recognizable in Israel and beyond because of the distinctive eye patch on his nearly bald head. Dayan reluctantly wore that eye patch after he lost an eye and part of the surrounding eye socket in combat, a 1941 skirmish against Vichy French forces in southern Lebanon in which Dayan, typically, was out in front. After a slow recovery, Dayan had returned to combat as a senior officer in the 1948–49 war, and in 1953 Ben-Gurion had elevated him to the job of chief of staff.

In the late summer of 1955, Ben-Gurion and Dayan were restlessly pushing against the more moderate impulses of the sixty-one-year-old prime minister, Moshe Sharett. Sharett (formerly Shertok) had come from Russian Ukraine to Ottoman Palestine in 1906 when still a boy. His was one of the founding families of the city of Tel Aviv. Able to speak Arabic as well as Hebrew, Sharett had been an interpreter in the Ottoman army before the British conquest of Palestine.

Sharett had been a kind of interpreter throughout his professional life, trying to bridge the gap across cultures and gradually build up the Jewish state. A slim man, the image of a cultured European gentleman down to his well-trimmed mustache, Sharett had been a kind of foreign minister for the Zionist movement since 1933, during the years of struggle, and then became the foreign minister of the new state.

Sharett's style was cerebral and careful. He had reached the point where he sometimes needed Ben-Gurion's leadership yet often resented its substance and style. Perhaps "Moshe Sharett was not a leader but a statesman and, as such, was hard-wired for compromise by personality and political outlook." In 1955 Ben-Gurion declared: "Our future depends, not on what the *goyim* [non-Jews, the rest of the world] say, but on what the Jews do." To which Sharett commented: "Correct. But it is also important what the *goyim* do."[5]

In 1955, Sharett had not given up hope of reconciling Jewish and Arab aspirations in Palestine. So, in opposing disproportionate reprisal raids, he was trying to find a way out of the cycle of violence and revenge.

Dayan, on the other hand, regarded conflict as inevitable. So for him, at that time in his life, peace was likely to be only a temporary condition, to be induced by Israeli strength and the evident will to use it. In this basic judgment, Ben-Gurion was in agreement. Where Ben-Gurion held Dayan in check, it was because the old man felt he had to balance his young subordinate's desire for action against all the elements in the wider Israeli and global picture.

At the end of August 1955 the back-and-forth with Egypt seemed about to boil over into full-scale war. After a violent tit-for-tat in February 1955, the populated area of the Israeli-Egyptian border, near the Gaza Strip, remained quiet until about the middle of May. Then there was another incident, a mine killed three Israeli soldiers, and the Israelis retaliated. Then more quiet. Israel held national elections in late July; the Mapai party of Sharett and Ben-Gurion did well, and negotiations to form a new coalition government commenced.

In mid-August 1955, for reasons that remain obscure, border violence resumed and intensified. In addition to clashes between soldiers on both sides, including Egyptian artillery barrages aimed at Israeli settlements and Israeli raids, the Egyptians dispatched terror squads of Palestinians called *fedayeen*. The last week of August saw more escalation, including the entry of Egyptian jet fighters into Israeli airspace, one of which was shot down. On August 31 the Israelis launched a massive raid against an Egyptian base at Khan Yunis; seventy-two Egyptians were killed and fifty-eight were wounded, while Israeli casualties were light. In early September the Egyptians stepped up the artillery attacks and air incursions.[6]

Ben-Gurion and Dayan prepared for war, planning to invade and occupy a significant portion of the Gaza Strip and set up a military occupation government there. This was barely averted by acceptance of a UN-proposed cease-fire, although Egyptian-sponsored fedayeen raids were also mounted out of Jordan and Lebanon. This was the context in which Israel learned that the whole military situation was about to be transformed.

THE "CZECH" ARMS DEAL AND THE QUESTION OF PREVENTIVE WAR: SEPTEMBER–DECEMBER 1955

In late September 1955 the news became public: Egypt was going to be armed on a large scale by the Soviet bloc (the nominal supplier was Czechoslovakia). The exact numbers were unclear, but the planned transfers would include 100 to 200 MiG-15 and MiG-17 jet fighters, up to 75 Ilyushin jet bombers, up to 300 medium and heavy tanks, hundreds of artillery pieces, other armored vehicles, and warships, including submarines.

To put these numbers in context, in the autumn of 1955 Israel had only about 50 jet fighters, none of them as good as the MiGs. It had about 100 tanks, none as good as the Soviet models. Until the deal was announced, Israel assumed that its superior mobilization and training of forces, in comparison to the large but weakly organized and armed enemy states, would give Israel effective military superiority—as had become apparent toward the end of the 1948–49 war.

Thanks in part to the arms sales controls put in place by the 1950 Tripartite Declaration (an agreement among Britain, France, and the United States), this had been a Middle East in which people argued over arms sales with a dozen tanks here or ten older planes there. Now the whole scale of possible buildup felt different.

The news of the arms sale shook Israel. Sharett wrote in his diary that the Soviet bloc's entry into the Middle East was "a frightening military factor."

Reflecting on the deal, he commented that he felt a "deep concern to our security, the likes of which I have never experienced since the days preceding the establishment of the State [of Israel]."[7]

News of the Soviet bloc's entry on Egypt's side seemed "earth-shattering, tectonically shifting the balance of power in the Middle East." Part of the problem was that, during the initial months, Israeli intelligence—a relatively small operation in a new state—simply did not have the ability to offer much clarity or analysis about the scope and impact of the arms deal.[8]

To Israelis at the time, it seemed that "the Czech deal changed everything." Dayan and Ben-Gurion assumed Egypt would go to war "when they feel they can win." The issue was no longer just border security. "From now on, the Israeli leadership would have to focus their sights on national survival."[9]

The conventional assumption was that the crossover point, when Egypt would have absorbed the new arms and be ready for war, would probably come in the summer of 1956. One of Dayan's aides recalled in 1958: "From [October 1955] onwards, the whole nation, and in particular the IDF [Israel Defense Forces], was living under the threat and strain of this motto: 'There will be war in the summer of 1956.' Everyone was talking about this forthcoming war with complete certainty, as though it was just one stage in a thoroughly worked-out plan."[10]

As Israel digested this news during October 1955, the border incidents and retaliatory raids flared up again. Egypt had already closed the Suez Canal to Israeli shipping (which was unlawful under the international convention that was supposed to govern the canal's use). Now Egypt also used its geographic position to close the Straits of Tiran, which ran from Israel's one potential southern port, Eilat, out through the Gulf of Aqaba to the Red Sea.

While Sharett traveled to Geneva to plead for the great powers to offer arms or security to Israel, the Israeli consensus from sources as diverse as the Israeli intelligence chief to the Israeli embassy in Washington (headed by the urbane ambassador Abba Eban) was that Israel had to consider some sort of preventive war, ideally, as Eban and his colleagues put it, "to overthrow Nasser's regime, be it on our own or jointly with the Western powers." Or, as the intelligence chief argued, "Israel therefore cannot wait until the initiative passes to Egypt. Egypt's present regime . . . must fall and the Egyptian army must be broken before it has time to use the arms." Ben-Gurion and Dayan concluded that Israel should plan to launch a preventive war against Egypt.[11]

Ben-Gurion decided that, once again, it was time for him to resume leadership of the government. He readily persuaded Sharett to step down and go back to his job as the foreign minister. On November 2, Ben-Gurion became both prime minister and defense minister.

The Israeli government was aware that if it launched an openly preventive war against Egypt, it could well find itself isolated internationally and possibly even face a military confrontation with the Western signatories of the Tripartite Declaration (the United States, Britain, and France). The task, then, was somehow to lure Nasser into striking first. The Israeli response could then be justified as an act of self-defense.

As Dayan explained on October 23, the confrontation "must be effected by escalation. Since it is imperative that Israel's actions can be justified in the international arena, she must not do this through any blatant provocation that can ultimately be exposed." But this was not a problem, for Egypt was constantly providing provocation. All Israel need do was to "stubbornly insist on her rights and retaliate sharply for each act of Egyptian aggression." Then, as the Egyptians escalated, the Israelis would launch their massive assault.[12]

In the preventive war plan, the hope was that the war might disrupt Egypt's military buildup and, perhaps, even unseat Nasser. But, more concretely, the war plan anticipated an Israeli occupation of most or all of the Gaza Strip as well as moving down the southeast coast of the Sinai Peninsula to its southern terminus, Sharm el Sheikh, from which point Israel could reopen and protect access through the Straits of Tiran. Initially the operation was set to begin at the end of December.

With the Israeli population feeling "a heavy sense of dread," with elderly people and schoolchildren joining a national voluntary fund drive to contribute coins to help Israel buy more arms, on November 2, Ben-Gurion replaced Sharett as prime minister. He addressed the Israeli Knesset:

> It is my duty to tell all powers that rule the world, with the modesty becoming a representative of a small nation in political affairs but with a moral force of a son of the Jewish people: The people of Israel in the Land of Israel will not be led like sheep to the slaughter. What Hitler did to six million helpless Jews in the ghettos of Europe will not be done by any foe of the House of Israel to a community of free Jews rooted in their own land . . . Our aim is peace—but not suicide.[13]

But as November went by, Ben-Gurion, fully in charge again, expressed a more cautious attitude toward war. Sharett was confused. He wrote in his diary:

What does Ben-Gurion intend? Just to react or to provoke war? When he says that an initiated war is impossible, where is the stress, on the first word or the second? . . . Does he not want war or does he indeed strive for war with Egypt on condition that it not be perceived by the world as a war initiated by us but rather imposed on us?[14]

The more Ben-Gurion thought about it, the more questions he could not answer. If Israel succeeded in its initial operations, what then? Egypt would continue its military buildup. Nasser would still be in power. The whole world might be inflamed against Israel as Egypt gathered strength. Meanwhile, Israel's underlying military inferiority would go unremedied. In such a situation, would Israel really be safer?

Dayan kept pushing for the strategy of "escalation," using some border episode as the basis for a major move. Ben-Gurion resisted. On November 17, he explained to Dayan that if Israel started a major war, all its sources of weapons would disappear and the country would be isolated. "It's not a case of being able to shoot and end it," he said. "Afterward, are we to flee? Where to?" Sharett moved to bring the debate to a close. On December 4 he asked the Israeli cabinet to take a formal vote against such offensive moves. Ben-Gurion joined most of his colleagues in going along with Sharett's motion.[15]

Yet the next week, on December 11, Dayan organized another reprisal raid, this one against Syria, just when Sharett was in Washington asking for American military aid. Ben-Gurion had approved the raid without consulting the cabinet.

An angry cabinet then demanded to approve every future reprisal raid. Embarrassed, Ben-Gurion made it clear that, for some months to come, the Israeli posture would go over to the defensive, to make itself "ready for an Egyptian attack." Ben-Gurion assumed "that we will survive it, but at a very high cost." It would be "harder than in 1948." There could be bombings in the cities, "farms laid waste."[16]

PEACE AND ARMS DIPLOMACY WITH
THE AMERICANS: JANUARY–MARCH 1956

Through 1955 Sharett's alternative to military escalation was to build a security partnership with the United States. In these efforts he was aided by his articulate ambassador in America, Abba Eban.

The American response from the State Department, led by Secretary of

State John Foster Dulles, had usually featured some version of the same three points, repeated in various ways. They were that, first, under the 1950 Tripartite Declaration, the United States already felt a general obligation to prevent aggression by either side (and to join the others in regulating arms supplies).

Second, the Israeli practice of reprisal raids further discouraged the United States from wishing to add to Israel's military power. Right after news of the Soviet bloc arms deal, Dulles had indicated some willingness to consider selling "defensive" arms. This was deferred after news of the December 1955 reprisal raid against Syria.[17]

Third, the Americans insisted that the real solution was to advance a durable Arab-Israeli peace. In August 1955 Dulles had publicly embarked on a significant peace effort, called project Alpha, that linked Israeli territorial concessions to U.S. commitments. If Israel made sacrifices to attain such a peace deal, the United States would be prepared to support Israel with a deeper security partnership. The initial reaction to these public moves was discouraging on all sides.[18]

After word of the Soviet bloc arms deal with Egypt, Israel redoubled its efforts to get American military aid, at least the willingness to sell advanced American arms—such as jet fighters—to Israel. The Israelis made their interest public, to enlist congressional pressure on the administration as it headed into the election year, 1956.

By 1956 the Israeli campaign to obtain weapons was pushing on two fronts. The "Washington school," led by the Foreign Ministry's Moshe Sharett and Abba Eban, worked for an arms deal with the United States. At the same time, the "Paris school" sought to obtain arms from France. That effort was led by one of Ben-Gurion's subordinates, Shimon Peres. Peres was the young (thirty-two-year-old) director-general of the Defense Ministry.[19]

Britain was discounted as a possible source of arms. British-Israeli relations remained strained, and British defense relationships were mainly oriented toward London's Arab friends, especially Jordan and Iraq. When British prime minister Eden weighed in with his views on Arab-Israeli peace (in November 1955), Ben-Gurion's reaction was scornful. He complained to the American ambassador that Eden was attempting "to eliminate Israel" because his government considered Israel "a nuisance and feels it could make a deal with the Arab states if Israel no longer exists."[20]

The United States accepted the urgency of Israel's situation. Yet, putting off discussion of more arms, the U.S. response was to redouble efforts to make progress toward peace. On January 9, 1956, President Eisenhower wrote to

Ben-Gurion (and to Nasser) asking them to receive a secret presidential envoy, traveling with CIA assistance, who would endeavor to facilitate dialogue about the major problems facing Egypt, Israel, and the Middle East as a whole. Eisenhower's letter promised that his envoy, Robert Anderson, "fully understands my personal concern and hopes in this area, which I am sure you and he will want to explore completely."[21]

The Israeli and Egyptian leaders separately agreed to receive Anderson. After talks in Cairo, Anderson arrived in Israel on January 23 for the first of several sets of meetings, shuttling back and forth, that continued into March.

At the same time, Sharett and Eban renewed their arguments to the United States for arms. Sharett called in the American ambassador to stress that Soviet arms were already flowing to Egypt. Nasser would not hesitate to use them, and Israel could not, he said, "rely on external intervention on its behalf [under the Tripartite Declaration] since there was no such commitment [to intervention in the vague Declaration], and even if there were, it was unable to guarantee that Israel's cities and towns would not be devastated before it materialized." The time for decision had arrived.[22]

In Washington, Dulles replied to Eban that "the preservation of Israel in all its essentials was a central aim of the policy of the United States government." But Dulles stressed that the United States was waiting on the results of the Anderson mission. The United States was "pinning its hopes on it and would not do anything to imperil it." The United States had some points of leverage with Egypt and, until "all hope had vanished" for the Anderson mission, the United States could not say yes to Israel's arms requests.[23]

In a series of meetings, Anderson made a good impression on the Israelis. He told them Nasser was very worried about the need to keep these talks secret. Nasser, he said, was flexible on the question of return of Palestinian refugees, but he was inflexible on territory. Nasser insisted on "territorial continuity" between Egypt and Jordan. The main idea, which Americans had worked up during 1955, was that Israel would cede territory in the Negev to Egypt and to Jordan in the shape of a geometric bow-tie, two triangles based in each Arab state and with their points meeting at a narrow point (perhaps even a bridge) in the middle, the "kissing triangles" meeting in some part of the Negev, in southern Israel.

The Israeli position was also to be flexible, arguing that there were no inherent, substantial conflicts of interest between Israel and Egypt. But the Israelis were adamant on two points. The Israelis "rejected outright the demand for territorial continuity." They would not cede more territory carved out of an Israeli state they thought was already small and fragile. On this point, Sharett was as firm as Ben-Gurion.

The Israelis also insisted on direct negotiations between Egypt and Israel as "an absolute condition for any progress." Such a meeting should be unconditional and open-ended. It could be in Cairo. The Israelis promised to keep Anderson's mission secret, as well as any direct contacts.

The Israelis also returned to the issue of arms. Ben-Gurion summed up: "If the United States is unable to bring about peace, its obligation is at least to prevent war, and this could only be through supplying arms."[24]

By March 1956 it had become clear to the Americans, and from them to the Israelis, that the Anderson mission had failed. From their contacts at the State Department, below the level of Dulles himself, the Israelis gathered that the Americans believed the problem was more on Nasser's side. It was hard to come to any preliminary bargain with him on substance and Nasser was unwilling to go along with direct talks.

The Americans told Israeli diplomats that Nasser refused to adopt any position that was not joined by the Syrian president and Saudi king. Therefore he could not meet with Israelis "at any level whatsoever."

The American side was depressed and disappointed. A key State official told an Israeli diplomat that "the Czech deal and Nasser's achievements in the Arab world had gone to his head. The United States had to reappraise its policy in the Middle East." State Department officials thought that if Anderson failed, the U.S. government might be likely to approve an arms request and encourage other states to help, too. The United States might also consider a more elaborate security guarantee for Israel.[25]

Summing up the situation with Anderson, Ben-Gurion warned that if Nasser began "murderous provocations" then Israel would react. War, he said, was marching toward Israel "like an unfolding Greek drama." The only way to avoid it was to provide Israel with the arms it needed. There was no use in further negotiations unless and until Israel could better arm itself. Sharett concurred.[26]

Ben-Gurion elaborated on these points in a letter to Eisenhower. In a recent press conference, Eisenhower had spoken of the futility of trying to give Israel more arms when it was a country of just 1.7 million facing 40 million Arabs. Eisenhower was making the case for a political agreement. Ben-Gurion was anxious to answer that.

Israel's military situation was not hopeless, he wrote. "The respective numbers capable of handling modern arms stand in no proportion to the population figures." Egypt would strain to absorb all the arms it was getting; Israel "is yet far from the saturation point." In 1948, then with only 600,000 inhabitants, Israel had the "essential minimum of arms" and had repelled the forces of five Arab nations. There was already an arms race, Ben-Gurion stressed, except that "*it is one-sided.*"[27]

The American answer to Ben-Gurion's plea, conveyed by Dulles on March 28, conceded that Nasser was indeed "no longer entitled to preferential treatment." The United States was still thinking about what to do about that. As for arms, "in the view of the United States it would be best to concentrate Israel's purchasing efforts mainly in European countries." The United States, he said, would be sympathetic to such European sales.

Sharett regarded this answer "as a most disappointing end to an intensive and lengthy affair which has been going on already for five months." Dulles, he thought, "had reneged on all his promises; the promises of the State Department people had turned out to be baseless." In his diary, Sharett wrote, "The failure of our effort to receive arms from the USA . . . cast a shadow on everything. For five months, I have invested all my enthusiasm and nerves in this effort. . . . I believe at this stage of our relations with the USA wrath is more effective than supplications."[28]

Replying to Sharett's anger, the urbane Israeli envoy in Washington and at the UN in New York, Abba Eban, offered a more nuanced assessment of the American policy. The Americans had tried to work through Nasser and failed. The Americans "had despaired of Nasser but not of all chances of influence in the Arab world." There was "still an essential need," Eban argued, "to maintain and enhance the influence of the United States in the parts of the Arab world that are not lost." That was why Israel had to meet its defensive needs in a way "that will not imply that the United States is identifying wholeheartedly with Israel against the Arab world."

The Israeli government should therefore bank on some informal American help with these other ventures, while the United States was also being supportive of Israel's efforts on other subjects, such as Jordan River waters, and financial assistance. That needed a friendly atmosphere. Eban advised against a political confrontation that attacked the Eisenhower administration. Israel "would not succeed in progressing in an atmosphere of open conflict with the United States."[29]

THE FRENCH PARTNERSHIP: APRIL–JULY 1956

Israel's relations with France had been warming since 1954, when the French government invited Dayan to come for an official visit. The Algerian revolt had put France in conflict with the political position of the Egyptian-led Arab League. Nor had France welcomed the British push, with mild American support, to create the Baghdad Pact. But while there was more openness to Israel, the French Foreign Ministry still placed highest priority on France's relations with the Arab world.

Thus, throughout 1955, the usual pattern was for coolness in dealings with the French Foreign Ministry yet friendly contacts between Israeli and French defense officials, led on the Israeli side by Shimon Peres. As Peres recalled later,

> The dalliance with France was contrary to the pronounced Anglo-Saxon orientation of virtually the entire top political echelon in Israel at that time. . . . It was into this settled and fairly homogeneous policy-making group that a *tsutsik* (young imp) like me came along and announced that only France would save Israel! There was not another Francophile in the whole Israeli establishment.[30]

Dayan, whose eye had been shot out fighting the Vichy French, was also ready to deal with these French. He, like Peres, well knew that the Frenchmen now taking power were more from the wartime Resistance; they had despised the Frenchmen who had served Vichy.

On the French side there was still trouble with the Quai d'Orsay (the nickname for the French Foreign Ministry, whose offices were located by this quay on the Seine riverbank). The French Foreign Ministry would protest Israel's reprisal raids. The French Defense Ministry officials were not so bothered, instead being impressed by demonstrations of Israeli military prowess.[31]

Peres noted in a journal that French "defence institutions will be delighted to fill any further orders from us, and will promise delivery. . . . The only obstacle is the Foreign Ministry, which does everything it can to ensure that our requests are turned down, using underhanded methods."[32]

During 1955 a deal had come together for about a dozen new fighter jets. The jets were finally transferred to Israel in April 1956. Elections in France at the very end of 1955 had brought Guy Mollet to the premiership. On assuming office in January 1956, Mollet met with Peres. Shaking hands with the Israeli official, Mollet remarked, "Now you will see that I will not be a Bevin." Mollet was referring to the British foreign secretary who had been so antagonistic during Israel's struggle for independence.

Hearing these words, Peres felt he was present "at the start of a new era of Franco-Israeli relations." Mollet followed this private meeting with a speech in which he declared that he was opposed to any Israeli territorial concessions. Mollet promised to continue arms sales to Israel to ensure regional equilibrium.[33]

It was in April 1956, after the failure to get arms from the United States and in the midst of another surge of Egyptian-sponsored *fedayeen* raids inside Israel, among the worst yet, with new raids and barrages on the Gaza border, that Ben-Gurion brought his senior foreign and defense officials together, along with Israel's ambassador to Paris. "I have no other topic," he said. "I see this subject [arms] as the main problem." From now on that job would be out of the hands of Sharett's Foreign Ministry. The Defense Ministry would be in charge, concentrating above all on France.[34]

Diplomacy had not entirely disappeared. After the failure of the secret Anderson mission, the Americans had encouraged more activity by the UN, which made a concerted effort to get Israel and its Arab neighbors to abide by the 1949 armistice agreements. The UN truce supervision organization, encamped in a few spots along the border and headed by a Canadian general, E. L. M. Burns, often found itself in opposition to Israeli policies. The Israeli government, for its part, was uncomfortable with the UN presence, which it took to be a foreign force that was not answerable to Israeli authority yet was stationed on Israeli soil.

During the first week of April Burns attempted to restrain the Israelis. He requested that the controversy be brought to the UN Security Council.[35] Raids and counterraids, shelling and counter-shelling, escalated to an Israeli artillery barrage that struck the center of Gaza City, killing fifty Egyptians, most of them civilians. On April 10, Secretary-General of the UN Dag Hammarskjöld arrived in Israel in an attempt to settle the tension. Ben-Gurion agreed to withdraw soldiers 500 yards from the border; Nasser reciprocated.

But Egypt had already dispatched fedayeen squads. They attacked cars and homes, blowing up bridges and pipes. A squad attacked a bus on the road to Jerusalem, then lobbed grenades into a synagogue at a settlement. Forty children were studying inside; five were killed and many more were wounded, including the rabbi. "The atmosphere is that on the eve of war," Sharett wrote in his diary, "one of despondency and shock."[36]

After a couple of weeks of quiet, on April 29, Ro'i Rothberg, the military commander of Kibbutz Nahal Oz, across the border from Gaza City, set out on horseback to run off Arab infiltrators using the kibbutz fields. He was ambushed, killed, and mutilated.

Dayan had liked Rothberg, and he gave a bitter eulogy at the funeral. "It is not from the Arabs in Gaza that we should demand Ro'i's blood," he said, "but from ourselves. How we shut our eyes to a sober observation of our fate, to the sight of our generation's mission in all its cruelty." This "generation of settlers" had the burden of guarding the "gates of Gaza," and "without the steel helmet and the cannon maw we will be unable to plant a tree or build a home."[37]

Dayan's eulogy gave voice to Israeli anger, channeled into military resolve. Not only Dayan but Ben-Gurion as well grew disillusioned with Hammarskjöld, and he with the Israelis. Dayan recorded that their last meeting, on May 2, "ended without any agreement. Ben-Gurion was angry. Hammarskjöld was threatening."[38] Hammarskjöld submitted a report to the Security Council lauding the cease-fire. The border remained tense but relatively quiet.

A biographer sympathetic to Ben-Gurion describes this time as "one of the most difficult periods of Ben-Gurion's career. On the one hand, he had to contend with a dithering Cabinet, most of whose members followed the foreign minister [Sharett] in opposing vigorous action. On the other, he had to restrain the pressing demands of Chief of Staff Dayan for a pre-emptive war against Egypt before it was too late."[39]

Toward the end of May, Ben-Gurion decided Sharett had to go. It was no longer the time for statesmanship. It was a time to get ready for war. To a party colleague, Ben-Gurion wrote that Sharett would be "an excellent foreign minister . . . in a country like Denmark." Israel, "to my deep regret, is not Denmark."[40]

On June 18 Sharett announced his resignation from his post as foreign minister, to be replaced by Golda Meir. Meir, fifty-eight years old, had been born in Russian Ukraine but had grown up in America, mainly in Milwaukee. She and her husband had emigrated to Palestine in 1921, and she had become a leading figure in Zionist politics and foreign relations. She was a reliable ally for Ben-Gurion.[41]

Meanwhile, as Ben-Gurion forced out Sharett, his Defense Ministry men developed the concept of a French partnership that included arms but was much more. In this effort, Peres played a singular role. Not an especially senior official, he identified interesting people and their concerns and lashed them together with "an active, personal diplomacy of a most unorthodox sort."[42]

First, as to arms, when India canceled a large order for hundreds of French aircraft, Peres saw the opportunity for Israel to become the buyer—and not just of aircraft but also of large numbers of tanks, trucks, and more: a deal on a scale comparable to the Soviet-Czech deal with Egypt. The Israelis were willing to pay cash. The two sides began developing ways to smuggle equipment into Israel by air and sea.

But beyond that, Israel saw that all this could make sense to France in the context of a broader strategic alliance against Nasser. The French saw Nasser as a key force behind the troubles in Algeria that had become the French government's largest challenge by far.

Finally, there was a matter of process. Rather than have a situation in which the alliance and the huge arms sales had to be submitted to cabinet review by other coalition ministers in Paris or in Jerusalem, which could be problematic, the solution presented itself when the Israelis intercepted information about the Algerian rebels and shared it with the relevant French minister. Under French law, the French prime minister had the authority to form intelligence relationships with other states without going through the usual cabinet processes.[43]

On June 22, an Israeli Air Force transport painted with French insignia flew secretly to a military airfield near Paris. It carried Dayan, Peres, and the head of Israeli military intelligence, Yehoshafat Harkabi. They were whisked to a lovely private home in the suburb of Vémars north of Paris, owned by one of the brothers who ran the company that made Perrier water.

In these quiet, pleasant surroundings, in meetings usually chaired by the head of the French foreign intelligence service (the SDECE), the two sides spent three days hammering out the details of their agreement. When they were done the accord was signed by the two intelligence chiefs present at the meeting, thus making it an intelligence agreement outside the usual cabinet approval processes.

The French arms deliveries were scheduled to begin, in secret, in July. The Israeli-French intelligence and military cooperation against Egypt began right away, on a voluntary basis for both sides.[44]

Thus, by the beginning of July, Israel had both found a source for the modern arms it sought and forged a secret alliance with a major power. By this time, Israeli intelligence was also putting together a clearer picture of how well the Egyptians were absorbing their new Soviet equipment. This evolving picture did not dispel Israeli military worries, but it brought such anxieties down to earth and showed up areas of continuing Egyptian weakness.[45]

From a wider strategic perspective, then, Dayan could return to contemplation of opportunities for an offensive war against Egypt to address the border issues, including the closure of the Straits of Tiran, in a more lasting way. As in his earlier thinking of late 1955, Dayan envisioned the occasion for such a war coming out of the escalation of another round of border clashes. Ben-Gurion had not yet decided to back such a play.

But for Dayan, leading the armed forces, it was a time to get ready, while also remaining attentive to French concerns and interests. That meant that even though border violence was escalating on the frontier with Jordan, nothing premature should be done about Egypt. Dayan even tamped down proposed reprisal raids while Israel gathered its strength. As he explained internally to his colleagues: "The boiling point in Egypt-Israel relations should be reached later on, when Israel, having absorbed its new French weaponry, will be able to move in a carefully calculated way, both in terms of its military deployment and its system of political and propaganda groundwork."[46]

On the night of July 25, 1956, an amphibious cargo ship called an LST (for Landing Ship, Tank), longer than a football field, powered its way onto a deserted beach near Haifa, in Israel. The ship, originally built by the United States during World War II, had been transferred to France after the war. It was now called the Chelif, after a valley in Algeria. The ship carried thirty tanks, ammunition, and spare parts from France. Israelis moved the equipment to a nearby railhead.

Ben-Gurion, Dayan, and Peres were there to witness this secret unloading, the first of many. They boarded the ship and joined the captain in his cabin, where the Frenchman uncorked a bottle of champagne.[47]

PART ONE

PARIS

CHARLES G. COGAN

FRANCE IN THE 1950S: STRONG ARMY, WEAK GOVERNMENT

For France, as for much of the world, hopes for peace in the mid-1950s came against a background of uncertainty and danger in the early period of the Cold War. It was not known when the Soviets would strike next or whether their aggressive moves would go beyond the bounds.

France was still physically scarred by World War II, but the wounds ran much deeper. It all began, of course, with the swift and surprising defeat of the French army by the Germans in the spring of 1940. General Charles de Gaulle, the wartime leader of the Free French Forces in exile, recalled in a moment of candor, "For all the satisfaction of [the war's] denouement, it had left—and forever!—a secret grief in the depths of the nation's conscience."[1]

The Korean War in June 1950 had sent out alarms throughout Europe. The concern that West Germany might be the object of another proxy war à la Korea saw the formation of the NATO integrated military command at the end of 1950 and the attempt to make use of German military ability through the creation of a European army, the so-called European Defense Community (EDC). Though the EDC treaty was rejected by the French parliament on August 30, 1954, a swift compromise had been worked out by Anthony Eden, then Britain's foreign minister, and Pierre Mendès-France, the French prime minister. It allowed for Germany's integration into NATO and the reconstruction of the German army—as part of NATO.

De Gaulle, in a 1959 speech before the classes of the military schools following his return to power, would look back on the 1950s as a time in which "it could be asserted that the Free World was confronted with an imminent and unlimited threat and that we had not recovered our national personality."[2] Communism's universalist appeal was spreading in the 1940s and 1950s, impelled by the prestige of the Soviet Union as the main power responsible for the crushing of Nazi Germany.

To anticommunists—and the French leaders of 1955 and 1956 were very much anticommunist, or at least against the Soviet version of communism—the rising popularity of neutralism (or positive neutralism, to use its more pro-Soviet nuance) seemed, in part, a mask covering this spreading attraction of communism. The Bandung Conference in April 1955 signaled the emergence of the neutralist community. This seemed, in effect, a kind of Soviet front; at any rate, it served the Soviets' interests. Then in September 1955, with the conclusion of a massive Soviet bloc arms deal with Egypt, the possibility opened of a proxy war in Algeria—the jewel in the crown of French colonial possessions, where a nationalist revolt had erupted in November 1954.

In contrast to the other European powers, France had been at war constantly since the surrender terms signed by Germany and Japan in 1945. A full-scale nationalist revolt in French-controlled Indochina had led to years of war on the other side of the world. The 1954 battle of Dien Bien Phu, ending in French defeat and surrender, led to the Geneva Conference in the summer of that year, which wrote finis to the French Empire in Southeast Asia. By the spring of 1956, the last of the French units stationed in South Vietnam had left.

No sooner had France, under the brief prime ministership of Pierre Mendès-France (June 1954–February 1955), cut Southeast Asia loose from the rest of the French Empire than the long-simmering discontent in Algeria broke out into open revolt on All Saints Day, November 1, 1954. Algeria, though nine-tenths Muslim, had been integrated into France in the form of three French departments. Paris intended to keep things that way.

The overseas French army, at that time still a volunteer force, found itself transferred en masse from Indochina to Algeria, where the presence of a million European settlers, mostly of French origin, strengthened the military's resolve to hang on there. Some declared themselves determined "not to allow in Algeria the 'coup of Indochina.'"[3]

The French army had traditionally considered itself as apart from (and morally superior to) the French civilian government, and it began to take on an increasingly political role in Algeria. The army included important contingents from the French Foreign Legion, composed, in part, of former German soldiers.

The French government that came to power on January 29, 1956, was based on a coalition called the Republican Front—which was neither communist nor rightist. The Republican Front was the leading group that emerged from the legislative elections of January 2, 1956. The French Communist Party was still highly influential in the country, partly through its dominance of the trade union movement. But it had overreached with insurrectionary tactics in the late 1940s. The right had been largely discredited through its tolerance and support of the wartime Vichy regime.

The Republican Front in the postwar Fourth Republic exemplified the "republican" virtues inherited from the Third Republic (1875–1940). It represented the ideals of a secular state verging on the anticlerical; a centralized, accessible educational system producing an integrated model of French citizenship regardless of social or ethnic origins; a political class composed largely of persons prominent in the public sector (the "notables"), who tended to view the moneyed bourgeoisie with faint disapproval; an ideal of social and economic justice; and a governmental system based on the supremacy of the French parliament. That National Assembly was an inheritance from the French Revolution; its factionalism led to a certain French immobilism, which had inspired Alexis de Tocqueville to comment more than a hundred years earlier that France is a profoundly conservative country which dreams of revolution but rejects reform.[4]

The system had its weaknesses, notably the lack of a strong central figure to take over the country in a time of national emergency, as was the case in May 1940 when the Germans invaded. The French president under the Third Republic was only a figurehead. The same was true of the Fourth Republic. The National Assembly could turn out the government in a vote of no confidence, but the president could not dismiss the Assembly and call for new elections.[5] As a result, weakness became a prevailing image of French governments.

Yet the leaders of the Republican Front were not themselves weak men. The prime minister was Guy Mollet, who before the war had been an English teacher and then a wartime member of the Resistance. He had a reputation for sincerity and incorruptibility. He entered office hoping to end the war in Algeria by treating the Muslim Algerians as full French citizens. But as 1956 wore on, he saw his hopes frustrated by rejection both from the Algerian nationalists, who wanted a country of their own, and by the Algerians of European descent.

On Algeria, he worked closely with Robert Lacoste, another trade unionist and a former Resistance leader, who became the minister-resident in Algeria—France's proconsul—and a symbol of adopting a tougher policy against the Algerian rebels.

The foreign minister was another Socialist, Christian Pineau. He and Mollet had both risen through the ranks of the trade union movement but had always stayed out of the Communist Party. Pineau, too, had been active in the Resistance and had fled France during the war to escape capture by the Gestapo. He had already served as a minister in other Socialist-led governments after the war. Americans preferred Mollet. One American diplomat who knew Pineau later reflected, "Nobody can be more ruthless in playing power politics or more intellectually insolent than French Socialists, once they believe their ox has been gored. Pineau did not conceal his contempt for what he called American naivete."[6]

At Defense, the minister was Maurice Bourgès-Maunoury. He was from the centrist Radical party.[7] He, too, had been a Resistance leader and had been involved in linking the Resistance in France to the Free French Forces in Algeria. He had already held office in other postwar governments, including the ministry that had supervised Algerian affairs. He was very supportive of the new state of Israel and close to the French Algerians who were determined to keep Algeria French.

THE FRENCH APPRECIATION OF THE SITUATION: EARLY 1956

After World War II, France had lost its territorial interests in the Middle East. France was not especially engaged and, in fact, tended to oppose the mainly British promotion of regional security pacts. France was, therefore, returning to more traditional instruments of diplomatic influence, including cultural and commercial ties, as its government became more open to friendly relations with Israel, as well as with the Arabs, during 1954. But the Algerian revolt, which escalated into wider warfare during November 1954, became a pivotal feature for the whole course of French policy after that.[8]

As 1955 turned to 1956, French officials in the Foreign Ministry looked back on the Soviet-Egyptian arms deal and the aftermath. They developed an extensive assessment of the whole situation to share with their key ambassadors and with the British and American governments:

The aggravation of rivalries between the Arab countries, the intrigues taking place from one capital to another, the growing tension between Israel and its neighbors, the success which the maneuvers of the Soviets have encountered, the favorable terrain that they have found, particularly in Egypt, the hesitations of Colonel Nasser between the West and the East—these [are the] many elements which, combined with the exaltation of Arab nationalism and Islamic mystique, have contributed to creating an extremely dangerous situation.[9]   .

The French government had "very serious doubts" about the Baghdad Pact, a project on which it had not been consulted. France had opposed this initiative not only in principle but also because its idea of linking up the Fertile Crescent—Iraq, Jordan, and Syria—tended to undermine long-standing French interests and influence in Lebanon and Syria.

The Foreign Ministry assessment explained, "The threat which the Free World must face is much less military than economic and political." Any effort to extend the Baghdad Pact system further would "create new dissensions and new subversions, it would moreover encourage neutralism; finally, it would increase the tension between Egypt and the Western powers."

The French government acknowledged, "Whatever reservations one may have about the current regime in Cairo, one must conclude that, for all sorts of reasons, Egypt presently enjoys in the Muslim World a prestige that no other Arab country possesses." This, plus the Egyptian influence on the Algerian rebels, had led France to try to improve its relations with Nasser's Egypt, too.

In March 1956, Foreign Minister Pineau stopped in to see Nasser on the way back from South Asia, at the suggestion of Prime Minister Nehru. There Pineau received Nasser's "word of honor as a soldier" that he was not sponsoring training in Egypt for the Algerian rebels. On returning to Paris, Pineau repeated this remark to the French National Assembly.

Thus the French government had its own reasons for welcoming the British and American initiative to help Nasser with Egypt's Aswan Dam project. The French government also associated with the "constructive and prudent" American and British efforts to press harder for a peace agreement between Israel and its Arab neighbors. The French government believed the British ideas that Eden had articulated in November 1955 (where he indicated that Israel should retract its borders back from the 1949 armistice lines) were unfair to Israel. But France was "in favor of the principle of Western mediation" and was ready to help in any way it could, if "the vital interests of Israel would be respected."

In a quieter reaction to the Soviet arms deal with Egypt, the French government had already moved forward to start helping Israel in ways the British and Americans would not. The French would sell advanced arms. In December 1955 the Israeli foreign minister, Moshe Sharett, had met with and thanked Pineau's predecessor for the decision to sell twelve Mystère IV fighter jets to Israel, although this deal had been gestating well before the Soviet arms deal was announced. France had previously supplied an earlier-model jet aircraft (the Ouragan) to Israel in August 1954. The French were waiting on approval from the U.S. government for this new sale, since U.S. assistance had helped pay for the construction of the jets.[10]

At the end of 1955 it was not yet clear whether the French government would be willing to sell much larger quantities of arms to Israel, even though the Soviet deal with Egypt would transfer hundreds of fighters and bombers, as well as several hundred tanks and other armored vehicles. At the beginning of January 1956, Israel presented France with a new request for arms. The Israelis asked for an additional tranche of twelve Mystère IVs, ninety AMX tanks, and a variety of other weapons.[11]

As one knowledgeable historian explains, "The question of arms sales to Israel dominated the entire first half of 1956. It developed against a two-fold background of mistrust: among French official agencies on the one hand, and between the French, British, and Americans on the other."

Within the French Foreign Ministry, known colloquially as "Quai d'Orsay" for the spot on the Seine where its offices were located, the Middle East experts wanted to maintain good relations with the Arab world and thus keep Israel at a distance. The Defense Ministry and the intelligence services had a different view. Meanwhile, the French wanted the British and Americans to share the burden or blame for helping Israel.[12]

Among the French leadership, some felt a strong attachment to the newly created Jewish state. This attachment emerged from two mindsets: the French Resistance, on the one hand, and Algeria on the other.[13]

The civilian side of the French government, led by people who had participated in the Resistance, saw Israel's plight as a sort of sequel to the issues from that earlier period. Nasser's Free Officers movement, which had seized power in 1952, had been in its majority sympathetic to the Germans during the war. It had also reportedly engaged a number of East German advisers and technicians. And with increasing stridency, Nasser was threatening to wipe Israel off the map. To Mollet and Bourgès-Maunoury in particular, as former members of the Resistance, these attitudes and associations rekindled the anti-Nazi sentiments of the wartime period. The genocide of the Jews could not be permitted to take place again. And, since aiding Israel had to be done discreetly, these leaders reacted with the reflexes of the wartime Resistance, using clandestine meetings and other secret techniques.

On the military side of the French government, the rapprochement with Israel became a function of the Algerian War. Cooperation against the Arab revolt in Algeria developed between the paramilitary action arm ("Service Action") of the French external intelligence service (Service de documentation extérieure et de contre-espionnage, or SDECE), and the Israeli external intelligence service, the Mossad. As the Algerian revolt gained in intensity in 1955, the cooperation increased to include visits of Israeli operatives to Algeria to give assistance and advice to the French.[14]

General Maurice Challe was an air force officer who had been appointed chief of staff of the French Armed Forces in 1955. Challe's qualities as a military man did not include much of a reputation for political judgment. But Challe was a man of contrasts. He was generally considered on the left of the political spectrum, and his dynamism and effectiveness as a military leader were widely recognized, including by de Gaulle. In 1956, having been promoted to five-star general, he took charge of French air force operations. Challe was widely credited for the success of the French military in Algeria in the ensuing several years.

The other major French military figure in 1956 was the man who in the spring succeeded Challe as chief of staff of the French Armed Forces, an officer whose memoirs are as balanced as Challe's are not, General Paul Ely.[15] While not escaping the typical French conviction that the road to victory in Algeria led through Cairo, Ely was realistic in his view of Algeria' s long-term future. He saw it as folly to treat the three Algerian departments as no different from the other departments in metropolitan France.

An Israeli counterpart at the time, Moshe Dayan, has left this description of Ely: "Gray-haired, tall, and thin, he looked very much the intellectual. He had lost the use of one arm. He was treated with great respect by his officers, and he was clearly more to them than just their chief."[16]

On the civilian side of the French government, the contacts between the French and the Israelis went back to 1954. On both sides, contacts came to be handled mainly through the respective Ministries of Defense. For the Israelis the principal figure was Shimon Peres, who had become director-general of the Israeli Defense Ministry. On the French civilian side, the Quai d'Orsay was kept out of the picture and Defense Minister Bourgès-Maunoury and his aides were the main partners.[17]

FRANCE TAKES SIDES: SPRING 1956

Although Pineau and his colleagues in the Quai d'Orsay still hoped France might work with Nasser, Prime Minister Mollet and other government leaders were moving rapidly toward a darker view. The Algerian War was a catalyst. The rebels insisted on France granting independence as a precondition to any serious negotiations. For the French government, this was out of the question. Mollet and the others debated what they could do to improve the status and assimilation of moderate Algerian Muslims as French citizens. But to abandon Algeria not only meant abandoning more than a million Euro-Algerians and a territory that had, for a century, come to seem like an agriculturally rich part of France on the southern side of the Mediterranean. It also would mean giving up on the secular and civic appeal of French citizenship and yielding instead to the appeals of a violent ethno-religious nationalism. And Cairo appeared to be the great microphone for broadcasting these appeals, inciting war, and secretly arming and training the rebel fighters.

During the spring of 1956, with the war intensifying, the French government decided to restore order in Algeria as a prerequisite for political reform there. The army would transfer tens of thousands of troops to Algeria from their NATO deployments in eastern France or western Germany. Draftees would serve there, too.

In March 1956, Mollet went to England to spend time with British prime minister Anthony Eden at the prime ministerial country estate, Chequers. Eden was fluent in French. Mollet, the former English teacher, was obviously comfortable in that language, as he had also long been comfortable with the idea of a strong friendship between Britain and France.[18]

When the two men exchanged views about the Middle East on March 11, Eden's views on Nasser had been changing, too. Mollet offered a detailed exposition of how he saw the general picture in the Middle East.

He began with "the situation in Algeria, where France more than anywhere else needs the understanding of the Free World." Britain had given that understanding, Mollet acknowledged. "In the United States, by contrast, France runs up against a public opinion that has a reflex of elementary anti-colonialism."

The French records of this Chequers meeting continue:

M. Mollet then made several observations of a general nature. The present period will be decisive for the future of the world. After having contained the offensive of [Soviet] pan-Slavism, the West must now confront that of pan-Islamism, which is not without collusion with Soviet pan-Slavism.

Colonel Nasser, in his writings, has made his objective known: recreate the Islamic empire, centered on Egypt.

M. Mollet regrets the American indulgence towards Egypt. It is France which suffers the brunt of the consequences of this. France alone must carry out a policy of arming Israel which the other Western [powers] approve, but which they do not want to make known. She thus incurs the hostility of Egypt, the Arab country which is the most influential in North Africa, and Libya. . . .

However it is impossible for [France] to abandon Israel. . . . A victory of Egypt over Israel, should it ever take place, would sweep the West out of the Middle East as well as North Africa. Israel is a factor particularly important for the West in that its will to resist is exceptional.

M. Mollet fears that the Baghdad Pact is bringing the USSR into the Middle East, and that the USSR could also move into Africa in the wake of the nationalist movement. . . . If the Paris-Brazzaville axis is cut, all of Black Africa would give way either to the Islamic tide or the Communist tide.

Sir Anthony Eden declared he is ready to make a great effort to bring about a common policy for the region by the Western nations—France, the United Kingdom and the United States.

He cannot accept the thesis that the [Baghdad] Pact is at the origin of Soviet penetration in the Middle East. How can one help friendly countries without making a common front with them? The United Kingdom must absolutely support [Iraqi leader] Nuri Said. The Baghdad Pact has in fact reinforced the resistance to Soviet pressure in the region.

M. Mollet [believes that] the British and French must combine their efforts to have the United States acknowledge that its condemnation of colonialism—of what it wrongly calls colonialism—will end up dooming the Free World to grave failures.

M. Mollet declares that the closest and most intimate cooperation of France and the United Kingdom is indispensable in this region [of the Middle East and North Africa]. . . . There is only one game being played out in the Near East as in North Africa: that of the expansion of pan-Islamism.[19]

Years later Mollet explained the Suez crisis with a trio of historical reference points: "Algeria, Spain and Munich." Each of these words spoke volumes to his generation. "Algeria" meant Nasser's alleged role fomenting the Algerian revolt. "Spain" represented the parallel between Israel and the beleaguered Spanish Republic during the Spanish Civil War of the 1930s, when that republic was destroyed by the fascist side and the French government had stood by. "Munich" represented the failure of the democracies to stop dictators early (Nasser being analogized to Hitler or Mussolini) and Nasser's short book, *Philosophy of the Revolution*, was a sort of mini-*Mein Kampf*.[20]

The Americans having granted their approval, the French had gone ahead with their initial shipment of twelve Mystère fighters to Israel. Israeli prime minister David Ben-Gurion made a statement in the Israeli Knesset (parliament) on April 22, 1956, singling out France for praise as the sole supplier of arms to his country. This embarrassed the Quai d'Orsay.[21]

It did not embarrass other French officials. The success the Israelis were beginning to have in prying arms loose from the French government led Shimon Peres to go a large step further. Peres recounted that he "thought [it] was the appropriate moment to initiate a formal, though secret, conference between the senior military echelons of the two countries. . . . The French Defense Minister . . . immediately agreed, and we jointly set the time and place: June 22 at a delightful chateau at Vémars, outside Paris, belonging to the Leven family, the producers of Vichy and Perrier water."[22]

Peres, Dayan, and a few aides secretly flew to France on an Israeli aircraft. Dayan's personal assistant, who was present, felt the June meeting at Vémars between Israeli and French military and intelligence officers was the key event that cemented the relationship between the two defense establishments. The secret agreement they reached was a decisive step to enable Israel to compensate, in part, for the Soviet-Egyptian arms deal. In particular, Israel's tank numbers doubled, and provision was made for the secret delivery of many more Mystères to Israel.[23]

As Peres recounted, "By the end of the second day, all was worked out. The bill for the hardware—72 Mystère planes, 200 AMX tanks, large quantities of ammunition came to more than $100 million, a vast sum in those days. Without hesitation, I took out my pen and signed."[24]

The additional seventy-two Mystères had to be delivered covertly, unbeknownst to the Quai. The first of three "covert" tranches was to be delivered, flown out with French insignia changed to Israeli markings, by September 1. The other equipment would go by sea, also covertly, in three shipments beginning at the end of July.[25]

Despite the misgivings of the Quai about the damage being done to France's image in the Arab world, there was a remarkable degree of solidarity at the top of the French government in favor of pursuing the de facto "alliance" with Israel. All three top members of the government—Mollet, Bourgès-Maunoury, and Pineau, and particularly the first two—were known for their sympathy for Israel. Mollet was directly acquainted with Israeli Labor Party figures through their common membership in the Socialist International.

Pineau, Mollet's Socialist confrere, who had the habit of expressing the French "difference" by criticizing the Cold War, had a tendency to raise hackles, particularly in Washington. An often repeated theme of Pineau was that the Soviet threat had become more economic than military, and therefore the West's response should be essentially an economic one, centering on increased aid to the underdeveloped countries.

What Mollet and Pineau both eventually brought to the table, and what appealed to Eden, was their common desire to bring down Nasser. As one historian has written:

> Nasser had aroused the most fervent hopes among the [Algerian] revolutionaries. All sides alike were taken in. [French official] Jacques Soustelle, writing as late as 1957, still insisted that the original impetus for the [Algerian] revolt came from Cairo, that the explosion was caused by the conjunction of 'two inert chemicals . . . Egyptian pan-Arabism and Algerian terrorism'; it was a notion that would die hard.[26]

The French were, therefore, naturally following the course of America's outreach to Egypt, such as the proposed Aswan Dam project.

When the French ambassador to Washington, Maurice Couve de Murville, learned the Americans had withdrawn their offer to assist Egypt with the Aswan Dam, he was neither surprised nor disappointed. The break "had been envisaged for several weeks at the State Department. . . . The secretary of state had gradually found himself isolated in his position of fence-sitter ('attentiste'), whereas officials of the State Department had been won over, one by one up to the highest echelon, to the idea that this indecision was prejudicial to the interests of both the United States and the West."

Ambassador de Murville did regard the manner of the decision as "categoric and abrupt, and more brutal in its form than the [State Department] officials . . . who had recommended it were expecting." But de Murville felt he understood the reasons for the American move. These, he argued, were essentially political. The Americans would no longer "be subjected to blackmail by certain powers who profit from the fact that they do not take sides with one or the other Bloc. It was becoming a paying proposition not to take sides." The U.S. Congress did not like Nasser. It was unlikely to "accept that the Administration commit important sums [of money] to a man who adopts such a cavalier ('désinvolte') attitude toward the United States and democratic ideals."[27]

JILL KASTNER *and* DAVID NICKLES

THE PROBLEM OF NASSER

News of Nasser's "Czech" arms deal caused shock waves in London. Until that moment, Britain had managed to walk a tightrope, preserving its oil supplies and influence while maintaining workable relations with Israel, Egypt, and the Arab world. Now the Soviets were in Egypt, and the balance of power was skewed. With his move, Nasser had set Whitehall on fire. Prime Minister Anthony Eden was furious, torn between a "fear of driving Nasser irrevocably into the Soviet camp and a desire to wring the necks of Egypt and Syria."[1]

At the Foreign Office, rueful ministers considered the deal "a master stroke," with repercussions for the future not only of Britain but all of Western Europe. Officials believed there was "no doubt whatever that we are witnessing the major attempt by the Russians to undermine our position in the Middle East."[2]

First was the problem of the weapons themselves. Britain, France, and the United States had concluded the Tripartite Agreement in 1950 to prevent precisely this kind of arms flow into the region. The three powers had guaranteed the Arab-Israeli armistice lines of 1949 and agreed to monitor and limit weapons sales to Israel and Egypt. Now, with the influx of Czech (really Soviet) weapons, the Tripartite Agreement was gravely undermined.

The new muscle in the Egyptian military posed a real danger of war with Israel. Nasser had been quite open in at least his rhetorical desire to wipe Israel off the map. The new weapons could be the key to avenging the Arab defeat of 1949. Israel could also decide to launch a preventive war against Egypt before the Egyptian military learned how to use the new equipment. Hostilities would no doubt spill over into neighboring Arab countries. This was a particular headache because of Britain's strategic and political obligations to protect the Hashemite royal dynasties in Iraq and Jordan, kingdoms Britain had done much to create.

Then there was the problem of what came with the weapons: Soviet technicians, meddling, and influence. For Britain, a Soviet presence in the Middle East posed an existential threat. "On no account," Eden declared, "must we let the Russians into the Nile Valley." Nasser had allowed the Soviet Union to effectively leapfrog the newly minted Baghdad Pact, ratified by Pakistan only days before. The pact was supposed to be the defensive barrier preventing Soviet expansion into Southwest Asia, linking Turkey, NATO's southernmost neighbor, to Iraq, Iran, and now Pakistan. Nasser's move made the pact seem pointless.[3]

Eden's reaction was a complex mix. There were the policy arguments, of course. But he also had a long personal history with the region, particularly with Egypt. He had traveled with the diplomat Sir Mark Sykes (co-author of the Sykes-Picot agreement) throughout Mesopotamia during World War I. After the war, he earned a first in Oriental languages at Oxford, then was elected a member of Parliament (MP) and enjoyed a swift rise in the Conservative ranks, becoming foreign secretary at the age of thirty-eight. The Egyptian problem was well known to him; he had participated in base negotiations with the young Egyptian king Farouk in 1936.

Dashing and handsome, Eden was easily recognizable by his trim mustache and impeccable taste in clothes. He was lauded for his principles, having famously resigned in February 1938 over what he perceived to be Prime Minister Neville Chamberlain's appeasement of Mussolini. He was known as a skilled diplomat, much more flexible in his approach to decolonization than his mentor, Churchill. And, having lost two brothers and a son to war, he was regarded as a committed man of peace.

But like many of his class and generation, Eden was preoccupied with maintaining Britain's great power status. He understood that compromise would be necessary to stay in the game, and in an environment of a struggling British economy, thermonuclear weapons, and nationalist uprisings in the non-Western world, Eden believed Britain needed to wield international influence in more subtle ways than formal imperialism. As he put it, "New times, new methods."[4]

As a result, when Nasser came to power, Eden did his best to work with him. In October 1954, while still Churchill's foreign secretary and heir apparent, it was Eden who had negotiated the agreement with Nasser withdrawing the last British troops from the Canal Zone by June of 1956. As a result, his personal reputation became publicly entwined with the policy of supporting Nasser.

The 1954 agreement had proved wildly unpopular with hard-liners within the British public and government, who disdained the notion that Britain should ever give up its presence in Egypt. Eden was subjected to vituperative criticism, accused of being a "scuttler" who had weakened Britain's position in the Middle East and the world. The worst attacks came from a group of Conservative MPs, known as the Suez Group, who accused Eden of betraying British prestige and strategic interests by appeasing Nasser. Their repeated criticism in Parliament and in the press was a constant irritant for Eden.

A few months after the treaty's conclusion, Eden had met Nasser for the first and only time, in February 1955. Eden had found the colonel friendly and full of praise for the improvement in Anglo-Egyptian relations. But there were many sources of friction in the relationship, particularly the pending Baghdad Pact, which Nasser deeply opposed. There was also a personally awkward moment as Nasser grabbed Eden's hand during a photo session. Tensions aside, Eden reassured Conservative MPs on his return to London that the colonel was actually "the best sort of Egyptian" and far superior to the pashas of the past.[5]

Eden championed Nasser in part because Britain needed Egypt's help to achieve peace in the Arab-Israeli conflict. In December 1954, Eden and U.S. secretary of state John Foster Dulles had launched a secret Anglo-American venture, the Alpha project, designed to solve the Arab-Israeli dispute by reducing the Israeli frontiers in exchange for compensation and guarantees of support for Israel. The plan sought to create stability for both Egypt and Israel, despite potential Israeli opposition to the loss of territory. As one pragmatic British official put it, "If we are ever to bring about a Palestine settlement, we shall have to be nasty to the Israelis at some stage."[6]

But the Baghdad Pact had soured Nasser's attitude. It not only thwarted his plans for a pan-Arab approach to Middle East security but also seemed to favor Baghdad over Cairo in the struggle between the Nile and the Fertile Crescent that had been going on for millennia. To make matters worse, just days after the meeting between Nasser and Eden, an Israeli raid on the Egyptian military headquarters in Gaza had left thirty-eight Egyptian soldiers dead. To protect his country and his political future, Nasser began to support more organized raids by *fedayeen* fighters into Israel. He also began searching in earnest for weapons for the Egyptian military. His subsequent overtures to London and Washington proved fruitless.

Eden, meanwhile, finally ascended to the prime minister's office in April 1955. He immediately called a general election, substantially increasing the Conservative parliamentary majority from seventeen to sixty. With this comfortable margin, he could tackle the many diplomatic challenges ahead. West Germany had joined NATO on May 5. A treaty on Austrian independence and neutrality was followed by the "Big Four" Geneva summit in July. In the East, tensions flared over the islands of Quemoy and Matsu, and the Chinese threatened to "liberate" Taiwan. Eden the diplomat was now Eden the world leader. It suited him well.

But the economy was weakening. Sterling had returned to convertibility in September, and the value of the pound was barely holding at the fixed rate of $2.80 to the £1. British wages had been rising, and with them, inflation. Eden was forced to consider wage and credit controls to stop it. If Nasser were to unite the oil-producing countries against Britain, and if Britain were stopped from trading freely, sterling could cease to become a reserve currency. These were problems for which his diplomatic skills had not prepared him, and his poll numbers began to fall. By the autumn of 1955, he had become politically vulnerable.

Unpopularity did not sit well with Anthony Eden. Despite his Hollywood looks and political success, he was thin-skinned and vain. R. A. "Rab" Butler, a political rival and chancellor of the Exchequer during Eden's first months as prime minister, remarked, "Anthony's father was a mad baronet and his mother a very beautiful woman. That's Anthony—half mad baronet, half beautiful woman." Eden thought and spoke in rapid, affected animation, charming one moment, vicious the next, contrite afterward. Those who worked with him over long periods became accustomed to his outbursts, but it was clear he could react badly under stress. Indeed, the criticism over the 1954 agreement with Egypt had devastated him.[7]

Part of the problem lay in the fact that he was physically a ticking time bomb. In 1953 his bile duct had been severely damaged during a botched gallbladder operation. Sir Evelyn Shuckburgh, for a time Eden's private secretary, wrote, "He was constantly having trouble with his insides. We used to carry round with us a black tin box containing various forms of analgesic supplied by his doctor, ranging from simple aspirins to morphia injections, and we dealt them out to him according to the degree of his suffering." When Shuckburgh raised his concern about the painkillers with Eden's doctor, the doctor "replied that he was responsible for a very important national figure and conceived it to be his duty 'to keep him on the road.'"[8]

To counter the lethargy brought on by the painkillers, Eden took a daily regimen of amphetamines. Even moderate doses often produced insomnia, restlessness, anxiety, irritability, overstimulation, and overconfidence. This was a toxic cocktail when combined with Eden's already high-strung nature.[9]

And now Nasser had made a deal with the Soviet Union that turned British policy on its head. For Eden, it felt like a personal betrayal. Nasser's move seemed to prove his critics right.

REACTION AND ACTION

The scramble to deal with Nasser's move began with the realization that Britain had been caught unaware. The news had reached the Foreign Office on September 21 through the American ambassador in Cairo, revealing a complete lack of British intelligence on the ground. That was not a new problem. Britain's intelligence sources in Egypt had been in the royal household and the Wafd party, one of the political groupings that had dominated Egyptian politics under the monarchy. The British Secret Service, MI6, had completely missed the preparations for the coup that overthrew the king and brought General Naguib to power in 1952. An understanding of Nasser's role in the new government had also emerged only slowly.[10]

As for the arms deal with the Soviets (handled nominally through the Czech government, a Soviet satellite), even the MI6 spy at the Egyptian embassy in Prague, the Czech capital, had failed to report the deal. The Joint Intelligence Committee (JIC) admitted the news "had taken us by surprise," and JIC chair Patrick Dean ordered an investigation into why there had been no warning.[11]

On September 26, the day before news of the arms sale became public, Foreign Secretary Harold Macmillan met with U.S. secretary of state Dulles in New York. The two became increasingly agitated as they discussed rumors of the deal. Macmillan was particularly incensed, declaring: "Nasser cannot have thought out all the consequences of this move. . . . The world will not allow the USSR to become the guardian of the Suez Canal." He was indignant at the idea of Soviet technicians sitting on airfields built by Britain and gratified that Dulles shared his umbrage.[12]

Macmillan and Dulles decided to join forces with French foreign minister Antoine Pinay and "have a word" with Soviet foreign minister Vyacheslav

Molotov, who was also in New York in September 1955 for the opening of the United Nations General Assembly session. Perhaps Nasser was bluffing. Molotov had said, at least up until his departure from Moscow, that "not a single rifle or bullet" had been sold to Egypt. In case Nasser was not bluffing, the British and Americans instructed their diplomats to let Nasser know of their disapproval of his actions and try to get him to abandon the deal.[13]

But if he did not, what should Britain do? Overthrowing Nasser was an obvious option to consider, especially in light of the recent coups in Iran in 1953 and Guatemala in 1954. The British and Americans had secretly worked together to support the Iranian upheaval; the Americans had organized the Guatemalan overthrow. As Macmillan told Dulles, "We could make life impossible for Nasser and ultimately bring about his fall."[14]

But at least for the moment, overthrow was not within Britain's grasp. Nasser had rounded up or eliminated his opponents after taking power. He was firmly in control in Egypt. Eden requested an assessment from Sir Humphrey Trevelyan, the British ambassador in Cairo. Trevelyan reported there were "at present no reliable signs of the regime losing its grip . . . or of its opponents gaining ground. On the contrary, the acceptance of Soviet arms has added to [Nasser's] prestige and given him, at least temporarily, what he had always lacked, a measure of personal popularity."[15]

By October 3, after Trevelyan had spoken to Nasser, it was clear the Egyptian was not bluffing about the Soviet arms deal. Meeting in Washington, Macmillan and Dulles concluded they had no choice but to accept it. They agreed to "wait a decent interval" and then approach Nasser to see if he would consider limiting his arms purchases in exchange for political concessions over the division of the Jordan waters, or perhaps progress on a settlement with the Israelis.[16]

For his part, Eden suggested seeking Four Power consultations between Britain, the United States, France, and the Soviet Union. But Dulles, Macmillan, and advisers on both sides vehemently opposed that idea, as it would set a precedent for consulting the Soviets on Middle East issues. Eden tried another tack. In mid-October, he wrote a reproachful letter to Nasser asking him once and for all whether he sought to be a friend or enemy of Britain. His private secretary, Guy Millard, warned him off. "Should we not be making ourselves look rather silly?" he asked. "How would it look if it becomes public?" The letter was never sent.[17]

Eden was hamstrung by Britain's need for oil. Although Egypt itself was not an oil supplier, opposing Nasser too forcefully might provoke more nationalist trouble for British allies in Jordan and oil-rich Iraq. And any British alliance with Israel against Egypt would turn the entire Arab world against Britain, threatening its oil supplies.

In the end, the cabinet concluded that the best course was to keep working with Nasser. Although Britain opted to "leave Nasser to stew in his own juice for awhile," issuing a statement supporting Sudanese independence (a sore point with Nasser) and loudly announcing support for friendly countries like Iraq, it eventually made overtures to the Egyptians on a topic close to Nasser's heart: the construction of the Aswan High Dam. Britain's plan was for the West (mainly the Americans, who had the money) to give Egypt support for this massive development project, which had been in talks since early 1955. This might keep Nasser in the Western camp while undercutting Soviet efforts to fund the project.[18]

The Americans were at first reluctant. But by late October word had reached London that the Soviets were making offers. Eden and the cabinet thought it crucial to prevent this further blow to Western prestige in the Middle East, and they began lobbying Washington hard for progress on funding for the dam.

American support was critical, but it was an uneven partnership. British officials liked to downplay the asymmetry in power between the two nations, recalling how the clever Greeks had manipulated and tutored the mighty Romans. But competition between the two countries over influence in the oil-rich regions of the Middle East was fierce. The United States, particularly, sought to displace Britain from the oil business in Saudi Arabia and Iran.

In addition, many Englishmen considered American anti-imperialism naïve and hypocritical. Eden shared this irritation, grumbling that the Americans were "always unprepared to act." He believed Britain must be willing to pursue its own interests while cultivating American support. With its long history in the region and dependence on oil, Britain's interests in the Middle East were greater than those of the United States. As Eden put it, "We should not . . . allow ourselves to be restricted overmuch by reluctance to act without full American concurrence and support. We should form our own policy in the light of our interests in the area and get the Americans to support it to the extent we could induce them to do so."[19]

This attitude led Eden to provoke a crisis with the Saudis—and the Americans—over the Arabian oasis of Buraimi, in the southeastern corner of the Arabian Peninsula. The sheikdom of Abu Dhabi (now part of the United Arab Emirates) and the sultanate of Oman claimed the right to jointly administer this territory and Britain, which protected both the sheikdom and the sultanate, represented their interests. Saudi Arabia claimed Buraimi. Eden deliberately avoided informing the Americans of his decision to break off international arbitration with the American-allied Saudis and kick them out of Buraimi, which was thought to have oil deposits. Britain also supported the sultan of Oman's suppression of Saudi-backed rebels in the area. These events did little to endear the British to U.S. under secretary of state Herbert Hoover Jr., a former oilman whose blessing was urgently required for the dam funding.[20]

Eden's attitude toward the Americans was influenced too by his close relationship with American president Dwight Eisenhower, formed during their years of work together during World War II. But Eisenhower had suffered a heart attack on September 24, leaving Dulles to deal with the situation. Eden had always had enormous difficulty dealing with Dulles. The two had clashed over policies in Indochina and Guatemala, and the British government tended to blame Dulles for the Eisenhower administration's decision to pursue an independent course in the Middle East.

Personally, whereas Eden was glib, quick-witted, and urbane, Dulles was ponderous, slow-speaking, and legalistic. He got on Eden's nerves to the point where Eden once described him with the quip, "Dull, Duller, Dulles." Try as he might, Eden just couldn't make out what the American was trying to say. As one observer noted, "Foster talks so slowly that [Eden] does not wait to hear what he has to say, while our man talks in so roundabout and elusive a style that the other, being a lawyer, goes away having failed to make the right guesses."[21]

Unlike Eden, Harold Macmillan enjoyed good relations with Dulles. He prided himself on his ability to work with the secretary of state, boasting that despite Dulles's "overlegalistic and often seemingly devious approach. . . I had not found it too difficult to bring him round to our point of view. But it needed a lot of patience and a great capacity for listening." Eden, for whom Macmillan had long been a political rival, was less impressed with his foreign secretary's talents. He wrote in his diary that Macmillan "follows Dulles around like an admiring poodle and that is bad for Foster and worse for British interests in the Middle East."[22]

ISRAEL, JORDAN, AND THE BAGHDAD PACT

Meanwhile, the threat of an Israeli attack on Egypt intensified. On October 26 Israeli prime minister Moshe Sharett, who would soon be replaced by the bellicose David Ben-Gurion, visited Macmillan to make a plea for arms and security guarantees. "He gave us the impression that his chances of avoiding a preventive war by Israel are very slender unless we grant him his demands," Macmillan wrote. By November 1955 British intelligence was reporting that the Israelis planned to "drive to Suez across Sinai in an endeavor to trap Egyptian forces, thereby causing Nasser's downfall."[23]

While Nasser's removal might be a good outcome, there was a danger that Israeli action could also involve Jordan, which Britain was committed to defend. As a result, British officials began to discuss plans for retaliation against Israel if it were to attack Jordan.

To many British ministers, support for Israel had long seemed incompatible with British interests. Strategically, Britain needed oil, the canal, and the bunkering facilities of the Port of Aden more than it needed Israel. In official circles there was some irritation with the Israelis stemming from a combination of anti-Semitism and a lingering resentment at the Zionist terrorism that had been directed against British forces during the bitter struggle over Britain's Palestine mandate, which had been dissolved in 1947.[24]

Outside of the Foreign Office, many of Britain's politicians, notably Churchill, Macmillan, and the new Labour leader, Hugh Gaitskell, were much more sympathetic to Israeli aspirations. Eden, while sometimes complaining about what he perceived as a pro-Arab bias in the Foreign Office, was also known as a friend to the Arabs. In 1954 he had even privately defended Nasser's ban on allowing Israeli shipping to use the Suez Canal.[25]

Whatever their personal bias, nearly all British leaders believed in the power of Israeli influence on their American ally, particularly in an election year. Macmillan regarded August 1955 as the final opportunity for constructive public declarations by American statesmen; afterward, politicians would begin "blatant wooing of the Jewish vote." This belief in Jewish influence was partially the result of having dealt with the United States in the period of the Palestine mandate, but it also came from the Americans themselves. Dulles, for example, urged the British to move quickly to support Project Alpha—the American effort to mediate a peace settlement with Israel—because the upcoming election would soon paralyze American policy. Later, in March 1956, Dulles warned Macmillan's successor as foreign secretary, Selwyn Lloyd, that a crisis over U.S. relations with Israel "would be the one thing that might rob President Eisenhower of victory" in the presidential election.[26]

Therefore, in addition to a push on offering funding for Egypt's Aswan Dam project, British policy in the autumn of 1955 included further efforts toward an Arab-Israeli settlement. The British made this point publicly, emphasizing

Israeli territorial compromise in a way that seemed especially pointed against Israel. In a major address at London's Guildhall on November 9, Eden offered his services as a mediator. In response, Israeli prime minister David Ben-Gurion informed the British that if they wanted Israeli territory they would have to send in the army to get it.[27]

Overall, the initial British reaction to the Soviet-Egyptian arms deal was to try to find a way to work with Nasser, emphasizing incentives rather than threats. The British then worked hard to persuade the Americans to go along with this approach.

But if incentives did not work, a tougher strategy also needed to be readied. Sir Ivone Kirkpatrick, the hard-line permanent under secretary at the Foreign Office and Eden's close confidant, counseled that efforts "should be made to prevent Egypt falling completely under Russian domination. If this fails we must try ruthlessly to isolate Egypt."[28]

One way to do this was to strengthen the Baghdad Pact. Kirkpatrick believed the British government should place great pressure on Jordan to join up. Iran had signed on in October 1955. Jordan should be next.

Eden wondered "whether it was wise to press Jordan hard to join the pact. This might rile the Egyptians, who were showing signs of being reasonable." Ambassador Trevelyan, in Cairo, agreed that such a move would be "unwise." Eden also believed the Soviets had been angered by the recent inclusion of their neighbor Iran in the pact; it was not clear how they would respond to new members. Pressuring Jordan might also cause trouble with the Americans. Eden's great hope was for the United States to join the Baghdad Pact. But American accession to a pact containing Jordan, a country bordering on and antagonistic toward Israel, was unlikely.

But Macmillan, following the advice of those like Kirkpatrick, who saw the Baghdad Pact as the instrument of British regional power, finally persuaded Eden to go along with pressure on Jordan to join the pact. Britain was ready to threaten Jordan "that we cannot continue our financial and military support for a country which will not stay on our side in grave issues and then the Israelis will get them."[29]

In November, responding to overtures that also came from Turkey, Jordan's young King Hussein finally expressed interest in joining the pact. But, as Trevelyan and others had warned, the British high-pressure approach backfired. Angry anti-British demonstrations rocked the streets of Amman. Anti-British broadcasts on Radio Cairo were renewed, straining Anglo-Egyptian relations almost to the breaking point. One particularly sensitive issue was the fact that Sir John Bagot Glubb, a well-known English general, oversaw the Jordanian military. Glubb quickly became the focus of anti-British propaganda. Despite King Hussein's overtures, his ministers balked. By the end of the year, he had been forced to back away and renounce any efforts to join the Baghdad Pact.

In late 1955, as London debated what to do about Nasser and about Jordan, new intelligence began to arrive in London that portrayed Nasser in the worst possible light. The material came from a mysterious source code-named Lucky Break. MI6 claimed that Lucky Break was close to Nasser. The source reported that the Egyptian leader was now Moscow's puppet. The Lucky Break source also asserted that Cairo was planning a war against Israel in June 1956. The French, whom the British had kept at arm's length throughout 1955, were also reporting that the West had underestimated Soviet influence on Nasser, particularly in his support for Algerian rebels making trouble for the French in North Africa.

The Foreign Office was not persuaded. Its officials believed Lucky Break was a crank, or worse, an attempt by MI6 agents to mask their failure to find real intelligence. The French arguments were also discounted at the Foreign Office, with one official noting, "This sounds to me like a too clever French supposition."[30]

At first, the British used Lucky Break's threatening portrait of Nasser as ammunition to convince the Americans to fund the Aswan Dam project—the "carrot" idea that the British were pushing. So, though it may seem paradoxical, this dark view of Nasser was used as an argument for why the West should help him. Eden even sent a letter to Eisenhower, based on the Lucky Break reports, describing Egypt's alleged submission to Moscow, as an argument for U.S. aid to Egypt's project. British ambassador to the United States Sir Roger Makins promptly shared the letter with U.S. under secretary of state Hoover on November 27, and he believed it persuaded Hoover to change his stance and throw his support behind funding for the Aswan Dam.[31]

Makins cabled that at least these Americans had believed the reports that Nasser was going down the communist route. Hoover did ask if, instead of helping him, Britain had "thought of finding an alternative to Nasser somewhere." Macmillan responded that "it would be advantageous in any event to overthrow him if possible." Makins reported that the CIA had been considering it and wanted to compare notes. By December, a special code word cover was designated in London for discussions of overthrowing Nasser, with distribution limited to the prime minister, the foreign secretary, Kirkpatrick, and four other senior Foreign Office officials.[32]

Meanwhile, negotiations for the Aswan Dam funding continued. On December 14, the offer to Nasser was made.

From mid-December, British policy seemed more and more contradictory. The Arab-Israeli peace push was still proceeding, at least in theory. Meanwhile Eden's government pursued a policy of enticing Egypt away from Soviet influence through the Aswan Dam project. Eden was simultaneously encouraging subordinates to plot Nasser's overthrow. When Macmillan reported on a new revolutionary group that might prove useful, Eden encouraged discussions with the United States to "see what alternative possibilities to Nasser there may be and what we could do about it."[33]

With the Nasser issue still festering, Eden was forced to turn his attention to domestic politics. The economy was struggling, and press stories portrayed a weak and indecisive prime minister, dithering over changes to the cabinet and other problems. The normally Conservative-leaning *Daily Telegraph* ran an editorial noting that Eden, to drive home a point during parliamentary debate, would "clench one fist to smack the open palm of the other hand—but the smack is seldom heard."

Eden seemed "stricken" by the criticism. Lord Kilmuir, a member of the cabinet, recalled, "No one in public life lived more on his nerves than [Eden] did, and criticism which Churchill, Attlee, or Macmillan would have ignored seemed to wound Eden deeply. He had not been used to dealing with a rowdy House of Commons, and he found the regular scenes of uproar mentally and physically exhausting." Kilmuir delicately added, "There were indications that his health was not as good as we had hoped."[34]

When Eden finally shuffled his cabinet in December, he moved Harold Macmillan from the Foreign Office to the Treasury. Macmillan bristled at the change. He had enjoyed being foreign secretary, and during his stint at the Foreign Office he had often chafed at Eden's meddling in an arena where he had great confidence and experience.

The post of foreign secretary went to Selwyn Lloyd, whose lack of international experience made it perfectly clear that Eden intended to manage his own foreign affairs. When Lloyd had joined the Foreign Office four years earlier, he spoke no foreign languages, had only visited a foreign country in time of war, and had never participated in or even listened to a foreign affairs debate in the House. Although his knowledge had improved by December 1955, he constantly deferred decisions to the prime minister, shying away from any challenge to Eden's judgment. This may have been just what Eden intended.[35]

NEW YEAR, AND A CHANGING POLICY TOWARD NASSER

In late January 1956, Eden and Lloyd sailed for America to meet with Eisenhower and Dulles. Eden's recent mauling in the press and the House of Commons had left him in low spirits. To Sir Evelyn Shuckburgh, now the main diplomat working on the Middle East, Eden seemed "very suspicious of American intentions and absolutely distrusts Nasser. He seemed thin, nervy and in a curious way frivolous. I don't think he is at all well or at all happy."[36]

Nonetheless, the meetings in Washington went well. Eisenhower, apparently recovered from his September heart attack, was in good form. The conference participants even appeared to make progress on the Buraimi oasis dispute.[37]

As for Egypt, Nasser was judged to be still worth cultivating. Both parties agreed that negotiations for Anglo-American financing for the Aswan Dam should continue apace. Both also agreed that the governments of Iraq and Jordan should be strengthened, while consideration should be given to changing the regime in Syria. And the Arab-Israeli peace push was going ahead, now with a secret American mission, led by Eisenhower's trusted confidant, former secretary of the navy Robert Anderson.

The British leaders felt euphoric after their meetings. Eden cabled colleagues in London that "this is the best meeting in Washington we have ever had." Lloyd wrote, "We felt that we might argue away like members of a family but at the end of the day would never seriously fall out."[38]

On February 15, 1956, with Jordan having decided not to join the Baghdad Pact, Jordan did ask Britain to promise support in case of hostilities with Israel. The cabinet agreed to this request on the condition that Jordan did not precipitate the conflict. By this time, British intelligence was predicting that Israel would take "provocative action on or about 1st March." British troops were stationed in the region, under the code name Operation Cordage, prepared to come to Jordan's defense.[39]

Two weeks later, events in Jordan changed everything. On March 1, King Hussein unceremoniously fired General Glubb, who had trained and led Jordan's Arab Legion army since 1939. Long the target of Cairo's anti-British propaganda, Glubb was a towering figure, respected as one of the last great symbols of Anglo-Arab amity and of British prestige in the Middle East. Despite his twenty-five years of service to the Hashemite throne, he was given only hours to leave the country.

Eden was livid. It did not help that Lloyd had been in Cairo, meeting with a smiling and amicable Nasser at exactly the moment Glubb was sacked. Eden reacted "almost as if No. 10 itself had been attacked and a howling mob of Arabs were laying siege to Downing Street." It was his "absolute conviction that Glubb's dismissal was Nasser's doing."[40]

Lloyd's deputy at the Foreign Office, Anthony Nutting, suggested that perhaps it was King Hussein's need to assert his authority in his own kingdom that had prompted Glubb's dismissal. Eden was having none of it. Despite assurances from King Hussein and Glubb himself that Egypt had not been involved, Eden could not be dissuaded from his belief that Nasser was the culprit.[41]

The sacking of Glubb crystallized Eden's belief that Nasser was a sort of second Mussolini, an up-and-coming Arab dictator in thrall to the Soviet Union. After fresh reports arrived from MI6 sources about Russian influence in Cairo, he sought to impress on Eisenhower the seriousness of the situation. On March 5, he warned the American president that "the Russians are resolved to liquidate [the] Baghdad Pact. In this undertaking Nasser is supporting them and I suspect that his relations with the Soviets are much closer than he admits to us. Recent events in Jordan are part of this pattern. . . . I feel myself that we can no longer safely wait on Nasser."[42]

Not only was Eden not willing to wait on Nasser, he was eager to eliminate him. "It is either him or us," Eden declared, "don't forget that." The option of overthrow was definitely back on the table. Eden asked MI6 to contact Egyptians prepared to form a government in the event of a coup against Nasser.[43]

The Americans were let in on the scheme. Several CIA officials visited London in early April and met with MI6 deputy director George Young. He told his incredulous guests that Egypt, Saudi Arabia, and Syria were threats to Britain's survival and would have to be subverted or overthrown.[44]

How serious were Eden's attempts to assassinate Nasser? It is unclear just what ideas were being considered during the spring and early summer of 1956, but rumors abounded. Sir Dick White, who was then "C," or chief, of MI6, later implied that Eden had ordered Nasser's assassination and White had refused.[45]

Glubb's departure created massive political problems for Eden. Glubb had been a familiar and comforting figure for the British public, who laid the blame for the general's sacking at Eden's feet. Eden's December cabinet shake-up had not been well received, and further economic austerity measures had led to cuts in subsidies for bread and milk. There were rumors that Eden might resign. He did himself no favors by lashing out at the press.[46]

Both Labour and the Suez Group now used the Glubb episode to bludgeon the government in Parliament and the press. In a March 7 House of Commons debate, Eden delivered the worst performance of his career and was shouted down by MPs chanting, "What's your policy?" and "Resign!" A correspondent for the *New York Times* reported that Eden was "subjected to a storm of vituperation and abuse beyond anything heard in the Commons since the last days of Neville Chamberlain's prime ministership." A British columnist warned, "If the year goes on as it has begun, it will not be Sir Anthony but Mr. Harold Macmillan who reigns in Downing Street in 1957."[47]

The cabinet agreed with Foreign Office suggestions that Britain work with the United States to isolate and weaken Nasser. But when Eden was informed, he completely lost the plot. "What's all this nonsense about isolating Nasser or 'neutralizing' him, as you call it?" he shouted down the telephone line at Anthony Nutting. "I want him murdered, and if you and the Foreign Office don't agree, then you'd better come to the Cabinet and explain why!" A stunned Nutting protested that there was no good alternative to Nasser and that a coup would only produce anarchy. "But I don't want an alternative," Eden shouted, "and I don't give a damn if there's anarchy and chaos in Egypt!"[48]

Two days later, Eden sent Eisenhower another "most secret note," based again on the Lucky Break source, about Egypt's design for domination of the Arab world. He claimed Nasser's plans would mean the overthrow of the rulers in Iraq and Jordan, the end of the Baghdad Pact, and the establishment of purely Arab republics in Tunisia, Algeria, and Morocco. And in all these endeavors, Nasser was working with the Soviets.[49]

But while the Americans seemed to want to work with Britain, they were also sending mixed messages about just what they wanted to do about Nasser. Eden was frustrated with their ambivalence. Macmillan believed the problem stemmed from Eisenhower's "light rein" on Dulles. "Our proposals were not rejected," he later wrote, but "they were lost in a vast ocean of prolonged but unfruitful discussions. Eden, baffled by Dulles, was induced to address personal appeals to President Eisenhower," a tactic that was "neither welcome nor successful."[50]

British leaders were not ambivalent. Nasser now became the "arch-enemy." British policymaking went into a tailspin, in which "each telegram that comes in causes Ministers to meet, telephone one another, draft replies and curse everybody." Spurred by righteous anger and falling back upon his own prowess as a diplomat, Eden refused any advice that contradicted his impulses. He spurned unwanted information and excoriated his closest Foreign Office advisers as "no good, not on the job, unhelpful." The Chiefs of Staff and ambassadors were not spared. One official noted that "no one is trusted to the extent that his advice is regarded when unwelcome."[51]

With Glubb gone and further attempts at an Egyptian-Israeli settlement in tatters, the British and U.S. governments now both took a harder line toward Nasser. Lloyd, with Eden's approval, sent a paper to Dulles outlining long-term measures to isolate Egypt. These included strengthening the Baghdad Pact and cutting off any possible aid, starting with the Aswan Dam project that Britain had pushed so hard only a few months earlier.

The American thinking, in a secret plan dubbed Omega, overlapped but was different. It was more focused on the danger of an Arab-Israeli war, including possible arms sales to Israel from Canada and France. The Americans were ambivalent about whether to try and overthrow Nasser, and, while wanting to reach out to other Arab partners, such as the Saudis, they remained ambivalent about the Baghdad Pact as well.[52]

Amid this turmoil, in April 1956, Eden received a visit from Soviet leaders Nikita Khrushchev and Nikolai Bulganin. It became even clearer to the British that the Russians "would make as much trouble . . . in the Middle East as they possibly could." Khrushchev warned Eden that if the Israelis attacked, "the Arabs might get the help of volunteers skilled in the use of modern weapons." Khrushchev appeared to be suggesting that Soviet "volunteers" might play a part in a future Middle East war, similar to the part played by Communist Chinese "volunteers" during the Korean War.

Eden retorted that the uninterrupted supply of oil was "literally vital" to the British economy. "I thought I must be absolutely blunt about the oil," he declared, "because we would fight for it." By the time the Soviets departed, Eden believed they understood that, when it came to the Middle East and oil supplies, Britain would not back down.[53]

WITHDRAWAL OF THE ASWAN DAM FUNDING

The project to offer Western (mainly American) funding for Egypt's Aswan Dam seemed increasingly surreal from London. Britain's financial position was already fragile. Loyal allies such as Iraq badly needed funds. The *Sunday Express* of July 15 asked, "Does anyone in his right mind really want to give a £5 million present of British taxpayers' money to Colonel Nasser?"[54]

In addition, Nasser had recognized Communist China in May, infuriating Americans and Britons alike. Withdrawing the funding became part of the

American Omega plan to isolate Nasser and it was agreed to let the Aswan project "wither on the vine."[55]

On July 19, Dulles informed the Egyptians that the United States was withdrawing the loan offer. Upon hearing of the American action, Eden exclaimed, "Oh good, oh good for Foster. I didn't really think he had it in him," before adding, "I wish he hadn't done it quite so abruptly." Britain followed the American lead and pulled out of the project the next day, citing economic reasons.[56]

Since the policy toward Nasser had hardened so sharply a few months earlier, several British government departments had begun to study "what we can do to Egypt and what Egypt can do to us." The reports covered exchange controls, oil supplies, sanctions, and other economic leverage. The government analysis noted that Britain had serious vulnerabilities owing to its dependence on Middle Eastern oil and the Suez Canal. In contrast, because of the nature of its economy and its ties to the Communist bloc, Egypt was not very vulnerable to British economic pressure. And in June 1956, in accordance with the 1954 treaty, Britain had completed the last withdrawal of its troops out of Egypt, leaving behind its once vast base in the Suez Canal Zone.[57]

Eden and his Cabinet ignored the reports. The only Egyptian revenge they could imagine was that Nasser would accept Soviet financing of the dam. There was little consideration in London of the possibility that Nasser might nationalize the Suez Canal Company. British observers assumed the Egyptians would never be able to keep the canal operating. As the London *Times* noted, "An international waterway of this kind cannot be worked by a nation of as low technical and managerial skills as the Egyptians." Between July 19, when the United States rescinded financing for the dam, and July 26, shares in the Suez Canal Company actually increased in value. [58]

With August approaching, Eden and his countrymen began turning their thoughts to their summer vacation plans, far from the sands of Egypt and the Suez Canal.

WASHINGTON

PHILIP ZELIKOW

On September 23, 1955, Secretary of State John Foster Dulles telephoned his president, Dwight Eisenhower, who was vacationing in Colorado. Interrupting the president's golf, Dulles wanted the president to know that the Egyptians were going ahead with their deal to obtain "a massive lot of arms" from the Soviet Union.[1]

The president was disturbed by the news. That night he suffered a heart attack.

The sixty-five-year-old Eisenhower's former four-pack-a-day cigarette habit (he had quit smoking in 1949) probably had more to do with his myocardial infarction than that day's stress. But it *had* been disturbing news.

The big foreign policy story of the summer had been the Geneva summit of the Big Four in July. The atmosphere of the summit had seemed encouraging, but now the Soviets had opened a whole new front in the Cold War. The odds of another war in the Middle East had immediately gone up.

Eisenhower would not be able to guide his government's initial response to this Soviet-Egyptian move. First he was in the hospital, then later convalescing for weeks. He did not resume a routine work schedule at the White House until January of the new year, 1956.[2]

The press line was that, while the president was recovering, the government was running smoothly along established lines of policy. This seemed believable, given the way the outside world thought of how the Eisenhower administration worked.

As one former member of that administration recalled, "Much of the press corps in Washington, domestic and foreign, together with other elements with whom they interacted in that highly political city, wrote Eisenhower off as merely a constitutional monarch, a role which he very successfully performed." The reporters saw Eisenhower as a "non-intellectual, rather too much given to the temptation to relax," yet quite popular.[3]

The public liked their president, with his big, easy grin, blue eyes, pink-tan complexion, and balding, sandy hair. To a country that knew the military well, he did not seem too inflated by his status as a former five-star general. His occasional vein-bulging bursts of temper were kept private. His wandering, foggy answers in press conferences just seemed to go with his genial style.

It was Secretary of State Dulles who seemed to lead U.S. foreign policy. Dulles was a veteran international lawyer and negotiator. A lay Presbyterian church leader his whole life, he was also used to Washington and its ways. His aunt had been married to Woodrow Wilson's secretary of state. He was angular and briskly articulate, and his downward-turning lips seemed to accentuate his conservative temper.

In fact the president was very much missed. His role was much larger than was realized even among well-informed outsiders. Dulles was America's lawyer. He thoroughly embraced the job of representing the anticommunist side of a case. He could master the details of a policy debate and eloquently state his argument. But Dulles was not much of a strategist. In an uncertain situation Dulles could come unmoored, pushed by the current. This weakness did not always mix well with his gifts for argument. It was, perhaps, just this combination that prompted then prime minister Winston Churchill to confide to his doctor the previous year (1954) that Dulles was "clever enough to be stupid on a rather large scale."[4]

When it came to what to do next, to point the way, America's lawyer needed direction from his client. And that was Eisenhower. Dulles was at his best when Eisenhower could steer him. The former supreme commander of Allied Forces in Europe during World War II, Eisenhower knew how to steer.

Eisenhower did his steering out of the public eye. He actively chaired National Security Council (NSC) meetings, which met like clockwork practically every week, sometimes more. His cabinet meetings had a similar schedule. When written policies were developed for review, Eisenhower would frequently edit the final products himself before they were finalized for implementation.

In this system, members of the team had clear roles. State had the policy lead. On the Middle East, Dulles tended to rely on his deputy, Herbert Hoover Jr., the son of the former president. He and Hoover looked to a veteran cadre of career diplomats, most of whom had some sympathy for the rising young group of Arab nationalists.

A lot of the real diplomatic work in the new countries, and specifically in Egypt, was often handled with the informal help of roving veterans of the Central Intelligence Agency. The CIA was led by another Dulles, Allen Dulles, Foster's brother. Allen had been involved in the secret world during World War II and ever since. Allen Dulles was more affable than his brother. He relished the personalities and details of spycraft, though he took less of an interest in the dry analysis of intelligence estimates.

When it came to the Middle East, Allen Dulles leaned on Kermit "Kim" Roosevelt. Roosevelt, a grandson of President Theodore Roosevelt, was also a veteran of intelligence work from the war. Roosevelt and his handful of fellow CIA operators in the Middle East were younger men (Roosevelt was thirty-six). They, too, sympathized with the Arab nationalists. They believed American alignment with the nationalist cause was the best way to keep the oil flowing and the Soviets out.

U.S. diplomats and CIA people on the scene might clash with each other. But on Nasser they agreed that, as the U.S. ambassador in Cairo, Henry Byroade, put it earlier in 1955, "Nasser is basically pro-West and certainly anti-Communist."[5]

At the Pentagon, most of the strategy work fell to the armed forces, not the civilian secretary of defense. They were represented through the Joint Chiefs of Staff, then chaired by Admiral Arthur Radford. The chiefs tended to focus more narrowly on possible preparations for war with the Soviet Union. They had, therefore, wanted the United States to join the Baghdad Pact without much attention to the politics of it (specifically, that big U.S. support for it would infuriate, for different reasons, both Egypt and Israel).

In any case, the chiefs were preoccupied by their constant struggles with Eisenhower and with each other over service budgets (which the president was pushing downward). They were also wrestling with their president over the realism of their planning for general nuclear war (which the president did not think was nearly realistic enough).

In Eisenhower's NSC, the Treasury Department, too, had an influential voice. The secretary was George Humphrey, a lifelong business executive out of the steel industry. Adamant about restraining federal spending, Humphrey was instinctively scornful about proposals for foreign aid.

The insiders knew that only Eisenhower could knit this team together and point the way. But, having given direction, Eisenhower tended to defer the details of policy development and execution to his team. This, in practice, left a lot to the Dulles brothers.

General U.S. policy goals for the Middle East were straightforward: keep the Soviets out and the oil flowing. Avoid an Arab-Israeli war, since that could damage both goals, but meanwhile try to be impartial about the dispute.

The United States also tried to avoid taking sides in the Arab divide between Cairo and Baghdad. Nor did the United States wish to encourage the hostility of the Arab nationalists toward the British, America's ally in NATO. Yet the United States also did not want to be too closely identified with the British, who were so unpopular in parts of the Arab world.

INITIAL DEBATES AND CONFUSION:
SEPTEMBER–NOVEMBER 1955

At first the U.S. government tried to persuade Nasser not to go through with the Soviet arms deal. When the news broke, Dulles had a chance to talk with his British counterpart, Harold Macmillan, since they were both in New York for a UN meeting. Macmillan wondered about "the carrot and the stick." The carrot might be arms from America and Britain, plus American help with Egypt's great development project, the construction of the huge Aswan Dam on the Nile river. The stick might be that the British would stop the agreed pullout of their troops from their Suez base in Egypt (scheduled to be completed in June 1956). "We could make life impossible for Nasser and ultimately bring about his fall by various pressures."[6]

Dulles quickly sent a diplomat to Cairo, the head of his Near East bureau, bearing a letter expressing concern and offering some U.S. military aid. Nasser made it clear that the deal was done. The U.S. offers were too little, too conditional, and too late.

Eisenhower sent a message of concern to his Soviet counterpart, Nikolai Bulganin. Bulganin replied that the Americans had no cause for concern.

Dulles began to field requests from the Israeli government that the United States sell arms to Israel to balance the Soviet arms going to Egypt. Dulles did not want the United States to compete with the Soviet Union in a Middle East arms race.

He instead preferred to try to find a way to bring Egypt back into the fold. On October 3 Dulles told Macmillan that "Egypt wished the best of both worlds and hoped to play one against the other. Egypt as a neutralist would be more tolerable than as a Communist satellite." So Dulles "was more inclined to temporize regarding Egypt at this stage." Macmillan seemed to go along with this.

The NSC members agreed that the whole U.S. policy in the Middle East needed to be reviewed. The next week the CIA circulated a Special National Intelligence Estimate, prepared by analysts from across the intelligence community, that warned bluntly,

> In the absence of convincing evidence of Western determination to preserve the territorial status quo, there is very real danger that Israel will undertake "preventive war," possibly in the next few months, and it would almost certainly be more willing to take risks which could touch off a new round of hostilities.[7]

Later in October, Allen Dulles stressed that the intelligence community regarded the Soviet arms deal with Egypt "with the highest degree of gravity." These Soviet maneuvers, he said, "could easily have a devastating effect on the position of the Free World in the Near East."[8]

The top question was how to deter either Egypt or Israel from starting a war. Economic sanctions were a start. But when the NSC members turned to further options, such as a naval blockade against an aggressor (if an aggressor could be determined either by the UN or by the United States on its own) or ground military intervention to secure the peace (if Congress approved), the discussion dissolved into arguments. Vice President Nixon, chairing the meeting, saw an "impasse." He had trouble imagining any Congress approving U.S. military action against Israel.

Dulles was still opposed to offsetting military aid to Israel. Perhaps, he thought, it would be better to treat this Soviet arms sale as "a 'one-shot affair'" and downplay its long-term significance. As for a security guarantee for Israel, that seemed impractical. The Senate might not ratify it, especially if the boundaries had not been agreed on with the Arab states.

Dulles explained the issues preventing an Arab-Israeli settlement. He laid greatest stress on the border problem and Egypt's desire for Israel to give up the Negev, so that Egypt would border Jordan and reconnect the two parts of the Arab world.

His brother Allen felt "impelled" to comment that he thought neither side really wanted a settlement. He thought they were just using the issues "as a means of keeping their quarrel alive."[9]

Dulles then traveled to Geneva for a meeting of the Big Four foreign ministers. The discussions with the Soviets were a flop. The summer's "spirit of Geneva" was gone. But Dulles could work on Middle East policy.

While in Geneva, Dulles told his Israeli counterpart, Moshe Sharett (who was also then still prime minister), that there was little the United States could do. Israel should put its faith in the vague security assurances of the 1950 Tripartite Declaration, although Dulles did not hide his concerns about the practicality of doing anything to help. Therefore, Dulles concluded, Israel had to try harder to make concessions and get to a peace settlement with the Arab states, picking up on the project Alpha ideas the United States had been pressing all year long.[10]

In Geneva, Dulles also heard the preferences of his British and French colleagues. For France, the great issue was "the reentry of Russia in Middle East." It was time to support friends, and Egypt had to stop inciting rebellion in French North Africa.

The British had a more elaborate plan. For them, the Baghdad Pact came first. Iraq was the cornerstone. Now the British were supporting the October addition of Iran to the pact. The Americans grudgingly went along with that. Britain then made a big push to force Jordan to join the pact. The Americans kept their distance from that effort, which backfired in December, creating a political crisis in Jordan.

As for Egypt, the British still preferred carrots to sticks, but they needed to persuade the Americans to carry forward the policy and foot the bill for it. They had in mind a package deal for Nasser. The "trump card" would be mainly American financing for the cost of Egypt's Aswan Dam project, Nasser's great development initiative. Macmillan made headway in bringing Dulles along.[11]

The Israelis became more and more worried. November brought another major outbreak of violence on the Egyptian-Israeli border. Egypt, Syria, and Jordan publicly advanced planning for coordinating their military operations.

The first deliveries of Soviet arms were arriving in Egypt, and in coming months these and more would slowly be integrated into the Egyptian armed forces. The Egyptians had already closed the Suez Canal to Israeli ships and positioned artillery in the south of the Sinai Peninsula to also close the Straits of Tiran, the only access route to the Gulf of Aqaba and Israel's southern port of Eilat.

The Israelis lacked any firm foreign supplier of advanced weapons. They felt their military superiority was trickling away like sand through an hourglass. Israeli politics turned more warlike. Elections restored David Ben-Gurion to the prime minister's job, and he held the defense portfolio, too. The more diplomatic-minded Sharett remained as foreign minister.

Sharett visited the United States in November. Making his case in person, he argued that the West should isolate Egypt and transfer appropriate defensive arms to Israel (for example, fighter jets, anti-aircraft weapons). He and his ambassador also asked the United States for a security guarantee. If the United States would do that, then Israel would understand and accept U.S. adherence to the anti-Soviet (and anti-Nasser) Baghdad Pact.

U.S. POLICY FIRMS UP: THE OFFERS TO NASSER, NOVEMBER 1955–MARCH 1956

In the last weeks of 1955, as Eisenhower slowly began returning to work, a U.S. policy began taking clearer shape. The formative period was during the weeks that Dulles and Macmillan and their key aides were together for the ministerial meetings in Geneva in late October and the first half of November.

The British government played a lead role in crystallizing a joint policy direction. The planning document had originated as an October 30 draft prepared by British official Ivone Kirkpatrick. Kirkpatrick passed it to State's key Arab-Israeli expert, Francis Russell, for Dulles. Russell also sent it to Washington on November 3, for Hoover and the Near East bureau to comment, which came a couple of days later.

Dulles and Macmillan then reviewed the issues at length on November 9. Russell was the U.S. notetaker. Kirkpatrick was there, along with another key British diplomat, Evelyn Shuckburgh. That same day, Hoover told Eisenhower that State hoped to use his friend, a former Texas oilman and defense official named Robert Anderson, as a secret Arab-Israeli mediator.

The day after the Dulles-Macmillan meeting on November 9, the key policy document was redrafted, probably by Russell working with his British colleagues, who were working with their own ministers. The ministers planned to use the paper as a basis for their discussions with the French. Still classified "top secret," the document was sent back to Washington for another round of comments, which came back to Geneva on November 14.

The core of the policy was aimed at Egypt. The policy's goal was "to prevent Egypt falling completely under Russian domination. Only if this is seen to have failed should we have recourse."

Toward Israel, the policy would be to avoid a security guarantee. Only a limited quantity of arms would be made available. "Our guiding principle is that we should not seem to be moving in to supply Israel with arms on a large scale to offset those supplied by the Iron Curtain."

Britain and the United States would push Israel hard to agree to a peace settlement with the Arabs. "If she [Israel] is to survive, she cannot afford to pursue a policy which estranges the Arabs from the West." The settlement would have to involve some territorial concessions by Israel.

Toward Egypt, they would make generous offers to Nasser to seek a deal. There were two principal objectives. First, Egypt would "be willing in effect to turn away from Russia as a source of arms," limiting future purchases. Second, Egypt would "agree to open negotiations for a settlement with Israel," including support for a promising plan that had been developed for the problem of Jordan River water.

In exchange, the British and Americans would offer to supply Egypt with its "reasonable arms requirements." Most important, they would assist in financing the enormous Aswan Dam project.

Further, the countries agreed they would pressure Israel to "agree to a just settlement, and help Egypt to play a role of leadership in the Arab world." The behavior of Egypt and its Arab allies would determine whether the United States continued to keep its distance from the Baghdad Pact.

"If all this fails," the Anglo-American planning document explained, "and Egypt is clearly lost to Western influence, we should have to consider policies which would minimize the harm which she could do to Western interests."

The policy laid out a script that the United States followed carefully for the next five months. Foster Dulles, that good lawyer, stuck to these agreed-upon positions in all his meetings during the coming weeks.[12]

The key policy document was never circulated and discussed in Eisenhower's NSC system. The two Dulles brothers, and their chief aides at State and CIA, appear to have fully understood it. Eisenhower was kept appraised about certain key elements as he began returning to work at the end of the year.

The Aswan Dam side of the plan was visible. It was a huge incentive. The British worked hard to line up a plan. They spurred the Americans on, warning that Egypt might instead seek Russian support for it.

In the Aswan plan, about half the major financing would come from an international organization created after World War II, the World Bank (the International Bank for Reconstruction and Development). The head of the bank, Eugene Black, was willing. He acknowledged that "this was the biggest single undertaking the Bank had ever gone into." It would be one of the largest construction and development projects in the world.

The other half of the financing would come from the American and British governments. Between them the Americans would have to shoulder almost all—80 percent or 90 percent—of that burden.[13]

The Aswan plan was reviewed in the NSC. Eisenhower eventually had to intervene personally to quash Humphrey's constant and strident objections.

Writing to Dulles in early December, as he continued to rest and reflect about the world situation, Eisenhower thought the basic struggle "between the Communistic and the free worlds" was changing. The United States had countered the threat of force by showing that Soviet aggression would lead to "a major war" with the United States, a nuclear war.

So he thought the Soviets were shifting to a "challenge with economic weapons." This should be an arena in which America had great advantages. But the United States was playing defense, and in the wrong places. It needed strategies of economic associations with key countries, planning "together over the long term." Instead the United States was "busy rescuing Guatemala or assisting Korea and Indo-China" while "they make great inroads in Burma, Afghanistan and Egypt." The United States had to start taking the initiative with these long-term partnerships, "with the kind of selectivity and smoothness that will largely rob the Soviets of the initiative."[14]

State prepared a large foreign aid budget item for Congress, as part of its 1956 request. The Aswan Dam funding was the biggest item in it. Eisenhower and Dulles knew this would be a tough sell, but they began working on it with key members of Congress, early in 1956.

The secret side of the Anglo-American Middle East "carrot" policy with Nasser was the U.S. mediation between Egypt and Israel. This mediation was to prepare the way for a possible settlement and for Egyptian leadership in the Arab side of the negotiations. This mediation was conducted as an extremely secret undercover operation managed by the CIA, with State Department help. The world was not to know that the envoy was meeting with Nasser or Ben-Gurion. Nasser was fearful of any hint that he was negotiating about Palestine with Americans and, indirectly, with Israelis.

Eisenhower had agreed the mission would be led by his Texan friend, Robert Anderson, who had already served in the administration as the secretary of the navy and as the deputy secretary of defense. Eisenhower had enormous regard for Anderson, whom he considered potential presidential material, "one of the most capable men I know."[15]

Other elements of the agreed-on Anglo-American policy line, such as the tough stance toward Israel and reticence on the Baghdad Pact, were also kept secret, even within the U.S. government. Early in 1956, for example, the Joint Chiefs of Staff kept recommending that the United States join the Baghdad Pact, only to have those recommendations shot down by the leadership at State and CIA.

The Israeli foreign minister had two lengthy and difficult meetings with Dulles during November. Dulles implemented the agreed-on policy stance practically to the word. The Israelis had submitted their detailed request for defensive arms. Dulles stalled, promising that the Pentagon would analyze it.

At one point, in early December, Dulles went out to see Eisenhower at the presidential retreat, Camp David. Dulles told him that he and Defense officials were still analyzing the Israeli request for defensive arms. Eisenhower replied that "we could not very well refuse to let the Israelis buy some defensive weapons."

Dulles assured the president he was working on it, though warning him that any sale of arms to Israel would cause problems in the Arab world. Later in December, after another large Israeli retaliation raid, this one a relatively unprovoked raid against Syria, Dulles converted his stall on the Israeli request to a no.

Eisenhower went along. He agreed that if there was a peace settlement the United States could do much to help Israel and Egypt, especially with economic aid. As for arms, "the interests of this country will not be served by attempting to arm one against the other."[16]

To get a peace settlement, Dulles insisted that Israel had to be prepared to make some important territorial concessions, of which the Negev cession was most important on the list. The Israeli envoys were flexible on everything— except to allow the southern part of their country to be sliced off through the Negev.

Sharett, who was very much the leader of the moderates within Israel's own government, protested that such territorial concessions might be a slippery slope. Dulles forcefully disagreed. There was a chance of a settlement; how much no one could say. The United States had to push for it. Israel had to be willing to say what it would give up. Dulles did not put on the table any "carrots" for Sharett. Instead he had a warning.

If an Israeli no was "the last word, then Israel is putting us all in great peril," he said. "If we have to make a choice of sticking to Israel in the face of all that the Middle East is to the safety and continued existence of the free world, Israel will be forcing us to make a very grave choice."[17]

The Americans kept the British well informed about what was going on. Eden corresponded with Eisenhower about the Aswan Dam financing plans.

The two capitals arranged for Eden to visit Washington at the end of January to coordinate policy in person with the president.

Early in January 1956, Eisenhower returned to his regular routine in the White House. He also finally decided, after weeks of deliberation and discussion, that he would definitely run for reelection, a decision he announced publicly the next month.

The larger Cold War context was still constantly on his mind. In one of a series of NSC meetings about preparations for nuclear war, Eisenhower unloaded his angry sense that "none of the members of the Council had withdrawn into a quiet room and contemplated for a period of time the real nature of a future thermonuclear war." No one would "be the winner" and "we might have ultimately to go back to bows and arrows."[18]

In the last days of January Anderson completed his first round of secret talks with Nasser and with Ben-Gurion. He used all the arguments in the Anglo-American plan, including assurances about further distancing of the United States from the Baghdad Pact. Nasser downplayed hopes of rapid progress. On the toughest substantive issue, future borders, Nasser argued for Israeli cession of its southern portion, the Negev desert, from the town of Beersheba south.

In any case, Nasser explained, it would take many months, at least, for him to be able to begin bringing the Arab world around to a possible peace. He kept coming back to the regional context, to British-inspired efforts to expand the Iraqi-led Baghdad Pact into countries like Jordan. "The only result" of any public sign of Egyptian openness to Israel, he said, "would be to give Nuri Said a weapon with which to destroy him."

On the Israeli side, Ben-Gurion wanted face-to-face peace talks. While Israel was flexible on many points, he gave absolutely no ground on any cession of Israeli territory in the Negev. The Israelis feared they were being strung along as Egypt completed its military buildup.

Dulles followed the talks closely, offering guidance at every turn. He, at least, hoped the two countries could narrow and itemize their differences.

Anderson replied, "I find little or no disposition on either side to catalogue items they will discuss." Dulles was becoming increasingly alarmed. He did not think the status quo could hold for another six months.

From the CIA, his brother Allen strongly agreed with this assessment. Either Israel would destroy Nasser or the United States would give way to the great public and opposition Democrat pressure to proceed with U.S. arms shipments to Israel.

The secretary of state was getting more impatient with Nasser. To him, it seemed like a good time for Egypt to make a move. Egypt's armed strength was growing. "West is temporarily denying arms to Israel. He [Nasser] has Aswan Dam within his grasp. He has possibility of acquiring our support for Arab unity and Egyptian leadership in it." He urged Anderson to keep at it, to "make [an] all out effort" to get some secret understanding on eight or ten key issues.

Anderson kept at it. But he finally reported that he could not break the "vicious circle" unless the United States was willing to detail and impose some kind of settlement, with "appropriate pressures," warning the parties they would have to "face the alternatives which we would outline to them." American experts had peace deal plans drawn up, for a significant cession of Israeli territory in the Negev or placement of this territory under a UN trusteeship for multinational use. But they had not worked up a plan for the "pressures" or "alternatives" that might further persuade or coerce the countries to accept a settlement.[19]

Meanwhile, Eden arrived in Washington. He brought with him a new foreign secretary. Eden had reshuffled his cabinet, moving Macmillan over to Treasury and replacing him with the much less experienced lawyer Selwyn Lloyd. It was a signal that Eden, so often having held the job of foreign secretary himself, was planning to keep a more direct grip on foreign policy.

The major takeaway for the Americans from the Eden visit was that the British now doubted, as Eden put it, "whether Nasser could be dealt with. If so, our course of action in the Middle East could go one way; if not, it should go another."

Eisenhower pressed Eden. Had the British "lost confidence" in Nasser? Eden replied that "it was difficult to evaluate Nasser who was a man of limitless ambition."

Dulles chimed in that ambition did not bother him. But he wondered if "Nasser might have become a tool of the Russians." On that point the ongoing secret mediation efforts "might be revealing."

Eisenhower said he had heard encouraging things about Nasser from a visiting American businessman who thought the Egyptian leader "was going about his business in an intelligent way" and was not a man "who would cut off his nose to spite his face."

Dulles was not sure. Yes, Nasser "talked intelligently and made a fine impression. However, he made violent anti-Israel statements on the one hand, while on the other saying privately that a settlement was possible. When recently presenting the new constitution, Nasser said its main purpose was to create a core uniting the Arab world from the Atlantic to the Persian Gulf and to put back into that core a heart that had been plucked from it: Palestine. This was, of course, inflammatory," Dulles pointed out. It "would argue against Nasser's sincerity in stating he would like to find a settlement and line up the other Arab states."

Since November 1955 the British secret service, MI6, had been receiving reports from an agent code-named Lucky Break, supposedly in Nasser's inner circle, who argued that Nasser was being duped by the Soviets and was willingly serving their interests. These reports were being shared with the American government, including the State Department. Neither Dulles brother was entirely persuaded by this intelligence. With some cause, the CIA tended to think they knew Nasser and his inner circle much better than the British did. Yet, as John Foster Dulles said separately to Eden in their own meeting, "we might soon know whether our whole attitude toward Nasser would have to be changed."[20]

Another theme in Eden's visit was speculation about how the United States and the British, invoking the 1950 Tripartite Declaration, might show their readiness to intervene with military force if one side or another started a war. There was much talk about a demonstration of readiness, perhaps with ship movements in the Mediterranean. But neither side could credibly specify just what their forces would do, either against Egypt or against Israel. Eisenhower also stressed that the United States could not engage in any military intervention without authorization from Congress, which seemed unlikely.

Anderson returned to the region, continuing his secret work on a peace settlement, but neither side budged. In Cairo the CIA representatives, helping Anderson, at least wanted to get enough of a thaw to shift the issue to the UN. Then the UN work might transition to high-level negotiations in which Egypt would play a key role.

The UN truce supervision chief did believe that an enhanced UN presence might deter a major land attack by either side. A big problem, though, was the danger of an Egyptian air attack with their newly acquired jet bombers. Pointing to that threat, Israel had asked the United States for forty-eight F-86 fighter aircraft, among other items, and the United States was considering whether to approve an Israeli purchase of twelve Mystère IV fighters from France (U.S. approval was needed because the French production was connected to U.S. military assistance to France for NATO needs).[21]

But Anderson could make no progress. He could not get Nasser to take any step forward. Nasser, instead, stressed his unhappiness with the whole trend in the region, "all simmering down to the proposition that the British and

American activities in support of the Bagh[dad] Pact were creating internecine warfare among the Arab states." Those Arab rivalries forced Nasser, Anderson reported, "to soft pedal or abandon what he would consider 'Constructive' conduct in the area."[22]

Warned that the United States might decide to sell arms to Israel, Nasser angrily made it clear that any such move would scrap any peace talks. He would just get more Soviet arms.

State and CIA representatives cabled home, as vehemently as they could, that any U.S. transfer of arms to Israel would do immense damage to the U.S. position in the Arab world. That warning was backed up by a Special National Intelligence Estimate circulated at the end of February. The intelligence agencies also continued to believe the Soviet arms supplies flowing into Egypt had "substantially increased" the risk of another Arab-Israeli war.[23]

In public and private, Dulles remained firmly opposed to arms sales to Israel. Nor would he consider a security guarantee for Israel unless Israel's borders had been agreed to in a broader Arab-Israeli settlement. He repeated that the United States would do something about aggression in the region, referring to the Tripartite Declaration, but did not say what. The Israeli government was furious. President Eisenhower, also, was getting anxious.

On February 29, Eisenhower told Dulles's deputy, Hoover, that "perhaps we were being too tough with the Israelis with respect to arms. He had in mind particularly [fighter] interceptors" and antiaircraft missiles. He was thinking of making a statement about it.

Hoover persuaded the president to hold off. Anxious about domestic political pressure while he was out of town, stimulated by press comment about a long-scheduled shipment of a few surplus American tanks to Saudi Arabia, Dulles went back to Eisenhower a couple of days later and again asked him to hold off on arms to Israel. Dulles promised a deliberate policy review.[24]

During the first weeks of March 1956 there was another crisis out of Jordan, this one about the dismissal of British general Glubb, but for Washington that was not such a big deal. Much more important to Dulles and Eisenhower was their sad conclusion that the Anderson mediation effort had failed.

Concerns about Nuri, the British, and the Baghdad Pact were a main theme in Anderson's last discussions with Nasser in early March. Nasser was open to more UN truce supervision of the border with Israel. But on the substance of an Arab-Israeli settlement there was nothing new.

Nasser seemed to step backward. Even if progress was made on the content of a possible settlement, Nasser said that Egypt would not join in sponsoring such a proposal. Others must put it forward. Then the Arab countries would decide.

To Anderson, Nasser seemed "completely haunted" by the memory of the assassination of Jordan's King Abdullah in 1951. "You [the United States] will have to solve the problem of Israeli aggressiveness."[25]

On March 5 Eisenhower received a message from Eden declaring "we can no longer safely wait on Nasser." Eden believed it was time for the United States to join the Baghdad Pact and join in a program of military aid to Nuri's Iraq.

"Certainly we should accept," Eden wrote, "that policy of appeasement would bring us nothing in Egypt. Our best chance is to show that it pays to be our friends."

Eisenhower's focus was different. Still more concerned about an Arab-Israeli war, he wanted to get the UN more involved in preventing a war. UN secretary-general Dag Hammarskjöld was ready to help improve the border truce supervision, but Eisenhower believed the United States would have to help defeat a major Egyptian attack, an assault that might have Russian help.

"We might rapidly be reaching the point where we would have to take military action in the area. [Eisenhower] felt that the Russians did not want to get into a war at this time and under these circumstances would probably back down if forced to make a clear-cut decision." Hearing this, the State Department's Hoover agreed. But he said the U.S. government would have to think this through "with extreme care if we wished to avoid the enmity of the Arab nations for many years to come."

The next day, March 6, Eisenhower said that if the Soviet arms deliveries continued, he thought it might be necessary to give defensive arms to Israel. This time he stressed necessary ground equipment, since he believed outside sources might be able to supply Israel with needed air and naval equipment.[26]

THE NEW POLICY TOWARD NASSER: CONTAINMENT AND ISOLATION, MARCH–JULY 1956

As the Anderson mission failed, the U.S. government began a thorough reconsideration of its policy. Eisenhower noted in his diary that it did seem to him "as if Egypt, under Nasser, is going to make no move whatsoever to meet the Israelites in an effort to settle outstanding differences. Moreover, the Arabs, absorbing major consignments of arms from the Soviets, are daily growing more arrogant and disregarding the interests of Western Europe and of the United States in the Middle East region."

"It would begin to appear," Eisenhower noted, "that our efforts should be directed toward separating the Saudi Arabians from the Egyptians and concentrating, for the moment at least, in making the former see that their best interests lie with us, not with the Egyptians and with the Russians."

As for Israel, Eisenhower was open to making a treaty or other statement "that would protect the territory." An isolated Egypt "with no ally in sight except Soviet Russia" might "very quickly get sick of that prospect and join us in the search for a just and decent peace in that region."

The next week, after talking directly to Anderson, Eisenhower confided more of his thoughts to his diary. He could see "no easy answer" to the war danger. Europe depended on Arab oil and the United States depended on Europe. Yet Israel was in a difficult place and "has a very strong position in the heart and emotions of the Western world because of the suffering of the Jews throughout twenty-five hundred years of history." It seemed to Eisenhower "that our best move" might just be "to prevent any concerted action on the part of the Arab States."[27]

Eden pushed Eisenhower hard to join Britain in targeting Nasser. In March he passed another British intelligence report directly to Eisenhower, noting that "we are entirely confident" about the report's authenticity. The report said Egypt planned to unify the Arab states under Egyptian leadership. The Egyptians would plan to overthrow Nuri and the Hashemite monarchies in both Iraq and Jordan, as well as junking the Baghdad Pact. They would also try to overthrow the monarchy in Libya. Saudi Arabia would be isolated as the last Arab monarchy. The Soviet Union would support this plan. In his diary, Eisenhower noted that Eden had given him "some very exact intelligence on Nasser's intentions."

Lower-level American officials heard their British Foreign Office counterparts refer to Nasser as comparable to Benito Mussolini, the fascist dictator who had recently led Italy to ruin as Hitler's ally. British analysis of Nasser, passed to the Americans, also predicted an Egyptian attack against Israel during the summer of 1956, after British troops completed their withdrawal from the Canal Zone.[28]

Studying the Arab-Israeli military situation, U.S. military experts believed that in the near term, Israel could rapidly win a war against all its enemies. But after midsummer 1956 the experts believed the balance of power on the ground would start shifting toward the Arabs. In the air, the two sides might reach a standoff by the summer of 1956. At that point either side might be tempted to launch a surprise attack, in light of how few airfields the other side had.[29]

To start working up a new policy approach, the State Department took the lead. Top State and CIA officials got together at John Foster Dulles's home for a long discussion of the analytical issues.[30]

A first major step was a U.S. push to support the efforts of UN secretary-general Dag Hammarskjöld. In April Hammarskjöld was able to announce agreement on a modest but meaningful reinforcement of the UN Truce Supervision Office, which attempted to monitor and prevent incursions on the borders set by the Israeli-Arab 1949 armistice agreements.

The rest of the State-developed approach, which carried the code name Omega, was approved by President Eisenhower on March 28. Omega started out mainly as a political effort to diversify the U.S. portfolio in the Arab world, so to speak. The U.S. government would quietly disinvest in Nasser but keep a bridge open to rebuild that relationship. Meanwhile the U.S. government was to bulk up its relations with virtually every other Arab leader, especially to explore how much progress could be made with King Saud in Saudi Arabia.

The military side of the work involved extensive contingency planning and preparations for a possible Arab-Israeli war. That planning picked up steam during April.[31]

The six most important elements of Omega were:

- The United States would secretly work on coordinated U.S.-British military planning for the contingency of military intervention against Egypt, to protect Israel's survival.

- The United States would secretly build up a significant stockpile of arms to be held in escrow, in or near Cyprus, to be offered to whichever side was the victim of aggression. The stockpile for Arab states, if they were attacked by Israel, would be a cargo ship full of antitank and antiaircraft weapons. The stockpile for Israel, if it was attacked, would be 24 F-86 fighter aircraft already in Europe, along with spare parts and ammunition.

- The United States would not itself sell defensive arms to Israel, except maybe for a few niche items. But the United States would acquiesce as Israel bought the arms it needed from other states like France or Canada. The Americans believed the Israelis could meet their needs from these sources.

- The U.S. government would let its financing for the Aswan Dam project "languish," even though the World Bank had successfully completed the negotiations over its half of the loan. Other foreign aid for Egypt would also be stalled.

- The United States would help build up Saudi Arabia, and King Saud, as an alternative pole of leadership in the Arab world. It would be ready to provide military assistance to Saudi Arabia and to Baghdad Pact member states. The United States would also try to help Libya, keep Syria relatively neutral, and buck up British support for Jordan.

- The United States would still not join the Baghdad Pact. Such formal adherence would probably require a security pact with Israel, too, yet such an open deal with Israel would be intolerable to Nuri's Iraq. But the United States would give increased support to the pact without formally joining it.

The leaders agreed that the choreography of the Omega program would need dedicated leadership. That job went to the State Department's counselor, a kind of deputy to the secretary. This was Douglas MacArthur II, the nephew of the famous general. All these plans and decisions were shared with the British government through their trusted ambassador in Washington, Roger Makins.

In the climactic White House meeting on the new policy on March 28, Eisenhower, Dulles, and JCS chairman Radford agreed that, although there would be no formal security pact with Israel, the United States would in fact plan to protect it. "If Egypt were to attempt to liquidate Israel, there is no question that war would be forced upon us." Such a war might require the United States "to occupy the entire area, protect the pipelines and the Suez Canal, etc."[32]

The U.S. government proceeded in line with all the elements of the new Omega policy during the spring and early summer of 1956. Omega did not have an important CIA covert action component. Only State and DoD officials came to the key Omega policy meeting.[33]

Nonetheless, during the first week of April Kim Roosevelt and a CIA team visited London to confer with their counterparts in Britain's MI6. The Americans were shocked by what they saw and heard.

The Americans were developing a mainly political program of graduated pressure and military contingency planning, which is what they thought the British Foreign Office also wanted. Yet, though it was supposed to be supervised by the Foreign Office, the British secret service seemed to be going to war. Their people talked of assassinating Nasser and mused about coup plots in Syria and Saudi Arabia.

The CIA men were unimpressed by the wild talk and the talkers. They recalled it with words like "madhouse" and "insanity." "There wasn't a James Bond in the bunch," one of the CIA officials recalled later. The Americans did not like any of the British covert action plans.

In fact, a month later, the CIA station chief in Cairo cabled to urge Washington officials not to get into "direct combat with Arab nationalism." He warned that such a battle would probably "lead to the defeat of Western interests in this area." Covert political action, he thought, would boomerang. Even though some of these same CIA men had secretly supported the overthrow of Iran's leader in 1953, they thought that in that case, they had supported a genuine popular Iranian uprising, not some American-made artifice.[34]

As April turned to May, U.S. officials were still hoping Egypt might come around, even though Egypt had annoyed Dulles by recognizing Communist China. A "head-on public clash" still seemed premature.

By July, however, the United States felt ready for that public clash with Nasser. State Department officials painstakingly summarized the record to show how hard the United States had tried to cooperate with Egypt "at considerable political cost, both domestic and foreign, relying upon repeated assurances Egypt intended [to] work with [the] West."

Now the United States was done with "appeasement" with nothing more "than vague hope of eliciting positive Egyptian response." The Nasser regime "bears responsibility for emergence of forces which it now may be powerless [to] control and which pose serious problem for US future in Middle East."[35]

Dulles was already considering when and how to pull the plug on the lingering issue of U.S. government financing for the Aswan Dam project. He met with World Bank president Black, who said the bank was ready to go ahead with the project.

Dulles was not. He argued that Egypt would not be able to afford its end. He complained about problems he would have getting the U.S. government portion through the congressional appropriations process. Black pointed out that the Soviets might try to step forward to help with the project. Dulles admitted this would be unfortunate.[36]

When the NSC met a few days later, it seemed the Soviets had made an offer to help with the dam. Treasury Secretary Humphrey was not a bit disturbed. In fact, he said he was glad to hear of it. If the Egyptians took Russian money instead of American money for the project, "that was the best possible thing that could happen for the United States." Dulles went along, saying that the project might prove to be burdensome and unpopular in Egypt, and "a terrific headache to any nation that undertook it."[37]

After further debate about how to handle the Aswan matter, including with the British, the State Department's Near East bureau recommended that Dulles explicitly withdraw the funding offer and so inform Egyptian ambassador Ahmed Hussein. The bureau did warn that "the Dam has become symbolic of the Western attitude towards Egypt. Therefore, we should not underestimate the strength of Nasser's reaction." But there was no specific analysis of possible Egyptian reactions, except that there might be anti-Western propaganda or a possible request for Soviet help.[38]

On July 19, Dulles met with Ambassador Hussein at the State Department and gave him the news. The decision was "final."[39]

Dulles felt good about the way the Omega program was unfolding. He conducted an off-the-record briefing with top journalists from America's most influential newsmagazine, *Time*.

Time's July 30 issue, which came out around July 24, used that background interview and played Dulles up as a diplomatic star. Headlined "The Dramatic Gambit," the story was edged by photos of Nasser and Dulles, each photo seeming to face the other.

"On the broad chessboard of international diplomacy," the story began, "the U.S. moved decisively last week in a gambit that took the breath of professionals for its daring and won the assent of kibitzers for its instinctive rightness. With an open show of sternness, Secretary of State John Foster Dulles advised Egypt's Gamal Abdel Nasser that the U.S. is no longer interested in building the $1.3 billion Aswan High Dam."

"In so doing," *Time* continued, "Dulles indicated to everyone around the board, neutrals, allies and Communists alike, that the U.S. remains unawed by bold Communist boasts of matching the West in economic competition—in particular in the financing and building of the high dam on the Nile. And if neutrals want to dart and barter between the two, this will be a kind of 'fearful risk' that they will have to worry about. They can no longer hope to seize the best of both worlds."[40]

As that issue of the magazine still sat on newsstands around America, the world learned of Nasser's reaction to Dulles's "daring" move.

PART ONE
CAIRO

JON B. ALTERMAN

HIGH HOPES: 1952–1955

Following Egypt's July 23, 1952, revolution, the new leadership was thinking big. Egypt was a large and impoverished country, but it needn't be, they thought. They argued that the monarchy had surrendered Egypt's sovereignty and gotten very little to show for it. The ambitious army colonels who now ruled Egypt had a different idea: They would reassert Egypt's sovereignty, and they would get Egypt its due.

The United States was an obvious source. It had put billions of dollars into Europe and Asia, and it had shown signs of interest in supporting Egypt. U.S. officials made no secret of their interest in preventing communism from taking root in the Middle East, and Egypt's large and landless peasantry seemed like tinder for social unrest. In addition, Americans, who had gotten their own independence from England, seemed empathetic to the Egyptian passion for pushing out British troops that had arrived in 1882 to secure a debt and never left.

In January 1953 the Egyptian Foreign Ministry asked its embassies in countries "most similar to Egypt" in their strategic, social, and economic conditions to report on the U.S. aid those countries were getting. The Egyptian embassy in Athens reported that America had given a lot of aid to Greece in the preceding four years. Three thousand American experts in economics, agriculture, engineering, and other fields aided Greek efforts to rebuild after the war. From

Yugoslavia the Egyptian embassy reported $425 million in economic aid since 1945, and a slightly higher amount of military aid. A 1951 package of $120 million in aid combined the contributions of the United States, Britain, and France.[1]

Egyptians could use that kind of money. They were "thinking big" in terms of their own domestic development. In the autumn of 1952 the leaders of the new Egyptian government latched on to a proposed plan to build a high dam on the Nile River. Although the British had built a dam in 1902 that provided some relief from uncontrolled flooding, the project envisioned in 1952 would be a vastly greater project. It could harness the Nile for both irrigation and electricity generation. If the dam were built, Egypt could increase its arable land by 30 percent and boost its industrial output with the energy the dam would provide. American embassy officials immediately exhibited interest in the plan and moved quickly to help execute preliminary feasibility studies.[2]

The first significant tranche of American aid for Egypt arrived in March 1953. It was small, $10 million for a joint U.S.-Egyptian program of land reclamation and resettlement,[3] but Egyptian leaders hoped more would come, and the U.S. embassy told them it would.

Secretary of State John Foster Dulles arrived in Egypt in May 1953 as part of his regional tour in the first months of the Eisenhower administration. Egyptian foreign minister Mahmoud Fawzi was careful in his discussions with Dulles to demonstrate that Egyptians had internalized the language of American development assistance. He began his talk with Dulles by stating that it was internal weakness that made the Middle Eastern states vulnerable to aggression, and in this regard, "Social and economic problems are as important as political problems." He continued, saying: "Egypt was anxious to build up Egypt and Egyptian strength. It believes in self-help and is willing to spend up to its capacity on social and economic reforms."[4]

The new administration, however, was less interested in local development and self-help than its predecessor had been. Dulles stated bluntly: "The new Administration's policies will be based on the Communist threat,"[5] which he perceived mainly to come from outside a nation's borders.

In the months following Dulles's visit, Egyptians continued to wait for Americans to open up the aid tap.

But there was a new problem. Continued haggling in the Anglo-Egyptian negotiations over British evacuation of a large military base it maintained in the Suez Canal Zone overshadowed Egypt's foreign relations.[6] When the Egyptian finance minister visited Washington in September 1953, he met with the heads of the World Bank, the International Monetary Fund, and other institutions. All promised significant aid to Egypt—once a deal with the British was reached.

Such a deal did not come until 1954. Meanwhile, economic and military aid to Egypt was repeatedly pushed off. The Egyptians knew that the British were pressuring the Americans to hold up aid until their deal was concluded.[7]

Egyptian leaders began to hint that an alliance with the West might not be in the best long-term interests of Egypt, and they concurrently announced that Soviet economic aid might be forthcoming if they stayed out of the Western camp.[8] American officials refused to take the bait. They stated categorically that Egypt would receive no additional aid until an agreement was reached with the British.[9]

Egyptian government officials were stunned. They seemed to believe that the hundreds of millions of dollars of aid they believed they had already been promised was unconditional. They thought any aid following the agreement with the United Kingdom would be on top of that. And a new condition was looming. U.S. officials began talking of American aid coming only after Egypt signed a mutual defense agreement with the United States. Such an agreement, Egyptians feared, would represent a return to the status quo ante, and simply substitute American influence and power for British.[10]

Finally, when the deal with the British for withdrawal from their Canal Base was concluded in July 1954, the next day the State Department authorized U.S. ambassador Jefferson Caffery to begin negotiations with the Egyptian government over the terms of American aid to Egypt. Ambassador Caffery warned Washington that the amounts contemplated—about $20 million in economic aid and a similar amount of military aid—would be "greeted with dismay" in Cairo because of a long period of built-up expectations, but to little effect.[11]

In September 1954 Egypt informed the United States that it was no longer interested in receiving military aid because of the encumbrances the American government placed on that aid.[12] But as Egypt sought to shift the American assistance to purely economic aid, a new problem arose.

CIA officer Kermit "Kim" Roosevelt told the Egyptians that American elections were approaching and Zionist pressure would make it difficult for the United States to award as much aid as Egypt might have expected. Thus the "vast" aid Egypt had expected would not be possible in a single year but would be "very possible" over many years. The figure for the current year would be in the neighborhood of $40 million.[13] An agreement for that amount was signed in Cairo on November 6, 1954, with the money targeted for railway improvement, highway construction, and potable water projects.

In a four-hour dinner in Washington in December 1954, Egyptian ambassador Ahmed Hussein met with Roosevelt and Assistant Secretary of State for Near Eastern, South Asian, and African Affairs Henry Byroade, who was soon to leave Washington to become ambassador to Cairo. The Americans explained to him once more why the aid Egypt felt it had been promised did not arrive. According to Hussein's report:

> The two guests confirmed that Israel feels it is not gaining new ground in America and is in fact losing ground, or that it is beginning to moderate, although Zionist influence in America is a force that cannot be ignored. Byroade noted that Arab countries are only concerned with Israel and don't care about the Russian danger, which is the premier concern of the United States. He said that this region is weak and cannot be maintained in case of war, although it is of great strategic importance to the West. He said that these countries should not compromise their economic programs because of an expansion in militarization programs which are beyond their capacity. He said America wants to offer genuine military aid continuously to the Middle East, but they have yet to find the appropriate basis that would allow it to convince public opinion and Congress to get the necessary appropriations for this purpose.
>
> Finally, I mentioned to Mr. Byroade the new approach of the American government in trying to avoid war and relying on strong economic assistance to Asian countries to protect them against communism. [The United States has pursued this path] especially after it became apparent that Russia's assistance to communist China and its economic program had deeper and more rapid effects than American assistance, which was economically insufficient. Russia now is trying to follow the same policy with regard to Afghanistan and Indonesia.
>
> I told Mr. Byroade that I thought the Middle East is no less important or sensitive than Asia or Southeast Asia and I thought the next long-term assistance program should include this region. He said that he agreed and will exert all his effort toward this goal.[14]

SOVIET ARMS AND A WESTERN OFFER:
FEBRUARY–SEPTEMBER 1955

Ambassador Hussein was a mild-mannered and erudite gentleman who had earned a doctorate in economics in Berlin, worked in government to improve the plight of Egyptian peasants, and established Egypt's first social security system. He resigned his government position in the monarchy just before Egypt's 1952 revolution to protest official corruption. He returned to public service for the new government, a government that shared his strong instinct for change but whose leadership was his temperamental opposite.

Gamal Abdel Nasser was an impatient populist and a fierce nationalist, eager to overturn a regional order that had left Egypt subjugated for decades. The son of an Alexandria mailman, he was part of the first class of Egypt's military academy that had allowed in boys from non-noble families. He saw serious combat in the 1948 war with Israel, fighting fiercely for months to defend a besieged Palestinian village when few Arab units acquitted themselves well.

Abdel Nasser and his military academy classmates were only thirty-four years old when they overthrew Egypt's monarchy. He was not prominent in the first months after the 1952 revolution, but over time it became clear he was in charge. His broad-shouldered and square-jawed image came to dominate photographs, and he wore his resolve on his sleeve. He exuded confidence in a country that had felt oppressed by the British for more than three quarters of a century and to the Ottomans for centuries before that, continuing a trail of foreign rulers, reaching back to the Byzantines, who had co-opted the pharaohs. He promised self-determination to Egyptians and to the wider Arab world in speeches that were lively and blunt. He argued that Egypt's path to modernity was tied to genuine independence and not to continued subservience to European masters.

Abdel Nasser was part of a cohort of new nationalist leaders who came on the scene after World War II. While such leaders were a clear threat to Britain's efforts for an orderly unwinding of the empire, the United States was initially sympathetic to them, especially if these leaders steered clear of communist influence. To many in the United States, rising nationalism was an unstoppable tide. Confronting it was folly, so there was little to do but work with it.

Abdel Nasser sensed the openness and tried to build on it. After all, one of his key strategic insights was understanding that Egypt's foreign policy could be a national asset. He was certainly open to working closely with the United States, but he had no intention of being drawn into a bloc. That would be just one step above subservience. If governments wanted Egyptian support, they would have to pay for it, and they could count on him bargaining for maximum advantage.

Egypt's desires for a strong postcolonial order in the Middle East based on the Arab League were dealt a strong blow on January 12, 1955. Without any previous announcement, the Turkish prime minister arrived in Baghdad and signed a defense pact between Turkey and Iraq, under Western aegis. While Egypt had been willing to overlook Western defense agreements with non-Arab states such as Pakistan, Turkey, and Iran, the Egyptian government took Iraq's inclusion in this "Baghdad Pact" as proof of a Western design to split the Arab world and assert its control over weaker individual states. Demonstrators clogged the streets of Cairo and Damascus. The Egyptian press lashed out with vigor.

Meanwhile, the Israeli border was becoming more worrying. On the night of February 28, Israeli troops launched an attack on Egyptian troops in the Gaza Strip, killing thirty-eight and wounding thirty-two. One Egyptian wrote later:

> From the first moment the Gaza raid was a political operation more than a military one. And it was meant to achieve several goals at once: First, to embarrass Cairo and demonstrate its weakness before the Arab world, which had divided itself because of Western alliances, and then playing on that to upset the regime in Egypt, and finally to act as a warning to Egypt that its border with Israel was exposed.[15]

Writing for an English-speaking audience, that same author explained:

> The raid was intended as a message from Ben-Gurion to Nasser, and Nasser understood the message. This was that building hospitals and schools and steel mills was not going to protect Egypt from a ruthless neighbor who was set on ensuring that it should not be allowed to prosper. Only arms could do that. . . . All the messages that had been passed on to him via well-meaning intermediaries were designed to lull him into a state of false security. Israel was determined to challenge the rising star of Egypt by every means at its disposal, primarily by force.[16]

In the spring of 1955 the United States and Britain were involved in an effort to explore possibilities to negotiate a more durable peace between Egypt and Israel. The main issues were Palestinian refugees and territory, as well as whether any Arab state could afford—amid such inter-Arab competition—to be seen taking a leading role in even trying to make peace with Israel.

On the substance, the most difficult issue was territory. The basic Egyptian position was that southern Israel had to be given up. In 1955 Nasser explained: "I do not and will not consent to Israel's existence separating Egypt from the Arab world. Sooner or later, Israel will have to concede the Negev, and we are prepared to go to war for it."

Harking back to a long view of Egyptian history and territory going at least to the early nineteenth century, Nasser believed: "Egypt's separation from the rest of the Arab world is a long-standing imperialist plan . . . aimed at turning Egypt into an African country. But I am an Arab and want to stay Arab." In practice, this seemed to mean that peace with Israel implied Israeli willingness to cede its territory south of the town of Beersheba.[17]

Nasser knew that no Israeli seemed ready to consider any such thing. He was also consciously assuming a role of leadership within the Arab world given weakness in places like Iraq. For both reasons, Nasser placed a high priority on his military needs. In a meeting with now ambassador Byroade in Cairo March 10, Abdel Nasser told him: "The Egyptian army must have the arms which are required to carry out its responsibilities. If the United States is not prepared to sell us weapons, let it say that once and for all so we know what we will do."[18]

Sometime that spring, Egypt contacted the Soviet Union about acquiring Soviet arms. There was a conversation with the Communist Chinese foreign minister Zhou En-Lai on the way to a nonaligned conference in Bandung in April 1955. However, the idea does not appear to have been a new one. Soviet representatives in Cairo had for some time suggested that Soviet aid might be forthcoming if Egypt were to request it.[19]

Meanwhile, the Egyptian press, under government encouragement, agitated against an alliance with the West. In their telling, years of a pro-Western orientation yielded only additional conditions and delays, but aid had not flowed and would not.

On April 6, the Soviet ambassador to Washington told the Egyptian ambassador there that the Soviet Union would be willing to give aid to the Middle East if such aid were requested. He also expressed sympathy with Abdel Nasser's efforts to bring the Arabs together and indicated his pleasure with a *New York Times* article suggesting the United States and Britain would not interfere in the creation of an Arab defense pact.[20]

The American government, too, was putting on a charm offensive. In May, Kermit Roosevelt went out of his way to indicate American pleasure with the premier. He told the Egyptian ambassador to Washington, "Any doubt about the friendly intentions and stance of the United States toward Egypt have no possible basis in fact."[21]

Amid the high politics, Egypt's leaders could not ignore the condition of their economy and society. Tens of millions of Egyptians lived in poverty, endemic diseases like malaria and bilharzia savaged the countryside, and illiteracy rates were dauntingly high. Egypt's leaders were looking urgently for a solution.

In August 1955, the World Bank issued an internal report on the viability of the Aswan Dam project, on which so many hopes had gathered. The report praised the new Egyptian government. It "is tackling the problem of economic development with great vigor. In many respects its determination to do something for the economic and social advancement of the country has given the people, long accustomed to indifferent, dishonest government, new hope for the future."[22]

The report continued by noting that "further economic development . . . is now primarily dependent on a considerable expansion of agriculture. . . . An expansion of the land under cultivation, which in Egypt is synonymous with agriculture, is an inescapable necessity."[23] The Aswan Dam was estimated to cost a total of $1.347 billion (of which $407 million would have to come in "hard" currencies), and it would expand the arable land in Egypt by 30 percent.[24] Combined with programs already under way to improve agricultural productivity through improved drainage and seeds, Egypt's total agricultural production could increase by 50 percent over the level achieved in 1953.[25] Increased agricultural production would in turn raise agricultural income by 50 percent. That would create a market for locally produced manufactured goods, thereby boosting Egyptian industry. Such industry could rely in part on plentiful hydroelectric energy produced by the dam.[26]

The bank study suggested that the government of Egypt could afford the dam, provided it was prudent in its other expenditures. Egypt could likely meet its share of the spending during the first decade. Egypt had virtually no foreign debt, high foreign exchange reserves, and high annual production of long-staple cotton, the finest in the world. In addition, the country's income from the Suez Canal would rise when the canal concession expired in 1968 and ownership of the operating company returned to Egypt.[27] While the World Bank study did not wholeheartedly endorse the Aswan Dam project, it attested to its feasibility and to its necessity.

As the Aswan Dam plans matured in the autumn of 1955, the Egyptians announced they were obtaining arms from the Soviets.[28] In October, Ambassador Hussein had a long meeting with Secretary Dulles. According to Hussein's memorandum of that meeting, he told Dulles:

> It is pressing and necessary that Egypt senses American assistance in executing the High Dam project. I told him that although the Russian government is offering us conditions better than those of the World Bank to finance the project and execute it, we still prefer to deal with the World Bank. But I confirmed to him that the issue cannot be postponed for long since Egypt truly perceives the project as its largest vital economic project. And any new delay in its execution will embarrass the Prime Minister before Egyptian public opinion. And it is not in anyone's interest that the Bank delay its decision whether to finance this project so as not to create new pressure on the Prime Minister to accept the Russian offer.
>
> I reminded Mr. Dulles of American assistance in the current year and said we want to apply for 360,000 tons of American wheat in accordance with PL 480. Then I expressed on this occasion the hope of the Egyptian government that America does not take any measures under agitating pressure that would cause Russia to gain a long-term political victory in Egypt and in the entire Arab East while at the same time Egypt is keen that the operation remains purely commercial. . . .
>
> Mr. Dulles added that the American government promised Egypt military and economic aid after the agreement with the English, and it fulfilled its promise without hesitation. . . .
>
> Then he said that he trusts President Abdel Nasser and he repeats to his aides that he is the most important man in the Middle East, and we can trust him and rely on him. But Egypt's last action [to obtain Soviet arms] was a strong shock to the American government and its foreign policy, described by some as the biggest defeat of American foreign policy after its first failure in China. This encouraged some who are hostile to us and harbor malice against us, and it strengthened the position of Israel and its supporters in this country. They are the ones who opposed the withdrawal of the English from the Suez base claiming that would strengthen Egypt, which cannot be trusted in the future. They said that a strong Egypt will be a source of trouble.[29]

EXPLORING COOPERATION: OCTOBER 1955–MARCH 1956

On December 16, the Department of State issued an aide-mémoire to the Egyptian finance minister in Washington that indicated the U.S. government's intention to finance construction of the high dam at Aswan in cooperation with the World Bank and the United Kingdom.[30]

Egyptians were anxious about the conditions the World Bank attached to its management of the loan, worried that the bank sought a veto power over the Egyptian economy and its external relations. This aroused in Egyptian minds chilling reminders of what happened when the Egyptian ruler Khedive Ismail found himself in crippling debt in the 1870s, opening the way to the 1882 British intervention in Egypt, a British presence that Egypt had only just dislodged.

The CIA stepped in to try to smooth over the tensions. A week after the World Bank's draft plan was issued, Kermit "Kim" Roosevelt reassured the Egyptian ambassador that the two American political parties were trying to remove Israel as a political issue, and that the administration was delaying (and likely would deny) arms shipments to Israel. He also cautioned that "extremist elements" were growing in Israel and some were acting without gaining support of the central government. Roosevelt added, "It is not a probability but a very strong possibility that Moshe Dayan will act independently and begin a real war."

Roosevelt lamented that Israel possessed no strong central government like Egypt to keep fringe elements in line and indicated that the United States and Britain would immediately intervene in case of war. But he advised the Egyptians, as a precautionary measure, that they should keep their troops away from the border.[31]

A week later, an unnamed American official (probably Kim Roosevelt again) told the Egyptian ambassador that the United States would not give Israel arms. Instead the United States had privately decided to help Egypt build the high dam at Aswan. There would not be additional money now, he said.

> That is to avoid approaching Congress in the current election year, which would allow the issue to be exploited by some Senators and Representatives who want to curry favor with Zionists and attack Egypt, thus agitating the environment rather than improving it as the United States government wants.
>
> But any assistance in the second stage [that is, the execution] must be authorized by Congress in future years as is necessitated by the Con-

stitution. My interlocutor told me there is no hesitation on the part of the American government to continue aid to Egypt until the project is completed. Otherwise there would have been no reason to award assistance now.[32]

Roosevelt was right, at least to the extent that Israel was casting an increasing shadow over U.S.-Egyptian relations.

In late January 1956, presidential envoy Robert Anderson arrived in Cairo on a secret mission, assisted by the CIA, to revive work on Arab-Israeli peace, project Alpha, the Anglo-American plan to achieve peace in the Middle East. Alpha had been simmering since the beginning of 1955. Now the Americans were making an all-out effort to hammer out the elements of an agreement.

The Egyptians had approached the Americans in late March 1955 about a possible peace with Israel.[33] But after that, and after the Israeli raids and Egyptian decisions to sponsor fedayeen raids of their own, Egyptian interest in a peace deal was less clear. Egyptian leaders were also wary of being outflanked by their anti-Israeli rivals in Baghdad.

Meanwhile the Egyptians wondered whether there really would be Western assistance building the Aswan High Dam.[34] At least part of the problem had to do with the fact that American government officials continued to tell the Egyptians that such aid was being opposed by foes the Egyptians knew would not disappear: Zionists and British imperialists. U.S. government officials also continued to express concern over the increasingly vitriolic Egyptian press and to warn Egypt that there existed a real possibility of Israel starting a war in the region.[35]

Anderson returned to Egypt in early March 1956. He was disappointed to discover that Abdel Nasser told him that he lacked the political capital in the Arab world to move forward with a peace with Israel in the near term. Abdel Nasser tried to ameliorate American fears of war by suggesting that Israeli and Egyptian troops further separate their forces in Sinai, but such accommodations seriously misjudged the American position.

Perceiving the growing tension in the Egyptian-American relationship, the Egyptian diplomat Anwar Niazi warned in an internal memorandum:

American papers and magazines have recently begun to attack the Egyptian government and say that the American government is reconsidering its policy toward Egypt. While some attacks seem Zionist-inspired, the news of reconsidering policy toward Egypt seems inspired by the Department of State. This may be because the department had faith in its policy toward Egypt but is disturbed to think Egypt hasn't acted accordingly. And perhaps the reason for that is that the confidence of this department in the appropriateness of the policy it followed with regard to Egypt is wavering because it thinks Egypt did not act to express its appreciation for what the American government did for it, for example we mention the following:

1. Silence of the American government in the face of Israel and its supporters.

2. Not joining the Baghdad Pact.

3. Earmarking money for the High Dam roughly double what Israel will get in aid this year.

4. Allowing Egypt to buy 280,000 tons of American wheat in Egyptian currency, which relieved a grain crisis in Egypt.[36]

Niazi continued that if the Republicans won the next election, it would benefit Egypt because Zionists had less influence in the Republican Party than the Democratic Party. He suggested Egypt could maintain its nonaligned policy, the United States would grant Israel only limited aid, and thus the threat of a regional war would be reduced. To gain such an outcome, Niazi urged the Egyptian government to cut back its anti-American (and anti-British and anti-French) propaganda.

Such a policy of Egyptian restraint, Niazi argued, would produce a number of political and military benefits. The United States would continue its policy of not pressuring Arab governments to join the Baghdad Pact and keep its own distance from it. The United States would continue to withhold arms from Israel. The United States might be helpful on Algeria. The Americans could come through with their share of support for the Aswan Dam project and would keep the trade flowing to buy Egyptian cotton.[37]

RISING TENSIONS: MARCH–JULY 26, 1956

At the end of March, an unnamed U.S. official (described only as "a high-ranking official known to us and known to be friendly to Egypt and the Arabs," most probably the CIA's Kim Roosevelt) met with Ambassador Hussein in Washington. Roosevelt was delivering a warning. According to the Egyptian report, he made the following points:

1. He would not dismiss the idea that the Israelis would try to assassinate Abdel Nasser.

2. Recent critical articles in the press may be the work of the British, and quite possibly also indicated Zionist involvement.

3. A growing circle of countries doubt America's policy to Egypt, including the Philippines, Pakistan, Turkey, and Greece, and they oppose aid [to Egypt]. Further, it is not helpful that Egyptian papers are calling for Arab states to get Eastern [Soviet bloc] arms, and that Egypt is sending arms to Algerian revolutionaries. Also, further delay on beginning the High Dam project suggests that Egypt either hopes to avoid Western funding or fears the project is too large for the Egyptian economy.

4. It is not helpful that Egypt is creating a number of confrontations simultaneously. America's policy toward Egypt was based on trying in all possible ways to win its friendship, but America will at some point evaluate whether this policy achieved success or failure and assess its future stance toward Egypt in light of these results.

5. Cairo must take a position since its current position cannot be maintained. While Egypt is saying it is a friend to Western countries and requests various kinds of assistance from those countries, we find that Egypt is actually following a hostile policy toward those countries and does not refrain from attacking them and provoking people against them. Egypt must choose one of these two policies, and if it chooses hostility against the West, the West will have to decide its stance on that basis.[38]

A few days later, the director of the Voice of America's Middle East service, Gerald Dooher, met with the Egyptian embassy's press attaché and warned that Americans in Saudi Arabia were trying to widen the rift between the Saudi monarchy and the Egyptian regime. Dooher did not make clear during a three-hour conversation whether these Americans were acting on the behalf of the American government, but he did explain that "they are telling King Saud that Gamal Abdel Nasser, the extremist rebel, is more dangerous than British influence and British hegemony and more dangerous than the communists."[39]

By mid-April, another Egyptian diplomat observed that recent American approaches had common but ominous themes:

1. America's policy was in Egypt's interest and was intended to win Egyptian friendship, and then changed to a different policy when it became clear that Egypt did not appreciate what the American government did for it.

2. Egyptian propaganda has been and still is intense against the West and the United States is hoping Egypt will temper its campaigns.

3. Appearances of a change in American policy toward Egypt are based on newspaper accounts and attacks on Egypt that are Zionist-based.

The official surmised that because all these reports came simultaneously, they may have represented an indirect invitation by the United States for Egypt to meet it "in the middle of the road."[40] In fact, Egyptian propaganda invective against the West seems to have declined following these approaches. Ambassador Hussein was able to report in early May that the "general atmosphere had improved" as a consequence.

Whether this would make any difference for Egypt is unclear. Also militating against rapprochement with Egypt was growing congressional concern that aid to Egypt, and particularly aid for the Aswan High Dam, would hurt southern U.S. cotton farmers, who had to compete against Egyptian cotton. Tensions revived later in May and continued into June, including Egypt's establishment of diplomatic relations with the People's Republic of China.

Abdel Nasser apparently concluded by early July that Western financing for the dam would not be forthcoming. He told Ambassador Hussein to go ahead and accept unconditionally all the American terms for financing. When Hussein met with Dulles on July 19, Dulles informed him that the financing for the dam had been withdrawn. Dulles claimed that the Egyptian economy could not support the project.

While Abdel Nasser was expecting rejection, he seemed shocked it had been done in an especially humiliating manner. Not only did it seem to have been done in a way calculated to cause maximum embarrassment to the government of Egypt, but the text of the rejection was distributed to journalists before the meeting was completed, and, therefore, before the government of Egypt could prepare any response.

The American withdrawal of funding, and the public way it was done, posed a domestic threat to the leadership. Abdel Nasser's government had dealt with its internal enemies in 1954, including former President Naguib. But Abdel Nasser's domestic enemies had made a strong comeback during 1955. Many aspects of his rule were unpopular. The solidification of Nasser's dictatorship had driven more of the foes underground, but the regime knew they were out there. Abdel Nasser may have felt he needed to do something decisive to reaffirm his government's strength.[41]

Abdel Nasser developed a surprising possible countermove. The World Bank report on the Egyptian economy had certainly highlighted the importance of Suez Canal tolls for the future financial security of Egypt. What if Egypt could get the revenue stream from Suez Canal tolls much sooner, by taking over the foreign Suez Canal Company that was supposed to be allowed to operate the canal until 1968?

Abdel Nasser reportedly commissioned a secret series of studies in 1954 on the effect of nationalizing the canal company. Each study of a particular issue was so narrowly drawn that those doing the studies had no idea of the larger purpose those studies might serve.[42]

But concrete plans to nationalize the canal seem to have come together just in the last half of July 1956. According to one account, Abdel Nasser wrote an outline of his plan on seven half-sheets of foolscap paper on July 21. His outline read, in part:

Assessment of the Situation: The nationalization decision will mobilize the Egyptian people and the masses of the surrounding Arab Nation and will inspire in them the meaning of self-reliance. And nationalizing the Canal Company will also be a complete response to the Western policies, in the forefront of which is the United States of America, and will make clear to them that we are able to bear our responsibilities and that they cannot hereafter decide our destiny let alone confront us with insults.

But the West will not be silent and will confront us with threats and political campaigns and psychological warfare. Most probably, we will be faced with military threats that could turn into an actual war if we don't use our resources with caution.[43]

But Abdel Nasser considered the possibility of war unlikely. He reportedly told a confidant:

The United States will probably hesitate because its military entry against a small state like Egypt will mean political failure. Also, it would seriously embarrass the United States in front of its Arab friends in the region, particularly Saudi Arabia.

France cannot enter alone as she is preoccupied with the war in Algeria. And its international position, especially after the crisis in Indochina, doesn't enable it to mount a decisive armed operation against Egypt.

Israel might consider intervening militarily, but it cannot take nationalization of the Canal Company as its casus belli. An Israeli invasion of Egypt would be a war against the entire Arab Nation, and this will make it incumbent on America to "put the brakes" on Israel. Thus it is in Israel's interest to wait as the conflict between Egypt and the entire West deepens.

Finally, Britain is the corner from which a real invasion is feared, and the British position is the key to the entire issue, and thus the fundamental question is how will Britain react and how will Eden react?

Abdel Nasser assessed that Eden was in a weak position and, thus, most likely to use force. He estimated the likelihood of a British invasion in the week following the nationalization at 80 percent, the subsequent two weeks at 40 percent, and during the month of September 1956 at 20 percent.[44]

Abdel Nasser seems to have made, on his own, the decision to nationalize the Suez Canal Company. He reportedly informed his confidant and close aide Abdel Latif Baghdadi on the evening of July 21.

Abdel Nasser had planned to announce the nationalization on July 23, the fourth anniversary of the Revolution. But he waited until he received word from emissaries in Cyprus that British troops were, in fact, unprepared for war, and thus not able to attack Egypt quickly. That information was slow to arrive. Also, Abdel Nasser's army leader, Field Marshal Abdel Hakim 'Amr, had opposed a quick nationalization. So Abdel Nasser did not inform the other members of the Revolutionary Command Council of his intent to nationalize until the morning of July 24 and did not inform his cabinet until 7 p.m. on July 26.[45]

Two hours later, Abdel Nasser began his speech. Marking the fourth anniversary of the revolution, thousands of Egyptians surrounded the stage in the cool evening air in Manshia Square in Alexandria. Thousands more seemed to be listening from surrounding balconies. Millions tuned to their radios across Egypt and around the Arab world.

Abdel Nasser masterfully worked the audience with an account of all the offenses Egypt had suffered at the hands of the West and gave evidence that a new day had come. He complained about promised aid that never arrived, the seeming Western goal to dominate Egypt, and the success of the Egypt's 1952 revolution to turn the tide.

Standing erect and speaking in his trademark mix of formal and colloquial Arabic, Abdel Nasser particularly singled out for criticism Ferdinand de Lesseps, the retired French diplomat who was behind the construction of the canal. In Abdel Nasser's telling, de Lesseps had opened the door to almost a century of European domination of Egypt.[46]

But Abdel Nasser focused on de Lesseps for another reason, as well. The mention of his name was the signal for Egyptians to nationalize the Suez Canal Company.[47] He mentioned it fifteen times for good measure.

As Abdel Nasser read the nationalization decree to the crowd, pandemonium broke out. To Egyptians, it was an unimaginably bold step. To Abdel Nasser, in particular, it was a fitting gesture of resistance to powers that had sought to humiliate him and, probably, overthrow him. There was little he thought they could do. Rejecting financing of the Aswan High Dam project was intended as a humiliation. Abdel Nasser used it as an opportunity to assert his independence. He was not isolated in the Arab world. Instead, he was now its greatest hero.

Observations on Part One

PHILIP ZELIKOW

In each of the six viewpoints in Part One (and in the next two parts), we try to provide the information for analytical dissection but work it into a chronological narrative, a narrative without omniscience about what others were doing, without knowledge of what was to come, and without inserting our own later judgments of whether we think the leaders were right or wrong. It is a little more lifelike that way.

Naturally we are making editorial and authorial choices, but we do try to present these viewpoints reasonably "straight." This puts a bit of a burden on the reader to evaluate and compare these different viewpoints. It is meant to.

To help stir up those reflections, here are a few of my own. They are organized around the three sorts of judgments called out in the Introduction.

VALUE JUDGMENTS: WHAT IS THE PROBLEM? WHAT DO THEY CARE ABOUT?

The first point to notice, and the beginning of any wisdom, is that all six capitals are defining their problems so differently. Recall the three levels of conflict: the global Cold War, the regional "Arab" cold war (for example, Egypt versus Iraq), and the Arab-Israeli conflict.

- Having kicked down the arms race dam and opened a river of arms to Egypt, Moscow is mainly adopting an opportunistic strategy in a game of global influence, deciding not to care overmuch about Egyptian communists. It wants to undercut the Baghdad Pact, of course. But Moscow is not too engaged in the details of regional politics. It is even less interested in Arab-Israeli matters, though it does not seem to want a war. As the viewpoint from Moscow shows, Khrushchev also certainly has domestic politics to worry about, too, but it is not yet clear how they will relate to developments in the Middle East.

- The Israelis are riveted to their local problems. The ongoing arguments about how to evaluate the border security problem are swamped first by the alarm about arms to Egypt and later by troubles with Jordan.

- As 1955 turns to 1956, a new Socialist-led coalition takes charge in Paris, and Paris is more and more preoccupied by the Algerian revolt. It has, in some ways, the most distinctive set of viewpoints of all. It is a leadership driven by ideas and historical experience, pro-Europe and pro-Israel, and it sees the Algerian rebels as antimodern throwbacks, inspired by a pan-Arab dictator in Cairo and his propaganda machine.

- The British are less preoccupied by the global Cold War during 1955–56 and more by concerns about regional influence in the Middle East and the related partnerships or protectorates with oil suppliers. They are interested, somewhat abstractly, in Arab-Israeli peace. Eden's government is also concerned about the domestic political situation, prodded more by domestic pressure—within his party as well as from the opposition—than is the case anywhere else.

- Washington is uniquely burdened in its attempts to juggle concerns about all three levels of conflict—global, Arab, and Arab-Israeli. But it is not nearly as concerned as Britain about the Arab cold war. It does not share Britain's stress on the Baghdad Pact. It is also more relaxed about its oil relationships and wishes the Arabs would quit quarreling so much and focus on the Soviet menace instead. Washington tries harder than practically anyone to advance an Egypt-Israel peace deal, including the Egyptians and Israelis. There are plenty of domestic concerns, but these seem relatively manageable except for rising congressional opposition to doing anything for Egypt.

- Egyptian concerns are clear enough, but the trade-offs among them are not. The Egyptians care little about the global Cold War. They care quite a lot about leadership in the Arab world. They are also necessarily attentive to the Israeli enemy, though they do not regard that concern as existential. Britain often seems to loom largest on Nasser's list of potential and historic enemies, as a symbol of Egypt's profound drive to feel and be independent. The Egyptians are looking for ways to advance their economy but have trouble balancing those interests against all the others.

REALITY JUDGMENTS: WHAT'S GOING ON?

For all but Nasser, the hardest assessment problem is, How to assess Nasser? How big a problem (or, for Moscow, opportunity) is he? What does he really want or need?

The interesting consensus, shortly after the initial shock about the Soviet bloc arms deal wears off, is the Anglo-American agreement that Nasser is a man with whom one can try to make a deal. That judgment changes, first for the British leaders. The Americans also grow more negative, but are more doubtful and divided. At the core there are disagreements about how to assess Nasser himself and size up his agenda.

The assessment issues are nicely encapsulated by two lengthy quotations in the conversations among leaders. One is the exchange, provided from Washington's viewpoint, from the Eden-Eisenhower-Dulles meeting in January 1956. Another revealing exchange, in March 1956, came in the French record of Mollet's meeting with Eden.

Is Nasser a doctrinaire expansionist? Or is he a practical fellow, an opportunist? Eden and Mollet clearly incline to the former view. Eisenhower is inclined a bit, perhaps, toward the latter camp. Dulles seems somewhere in between; perhaps he is going back and forth.

The most important evolution is the marked hardening of British views in early 1956. There appear to be several reasons, very much including the questionable intelligence reports MI6 is providing to Eden.

Dulles is, at all times, a highly capable lawyer for his country. His professional habits are strong, but when it comes to sizing up what is going on, he is highly susceptible to British views (especially Macmillan's, while Macmillan was his counterpart) unless and until President Eisenhower gives him guidance and steers him.

The new French government has a more consistent view of Nasser, if lightly evidenced. Since its main attention is directed elsewhere, its reality judgments about Nasser and the Arab-Israeli situation are predictably thin.

In Israel, at first the whole country is alarmed about the new danger of war with Egypt, conventionally expected for the summer of 1956. But by the time summer rolls around, the Israeli assessment is rapidly evolving. The Egyptian menace no longer seems so immediate; Israel's own arms situation is being transformed by the June agreement with France and what may follow.

Egypt's own assessments are murkier and also appear to be evolving. For Egypt, a huge event is the just-completed withdrawal of British forces from the Canal Zone and their territory by the summer of 1956. The full implications of the Soviet bloc arms and the new political situation are still being digested. The Israeli reprisal policy is a menace, but Egypt does not feel too threatened by these raids, as it calculates how to keep the pot simmering but not boiling over.

Several of the countries—notably Britain, Israel, and Egypt—are paying more and more attention during 1956 to questions about how to assess the future of Jordan. They are also distracted by puzzles (or, for the British secret service, opportunities) in the future of Syria, a country where Egyptian ambitions run high.

ACTION JUDGMENTS: WHAT CAN BE DONE?
APPRAISING THE POLICY DESIGNS

In the autumn of 1955, London and Washington (and even Paris) sought some kind of deal with Egypt. At that time the British Foreign Office appears to have played a central role in developing a consensus approach, even if London looked to Washington to provide most of the diplomatic muscle (in working on an Israeli-Egyptian peace deal) and financial muscle (in the Aswan Dam project with the World Bank).

Cairo's policies are harder to appraise because they seem to go in every direction. During much of this period Nasser is simply trying to carry forward both the eviction of the British and the absorption of his new arms supplies. His star was rising; Nuri's in Iraq was fading. But did Nasser need more?

The evidence is not sufficient to say just what Nasser's objectives were with Israel, at least in the near term. Nor is it clear just what he wanted in national development. If he was determined to get Western support for the Aswan deal, he had made decisions that seemed to put that priority in second or third place.

By early 1956 the British policy lead falters. The British Foreign Office, formerly in the driver's seat (when led by Macmillan), seems to find itself more and more a passenger (under Lloyd). Eden seems to have a well-developed attitude, not a serious plan.

The Americans deserve credit for crafting the most well-developed policies on the Israel-Egypt problem during the first half of 1956. Their policies, therefore, invite more scrutiny.

It is the Americans, led by Eisenhower and Dulles, who are centrally focused on Israel-Egypt peacemaking. For the Anderson mission, the "Gamma" stage of the peacemaking project that began with Alpha, the State Department experts and their CIA colleagues had worked out quite detailed ideas. The toughest issue was territorial boundaries. The Americans chose to insist on significant Israeli concessions from the 1949 armistice lines.

The choice of these particular operational objectives was divorced from a solid reality assessment about what the Israelis could do. The Americans were decently informed about the political divides in Israel. On other issues they should have known that the Israelis had room for maneuver, but on territorial concessions they had none. Nor was it at all clear that the proposed concessions would have thawed Nasser's attitudes, since he sought much more territory than the Americans were trying to offer.

The American design for a peace settlement, developed at the level of the professional experts and strongly influenced by British views, may, thus, have been fatally flawed. What else could they have tried? An alternative would have been to focus entirely on how to stabilize the 1949 lines and see if Nasser could ever, by any inducement at all, be brought to publicly accept them (and this is doubtful).

Instead, led by Dulles, the Americans leaned hard on the Israelis, who would not budge a bit on the territorial borders issue. Nor are they likely to have given in even if the Americans had sweetened the deal with more detailed discussion of security guarantees or arms transfers.

Perhaps CIA director Allen Dulles was right all along when he mused, back in October 1955, that neither Israel nor Egypt really wanted to, or could, settle their conflict. Once the U.S. government reached that sort of conclusion, which it did in March 1956, then it had to redefine policy success. Its operational objective, at that point, was damage control—to deter or mitigate another Arab-Israeli war.

That is the key U.S. policy shift during the summer of 1956. Eisenhower, in particular, is organizing the Omega plan to orchestrate secret contingency work to deter or respond to a possible Israel-Egypt war. The first stage of war-management project Omega seems secret and creative. In these plans, Nasser is increasingly discounted as a constructive factor. Helping him with the Aswan Dam no longer seems worth the trouble.

Instead, while also trying to diversify their portfolio of Arab friends, Eisenhower and his aides are setting in motion military planning for U.S. (and British) military intervention to contain or stop an Arab-Israeli war. He is, thus, effectively moving his government toward a de facto ultimate security guarantee for Israel. He does this without any public promise, a promise that could have been misunderstood or abused.

The United States has begun accumulating stockpiles of arms to be transferred either way, for the contingency of aggression by either side. Of those, the fighter jets being amassed for Israel would be the most immediately meaningful if a war broke out.

Further, the U.S. government may feel that, quietly, it is also effectively addressing the Israeli arms problem. Washington would not publicly offer arms to Israel and, thus, antagonize its Arab friends, of which it still had some and hoped for more. Instead the United States tacitly approved supplies of advanced weapons to Israel from others, principally France.

The French diplomats at the Quai were unhappy about being put in this spot. But their colleagues in other ministries did not seem to mind so much. It is unclear to this day whether U.S. intelligence was aware of the full scope of the June 1956 French arms deal with Israel. But Paris had certainly seen Washington's wink.

For Eisenhower, his most important problem is being addressed. In May and June he was again sidelined by illness, this time in his intestinal tract. Dulles executed the change of course on the Aswan Dam project plans, which no longer mattered very much to what the U.S. government was trying to achieve.

Dulles handled the Aswan Dam project cancellation brusquely and played it for stage effect. Nasser then taught Dulles a lesson in how one actor can upstage another.

The Cairo viewpoint that closes Part One ends with Nasser's move to take over the Suez Canal. Hardly anyone sees this coming, even among Nasser's own officials.

To evaluate Nasser's big policy move, we have to consider the quality of his reality judgments, his assessments of what others may do. The Cairo viewpoint ends with some remarkable evidence about just how Nasser sized up the possibilities. In Part Two we will see how well Nasser, that veteran gambler, calculated the odds.

PART TWO

What to Do about the Crisis

Part Two

TIMELINE OF PUBLIC EVENTS

JULY 26   Nasser announces nationalization of Suez Canal.

AUGUST 1–2   U.S, British, and French talks in London.

AUGUST 16–23   London Conference on the Suez Canal Crisis.

SEPTEMBER 9   Nasser rejects "Eighteen-Nation Proposal" from London conference.

SEPTEMBER 19–21 Second London Conference, on Suez Canal Users Association.

SEPTEMBER   Border clashes between Israel and Jordan raise threat of wider war.

OCTOBER 5–13   UN Security Council debates Suez crisis and next steps.

WASHINGTON

EDWARD MERTA

At 11:00 p.m. on July 26, the American chargé d'affaires in London, Andrew Foster, answered a summons to report immediately to Number 10 Downing Street. There Foster attended an emergency meeting of the British cabinet, the chiefs of staff of the armed forces, and the French ambassador.

The subject was Nasser's speech that evening to a frenzied crowd of 250,000 in Alexandria. Nasser had delivered his response to the American and British withdrawal of Aswan Dam aid. Egypt, he roared to the masses, had nationalized the Suez Canal Company. Egyptian government teams took control of company offices as he spoke. European staff who refused to work for the Egyptian government would be imprisoned. Tolls collected from ships transiting the canal would fund construction of the Aswan Dam.

After the meeting, Andrew Foster cabled the State Department: Eden had ordered his military chiefs to plan for war. If it came, he wanted American support.[1]

DEFERRING THE CHOICE FOR WAR: JULY 27–AUGUST 16

Was Nasser's takeover of the Suez Canal worth going to war against most of the Arab world? Washington officials feared that British and French leaders believed the answer was yes.

At first, the American officials were startled and deeply worried. Nasser

133

had gone beyond simply flirting with the Eastern bloc and flinging about wild, anti-Western invective. He had seized a chokepoint vital to the economic and military power of the Western alliance.

The British navy relied on the Suez Canal to move vessels quickly through the Mediterranean Sea to the Indian Ocean, defending critical shipping lanes holding the empire together. Of the 2 million barrels of oil consumed by Western Europe every day, about 1.3 million passed through the canal. The remainder went through pipelines from Saudi Arabia and Iraq through Syria to Lebanon.

Nasser could now interrupt much of that supply if he chose, and his allies in the Syrian government could cut off the rest by blocking or sabotaging the pipelines. That would force oil tankers bound for Europe to go around the Cape of Good Hope and up the Atlantic coast of Africa, adding thousands of miles—and great expense—to their journey. In that scenario, the global oil tanker fleet could not keep up with European demand.

Oil shortages would quickly develop, threatening economic collapse and political chaos. The United States would have to deliver emergency supplies, leading to rationing on the home front, hitting the auto industry and the rest of the economy hard, with a presidential election a little over three months away. Moreover, Nasser's success in nationalizing the canal might itself trigger further nationalizations of foreign property, of oil production facilities, pipelines, or military bases.[2]

Eden cabled Eisenhower the day after Nasser's takeover. He asked Eisenhower to send a high-level American emissary to London to coordinate with Britain and France on military preparations and diplomatic pressure against Egypt. Eden declared his government "convinced that we must be ready, in the last resort to use force to bring Nasser to his senses. For our part, we are prepared to do so." The French, similarly, vowed to reverse Nasser's seizure of Suez by whatever means.[3]

On this occasion, Eisenhower's explosive temper did not appear. With Secretary of State Dulles still making his way home from the inauguration of Peru's new president on July 27 and 28, the president coolly dispatched Deputy Under Secretary of State Robert Murphy to London. Facing the prospect of allied military intervention and an interruption in Middle East oil supplies, the commander-in-chief ordered the State Department to notify leaders of both parties in Congress—secretly—that he might need to call a special session authorizing U.S. military action in the Middle East.[4]

Dulles, upon his return, said he "thought we should be prepared, if necessary, to use force to keep the canal going." He hoped, he added, that "a broad international basis for this could be developed.[5]

But the shock quickly wore off, as did the initial impulse toward military solutions. Eisenhower, the now-returned Dulles, and their top aides agreed in the last days of July that domestic and international opinion made early resort to military action risky at best. At home, public opinion, Congress, and the press would probably view early use of force without first attempting a diplomatic settlement as unwarranted support for naked European colonialism. Overseas, international opinion regarded Nasser as well within his legal rights, since nation-states enjoyed inherent power over their territory so long as they compensated foreign investors adequately and competently and impartially administered an international waterway like the canal.

Accordingly, Eisenhower and Dulles instructed Murphy to dissuade the allies from early military action. He was to press for diplomatic action to build an international consensus against Nasser.[6]

Upon Murphy's arrival, the United States and the allies agreed to pursue an international conference of the major canal users, to be held in London. The legal basis for the conference would be the Suez Canal Convention of 1888. That treaty guaranteed free transit of the canal to all nations, free from political manipulation by any one of them, including Egypt. Those provisions could be carried over into a new treaty that could create an international authority to take over operation of the canal from Egypt.

As the London talks continued, Murphy reported that America's allies seemed to regard the proposed conference only as a means to deliver an ultimatum to Nasser. They emphasized that his Suez takeover, if not reversed, would magnify Nasser's prestige with the Arab masses immeasurably. Then Nasser and his emboldened allies could endanger British and French interests throughout the Middle East.[7]

On July 31, Murphy relayed a message directly for Eisenhower. It was a stark declaration from Eden and Macmillan: Britain and France were going to war at the earliest possible date and that decision was final. They would go through the motions of a diplomatic conference only for show, as a prelude for preordained military action.

The British were planning to land three divisions in Egypt. They would spend whatever money and blood were necessary, even if it meant war with the Soviet Union. Eden and Macmillan believed that if the United States was "with them from the beginning," Murphy reported, then the "chances of World War III would be far less than if we delayed." The British and French would rather run the risk of global war than accept "another Munich leading to progressive deterioration of ME [Middle East] position and in the end inevitable disaster," leaving the former British Empire broken and irrelevant, "becoming another Netherlands," as Macmillan put it.[8]

Discussing Murphy's dramatic cable on July 31, Eisenhower and some of his top advisers realized the British had no idea how strongly Congress and the public would oppose American involvement in the use of force without first attempting diplomacy. The rippling effects of disrupted oil supplies would affect the U.S. economy. A British and French attack under those circumstances, CIA director Allen Dulles said, "would arouse the whole Arab world." Eisenhower "enlarged this to the whole Moslem world." Nasser, he said, "embodies the emotional demands of the people of the area for independence and for 'slapping the white Man down.'" Challenging him while he enjoyed international support, said the president, might "array the world from Dakar to the Philippine Islands against us."

Secretary of State John Foster Dulles hedged. After an international conference, "it would then be possible to take armed action if it became necessary with a good chance of retaining a large measure of world support."[9]

Eisenhower settled the issue. The United States would not stand by and let its allies go to war over Suez. At least not yet. Eisenhower ordered Secretary Dulles to fly to London immediately, to deliver a personal letter warning Eden that the United States opposed any use of force without first organizing an international conference based on the guaranteed right to international usage of the canal in the 1888 convention.[10]

Dulles followed his instructions. In talks with Dulles in London on August 1 and 2, Eden, Macmillan, Selwyn Lloyd, and French foreign minister Pineau grudgingly agreed to set aside the military option until after negotiations toward an international authority to run the canal had failed. A diplomatic conference to negotiate such an arrangement would open in London on August 16, the United States and its allies announced.

The allies weren't happy with this, Dulles knew. Still, the British and French seemed to concede the logic of his argument that successful use of force would depend on first building international support, most especially in the developing countries Europe had once ruled, where support for Nasser ran high. Diplomacy alone, Dulles argued, might compel Nasser to "disgorge" the canal.

For now, the allies would abstain from war in favor of suspending aid programs, freezing Egyptian assets in Western countries, and excluding Egyptian trade from Britain's sterling area. In the meantime, British and French preparations for the possible use of force would continue, ready to implement if diplomacy should fail.[11]

There was still division in Washington about whether the diplomacy was a determined effort to find a peaceful settlement or just a necessary prelude to war against a recalcitrant Egypt. In these first weeks after Nasser's announcement, officials in the U.S. government reevaluated their assessment of Nasser. One of Dulles's principal experts on Arab-Israeli matters, Francis Russell, held the pen for a paper, on August 4, that summed up the revised views within the State Department.

Before, he wrote, there were three hypotheses about Nasser. He could be regarded as (1) a progressive military dictator trying to modernize his country, (2) a symbol and leader of Arab resentment and bitterness, and (3) an aspirant for power on a large scale and without scruple. "Up to the present time," he wrote, "there has been room for divergence of opinion." But now the developments "point clearly to the conclusion that Nasser is an international political adventurer of considerable skill and with clearly defined objectives that seriously threaten the Western world, though probably with no definitely planned tactics or timetable."[12]

Some in the Eisenhower administration shared the British and French inclination toward going straightaway toward the use of force against Egypt. American military leaders, meeting as the Joint Chiefs of Staff, echoed the kind of arguments coming from Eden and Mollet.

They all, including JCS chairman Admiral Arthur Radford, believed that Nasser was hostile and that hostile control of the Suez Canal was militarily unacceptable. To Radford, Nasser was someone "trying to be another Hitler." Thus, by early August, the Joint Chiefs pushed for a full-blown debate in the National Security Council (NSC) over whether the U.S. government should support Anglo-French military action against Egypt in the event Nasser rejected international control of the canal.[13]

Eisenhower and Dulles thought it was too early to make such a formal policy decision on U.S. readiness to use force. But neither of them had categorically decided against it, either, at least not prior to the London conference.[14]

At an August 9 meeting of the NSC, Dulles acknowledged the uncertain prospects for diplomacy. He asked whether, if diplomacy failed, the United States should support Anglo-French military action. Or should the United States instead try to stop such military moves? Eisenhower did not yet answer him directly. He did say, ominously, that "Egypt had gone too far. He asked how Europe could be expected to remain at the mercy of the whim of a dictator." He ordered contingency planning for emergency oil shipments to Europe and studies of military options to continue. If war came, the United States would be ready.[15]

At an August 12 White House meeting, Dulles made it clear where he stood if diplomacy failed. He would endorse the use of force if it came to that. Dulles did not want a war. But if Nasser rejected a reasonable proposal from the London conference, he thought Britain and France would feel compelled to go to war against Egypt and, in that case, "it would seem clear that the United States should give them moral and economic support."[16]

STRATEGY AT THE LONDON CONFERENCE: AUGUST 16–23

By the second half of August, the initial shock and angry reactions had subsided. There was more time to think about a possible war, more time to consider Nasser's position, and more time to think about possible diplomatic moves to head off a potentially unnecessary war.

While preparation for military action might seem prudent, much of the State Department and the CIA feared, the harder they looked at it, that an Anglo-French invasion of Egypt would trigger massive anti-Western political convulsions across the Arab states and the decolonizing world more generally. They could see a preview of such tumult. Throughout August, U.S. missions in numerous African and Asian nations reported that Nasser's takeover in Suez had prompted ongoing street demonstrations and anti-Western hostility in newspapers, on the radio, and in conversations among politicians, bureaucrats, and military officers.

In places like Amman, Baghdad, Karachi, Bombay, Colombo, and Djakarta, Nasser's defiance had touched a nerve. It was all too easy to imagine that British and French tanks rolling into Cairo would turn simmering hostility into an inferno of rage. If Israel moved to take advantage of a European war against its chief Arab enemy, as seemed all too likely, the firestorm would be that much worse.

Governments already unwilling to criticize Nasser publicly might be forced to break relations with the West altogether. Ambitious young military officers might, as Nasser himself had once done, lead uprisings against the West. Such chaos would open new opportunities for Moscow to build alliances with Arab states, as they had been attempting to do with Nasser and his allies in Damascus. Only if Nasser brazenly defied world consensus in favor of internationalizing the Suez Canal would force become a viable option.[17]

When John Foster Dulles arrived in London for the opening of the conference on August 16, he had a busy first day of meetings. Immediately he sensed, and reported that night to Eisenhower: "The atmosphere on the whole is much more composed than two weeks ago. There is I think a growing realization of the magnitude of the task of military intervention and of the inadequacies of their military establishments to take on a real fighting job of this size."[18]

The original diplomatic strategy for London had, however, already been set "two weeks ago." The design for the London conference still reflected the "ultimatum" tone of the first week of the crisis. It still reflected Dulles's initial sympathy for that stance.

Therefore the substance of the "tripartite" U.S.-British-French diplomatic position going into the London conference was very tough. Developed at the time of Dulles's earlier trip to London, the substantive approach had been drafted in a tripartite working group and pretty well settled between August 2 and 4. In that crucial drafting, French officials had played a key role, supported by British work. The Americans had focused mainly on the process for the conference itself. The plan was very clearly for an "international authority" to take over the canal from Egypt, manage its money, and ensure that Egypt received "an equitable return."[19]

Naturally enough, given the origins of this plan, it was not designed to win over Egypt. It was designed more as an ultimatum, leaving only a road for Egyptian retreat. As the conference convened, weeks later, one question obvious to some delegations was whether there was room for any middle ground, some way that granted a sufficient measure of Egyptian authority and control yet gave the international community adequate security and guarantees. But Dulles was now identified personally with the tough full international control proposal.

Dulles had instead concentrated on the conference process and ways to isolate Nasser. He lined up developing countries as participants. Dulles successfully excluded Israel from the conference, preventing the Arab-Israeli conflict from causing any distraction.[20]

After securing reluctant British and French acceptance of a Soviet presence at the conference, Dulles also urged the Russians to intercede with Nasser on behalf of some form of international participation in running the canal. Moscow, he hoped, would view a successful compromise along these lines, rather than intransigent opposition, as the surest means to strengthen Soviet prestige. If he could push the parties away from abstractions like "colonialism" and "imperialism" and "get the problem onto a practical basis," focused on the logistics of running the canal, "there was a good chance of an acceptable solution."[21]

Nasser refused to send a formal Egyptian delegation to London. He denounced negotiations for an international authority over the canal as an attempt to reimpose colonial rule.

After some internal debate within Moscow, the Soviet government decided to attend and to send their foreign minister, Dimitri Shepilov. Shepilov impressed Dulles with his "frank and businesslike" approach. The Soviet minister appeared to want some sort of settlement but one with a more flexible approach to Egyptian authority.[22]

From Washington, Eisenhower studied the tripartite proposal that Dulles planned to put on the table as the U.S. proposal. He zeroed in on the same core issue that had troubled Shepilov—the insistence on full international control. "Nasser may find it impossible to swallow the whole of this as now specified," Eisenhower wrote to Dulles.

The president said he had no problem agreeing to an international board that had "supervisory rather than operating authority." The analogy he had in mind was to a corporate board of directors. He had no other comment "other than expressing the hope that the results of the conference will not be wrecked on the rigidity of the positions of the two sides on this particular point."

Dulles disagreed with Eisenhower. He thought the British and French would insist on international control of operations. He did not wish to soften the proposal before it was given to Nasser.

In reply, Eisenhower further explained his concern. But, deferring to the man on the spot, he said he would back whatever decision Dulles took.[23]

Dulles stood firm on full international control. There was, therefore, no chance of winning Soviet support for his approach. The Soviets eventually backed a proposal from India for an especially weak version of joint participation in which the users would have a mere advisory role.[24]

After the twenty-two attending countries had their debate, Dulles did secure an eighteen to four vote approving the U.S. proposal for an international board of directors to control the canal, with an Egyptian voice on the board. The London conference concluded on August 23.[25]

The conferees appointed a delegation of five countries, led by Australian prime minister Robert Menzies, to travel to Cairo, see Nasser, and present the eighteen-nation proposal for international control.[26] But Nasser insisted that he would accept nothing less than permanent Egyptian control, softened only by new guarantees of free international passage through the canal. He continued to enjoy acclaim across the Arab world and backing from Moscow for rejection of an internationalized canal. When the Menzies delegation arrived in Cairo for talks with Nasser, there would be essentially nothing to talk about.[27]

Time for a peaceful settlement of the Suez crisis appeared to be running out.

DOUBLING DOWN ON DIPLOMACY, NOT FORCE: THE USERS ASSOCIATION PLAN, AUGUST 24–SEPTEMBER 11

With the failure of diplomacy increasingly a foregone conclusion, the odds of an early attack by the allies on Egypt seemed to rise. Eden and Lloyd told Dulles that the ongoing buildup of British and French forces in the eastern Mediterranean would soon require a decision on whether to use them. Once the decision was made, Lloyd had warned on the last day of the conference, "in effect there would be a button pushed early in September and after that everything would happen automatically and be irrevocable."[28]

Dulles met with Eden the next day, August 24. He told the prime minister that Eisenhower's warning on August 1 remained valid: international opinion still would not tolerate the use of force. Dulles suggested that any further recourse would have to go through the UN Security Council (where the Soviet Union had veto power), or "if possible a situation created so that if force had to be used, the primary responsibility could be put upon Egypt through their perhaps using force to prevent transit through the Canal."[29]

Given the American support for a tough international control position at the London conference, Eden may have understandably believed that the Americans were just opposed to war because it was too soon. The Menzies delegation still had to present Nasser with the demand and give him a chance to retreat. Eden, therefore, wrote to Eisenhower a few days later saying that Britain wanted to "be in a position to act swiftly" once Nasser replied to the Menzies delegation.

If Nasser rejected the eighteen-nation proposal, Lloyd informed Dulles that Britain would seek a Security Council resolution condemning Egyptian defiance. That UN effort would thus clear the way for an Anglo-French attack. Dulles told Eisenhower "the British were determined to move militarily unless there was a clear acceptance of the 18-Power plan by Nasser around the 10th of September." By early September, both the press and U.S. diplomatic posts were reporting that Britain and France had begun evacuating their nationals from the Middle East in anticipation of war.[30]

Eisenhower and Dulles realized they might soon face the hard question: If Nasser rejected international control, would the U.S. go along with an Anglo-French war? Via a secret visit from presidential envoy Robert Anderson, Eisenhower pleaded with the king of Saudi Arabia to end his public support for Nasser and pressure the Egyptian leader to accept the Menzies delegation's proposal. The Saudis rebuffed this request.[31]

Nasser's position had grown stronger as Egypt ran the canal competently, without any hint of disrupting traffic or other provocations. Soviet support also backed Nasser up and Nasser could draw comfort from the growing voices in Britain itself opposing a use of force against Egypt.[32]

As the diplomatic alternative was sinking, both Eisenhower and Dulles settled more firmly on an assessment that the other option, war, would still be the wrong choice. At an NSC meeting on August 30, Dulles argued that Britain and France would find themselves pitted against the entire Arab world, potentially forcing them "to try to re-establish colonial rule over the whole area of the Middle East." The result would be "a morass from which it was hard for Secretary Dulles to see how the British and the French could ever hope successfully to extricate themselves." The resulting anti-Western upheavals could open the way to Soviet domination of the Middle East and its oil.

Dulles was still searching for some other kind of "intermediate situation," one that "would not mean a total success for Nasser, who might subsequently be successfully deflated." Key to that effort would be Nasser's rival leaders in the Arab world. They might want to see Nasser "deflated," but they did not see the Suez affair as the right occasion to challenge him.[33]

After he made this case to the NSC, Dulles was blunter about the war danger in a private conversation with Eisenhower. The British and French, he said, would be sucked into a colonial occupation of Egypt that would never end. "Everywhere they would be compelled to maintain themselves by force and in the end their own economy would be weakened virtually beyond repair and the influence of the West in the Middle East and most of Africa lost for a generation, if not a century." The Soviet Union would dominate those areas as a result, critically weakening Western Europe.

Eisenhower concurred. "This was not the issue upon which to try to downgrade Nasser." The Americans did what they could to rally other Arab governments to oppose or isolate Nasser. Also, at the beginning of August the State Department had asked the CIA to reconsider the possibility of some covert action against Nasser. The CIA was not interested. It was going along, unenthusiastically, with British plotting against Nasser's ally in Syria, but even there the CIA was not well informed about what the British were doing.[34]

The first priority, before trying to figure out a longer-term strategy to contain Nasser, was to end the crisis over Suez. To get to that outcome, Dulles and his aides devised a new idea to restart the diplomacy, even while the Menzies delegation was wrangling with Nasser in Cairo in early September. Switching from full international control, the State Department came up with a fallback idea to cede nominal Egyptian control, while the users of the canal actually ran it.

A users' association would exploit its ownership of ships passing through the canal. Instead of relying on the Egyptians, the association would hire its own pilots for ships, replace Egypt as the collector of transit tolls, and set its own shipping schedules, via ships anchored at either end of the canal as permitted by the 1888 convention. The association would propose needed maintenance and expansion of the canal to Egypt. It was as if the Egyptians would be left owning the physical canal and the surrounding real estate, while the users ran the operations.

If the users took over the operation of the canal, then Egyptian refusal to cooperate with them could be treated as interference with use of the canal. That, then, would be a breach of the 1888 convention. Such a breach could justify resort to the UN Security Council and the use of force. So Dulles could present his fallback "users' association" as a cession to formal Egyptian sovereignty but try to sell it to the British and French as an idea that still held open their options. Eisenhower was skeptical that the users' association could actually run the canal without Egyptian cooperation. But he approved the idea as a way to stave off war.[35]

Dulles, too, was really proposing a users' association as a way to forestall the use of force, not facilitate it. He sold the idea to British representatives as one more means to pressure Nasser, especially by removing his control over canal revenue.[36] But in the same breath he depicted the association as the path to a genuine diplomatic settlement with Egypt. He and Eisenhower saw the users' association as a basis for complicated, time-consuming international negotiations, first among the nations of the users' group and then, perhaps, at the UN.

It was important "not to make any mistakes in a hurry," Eisenhower said in regard to British and French insistence on military action, stressing "how important it was to go slowly." Dulles agreed, saying, "If we could work it out they would have to unmount." He meant that the British and French would eventually have to abandon their plans for war.[37]

"Every day that goes by without some outbreak is a gain," Dulles told White House speechwriter Emmet Hughes, "and I just keep trying to buy that day. I don't know anything to do but keep improvising." The president and Dulles apparently doubted the warnings from Britain and France that passage of time made them more likely to use force, not less.[38]

Eisenhower then made his position against the use of force as clear as he could to Eden. Replying in early September to a message in which Eden had described the Suez crisis as "the most hazardous that our country has known since 1940," the American president started off by reviewing all the upcoming diplomatic steps but, after considering "the diplomatic front," Eisenhower wrote, "I am afraid, Anthony, that from this point onward our views on this situation diverge."

The president warned his old wartime partner that he continued to oppose war with Egypt. American opinion was "flatly against it." Congress would not support it. International opinion was negative.

Then Eisenhower reviewed the substance of a possible military move. "I really do not see how a successful result could be achieved by forcible means." There were other ways to secure effective operation of the canal and to contain Nasser's influence.[39]

Eden answered immediately. He more fully unpacked his assessment of Nasser. He drew explicitly on the most powerful analogies: Hitler's unanswered aggressions during the 1930s and the Soviet Union's attempt to force the West out of Berlin during the Berlin blockade of 1948. "It would be an ignoble end to our long history if we tamely accepted to perish by degrees."[40]

Eisenhower promptly wrote back a long and careful rejoinder. He began humbly: "Whenever, on any international question, I find myself differing even slightly from you, I feel a deep compulsion to re-examine my position instantly and carefully."

But Eisenhower thought Eden was exaggerating the danger. He was "making of Nasser a much more important figure than he is." He rejected Eden's repeated assertions that extended negotiations would "inevitably make Nasser an Arab hero and perilously damage the prestige of Western Europe, including the United Kingdom, and that of the United States," inexorably triggering "an upheaval in the Arab nations" and the collapse of Britain as a major power. "This, I think, is a picture too dark and is severely distorted," Eisenhower wrote. The Arab world would rally to Nasser in an upheaval against the West only if the Europeans attacked him or the West capitulated to his seizure of the canal. Eisenhower tried to warn Eden of an additional dire consequence if he went to war now:

> The use of military force against Egypt under present circumstances might have consequences even more serious than causing the Arabs to support Nasser. It might cause a serious misunderstanding between our two countries because I must say frankly that there is as yet no public opinion in this country which is prepared to support such a move, and the most significant public opinion that there is seems to think that the United Nations was formed to prevent this very thing.

Because time wasn't against the West in the way Eden feared, Eisenhower maintained, a middle path existed between war and capitulation. He then outlined the new American idea for talks on a users' association to defuse the crisis and to isolate Nasser. Eisenhower also emphasized patient, long-term efforts to make the Suez Canal obsolete via new pipelines and tankers.

"Nasser thrives on drama," the president observed. "If we let some of the drama go out of the situation and concentrate upon the task of deflating him through slower but sure processes such as I described, I believe the desired results can more probably be obtained."[41]

On September 9, Nasser formally rejected the eighteen-nation proposal of the London conference.[42] The Menzies mission had failed, at exactly the early September interval when the British and French had said they would decide on the use of military force.[43]

Eisenhower publicly signaled his opposition to that course at a press conference on September 11, when asked whether the United States would back an Anglo-French attack on Egypt if Nasser remained intransigent. "I don't know exactly what you mean by 'backing them,'" the president replied. He later added, "We established the UN to abolish aggression and I am not going to be a party to aggression if it is humanly possible."[44]

THE RIFT—AND AN APPARENT SETTLEMENT AT THE UN: SEPTEMBER 12–OCTOBER 14

The British and French quickly demonstrated that they had a much different view of the proposed users' association. British and French diplomats were prepared to go along with the new U.S. idea. But they informed Dulles that they regarded a users' association as a basis not for negotiation but as a way for the allies to "resume physical control of the Canal" now that Nasser had rejected the Menzies proposal.[45]

When Anthony Eden announced the proposal in Parliament on September 12, he presented the association as an instrument to take over the management of canal traffic from Egypt, with transit tolls paid to the international organization rather than to Egypt. If Nasser didn't cooperate, the prime minister said, Britain would take the matter to the United Nations or "use other means."

At a press conference the following day, Dulles publicly contradicted Eden's presentation. He denied that the users' association was intended to impose a new management scheme against Egypt's will. Instead, he depicted it as a basis for working out a new arrangement for international participation in running the canal. If Egypt refused to allow passage of ships belonging to the new organization, Dulles said, the United States would send its vessels around the Horn of Africa. "We do not intend to shoot our way through," he said.[46]

The secretary raised a number of other objections to the positions of the allies, generating friction as he worked with Lloyd and Pineau to organize a second London conference on establishment of the users' organization. Dulles declined their rush to take Nasser's rejection of the Menzies proposal to the UN Security Council for action. He stalled, wanting to give the users' group a try.[47]

CIA field officers dealing with the Middle East understood the message to the British and French. They referred to the Suez Canal Users Association idea (SCUA) as "SCREWYA." Dulles also pressed the allies to begin preparations for an extended reduction in Middle East oil supplies. He warned them that Nasser might react to establishment of the users' organization by cutting off traffic of its members through the canal. British and French envoys refused to make such a commitment. Any interruption of oil supplies would, they said, be quickly ended by military action.

Such wishful thinking worried Dulles. But by late September the U.S. intelligence community, which had been very worried about the danger of war earlier in the month, thought the danger appeared to be easing. American opposition, ongoing diplomacy, world opinion, Nasser's determination to avoid provocations, and the specter of Arab backlash were, the estimate judged, likely to prevent the allies from resorting to force, despite their hatred of Nasser.[48]

For instance, one report found "softening" in French militancy now that the users' association offered a diplomatic means to pressure Nasser. The report saw hesitation in London amidst "serious British internal, as well as world-wide, opposition to the use of force." Another report, at the end of September, noted an "absence of any evidence of British-French intentions to act against Egypt through Israel, despite various reported rumors to the contrary." War remained a possibility, according to these analysts, but it no longer seemed imminent. [49]

A second London conference, held September 19 through 21, adopted the new SCUA proposal. The same eighteen countries that had backed the Menzies proposal for international control seemed to deliver a crucial victory for Dulles's middle path between war and capitulation.[50]

The Soviet Union was opposed, as expected. Moscow warned that it wouldn't tolerate foreign intervention. The British and French regarded this as empty bluster.[51]

Eden himself seemed to have gone along with SCUA as a convenient pretext for armed intervention. In a private conversation with Dulles during the conference, Eden emphasized his continuing readiness to use force.

Nor would Britain ration oil imports to prepare for war. Eden rejected that course as too costly compared to what he, like others in his government, thought would be a short, decisive military campaign.[52]

Hoping to persuade Eden that alternative means could undermine Nasser, Dulles proposed a joint Anglo-American working group on, in the U.S. conception, economic and political methods to weaken Nasser's prestige and hold on power. Such an effort would complement plans already under way for a coup in Syria. Eden agreed. The proposed effort against Nasser's regime would be designated as Operation Mask. Dulles hoped such steps might yet convince the British and French that Washington shared their aim of denying Nasser a victory over Suez.

But the Americans had only a set of political and economic pressures in mind. Dulles still believed that "the use of military force was not right." He had also "told Mr. Eden he did not want to get into CIA type work and," according to the State Department record, "Eden agreed."[53]

As the secretary flew home from the London conference, however, American hopes for trans-Atlantic unity suffered a major blow. Without consulting Dulles, the British and French governments went ahead to demand a meeting of the UN Security Council on Egypt. They emphasized Egypt's rejection of the original eighteen-nation proposal for full international control. The UN Security Council meeting would be held in early October.

Dulles was furious. Not only had he cautioned against such action, his allies had discarded the long-standing practice of consulting in private with Washington before taking any new diplomatic action. Now he wondered if America's European allies were sticking to the old game plan to set up an attack on Egypt.

British and French envoys in Washington told him they had intelligence information that the Russians were preparing to go to the UN themselves, necessitating quick action to beat them to the punch and line up support against the pro-Nasser resolution Moscow no doubt intended to seek. The United States had no such intelligence, Dulles shot back.[54]

Moreover, for almost two weeks after informing Washington of their intended move, British and French officials in Washington and across the Atlantic refused to give any American representative a straight answer on whether their proposed resolution would try to promote a peaceful settlement based on the SCUA framework or would, instead, be a pretext for war. They offered only maddeningly nonspecific declarations to the effect that strong action was critical in the wake of the London conference to keep pressure on Nasser, with the French particularly angered that the conference had been inadequate for that purpose. An exasperated Dulles complained frequently to aides and the president about the lack of communication.[55]

Amidst this uncharacteristic evasiveness from the allies, another crisis arose out of the Middle East. This one involved Israel and Jordan. After a frontier skirmish with Jordan on September 10, an Israeli battalion crossed the border the following night, assaulting Jordanian military and police units in a raid that demolished two buildings and damaged another. Additional skirmishes and major Israeli ground incursions followed, killing and wounding dozens on both sides.

Britain warned the Israeli government to desist, invoking its defense treaty with Jordan. With British support, Jordan's King Hussein appealed to Iraq, a British ally under the Baghdad Pact, to deploy Iraqi ground troops into Jordan as a deterrent against further Israeli attacks.

In Washington, the State Department and the intelligence community believed Israel might be moving to exploit the Suez crisis by seizing Jordan's West Bank in a full-scale invasion. The Joint Chiefs of Staff noted that such an operation could easily annihilate the entire Jordanian army. A defeat at the hands of Israel might cause the already fragile Jordanian government to disintegrate, opening the way to a partition of the country between Israel and Iraq. Washington would have a second Middle East crisis on its hands, on top of Suez.

Despite tensions over Suez with Britain, the State Department worked closely with the British and Jordanians to defuse this crisis and stabilize the Jordanian government. In early October, Dulles pressured Ben-Gurion into reluctant acceptance of a small, lightly armed Iraqi presence east of the Jordan River. But the Israeli leader quickly recanted on the pretext of Iraqi statements calling for a return to 1947 Israeli borders and alleged British endorsement of those views.[56]

No one in Washington seemed concerned when intelligence reports in early September revealed that France had secretly delivered forty-eight Mystère fighter-bombers to Israel sometime in early September, rather than the twenty-four the French had proposed to transfer just after Nasser's takeover of the Suez Canal. Reports increased the number to sixty in early October. The covert French shipment broke an agreement among the tripartite powers to consult on any Middle East arms transfers in the three-way committee they maintained for that purpose. The Pentagon saw little military significance in the move, believing Israel lacked the pilots and logistics to operate additional aircraft on top of those the Israelis already had.[57]

Nevertheless, as reports of the Mystère shipment surfaced, the CIA accelerated its schedule of surveillance flights by its very secret and brand-new U-2 spy planes. These had recently deployed to European bases for the first time. They conducted surveillance flights over the eastern Mediterranean, including Egypt, Israel, Jordan, and Syria, likely on direct orders from President Eisenhower. Once the flights began on August 29, they consistently revealed that the buildup of allied air and naval forces around Malta and Cyprus was much larger than the British and French had revealed to American officials.

Eisenhower was "greatly irritated" by this, according to a CIA source. He went so far as to dispatch CIA officials to London to show U-2 photos of the buildup to their British counterparts in person.[58]

Washington's reasons for worry about France went far beyond the Mystère shipment. With Mollet's government convinced that the Algerian war was Nasser's doing, U.S. diplomats and intelligence analysts had no doubt that the French continued to seek a crushing blow against Nasser in the Suez crisis. According to U.S. assessments, the French had relentlessly pushed Eden toward war. Now they wanted him to treat SCUA merely as diplomatic groundwork for an ultimatum to Nasser, to be followed by a decisive military campaign if he rejected it.[59] At an October 4 NSC meeting Dulles said the French all along had been "eager to resort to the use of force in the Suez area" to bolster their North Africa position, and he "believed that they had lined up the British behind this point of view but that we had pulled the British back."[60]

Dulles and U.S. ambassador Douglas Dillon in Paris saw extremism in French politics, not just about Suez but about foreign relations in general, as a potentially dangerous wild card in the Suez crisis. Dillon worried that the French were losing confidence in NATO. French politics was drifting in a direction that was "fundamentally anti-American." Incendiary denunciations of the United States increasingly filled the French press and parliament in the wake of the second London conference. They accused Eisenhower's government of appeasing the Fourth Republic's new Hitlerian nemesis in Egypt so as to destroy French rule in Algeria and open it to American oil companies. In this venomous, widely circulated conspiracy theory, Washington's treachery had proven the NATO alliance essentially worthless. Talk of abandoning the Western alliance in favor of neutralism toward the Soviet Union was becoming more common in the airwaves, newspapers, cafés, and conference rooms of Paris.[61]

The American alliance with Britain betrayed strains of its own as September turned to October, beyond differences over SCUA and UN action on Suez. In talks to prepare Operation Mask, MI6 and the British Foreign Office were demanding stronger action than the Americans could accept. Eisenhower told Dulles, as Dulles noted, "that we should have nothing to do with any project for a covert operation against Nasser personally." The canal issue was not the occasion for undermining Nasser. The United States would be better off "developing Arab leadership elsewhere, and [he felt] that this offered greater hope than a frontal attack on Nasser on the Canal issue." The United States needed "to maintain an independent position as regards the British and French until we knew definitely what they were up to."[62]

Dulles then put off British demands that he sign off on such plans. At a London cocktail party, the deputy director of MI6, George Young, berated the CIA representative on Britain's Joint Intelligence Committee, Chester Cooper, for America's failure to join British plans for "bashing the Gyppos." Young hinted at dark consequences of America's timidity, saying, "Your [CIA] friends at home had better come up with something constructive pretty soon."[63]

All these tensions over Suez unfolded amid growing controversy in NATO over other issues, thus helping to fuel the sense of alarm in Washington over the potential implications of the crisis. France had been pulling out forces from Germany to serve in Algeria. Eden opened up discussion of pulling down British forces, too, perhaps in favor of relying more on nuclear weapons. All this was making it harder for the West German chancellor, Konrad Adenauer, to maintain support for his own country's rearmament plans. The rift with the allies over Suez seemed to be part of a broader trend.[64]

Dulles publicly fueled such speculation at a press conference on October 2, refuting accusations that the United States sought to pull the "teeth" from SCUA by saying, "There is talk that the teeth were pulled out of it, but I know of no teeth. There were no teeth in it."

"No teeth"? That did not help the British and French much. But the secretary went further. He said the rift over SCUA was just a symptom of fundamentally different assumptions about the NATO alliance between America and its allies. The existence of NATO to defend Europe did not require the United States to endorse British and French policies everywhere in the world. In fact, Dulles added, American policy over the long run actively encouraged the dismantling of European colonial empires, albeit gradually and peacefully rather than abruptly and violently.

The secretary's remarks sparked a firestorm of condemnation in the press on both sides of the Atlantic. Critics berated the U.S. administration for enabling the disintegration of the Western alliance. Dulles apologized to Eden.[65]

But Dulles did believe that a larger historical process was at work. Writing to some of his ambassadors in Western Europe, he explained that some allies had come to believe they could count on a "blank check on the US for economic, military, and political support everywhere in the world." Dulles thought they were now confronted by the traumatic realization that their belief was mistaken.

"This Suez matter," he said to Dillon, "is bringing into the open the fact that they cannot count upon us outside the North Atlantic Treaty area automatically and without the exercise of our independent judgment." Dulles speculated that the long-range result might be to foster a more unified, independent Europe. He thought such a trend might actually be healthy and constructive, since such a Europe would still be generally aligned with the United States by common historical and cultural bonds.[66]

Everything depended on first settling the Suez crisis, and in early October Dulles made his last-ditch push to do that. He confronted Lloyd and Pineau personally on October 5, at the outset of the UN Security Council debate in New York City on the Anglo-French Suez resolution.

Dulles demanded they state, once and for all, whether their governments remained open to a final push for a diplomatic solution to avert war in the Middle East. Pineau was unenthusiastic, but Lloyd reluctantly said Britain would support such an attempt. After the conversation, Dulles cabled the president that the next week would be "make or break."[67]

In the glare of world press coverage, the UN Security Council debated the Suez crisis from October 5 to October 13. In public, Dulles and other foreign ministers considered a British and French resolution calling on Egypt to accept negotiations for a final settlement based on the first and second London conferences.

In secret, in the offices of UN secretary-general Dag Hammarskjöld, Lloyd and Pineau negotiated directly, at Dulles's urging, with Egyptian foreign minister Mahmoud Fawzi, with Hammarskjöld as mediator. After days of tense bargaining, the UN negotiations paid off on October 12. Britain, France, and Egypt publicly announced they had agreed on basic principles for further negotiations to end the crisis, based on a cooperative relationship between the Egyptian government and the Suez Canal Users Association. Further negotiations were tentatively set to take place in Geneva on October 29.[68]

The Americans felt a huge sense of relief. Dulles and Eisenhower believed, in the hours after the announcement, that this agreement essentially put an end to the Suez crisis. For the first time since Nasser nationalized the canal, after repeatedly rejecting Western proposals coming out of the London conferences, his country had agreed directly on a common diplomatic approach with the until-now militantly intransigent British and French.

The expected Soviet veto of a UN Security Council resolution endorsing the Hammarskjöld framework did nothing to derail negotiations to finalize it. As conflict between Israel and Jordan loomed, it seemed that a way out of the Suez imbroglio had been found at last.

Eisenhower went so far as to announce a resolution of the crisis during an interview on national television. "I have got the best announcement that I think I could possibly make to America tonight," he said. Egypt had agreed with France and Britain "on a set of principles on which to negotiate; and it looks like here is a very great crisis behind us."[69]

In private, the president and his secretary of state knew that much work remained to be done. There were still quarrels with the British about the details. But, Dulles said, "Enough has been said and done to make it virtually certain that the status quo will be preserved and there will be no use of force." The CIA analysts had a similar view.[70]

Egypt's president,
Gamal Abdel Nasser

Nasser at work.
Alexandria, July 1956

Israel's leader,
David Ben-Gurion

Israeli army chief of
staff, Moshe Dayan

Ben-Gurion's
Defense Ministry
aide, Shimon Peres

Moshe Sharett's
successor, the new
foreign minister,
Golda Meir

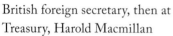

Britain's prime minister,
Anthony Eden

British foreign secretary, then at
Treasury, Harold Macmillan

Replacing Macmillan as foreign
secretary, Selwyn Lloyd

France's new government. In the center is Prime Minister Guy Mollet, eyeing his defense minister, Maurice Bourgès-Maunoury. Their cabinet colleague, François Mitterrand, is on the left.

French foreign minister Christian Pineau, British prime minister Anthony Eden, and American secretary of state John Foster Dulles emerge from a meeting in London.

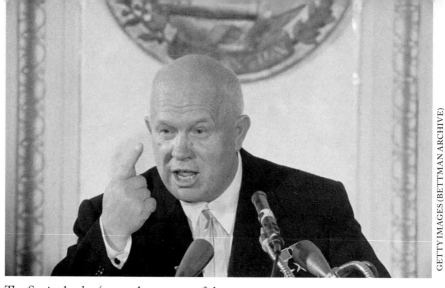

The Soviet leader (general secretary of the
Communist Party), Nikita Khrushchev

The new Soviet
foreign minister,
Dmitry Shepilov

The other Dulles, CIA
director Allen Dulles

Eisenhower and John Foster Dulles together go on
TV to explain the Suez crisis, August 3.

The Suez crisis moves to the UN Security Council.
British foreign secretary Lloyd is speaking, flanked by
Shepilov on one side, Dulles and Fawzi on the other.

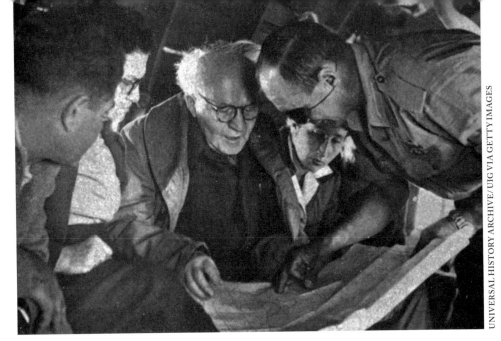

War—Ben-Gurion is being
briefed by Moshe Dayan.

Israeli soldiers display a captured souvenir.

PART TWO

CAIRO

JON B. ALTERMAN

FIRST MOVES: CAIRO FIGHTS THE LONDON CONFERENCE

In the weeks immediately following the nationalization of the Suez Canal Company, the leadership of the Egyptian government devoted much of its energy toward building Third World support for its action. Because of low levels of preparedness by the British and French militaries, Abdel Nasser had judged that an Anglo-French military attack could come only after several months of preparation. So Abdel Nasser spent the intervening time courting potential friends. In so doing, he hoped to fan the flames of public opposition so as to make an attack impossible.

The first step was circulating a memorandum to Egypt's missions abroad and directly to some allied governments detailing the legal bases for his nationalization of the canal company. The Egyptian side had a good case to make in international law and it had good lawyers to make it. Egypt had not confiscated anything. It had not closed an international waterway. It had nationalized an Egyptian company, which it was now operating in a wholly professional manner. The company had never been responsible for securing the canal or defending it; that was being done by the government of Egypt, and nationalization did not change that. While owners would have to be compensated, Abdel Nasser seemed to have the law on his side.

The law was one thing, but personal relationships were another. Immediately before the nationalization, Abdel Nasser had met his leading allies in the

153

nonaligned movement, Jawaharlal Nehru of India and Josip Broz Tito of Yugo-slavia, at Tito's summer resort in Brioni. Nehru had even stopped off in Cairo on his route back to India. But in hours of discussions, the Egyptian leader had not given any inkling that he was contemplating anything like the nationaliza-tion. It looked like Abdel Nasser had not been honest with his nonaligned col-leagues, and some egos needed stroking.

So, shortly after the nationalization, Abdel Nasser sent his chef de cabinet for political affairs, Ali Sabri, to meet with the Indian ambassador in Cairo. Sabri assured the ambassador that the decision to nationalize the canal com-pany was made only after Nehru had departed Cairo and that the Egyptian leader had not withheld any secrets.[1]

The personal approach paid off. In the early days of the crisis, Nehru pri-vately assumed the role of a kindly uncle to Abdel Nasser. Almost thirty years his senior, and with more than twenty years of nationalist, anticolonial politics under his belt, Nehru was a veteran. To the young and fiery Egyptian colonel, the weathered lawyer counseled patience and an adherence to international law. Perhaps in the back of Nehru's mind was the idea that Secretary of State Dulles was himself an international lawyer, and such an approach would serve Egypt especially well in winning American backing. At the very least, it held out the hope of securing American opposition to an extralegal offensive by America's allies.

Nehru wrote Abdel Nasser on August 3: "I venture to express the hope that you will decide to take the initiative yourself to call together all those interested in the international aspects of the development [that is, the nationalization] and on the basis of Egypt's sovereignty."[2]

The United States, France, and Great Britain had already taken the initia-tive for international discussions, however. They had issued a statement the previous day denouncing the Egyptian action to "threaten the freedom and security of the Canal" and called for an international conference on the matter to be held in London two weeks hence.

Sensing no satisfaction could come out of a conference in London, Abdel Nasser started looking for another venue to make his case. He transmitted an oral message to Nehru noting that he was thinking of taking the matter to the UN Security Council, where he would propose a new agreement to replace the convention of 1888.[3]

The problem with that convention, Abdel Nasser told Nehru, was that it charged the signatories to the convention with "watching over its execution" (that is, guaranteeing the security and free passage of the canal). Abdel Nasser viewed this provision of the convention as an infringement on Egyptian sovereignty in two ways: it ceded control over activities within Egypt's borders to foreign powers, and it implied Egypt's inability to administer the canal without foreign assistance. He asked Nehru to decline the British invitation to attend the London conference and, according to Abdel Nasser's confidant Muhammad Hasanayn Haykal, "begged Nehru to give him the benefit of his ideas."[4]

Replying to Abdel Nasser's message on August 5, Nehru counseled continued patience and conciliation. He wrote that, if India did decide to attend the London conference, "Our object would not be to weaken your position but, as you yourself have been doing, to work for conciliatory approaches. In this way it may be possible to prevent the proposed conference from being a barrier to settlement."[5]

The next day, Nehru sent a further missive, coaching Abdel Nasser to prepare a counterproposal, to "express yourself surprised at the UK convening a conference on the Suez Canal without consulting, or even referring to, Egypt and deciding on the countries to be inviting as well as indicating further action in regard to this," and to offer a counter based on the successors to the original 1888 signatories.

He urged Abdel Nasser to stay clear of the United Nations. "In the present state of the world the alignment of forces there may not be favourable. Further it can also lead to the interpretation of prior acceptance of international control."

Abdel Nasser considered going to London himself to attend the conference. But according to his friend Abdel Latif al-Baghdadi, he reconsidered this course when it became clear to him that he would not return a victor. Rather, the other conferees would diminish his position and insult him, until he returned having lost the battle.[6]

If Abdel Nasser could not succeed in the London conference, he would do what he could to ensure that the conference would not succeed either. As he saw it, the tripartite powers (Britain, France, and the United States) were working, at that time, in concert against him. Their arguments were "excuses to foist a new domination on us so that, having got rid of one [Britain], we will now have three dominating us in our territory." The list of invitee states was rigged in favor of "international control." Abdel Nasser made similar arguments to Tito.[7]

Also in early August the Saudis emerged as an intermediary between Abdel Nasser and the Western powers, especially the United States. One Saudi message to the Egyptians advised: "[The American ambassador] does not believe that the British will resort to force. President Eisenhower sent Dulles to head off this danger and prevent the use of force unless the Egyptians antagonize the

British by preventing their ships from transiting the canal or by continuing to insult them." The message ended with a query whether Saudi attendance at the conference would help Egypt's cause. Abdel Nasser reportedly discouraged the idea, and the Saudis did not attend.[8]

Abdel Nasser's efforts to persuade countries to boycott the London conference generally failed. Both India and the Soviet Union attended. The Egyptians were not surprised that the London conference resulted in a proposal for international control of the canal, although both the Indians and the Soviets dissented, along with two other attendees.

In late August, the Egyptian ambassador in Washington wrote in his diary that he had learned from a senior State Department official "that America agrees with Britain and France on the principle of internationalizing the canal, and if a war broke out, the United States would try to defuse it before it developed into a world war. The British regard this as an issue of life and death and he said that the British were determined to act." Another source had told him "there is fear of Egypt and its desire to found an empire to thwart Western interests. He concluded that if the London conference failed, and the two countries decided to take military action, America would not intervene to avoid later blame [from the two countries] except he confirmed that if Russia entered the conflict, America would enter it too."[9]

At the beginning of September, a delegation led by the Australian prime minister, Sir Robert Menzies, arrived in Cairo to deliver the results of the London conference to Abdel Nasser. "[Menzies made] clear to us that we were to wholly accept or reject the plan; we had no right to discuss or negotiate anything with them."[10]

According to Haykal, Abdel Nasser complained to outgoing U.S. ambassador Henry Byroade and veteran U.S. diplomat Loy Henderson (who was a member of the Menzies delegation)[11] that he was "prepared to discuss and study and come to an agreement, but 'not ready to welcome a man who acts like an Australian mule which Eden has sent, to scare me.'"[12] Egyptian sensibilities were further wounded by the fact that joint Anglo-French military exercises had begun on Cyprus just days before the Menzies mission arrived.

Abdel Nasser was unwilling to bend on his right to nationalize the canal company and impose Egyptian management on the canal. Menzies was unable to depart from his brief of working out some sort of international supervision for canal operations. According to Haykal, Menzies told Abdel Nasser, "Failure to arrive at an agreement will be the beginning of problems," and Abdel

Nasser replied: "If I accept your position, problems will arise with the Egyptian people, and if I do not accept it, there will be problems from your side. Thus, it appears to me that we will have problems in any event, and if that is the case, we will simply face up to our problems. We are prepared to do that."[13]

EGYPT SIZES UP THE NEW SITUATION

In early September, after the Menzies mission left Cairo in failure, the Egyptian government had to make some judgments about the next moves. The London conferees had made their demand. Egypt had rejected it. Now what? War? A fresh diplomatic move?

Egypt immediately made its own counteroffer for an international conference; it could draw on its own views and the advice it had received from India's Nehru as well as from the Soviet government. This was effectively preempted by the next Western move, the Dulles proposal for a users' association that would collect the tolls and operate the canal. To the Egyptians this seemed like just one more scheme for international control.

The Egyptian government was now constantly calculating the evolving risks of war. But to one of Abdel Nasser's aides, it seemed that the "idea of war was not uppermost in his thoughts and that war itself did not enter his plans as a serious possibility."[14]

Abdel Nasser did reach out to both Moscow and Washington. These probes were mainly handled through intelligence channels—the Soviet KGB and the American CIA. Through the Soviet KGB chief, in early October Nasser asked whether, in the event of an attack on Egypt, "the Egyptian government could count on the Soviets dispatching volunteers and submarines." The Soviet leadership apparently took no action on this request.[15]

Meanwhile, in mid-September, the Egyptian ambassador in Washington had already met one of his chief CIA interlocutors, Kim Roosevelt. Roosevelt was worried about Israel. The Israelis, he feared, would try to provoke Egypt to launch a massive reprisal raid against Israel that would then provide a pretext for war. Roosevelt added that the United States was pressuring Israel to avoid further escalation. Roosevelt also mentioned that Britain and France were afraid Egypt might emerge victorious from the canal crisis.[16]

On September 15, just before another meeting in London—this one to discuss the users' association idea, the Suez Canal Company's ship pilots walked off their jobs. The Egyptians had expected this and, weeks earlier, had put out an international call for pilots. Pilots arrived from the Soviet Union, India,

Yugoslavia, and even a few from the United States, in addition to available Egyptian pilots. The canal continued to operate smoothly, demonstrating Egypt's ability to run the canal without foreign assistance.[17]

On September 23, the British and French governments asked for a meeting of the UN Security Council to condemn Egypt's actions in the canal. The next day the Egyptians lodged a countercomplaint against those powers for taking actions "which constitute a danger to international peace and security."

The CIA continued its active role in diplomacy with Egypt. Meeting again with the Egyptian ambassador in Washington at the end of September, Kim Roosevelt said he now thought "war is a remote possibility, except if there are new incidents to threaten foreigners in Egypt or Jordan or if the oil pipelines in Syria are cut off, for example." Roosevelt was still worried about the Israeli dimension. He reiterated: "America had used pressure and threats with Israel to warn them against a war which the United States does not want. Roosevelt added that the American policy of economic pressure against Egypt was a firm one."[18]

The next week the Egyptian ambassador met with a senior State Department diplomat, Loy Henderson, freshly returned from the London Suez Canal users conference. Agreeing on their desire to reach an amicable solution to the conflict, Henderson said he didn't think war would break out, but he couldn't rule out the possibility.

Ambassador Hussein presented an Egyptian position that had some flexibility. Specifically, he emphasized "Egypt's desire to create a negotiating process . . . with the goal of reaching a solution which guarantees Egypt's rights and sovereignty while guaranteeing also free passage in the canal, instead of creating a situation predicated on attacks and aggression." Hussein stressed the role the United States could play, and Henderson told him he hoped "with all his heart" that the two sides could come to an agreement.[19]

Kim Roosevelt then made his way out to Cairo. In early October he met with two of Abdel Nasser's chief aides. They asked for U.S. help, not only to ward off a British attack but also—they said—to keep Egypt from becoming too dependent on the Soviet Union. Economic pressures were already driving Egypt to undue dependence on trade with the Soviet bloc. If the United States could not block British moves at the UN to set up a war, Abdel Nasser's aides hoped that Washington at least would share CIA estimates of British intentions, since surely the Americans would know what the British were up to. There is no evidence that the CIA followed up on this request, although

Roosevelt himself probably shared the same assessment he had offered back in Washington to Ambassador Hussein, which was that the chance of war now seemed remote.[20]

THE UN DIPLOMACY OF OCTOBER: MANEUVERS
TO BLOCK THE BRITISH AND FRENCH

In the first two weeks of October, the UN Security Council began its debate on the Suez crisis. Egyptian foreign minister Mahmoud Fawzi represented his country. Fawzi met UN secretary-general Dag Hammarskjöld, who told him he thought there was still a danger that Israeli extremists might push for war. Hammarskjöld added that while Egypt had gained some at the beginning of the crisis, it had lost what it had gained because others had seized the initiative. He also assured the Egyptian that the British foreign secretary, Selwyn Lloyd, really was truly interested in reaching a solution "despite the appearance to the contrary."

Soviet policy also began to get a little bit bolder. Soviet foreign minister Dmitri Shepilov was looking for a way to negotiate a solution without relying on the Security Council. He asked Fawzi about reviving the Soviet suggestion of a "Committee of Nine" to negotiate a settlement independent of the Security Council. Such a committee would presumably be more favorably disposed toward Egypt. Fawzi said Egypt had already proposed a committee of nine countries. Shepilov asked if Egypt had chosen the nine, and Fawzi replied that it was under study.[21]

On the matter of an American role, Shepilov suggested that while the Americans may have differed with the British and French over the means and methods of reaching an agreement, they agreed completely with them that there should be international administration of the canal. Shepilov, therefore, counseled that Egypt's goal at this point should be to create the facade of Western participation in canal administration while maintaining actual Egyptian control.

In response, Fawzi suggested Egypt might be able to live with some sort of international organization with advisory powers. The next day, Abdel Nasser wrote Fawzi, advising him of a meeting he had with the Soviet ambassador to Cairo. Abdel Nasser's summary of the Soviet position harmonized with what Fawzi had heard from Shepilov.

The Soviets were open to an "agreement accepted by both sides to protect

Egyptian sovereignty and the interests of the canal users." They recommended that Egypt suggest a committee of six countries to work on this, made up of "the four Great Powers, Egypt and India." This committee "would prepare for an international conference in which would participate the signatories to the 1888 convention, the Arab states, and the nations which use the canal. Russia will support the suggestion if Egypt wants, and would be willing to propose it herself."

Egypt should also be ready to volunteer its acceptance of an international advisory committee. This suggestion may strengthen Egypt's position and that of the countries which support it, by making clear Egypt's dedication to international cooperation in the interests of free transit. Abdel Nasser instructed Fawzi that the Western powers would probably reject a "Committee of Six," and therefore he suggested Fawzi contemplate a committee of ten or twelve. "With regard to announcing our position on the advisory committee, I have no objection to its announcement and leave you freedom of action."[22]

The next day Fawzi met with Secretary Dulles. Dulles explained he felt compelled to accept the British resolution in the Security Council to prevent mayhem from breaking out. He complained to Fawzi that he was unable to "steer" the British and French in Suez as he could in the earlier Formosa and Korean crises.

Fawzi responded that the issue at hand was not transit or tolls but rather administration. Egypt would accept neither an international administration in which Egypt participated nor an Egyptian administration with international participation. It would have to be wholly Egyptian. Fawzi did not yet float the emerging Soviet and Egyptian compromise ideas.

Apparently trying to assure the Egyptians of his good intentions, Dulles mentioned the Aswan High Dam to Fawzi at the end of the meeting. Dulles explained the project

> would add to the economic burden of Egypt, and it would have engendered hatred for America when the Egyptian people felt deprived because of it. For that reason he had no objection to the Soviets building it. But he added that Egypt could in his opinion fund the High Dam with Suez Canal revenues because this was a sounder approach and will prevent any country which advances the necessary money for the plan from incurring Egyptians' hatred.[23]

Then Fawzi discussed strategy with Shepilov. They came to agreement on an unspecified "negotiating committee of eight or nine states," believing that designating members in advance would lead to its rejection. The Egyptian mission's gloss was that "America differs greatly with Britain and France in the particulars of a solution to the problem. This became apparent in Dulles' meeting with Dr. Fawzi. In addition, America hopes the canal improvement works will be assigned to American companies, and this makes the American position more inclined toward a solution of the problem along the lines of negotiations per our suggestion."[24]

The Saudis continued to play a role as intermediaries, perhaps encouraged by the fact that Abdel Nasser visited Saudi Arabia for several days in late September.[25] The king reported to Abdel Nasser the results of discussions with Nehru. The letter claimed the Saudis asserted their "full support for Egypt's position, and explained to [Nehru] Egypt's preparedness to be reasonable, on the basis of preserving its rights and sovereignty."

Nehru, according to the Saudis, had replied that India supported "the right of Egypt to nationalize [the canal company], together with preserving the interests of other nations in [maintaining] free traffic and moderate tolls. That was something on which mutual agreement could be reached with a supervisory [international] authority. If differences arose, they could be adjudicated in an international court." The European psyche, Nehru reportedly said, was bothered by the shrinking European influence. "It is thus our duty to ease the withdrawal for them in peace and tranquility and mutual understanding, as did India."[26]

As the various countries made their arguments in the Security Council, Fawzi continued to work on strategy with Shepilov. But he also reached out to U.S. diplomats, like the new head of the State Department's Near East bureau, William Rountree. Fawzi complained that the United States wanted to "finish with the present regime in Egypt."

But Rountree believed the crisis was solvable. In the Egyptian account, he admitted "that the difficulty in solving it derives from Britain and France's fear for their prestige. Rountree has concluded that it is possible to arrive at a solution in terms of canal operation, and he expressed his hope that we appreciate America's role in preventing war."[27]

After all these exchanges, a growing consensus seemed to be emerging in New York. The diplomacy was moving toward acceptance of Egyptian administration of the canal with some sort of international committee, sometimes called advisory and sometimes called supervisory, to represent the users and allow the British and French to save face.

Hammarskjöld told Fawzi privately that the British foreign secretary,

Selwyn Lloyd, finally seemed interested in compromise. To Hammarskjöld it was the French foreign minister, Christian Pineau, who seemed bent on obstruction. He advised Fawzi to try to win over Pineau without disclosing the accommodation to Lloyd.

That afternoon after meeting with Hammarskjöld, still on October 12, Fawzi met Secretary Dulles. Dulles told Fawzi that "France was trying to sabotage the agreement and enter into a battle over the Suez Canal, and was looking for allies to join in the invasion [word unclear in Arabic original] and that it [France] is working foolishly in that direction. And Britain would not share in [an invasion] because it would bear the burden itself." Fawzi was encouraged. He believed Dulles sincerely wanted to resolve the crisis.[28]

Later that same day, Fawzi met with World Bank president Eugene Black at the latter's request. Black had more good news. He held out the prospect of international help on the Aswan High Dam and improvements to the Suez Canal if the present crisis were resolved amicably.[29] In so doing, Black seemed to be reinforcing the message Secretary Dulles delivered a week prior, that Egypt stood to gain far more from cooperation rather than confrontation with the West.

When Fawzi, Pineau, and Lloyd met in Hammarskjöld's office on the morning of October 12, Fawzi stressed his willingness to keep negotiating. He told the parties he was not in New York for any fixed period of time. He said he would be available "in any place and at any time" to meet to discuss the Suez Canal issue.

Throughout the meeting that morning and a subsequent meeting in the afternoon, Pineau maintained his hard line. He pushed Fawzi to negotiate based on the principles of the first London conference, the position of full international control.

Fawzi repeatedly refused. Egypt would not negotiate on Western terms just as the West would not negotiate on Egyptian terms. He suggested finding new terms for negotiations that represented a compromise. Fawzi and Hammarskjöld were even more convinced that the British minister, Lloyd, was far more interested in negotiating than was the French minister, Pineau.[30]

The next day, October 13, Hammarskjöld wrote up the emerging compromise consensus. He gave Fawzi a list of principles to govern a future agreement, based on the discussions the three foreign ministers had had thus far. The principles seemed to meet Fawzi's objectives.

They were:

1. There should be free and open transit through the canal without discrimination, overt or covert; this covers both political and technical aspects.

2. The sovereignty of Egypt should be respected.

3. The operation of the canal should be insulated from the politics of any country.

4. The manner of fixing tolls and charges should be decided by agreement between Egypt and the users.

5. A fair proportion of the dues should be allotted to development.

6. In case of disputes, unresolved affairs between the Suez Canal Company and the Egyptian government should be settled by arbitration with suitable terms of reference and suitable provisions for the payment of sums found to be due.[31]

In the course of their private conversation, Hammarskjöld told Fawzi that he and Lloyd had been trying since the previous evening to prod Secretary Dulles to intervene to help soften Pineau's position.

Later on October 13, Hammarskjöld proposed his list of principles to the full membership of the UN Security Council. Lloyd and Pineau proposed to amend those principles by adding the resolutions agreed to by the eighteen nations in London. The Soviet Union promptly exercised its veto over that addition, thus leaving Hammarskjöld's principles intact.

Understanding that the principles formed only the basis for the next round of negotiations, and were not themselves a final agreement, Hammarskjöld proposed reconvening negotiations in Geneva to prepare such an agreement. This Geneva conference would be held in two weeks, at the end of October. Hammarskjöld's proposal was accepted.

As he left New York, Fawzi could well feel a sense of satisfaction for himself and for his country.

PART TWO

MOSCOW

CAROL R. SAIVETZ

Nasser's nationalization of the Suez Canal presented Nikita Khrushchev and his colleagues in the Communist Party of the Soviet Union's (CPSU's) Politburo with both opportunities and dilemmas. On the one hand, backing Nasser's action would help solidify the USSR's ties to Egypt and prove the Soviet Union would support the nonaligned states. On the other hand, by supporting Egypt, the Kremlin ran the risk of directly confronting Britain and France. This dilemma was being faced amid the continuing split in the ruling Politburo, mentioned in Part One, that had been caused by Khrushchev's public break with Stalin and Khrushchev's announced agenda for reform.

Khrushchev's leadership was being watched by opponents like the just-relieved former foreign minister, Molotov, pushed out of that job in June 1956, who was down but not out. There was also plenty of turmoil in the governments of the Soviet satellite states in eastern Europe. Major riots in the Polish city of Poznan had been put down in June with substantial loss of life.

THE INITIAL SOVIET RESPONSE TO NASSER'S NATIONALIZATION OF THE CANAL COMPANY

Moscow was blindsided by the nationalization. According to Nasser confidant Muhammad Haykal, Foreign Minister Shepilov later chided the Egyptian ambassador to Moscow, saying, "At least you, our friends, should have consulted us."[1]

Caught by surprise, Moscow waited a full twenty-four hours before responding. According to Sergei Khrushchev, his father proceeded carefully because, his father said, "we didn't have a common border [with Egypt] and it was necessary to understand what the true position of the Egyptian government [was]. It was possible that they were only playing, trying to extract from the West a larger sum [of money]."[2]

The day after the announcement, the Egyptian ambassador to Moscow met with Shepilov. Egypt was looking for direct and overt Soviet support. Soviet indecision was evident: Shepilov expressed understanding that Egypt had taken steps to "secure" its "political freedom," but he urged Egypt to develop its economic base. While noting that the original 1888 document affirmed the canal as an integral part of Egypt, Shepilov underscored that the USSR would also work to prevent war resulting from the nationalization of the canal.[3]

The USSR—as directed by the Foreign Ministry—opted to conduct a well-orchestrated press campaign in support of the Egyptian action.[4] At the end of July, Khrushchev, in what should be seen as the first official pronouncement on the developing crisis, said the Soviet Union "considers that there are no grounds for showing nervousness and alarm. . . . We are convinced that the situation in the Suez Canal Zone will not become tense unless it is artificially aggravated from outside."[5]

The Kremlin simultaneously used the crisis to carve out a major role in any future deliberations. On July 30, "sources" revealed to the *Washington Post* that the Soviet Union was willing to discuss an "international solution" that would permit unrestricted passage for ships but allow Egypt sovereignty over the canal. The same source confirmed that despite USSR sympathy for the Egyptian position, Moscow was alarmed by the West's strong reaction to the nationalization and worried that events in the region could lead to a "shooting war."[6]

This Soviet balancing act included decisions about whether or not to participate in the London conference proposed by Britain, France, and the United States. Nasser had asked the Soviet government to follow Egypt's lead and refuse to attend the conference, and at first Khrushchev was inclined to go along with Nasser and refuse.

Then, as the daily news added to concerns about a possible war initiated either by the British or by rash Egyptian actions, Khrushchev decided the Soviets should help mediate the crisis. The Soviet government had received intelligence reports of possible British and French planning for a war.

It was clear that some of his rivals on the Politburo thought the Soviet government, under Khrushchev, might already have gotten too close to the

Egyptian hothead. A few days later, Georgi Malenkov, a deposed rival who was still a member of the ruling Politburo, commented, "We should never be the prisoners of Nasser's political enthusiasms."[7]

On August 7, U.S. ambassador to Moscow Charles "Chip" Bohlen met with Soviet premier Nikolai Bulganin. Following instructions, he urged the USSR to participate in the planned conference, ostensibly because the United States was having trouble restraining its allies.[8] Bulganin indicated his government's indecision. The premier then acknowledged "that there seemed to be between the United States and the Soviet Union a common position in that both felt this matter must be settled by peaceful means." Bohlen made it clear that Soviet refusal to attend the conference could make a peaceful solution less likely.[9]

Finally, on August 9, 1956, the Soviet Union circulated to embassies in Moscow a long letter in which it accepted the invitation to participate in the London conference while denying its authority. The full statement was published in *Pravda* the next day.

> The government of the Soviet Union has taken note of the statement by the Egyptian government [guaranteeing freedom of navigation] and considers that there is no reason for any uneasiness in this respect, the more so since Egypt, through whose territory the Suez Canal passes, is interested in and can ensure normal navigation through the canal no less than any private joint stock company. . . .
>
> The Soviet government regards as utterly inadmissible the measures now being turned out by the British and French governments and considers them a challenge to peace. . . .
>
> Attention should be drawn to the fact that the list of the countries invited to the Conference reveals a biased approach designed to ensure that most of its members would support the proposals drafted in advance by the United Kingdom and France. . . .
>
> In view of the foregoing, the Soviet Government considers that the above-mentioned Conference cannot in any way be regarded, either in its composition or in character and purposes, as an international meeting authorized to take any decisions whatever on the Suez Canal.

Therefore, "the Soviet Government's participation in the Conference in no way commits the Soviet Union to any restrictions or obligations . . . which may damage Egypt's sovereign rights and dignity."[10]

THE LONDON CONFERENCE

Shepilov cut a different figure from other Soviet officials. While never abandoning Soviet objectives, he at times sounded conciliatory and flexible. With the Soviet Politburo internally divided about how tough a line to take, Shepilov had some authority to seek a solution.

Shepilov's public position was "that the Egyptian Government, in nationalizing the Suez Canal Company, was acting within the standards of international law." The American proposal insisting on full international control, taking the canal away from Egypt, went too far. It took into account "neither the real situation nor the legitimate national demands of Egypt." Nasser's guarantees of unrestricted passage should be trusted.[11]

Privately, Dulles met with Shepilov. He was impressed by how "frank and businesslike" the Soviet minister was, presenting "the best statement I have ever received from any Soviet Foreign Minister." Shepilov floated a compromise possibility centered on "the principle of Egyptian operation [of the canal] with participation of other countries for the purpose of guaranteeing the free and efficient functioning of the Canal."[12]

But at the conference Dulles held to the tougher line where he, the British, and French had begun. Rather than allowing for some mix of Egyptian control with international participation, they pushed to take the canal out of Egyptian control and create a new structure for international ownership and operation of the canal. Shepilov did not, however, publicly propose his joint participation compromise.[13]

Instead, when India's delegate, R. K. Krishna Menon, proposed an even weaker version of joint participation, consigning users to a merely advisory consultative body, Moscow quickly supported the Indian initiative. In a long speech, Shepilov took a hard line against the Western position, labeling the Dulles plan a new form of colonialism. Dulles reported to Eisenhower that Shepilov's position was especially "disappointing" because this stance "was I think deliberately calculated to make it difficult for Nasser now to accept our program unless it is heavily disguised."[14]

The tougher "international control" position won a large majority support at the London conference, a vote of eighteen to four among the participants. Around this point, opinion hardened among the Politburo.

Khrushchev was angry that the West was not going along with the "consultative" alternative for international participation in management of the canal. He was still worried about the danger of war. As the London conference was ending, he chose a reception at the Romanian embassy in Moscow to scold and warn the British ambassador. There are several versions of what he said. One version is: "Even if you have interests, do you need to mobilize armies and threaten war to protect them? Don't forget that if a war starts because of what you are doing, all our sympathies will be with Egypt. A war of Egypt against Britain would be a sacred war, and if my son came to me, and asked me if he ought to volunteer to fight against Britain, I would tell him he most certainly should do so." The gist of this account is corroborated by a page one *Washington Post* dispatch dated August 24 and by the *New York Times*. According to the *Times* report, Khrushchev said: "The defense of Egypt in case of a Western attack would be justified." This account added that Khrushchev said that "volunteers" would come to the defense of the Arab states.[15]

Shepilov was ordered to give a final public statement that "hit these imperialists on the snout!"[16] Shepilov remembered:

When the London Conference of Canal Users was coming to an end, I suddenly received a coded telegram signed by Khrushchev and Bulganin. It said: "At one of the last press conferences make things hot for the imperialists, spike their guns. . . ."

When it was all over, victory was ours. We found ourselves in agreement with India, Indonesia and Ceylon, and the Dulles proposals were not accepted. So I thought: "Why should I aggravate relations at a final press conference?" and I played things calmly. . . .

Well, after the London Conference, he [Khrushchev] asks me to come and he says: "Look here, why didn't you carry out my and Nikolai's orders? Why didn't you hit the imperialists in the mug?"

I say to him: "Nikita Sergeevich, there was no need. The Conference was a success, we won, the Egyptians retained the canal. . . . So what was the point of aggravating relations? We have gained one thing, so why should we spoil the other? Why should we spoil relations with other countries, with the United States, for example? It wasn't necessary."

He says: "Yes, indeed you are a dangerous man, you are very dangerous. Do you want to conduct foreign policy yourself?"

I say: "I don't want to conduct it myself. I know perfectly well who conducts the foreign policy here. Please understand me correctly, there was no need. Under the circumstances, I assure you, there was no need for any mug-hitting."

"No, no, no! You are a dangerous man. We appreciate your good work at the Conference, but we have also noticed that you didn't follow our instructions."[17]

MOSCOW RETURNS TO DIPLOMACY

The Soviet propaganda effort completely supported the Egyptian rejection of the London proposal. *Pravda* quoted Nasser's description of the Suez Canal Company as a "vestige of imperialism" and a "state within a state," while an article in *International Affairs* called the Menzies plan an attempt to "Panamize" the Suez Canal. The same article went on to justify Soviet support for Egypt in the event of war. "It is clear that in the event of a colonialist attack upon Egypt, the war of the Egyptian people against the foreign enslavers would be a just war of liberation. Therefore, Egypt would have the warm sympathy and active support of the whole of progressive mankind."[18]

That was the public line. Privately the Soviet leaders worried about war, though their arms kept flowing into Egypt.[19] On August 31 the Politburo approved a policy approach that called on Egypt to make a counteroffer to the London move. The counteroffer should reassure the international community about Egyptian administration of the canal. It was a compromise approach that would place control under an independent agency and guarantee rights of passage to all (presumably including Israeli ships) without discrimination. Egypt should be open to the use of foreign specialists in operating the canal and invite creation of an international consultative entity to advise and help. Egypt should call an international conference of its own to draft a new canal treaty that would replace the 1888 convention and protect user rights.[20]

Nasser adopted his own version of these ideas and made the call for a new treaty conference right after the disappointed Menzies delegation left Cairo. The United States also made a fresh diplomatic move.

Dulles advanced the idea for what came to be called the Suez Canal Users Association (SCUA), which still did not cede as much control to Egypt as the other compromise plans did. Most of the participants of the first London conference accepted invitations to a second meeting, also in London, to discuss the new proposal.

Prior to the second London conference, Soviet premier Nikolai Bulganin sent warning letters dated September 11 to both Anthony Eden and French prime minister Guy Mollet. To Eden, he wrote, "It is not Egypt who concentrates forces and threatens military action against anyone. . . . How in such a situation and guided by the noble principles of the United Nations, can one help standing on Egypt's side?" And, in his letter to Mollet, Bulganin warned "of severe consequences."[21]

The Soviet government denounced the new American alternative for a users' association that would control the canal. Moscow refused to attend the second London conference. The USSR statement called the American proposal a "provocation" designed to create "artificial" incidents that could be used as a pretext for the use of force against Egypt.

The Soviet statement publicized threats against France and England. "There can hardly be any doubt that a military attack on Egypt and military actions in the region would lead to immense destruction on the Suez Canal and also in the oilfields. . . . The USSR as a great power cannot stand aloof from the Suez question . . . because any violation of peace in the region of the Near and Middle East cannot but affect the interests and the security of the Soviet state."[22]

By the end of September, the Soviet government was receiving mixed assessments about the danger of war. Its diplomats were doubtful about it. They thought Eden's government and the British public were now very divided about whether to go to war. A pair of former British officials, who had fled to the Soviet Union after being discovered to be Soviet spies, also advised their Moscow friends that the British government did not have the will to fight—a view confirmed to Soviet leaders by a British Labour Party leader who visited Moscow.

But the Soviet intelligence services offered a more ominous picture of British and French military preparations in the eastern Mediterranean. Also, Soviet diplomats in Paris observed that the French government seemed remarkably unified behind a tough determination to go after Nasser. The KGB also believed there might be a Western plot to assassinate Nasser. It flew officers to Cairo to help Nasser's security detail.[23]

At this point, in late September and early October, the diplomatic focus shifted to the United Nations. The British and French had now insisted on taking the Suez issue to the Security Council, a possible prelude to war.

THE SECURITY COUNCIL DEBATES

On September 23, Great Britain and France decided to bring the Suez Canal question to the UN Security Council. In the lead-up to the Security Council meetings, there were rounds of consultations in both Cairo and Moscow, as well as between the Soviet and Egyptian delegates to the UN.[24]

Formal deliberations began on October 5. During the discussions, Shepilov stuck to the line opposing international control of the canal.[25]

On October 7, the Soviet intelligence service (KGB) chief in Cairo reported to Moscow that Nasser wanted to know whether "in the event of an attack on Egypt, the Egyptian government could count on the Soviets dispatching volunteers and submarines." Khrushchev put off a firm answer to Nasser's plea. He still preferred to rely on diplomacy.[26]

Consistent with the earlier Politburo guidance from August 31 and Nasser's own proposal, Shepilov, hoping to protect Egypt, proposed the creation of a committee to be composed of Egypt, Britain, India, France, the United States, and the USSR to draft a new convention governing the canal. The Soviet Union seemed willing to counsel Egypt to accept a negotiating body in which there would be "balanced representation" as long as Egyptian sovereignty over the canal was assured.[27]

As the drama played out in the Security Council, it was clear that Shepilov operated with the Soviets' somewhat conflicting goals in mind. Publicly, he condemned all the imperialists—including the United States. "You have urged us to appeal to the UN. We have done so, but as you see it is powerless. It can do nothing. Other steps must be taken. Egypt is guilty. Crucify it."[28]

Privately, Shepilov counseled that the West needed an honorable means of retreat; however, the Americans were not to be given any role.[29] Seek some accommodation and allow for international involvement with the canal. But, with Soviet assistance, keep the Americans out of the region.

Toward the middle of October, it seemed that the UN Security Council would resolve the ongoing conflict. Both sides agreed to six principles to govern operation of the canal: free transit without discrimination; agreement between Egypt and the users on tolls and charges; the allocation of a fair amount of dues for development; arbitration to settle disputes; respect for Egypt's sovereignty; and insulation of the canal from politics.

Moreover, Egypt also effectively accepted an association of canal users that would operate under these principles. Egypt seemed to be so flexible in the diplomacy that Shepilov cabled home his concern that Cairo, fearing a military attack, was making too many concessions.[30]

The first part of the resolution, the six principles, was adopted by the Security Council. At the last minute, the French offered an amendment adding that Egypt would still have to accept the original London proposal for international control. That amendment was vetoed by the Soviet Union.

By its exercise of the veto on October 13, the USSR upheld both its support for Egypt and its anti-imperialism. The veto also possessed tremendous political value. One of the Soviet Union's top diplomats in a later generation saw the veto as another reminder that the USSR had a role to play in the resolution of the crisis.[31]

Shepilov was satisfied with the results of the diplomacy in New York.[32]

PARIS

CHARLES G. COGAN

The French press was nearly unanimous in reacting immoderately to the news from Egypt: "overall, the Press spoke of Nasser in hostile terms; it was profoundly shocked by the laugh which accompanied [Nasser's] announcement of the nationalization of the Canal."[1]

As for Christian Pineau, the foreign minister, he was shocked in another way. What on earth did relations with Britain and France have to do with the American decision about the Aswan Dam?

> If the unexpected refusal of Foster Dulles to help Egypt construct the Aswan Dam had both surprised and disturbed us, we did not imagine there would be a reaction of the "Rais" [Nasser] against the Canal. A priori there was no relation between the two problems. This lack of foresight was no doubt an error. But we could not see any reason why Egypt should attack Franco-British interests to avenge itself against an affront inflicted by the United States.[2]

French prime minister Guy Mollet had already made up his mind about Nasser. "The events of the last few days have brutally confirmed [my position]."

What else did Colonel Nasser declare in his sensational speech? "We will pursue our efforts to unify the Arab World from the Atlantic Ocean to the Persian Gulf." This is the striking proof, coming at a dramatic moment, of the theses developed in his brochure, *The Philosophy of the Revolution*.[3]

Gamal Abdel Nasser had nationalized a private company operating in Egypt whose headquarters was in Paris and whose largest shareholder was the British government. The nationalization was due to take place anyway in 1968. In nationalizing the canal company now, Nasser promised to indemnify the shareholders according to the price of the stock at the Bourse of Paris the previous day (July 25, 1956). However, Nasser accompanied the act of nationalization by the simultaneous takeover of the Suez Canal Company's offices in Egypt by Egyptian forces.

Strictly speaking, the only international aspect of the Suez Canal was that the right of passage through the canal for all countries was guaranteed by the world's major interested powers in 1888.[4] This convention had already been violated by Egypt, well before Nasser's nationalization speech, so there was no new violation per se. In September 1954 Israel had tested its right to use the canal. The Egyptians had confiscated the ship and imprisoned its crew for three months. (Technically speaking, Great Britain had also violated the 1888 convention in World Wars I and II when it closed the canal to various signatory powers.)

Christian Pineau, a leading advocate of the "free passage" principle, emphasized that "there had to exist, we thought, sufficient means of pressure to compel Nasser not to go back on his nationalization of the Canal but on his will to control international navigation."[5]

As one expert has pointed out, "The fact that the character of the Suez Canal Company was French, with its principal headquarters in Paris, while the British Government was the principal shareholder, made for an Anglo-French alignment."[6] While Britain and France's interests were interlocked, and therefore they were compelled to act together, there were a number of anomalies and tensions in the background of this situation.

The canal had been built on the initiative of a Frenchman, Ferdinand de Lesseps, and in 1854 the French project was created under the name of the Compagnie universelle du canal de Suez. After the canal was opened in 1869, the British eventually edged the French out of Egypt, but then came the Entente Cordiale at the beginning of the twentieth century, and Britain and France became allies after a thousand-year rivalry. However, the ancient fault lines were still there, hardly under the surface.

PREPARING FOR WAR AND A DIPLOMATIC
ULTIMATUM: THE LONDON CONFERENCE

The British and French reacted to Nasser's announcement with a sense of emergency. At 11 p.m. on July 26, following Nasser's speech earlier that day, Jean Chauvel, the French ambassador in London, was summoned to the prime minister's house at 10 Downing Street along with a representative of the U.S. embassy, to join a meeting with the British leadership.[7]

Although for the company it was a legal problem, for the governments it was a political one. Eden said he regarded the affair as a test of wills that Nasser could not be permitted to win. It was imperative, Eden stated, that the foreign ministers of the United States, Britain, and France meet without delay. The problem was that Dulles was on a tour of Latin America.[8]

On July 29, Pineau arrived in London, and that evening took part in a three-way meeting with British foreign minister Selwyn Lloyd and Robert Murphy, whom Washington had sent to London instead of Dulles. Pineau presented the essence of France's concerns. To him the Suez crisis was a North African crisis:

> If the action of Egypt remains without a response, it would be useless to continue the struggle in Algeria. Also, the question is not juridical but above all political. I recalled the warnings that Hitler had provided to the democracies and of which none of our three countries had taken into account. This lesson should inspire our action.[9]

The discussion at the three-way British-American-French July 29 meeting, as reported back to Paris by Pineau, focused on two principal points:

1. Military preparations. Selwyn Lloyd made the point that one of the objects of our meeting was to examine together the different dispositions of a military nature which should be taken as a last resort. Obviously, it is not a question at this point of military threats, but given the delays [required], particularly the logistics, it was necessary as of now to draw up plans in common. In any case it is appropriate that Nasser be aware that a military option is not excluded. Without that, no economic pressure will have an effect on him.

2. The proposition for an international conference. M. Selwyn Lloyd and myself suggested that it might be appropriate to hold an inter-

national conference of the principal countries using the Canal. . . .
M. Murphy stated that since the question had not been studied in
Washington, he could not take a position. Nevertheless, he thought
the American Government in principle would be in favor of such a
conference.[10]

The American government did indeed favor the conference, and ministers
would soon meet to go over the planning for it.

In the meantime, the pent-up French military had not even waited for the
go-ahead from their government before getting together with their British
counterparts. On July 30, a joint British-French planning group set to work.
On July 31, the French side presented a list of units the French were prepared
to dedicate to a joint operation.[11] Yet as one French scholar of the crisis noted:

> If the British were astonished by the firmness of the French and the sac-
> rifices they were prepared to make (two divisions taken from the French
> forces in Algeria), the overall picture was not very favorable. Neither
> France nor Great Britain, integrated into the NATO system [that] by
> principle was opposed to autonomous and independent forces, had an
> integral and substantial intervention force capable of operating several
> thousand kilometers from its bases.[12]

This sobering estimate was borne out by a contingency plan submitted to
the French government by General Paul Ely, chief of staff of the French Armed
Forces, at the end of July. As Ely recounted in his memoir:

> From the start of the crisis, the General Staff of the Armed Forces had
> undertaken detailed studies, intended for the Government, of the pos-
> sibility of an intervention in Egypt. These studies examined . . . the vari-
> ous hypotheses of possible interventions:
>
> • France alone
>
> • France and Israel
>
> • France and Great Britain
>
> • France, Great Britain, and Israel
>
> • France, Great Britain, and the United States[13]

The first option was ruled out because of Egyptian air strength, on the one hand, and France's limited means on the other: no air base near Egypt and no aircraft carrier for jets. The second, third, and fourth options involved delays varying from a month to a month and a half. The fifth option was considered unlikely.[14]

Given its recent secret work with the Israelis, the French Defense Ministry immediately began to cut the Israelis in on their thinking. On July 27 in Paris, Defense Minister Bourgès-Maunoury met with Shimon Peres, the director-general of the Israeli Defense Ministry, at the French minister's request. According to the minister's cabinet director, Abel Thomas:

> In the name of the confidence that he had in us, we suggested that his country organize [a military response] but not unleash a premature operation. We promised that we would get together with him at the right moment to go over with him in what measure Israel could possibly lend us assistance, if that appeared necessary (whether in the matter of bases, or logistical support, or diversion operations).[15]

Peres recalled: "How long, [Bourgès-Maunoury] asked, would it take the IDF [Israeli Defense Forces] to fight its way across the Sinai and reach the Canal?"

"Two weeks," Peres replied.

"Bourgès-Maunoury then followed up with another question. . . . Would Israel be prepared to take part in a tripartite military operation in which Israel's specific role would be to cross the Sinai?"

Peres replied "without hesitation" that "under certain circumstances I assume that we would be so prepared."

Bourgès-Maunoury then briefed Peres on the embryonic British-French planning to land troops in Egypt. Peres noted that Israeli-French cooperation of this sort would have to be decided at the highest level. They agreed to schedule a ministerial meeting in Paris as soon as possible.[16]

Secretary of State Dulles arrived in London on the morning of August 1. Dulles called on Pineau.

> M. Dulles: It is very important that this operation not end in a gain for [Nasser]. The United States Government does not believe that military action would be justified at the present moment. . . .
>
> Consequently, a real effort should be attempted to have Nasser re-

nounce the initiative he has taken and agree to place the Canal under international management. It is probable that this effort would achieve its objective if it is supported by an important group of nations using the Canal. If on the other hand, after this effort has been made, Nasser rejects the conditions presented to him, the basis would exist for a strong action which would be supported by many countries in the world and by the United States. As regards Washington, this support would be moral. M. Dulles emphasized the difficulties involved as to the participation of American troops in a military action.

M. Pineau [said that] from the French point of view, the important thing is that Nasser, supported by the USSR, has established considerable influence in the Arab World. This influence is such in North Africa that, according to very reliable information, we have only several weeks left to save North Africa. Obviously, the loss of North Africa would be followed by that of Black Africa, and thus the European role and influence in Africa would disappear.

This is why it is absolutely essential for us to oppose such developments. Our conviction on this point is so strong that even if the Americans refused us their moral support and the English their concrete cooperation, we would be obliged to act militarily. [However,] there would be all the more reason that we would not hesitate to launch such an action if the British were with us.

We agree, however, that we should first try other means . . . [provided] the solution proposed to us is a good one. . . . It is not enough, from our point of view, to get Nasser to renounce the nationalization of the Canal. On the contrary, we should make it appear that the position we are taking is not solely, nor even especially, aimed at assuring the protection of French private interests. . . . We propose to substitute for the former company an international management company. . . . We must agree on a new statute for the Canal. . . . For us the criterion . . . is the possibility of a quick outcome. It is necessary to propose a solution to Nasser as soon as possible. If he accepts it, we will have satisfaction. If he does not, we will intervene with the British. If the Americans do not join this intervention, we would expect of them that they would take a position such that it would convince the Russians not to intervene.

M. Dulles does not see that there are divergences between what M. Pineau just said and what he himself thinks of the situation.[17]

Pineau believed that "despite his military prestige, Eisenhower is a weak man. Dulles is his backbone."[18]

The next day, August 2, the three foreign ministers, Dulles, Pineau, and Selwyn Lloyd, agreed on a common approach. Pineau reported that Dulles had gone along with the French and British concept for demanding "international management of the Canal, whereas until now the American delegation envisaged only international monitoring [*contrôle*]."[19]

If Nasser rejected the conference plan, the French understood that the Americans would not act jointly with England and France but would accept Anglo-French action.[20] The French thought of this as American "moral support," enough to keep the Russians at bay.

As the London conference was being prepared, the French were pressing forward with military preparations. As noted earlier, a preliminary estimate drawn up under the aegis of the chief of staff of the French Armed Forces on July 29 ruled out the possibility of a French attack alone on Egypt.[21] The French had neither bases near Egypt nor aircraft carriers that could take jet planes. Thus the French were in no position by themselves to take out the potentially powerful Egyptian Air Force.

So the French gravitated toward the British for military support, as the British were the most aggrieved party in Nasser's Suez seizure: the British government was the majority shareholder in the Suez Canal Company. The French had only private shareholders (albeit 80,000 of them). The Canal Zone had been under the control of the British until the last of their soldiers evacuated it in June 1956. And the British by the terms of the Anglo-Egyptian accord of October 19, 1954, were entitled to reoccupy the Canal Base in certain circumstances; Article 4 of this accord specified that in the event of an attack by a foreign power on any of the signatories of the Arab League defense pact of 1950, or on Turkey, Egypt would allow Great Britain to use the Canal Base.[22]

As noted, an informal working group of British and French officers was set up in London as early as July 30.[23] By the beginning of August, it was decided to institute a British-French joint committee that would be independent of NATO, with access tightly controlled under the code name Terrapin.[24]

At the start of the British-French joint planning activity, four possible scenarios were envisaged, under the overall objective of taking over the Canal Zone and placing it under international control:

- "A massive assault on Port Said, coupled with the capture by parachutists of the airfield at Abu Sueir, 80 kilometers to the south.

- A massive assault on Alexandria, the capture of the port area and the airfield there, and then progression toward the canal via the Cairo region.

- A limited operation against Port Said followed by a larger-scale operation against Alexandria.

- A limited operation against Alexandria and a massive assault on Port Said."[25]

Although the military planners initially preferred the second option, as it was the most likely to topple Nasser, the British government's preference was for the last option, as it was a limited one and concentrated the action on Port Said, which was focused on the principal aim of the operation, gaining control of the Suez Canal.[26] Initially, the Anglo-French joint committee began to elaborate an operational plan based on this last option, mainly focused on the canal.[27]

On August 8, the Anglo-French planners drew up a paper designating which of their military chiefs would be assigned to the operation.[28] The senior French officer was to be Admiral Pierre Barjot, who would represent all three French armed services at the level of the British Middle East Command (the "theater" level).

A key piece of British understatement in the August 8 memorandum set the hierarchy: Barjot was described in the following terms: "This Flag Officer stands on the level of the three British Commanders in Chief, Middle East."[29] In other words, Barjot would not be the overall commander of the operation; that would be a Britisher: General Sir Charles Keightley. The French also suggested in this paper that, at the next opportunity, the British commanders-in-chief at the theater level come to Paris to brief the French General Staff.[30] This was never done by the British, apparently out of concern for security.

The following day, August 9, General André Beaufre, who had been stationed in Algeria, arrived in London at the head of a delegation to participate in the work of what was now termed the French-British Planning Committee. The committee held its sessions in an underground headquarters on the banks of the Thames, an installation that had not been used since World War II.

The arguments in favor of overall British command were compelling. The British had a base from which to operate against Egypt (Cyprus). They would be contributing more forces than the French (50,000 as against 30,000). But

General Beaufre, who was to command the French theater land forces (Force A), commented that the integrated command system "seemed to me a difficult beginning, and right then I anticipated all the problems that this was going to create in case of disagreements . . . this decision was unquestionably an error."[31]

The first meeting of the allied task force commanders took place on August 10. By the time of this meeting the British government's preference for a limited operation against the canal rather than a massive attack on Alexandria had become known. However, the military planners attacked this idea. They argued instead for the "second" option, the massive assault on Alexandria, securing the port and airfield, and then a move on Cairo and the canal.

The planners contended that "the arrival of the Allied forces before Cairo would be sufficient to topple Nasser; the landing would be more rapid, the advance toward Cairo more assured; and the probability of progressively defeating the Egyptian Army greater.[32]

This option, a large-scale attack on Alexandria as advocated by the military chiefs, especially by Beaufre, quickly gained the day. It seemed to be the best means of getting rid of Nasser. For the French, particularly, this was their top priority in the venture. A new plan, called Musketeer, was finalized in London on August 15, with implementation to take place around September 15.[33]

The diplomatic part of the plan slowly rolled into place as well, as the London conference was held during the third week of August. The majority resolution of the conference stayed with the French objective of demanding an international management authority to operate, maintain, and develop the canal. The proposal would recognize Egyptian sovereignty and give Egypt a fair share of the profits, but also protect the canal from being used as an instrument of national policy.[34] It was adopted by eighteen of the twenty-two nations present but was promptly rejected by Nasser.

The Western powers sent a five-power delegation to Nasser, headed by Australian premier Robert Menzies, to present the findings of this "Group of 18." The Menzies mission (September 3–9) also failed.

As the London conference ultimatum was rejected, the Anglo-French military planning was expected to move into the foreground. Communicating this threat of force was part of the Anglo-French strategy. On August 19, a communiqué of the French Foreign Ministry announced that "Great Britain [has given] its agreement to the temporary stationing of French forces in Cyprus."[35] On August 26, the first elements of a French airborne operations base were set up at Tymbou in Cyprus, and on September 7 the first French troop contingent arrived on the island.[36]

But behind the scenes, the military planning was going through a major change. On August 26, at the first plenary session of the theater-level commanders-in-chief at London, the deputy commander—French admiral Barjot—made his presence felt. Although the meeting was held for the purpose of finalizing details for Operation Musketeer, Barjot proposed a new plan. Apparently on his own initiative, he wanted to go back to ideas for a direct assault on the Canal Zone, at Port Said.

Barjot's recommendation was not accepted immediately: "The British were aghast: after 12 days of studies and within two weeks of the start [of the operation] how could one go back on a decision taken by the two governments? The malaise was lifted when Gen. Beaufre suggested that [his] Port Said plan be studied as a variant of the original plan. Gen. Keightley even found a formula for it: the version Port Said would be kept 'in the pocket.'" Yet the "Port Said Plan" was the one eventually chosen, in the following month. It was to become known as Musketeer Revise (Mousquetaire Révisé).[37]

The French government began receiving indications about Moscow's possible reaction to Anglo-French military moves. On August 28, on the occasion of a dinner in honor of the visiting former French prime minister, Edgar Faure, the French ambassador in Moscow reported that Nikita Khrushchev had warned that any attempt to resolve the question of Suez by force would set the whole area of the Near and Middle East on fire. Khrushchev was not sure the conflict could be limited to that area. He said he was not intending to make a threat but he wanted to express clearly his thinking.[38]

On September 11, French ambassador Maurice Dejean confirmed what he described as "real concern" on the part of the Soviet leaders concerning Anglo-French military preparations. The previous evening, Anastas Mikoyan, flanked by two other Politburo members, Mikhail Suslov and Mikhail Pervukhin, made the following statement to Dejean:

> Do you really want to make war on Egypt? What other meaning could there be for your troop disembarkments in Cyprus, your concentration of naval forces in the Mediterranean, the recent speech of M. Pineau,[39] [and] the tone of your press? Does the France of 1789, the France of the Great Revolution, really want to make war on the Egyptian people? You believe there will be an easy victory. But you are going to launch yourself into an adventure. Haven't you [had] enough of war in Algeria? You have not the slightest reason for a recourse to force . . . all the Arab

World will stand against you. The war will be without end. You will wind up in a quagmire.[40]

On the same date, Ambassador Dejean gave his assessment of what the Soviets would actually do. "The generally acknowledged opinion—which I personally share—is that in case of military operations, the USSR will not intervene directly as long as the United States itself abstains."

What the Soviet Union would more likely do, Dejean estimated, was "furnish war materiel, facilitate the recruitment of foreign volunteers and even send specialists chosen from among its numerous non-native populations. Any Anglo-French decision to intervene militarily should take into account these formidable risks and weigh them against the grave consequences that a success of Nasser would have vis-à-vis the British and French positions in Africa and Asia."[41]

ANOTHER ROUND OF DIPLOMACY, REVISED PLANS FOR MILITARY ACTION

In early September the Americans responded to the failure of the London conference proposals for international management of the canal with another diplomatic suggestion, to discuss a possible association of canal users that could provide control over the canal. A second London conference was convened to discuss this SCUA plan, composed of representatives from the eighteen countries that had passed the majority resolution of the first conference.

At the outset of the Anglo-French military planning, an American general remarked to a group of French officers that "the problem for you is going to be British slowness. The British require for every move twice as much time as is needed to accomplish it."[42]

This legendary British *lenteur*, combined with London's hesitations at the diplomatic level, were causing the military planning to slip. This hesitancy, which stemmed largely from the continuing American disapproval of a military solution, became apparent to the French when Eden and Mollet came together for a summit discussion in London on September 10 and 11.[43]

Discussing the American proposal for a canal users association, Pineau had urged that "we must do something," Eden had expressed his doubts about the users' association idea, and Lloyd had said that the only weapon at their disposal was the withdrawal of the canal pilots; everything else was absurd.

Eden and Mollet reluctantly agreed to go along with this new diplomatic effort and another London conference to discuss it.[44] In a dramatic and unexpected display of solidarity, Mollet then proposed to join the two countries in a union with common citizenship and Queen Elizabeth II as head of state. This radical suggestion, which Mollet followed up several weeks later with an alternative proposal for France to join the Commonwealth, was designed, no doubt, to show the British ministers France's total commitment to resolving the Suez issue as part of a commitment to greatly enhanced European integration, anchored in an Anglo-British confederation. A stunned and skeptical Eden agreed to study the issue, which the British quietly rejected soon thereafter.[45]

It was also at this Anglo-French summit meeting on September 10 and 11 that an important military decision was taken (not reflected in the diplomatic record): the operation against Egypt was postponed to October 1. The new "Port Said" plan targeted directly on the canal (Musketeer Revise) was to be drawn up.[46]

The British would land at Port Said on the west side of the canal, and the French would land at Port Fouad on the eastern side. They would then proceed down both sides until they reached Ismailia and Suez City and occupied the canal entirely. Subsequently there would be a move on Cairo.[47]

It seemed the original Musketeer plan "appeared less and less adapted to the international situation: a massive attack against Alexandria and Cairo would now produce a wave of general reprobation and could lead to a Soviet intervention." The military staffs were also getting worried about Egyptian troop reinforcements near Alexandria and possible press leaks about the Anglo-French plans.[48]

The decision to change Musketeer and postpone the military operation was very sudden. On September 9, General Beaufre, commanding Force A (the French land forces) at Algiers, waited in vain for the telegram to arrive confirming the operation was to go ahead. He then flew on his own initiative to Paris, where on September 10 he was informed by French chief of staff General Paul Ely that the French and British governments had given up the idea of an attack on Alexandria and a new plan had to be drawn up targeted on Port Said and the canal. Beaufre replied, "Thus, after one month of studies and preparations, we came back to square one, and this six days before the date when the transport ships were to depart."[49]

In fact, this was the second postponement of the military operation. In the first, the landings had been put off until September 25. Now they were to be put off until October 1.[50] The logistical plan for the original operation would have to be used for the Port Said operation as well, with minor adaptations.[51]

The second London conference agreed on a text on September 21. It established the main lines of the Suez Canal Users Association (SCUA).[52] However, as Dulles pointed out at the start of the conference on September 19, "Participation in the Association would not imply, for the countries belonging to it, any obligation."[53]

As French diplomats reported from London, Dulles had hoped to use this effort to delay any move to bring the canal crisis before the United Nations. The British and French governments did not feel so constrained.[54]

On September 22, with Dulles having just left London for Washington, the British government decided to take the issue to the Security Council that evening. The British had sought and received French assent.

The French government concluded that even though the appropriateness of going to the UN at that moment might be questioned (an apparent reference to the possibility that, as a result, the two countries might find their hands tied), Paris was anxious above all to preserve Anglo-French solidarity. It, therefore, supported the British action.[55]

Pineau sent a message to his key embassies assessing the SCUA idea and the results of the second London conference. He noted that the SCUA plan was weaker than France would have liked. Nevertheless, France went along with the canal users association idea. But France, concluded Pineau in his circular note to the ambassadors, did not intend to compromise on the principle accepted by the Group of 18 at the first London conference, the principle of international management of the canal. The key point, Pineau emphasized, was that France intended to retain its freedom of action.[56]

On September 26, British Prime Minister Eden and Foreign Secretary Lloyd arrived in Paris to coordinate plans for the upcoming UN Security Council debate. The debate on the British-French resolution was scheduled to begin on October 5, with a vote probably due on October 13 or 14.

With this further diplomatic shift—a new phase at the UN—the military plans had to be changed again. From September 12 to 19 the new plan targeted on Port Said—Musketeer Revise—was drawn up. On September 20 the new plan was presented to the military chiefs.[57] But the British decision on September 22, backed by the French, to take the Suez matter to the UN Security

Council put off the landings until October 8. Ships would have to start moving on September 29.[58]

Once the military realized the Security Council debate on the Anglo-French resolution was not even due to begin until October 5, a further delay was needed. What is more, a new plan, the Winter Plan, was under study.[59] "The Winter Plan, approved on October 12 by the British Chiefs of Staff, virtually buried the idea of an imminent military action in the Middle East."[60] The Winter Plan represented a modification of Musketeer Revise to take into account unfavorable meteorological conditions as winter approached. Theoretically, implementation of the plan would finally begin on October 21.[61]

INTENSIFYING PREPARATIONS WITH THE ISRAELIS

In September the French believed British leadership was wavering in its determination because of an erosion in parliamentary and public support. The French turned their attention more and more toward Israel.

Armed Forces Chief of Staff General Ely recalled that "the leading players in the negotiations [were Defense Minister] M. Bourgès-Maunoury, with the aid of his cabinet director, M. Abel Thomas, a man of exceptional dynamism and, from the Israeli side, M. Shimon Peres who, in contact with all the French milieu likely to aid him in his enterprise, was the real animator of the French-Israeli rapprochement."[62]

On September 18, Shimon Peres was again back in Paris, where he and his key aide, Yosef Nahmias, met with Bourgès-Maunoury and Thomas. By this time, the House of Commons debate had been held, clearly revealing the degree of Labour Party opposition to Eden. The military operation had been revised and postponed to October 1, in part because of the need to wait for the outcome of the second London conference. Bourgès-Maunoury (though there were few with him on this issue at that point) began to consider seriously the alternative: a bilateral French-Israeli operation against Nasser.

After Peres returned to Israel, Prime Minister Ben-Gurion decided to send a delegation to France headed by Foreign Minister Golda Meir.[63] At these meetings, which took place in Paris (September 30–October 1), the French discussed a commitment of air and naval support for Israel. The meetings represented the first in-depth discussions of joint French-Israeli military operations against Egypt. Before that time there had been some discussions of joint planning chiefly in the context of French operations in Algeria.[64]

The September 30–October 1 meetings, sometimes confusingly referred to as the "St. Germain" meetings because the Israeli delegation overnighted there, were held at the home of Colonel Louis Mangin in the Sèvres-Babylone section of Paris. In the dining room hung the portrait of Mangin's father, General Charles Mangin, a famous French general who had been associated both with successes (Verdun) and failures (Chemin des Dames) in World War I.

The leader of the Israeli delegation, Foreign Minister Golda Meir, was accompanied by Israeli Armed Forces chief of staff Moshe Dayan, Peres, and Moshe Carmel, a cabinet member, former general, and fluent French speaker. On the French side the delegation was led by Pineau, backed up by Bourgès-Maunoury, Abel Thomas, and Air Force chief General Maurice Challe. Meir was annoyed that Mollet was not with the French group but was partially mollified when Mollet agreed to receive her privately in his office.

Pineau led off. France had decided the time had come to use force against Nasser. This would best be done in October, before the weather turned bad and before the U.S. presidential election in early November.

Would the Israelis, Pineau asked, be interested in joining the French in a military operation if the British dropped out? The Israelis agreed that force had to be used against Nasser, but the big question mark was what the British role would be if, for example, hostilities broke out between Israel and Jordan. Would Britain honor its defense treaty with Jordan? Pineau said he expected to have a definite answer on the British overall attitude by the end of the Security Council debate in mid-October.[65]

The military phase of the discussions, which began that afternoon, continued the next day, October 1. At that point, Dayan's French counterpart, General Ely, who had been kept abreast of the French-Israeli military relationship, entered into contact with the Israelis for the first time. Ely met with Dayan at Mangin's home.

Without entering into much detail, Dayan gave an overview of how Israel planned to conduct a campaign in the Sinai. Dayan accompanied this with a new list of requested equipment, which included another 100 tanks. Ely said he would support this request with the government. Dayan told Ely it would greatly help if the British and French launched an attack against Egypt at the same time the Israelis entered the Sinai.

Ely said a British-French attack would not be possible except after a delay of several days.

Dayan said he understood.[66]

Although impressed with Dayan and his presentation, the French decided more firsthand information was needed on the capabilities of the Israeli forces.

Accordingly, when the talks ended on October 1, three French officers accompanied Dayan back to Israel: Air Force chief General Challe and two of Ely's top officers.

Following the French-Israeli ministerial-level talks in Paris from September 30 through October 1, a separate element of French air support to Israel was created on October 4. Quite apart from the Anglo-French planning, a French squadron of Mystère IVA jet fighters was based in Israel, at Ramat-David, and charged with air protection of the southern part of Israel. Another squadron of French fighter-bombers was based at Lydda airport near Tel Aviv and several French transport planes were based at Haifa.[67] By the end of October, all these aircraft were in place in Israel.

In the meantime, a new and massive seaborne shipment of arms for Israel had been arranged. Three shiploads left Toulon one after another, carrying 100 tanks, 200 half-tracked armored vehicles, and 300 four-wheel-drive trucks, along with plenty of ammunition, fuel, and other equipment. It all reached Haifa during the last days of October.[68]

THE UN SECURITY COUNCIL DEBATE
AND THE SOVIET VETO

As the French saw it, British resolve was clearly weakening. In mid-September the Labour Party changed course and decided to attack the government over its handling of the Suez affair. Eden and Lloyd had gone to Paris for another Anglo-French summit, this one on September 26–28.

The French did not wish to concede one millimeter from the original demand for international management of the canal. They wanted to be ready for imminent military action by the end of October, before winter weather compromised Mediterranean operations.

The British seemed inclined to find some negotiated diplomatic solution to the crisis. Nonetheless Eden's charm and fluency in French made a good impression. The French alluded vaguely to the possibility of coordination with Israel. For the moment there still seemed to be a united Anglo-French front.[69]

On October 1, the French ambassador in London, Jean Chauvel, reminded his government that "British public opinion . . . has adapted to the idea of a negotiated solution." He feared that the just-concluded Eden-Lloyd visit to Paris might "have left in the minds of their interlocutors an overly strong impression of firmness on the part of the British Government with regard to the Suez affair."[70]

Selwyn Lloyd, claimed Chauvel, had shown himself to be "hesitant and uncertain." The British foreign secretary, he added, had gone to the Paris summit
meetings in favor of a "committee of negotiation" to try to settle the Suez
issue. This idea had been floated some time earlier by UN secretary-general
Dag Hammarskjöld, who visualized that a restricted committee of the Security
Council could be charged with seeking a compromise solution or at least with
recommending a procedure to follow. In the September 26–28 summit meetings in Paris, however, the British were persuaded by the French not to accept
this idea.[71]

The Security Council debate on the Anglo-French resolution began on
October 5. Debate was to follow on a rival Egyptian resolution, condemning
French and British measures against Egypt. The Americans were giving, more
and more, the impression they were trying to mediate impartially between the
Anglo-French position and the Egyptian position. This impression was reinforced by a press conference of Dulles on October 2, in which he mentioned
that the United States had to play "a somewhat independent role" in the problems of "colonialism" and the "shift from colonialism to independence."

This was the same press conference in which Dulles had conceded there
were "no teeth" in the SCUA proposal. "There never were 'teeth' in it, if that
means the use of force."[72] Two days later, on October 4, Eden told the French
ambassador, Chauvel, that this was just "the latest in the series of surprises
which the American Secretary of State has reserved for us."[73]

On October 5 in New York, Dulles, Pineau, and Lloyd gathered in a preliminary meeting prior to the opening of the Security Council debate. According to Pineau's report:

> M. Dulles thought that it was first of all indispensable to have an in-
> timate interview in which a frank discussion could be held among the
> three of us concerning the misunderstandings and differences of opinion
> which might exist. . . .
>
> The Secretary of State repeated that his Government held to the
> principles contained in the resolution of the 18 powers, but he still con-
> siders that these principles can be implemented by peaceful means. Ac-
> cording to him, a recourse to force would be disastrous for the Western
> position in the Middle East [and] in Asia [and] Africa.[74]

Both Lloyd and Pineau maintained that time was on Nasser's side in the
situation (with Dulles arguing the opposite). Pineau, for his part, said that

France was ready to negotiate with Egypt but only on the basis of international management of the canal as originally proposed by the Group of 18. He was not in favor of negotiating with Egypt outside that basis through a United Nations committee.

For the moment, the powers agreed on a phase of quiet negotiations. But they also agreed not to deviate from the proposals of the Group of 18. Dulles also agreed, at Pineau's request, not to support amendments to the Anglo-French resolution without discussing such an American move first with himself and Lloyd.[75]

The decision taken at the tripartite meeting on October 5 paved the way for Hammarskjöld to open up private discussions with Pineau, Lloyd, and the Egyptian representative, Mahmoud Fawzi. On October 12, the Security Council met in a closed session. Hammarskjöld announced that the private talks had produced an agreement on principles, and it now remained to agree on how to put them into execution.

The principles were the following, stated Hammarskjöld, according to the report of the French ambassador to the UN:

- Transit through the Canal would be without discrimination . . .

- The sovereignty of Egypt would be respected.

- The functioning of the Canal would be exempt from the politics of any country.

- The method of fixing tolls and charges would be determined by an accord between Egypt and the [Canal] users.

- A part of the revenues of the Canal would be devoted to an improvement of the latter.

- In case of disagreement, pending matters between the Suez Canal Company and the Egyptian Government would be settled by an arbitration tribunal.[76]

Fawzi then spoke, saying that while he could not subscribe to all the points of the secretary-general's language, an accord had been reached in principle and now the means of application had to be found. Lloyd cautioned against too much optimism and said there were still important divergences regarding the application of these principles. He thought the recommendations of the Group of 18 remained the best formula for this application.

Pineau seconded this, stressing the validity of the principle of international management of the canal. He concluded, however, that some progress had been made.[77]

Commenting in a telegram at the end of the same day, October 12, Pineau began by saying, "Today was a much better day." He went on, "We have put together with M. Lloyd, who is in a much better disposition, the following procedure. We are going to prepare a resolution comprising two parts: [First,] The enunciation of the six principles [of M. Hammarskjöld]. [Second,] The essential points of our earlier proposition [Group of 18 London proposals]."[78] Pineau apparently believed that UN Security Council approval of the first part of the resolution (the six principles) and a Soviet veto on the second part (international management of the canal) would be a tolerable outcome for France.

When the vote came, the first part of the resolution (the six principles) passed unanimously; the vote on the second part was nine to two, with Yugoslavia and the Soviet Union voting against. Since the USSR was a veto-wielding member of the Security Council, the second part was considered vetoed.

The public mood was cautiously optimistic. Dulles announced he was encouraged that some progress had been made.[79]

BUT THE FRENCH HAVE ANOTHER PLAN

What Pineau knew about, and other delegates in New York did not, was a report from a French general, Maurice Challe, who had just had a very interesting trip to Israel. A former chief of staff of the French armed forces, Challe had been replaced in that position in early 1956 by General Ely and was assigned as chief of air operations in Algeria.

However, Challe had earlier been deputed by the French leadership in 1955 to establish high-level contacts with the Israeli government, and Mollet had continued to rely on him in this role. Challe had been present at the military and intelligence conference with the Israelis in June that had been so important and at the ministerial-level French-Israeli talks in Paris on September 30 and October 1, and he had just led the French military delegation to Israel immediately after those talks.

Challe and his delegation had returned from Israel on October 5. They were exceedingly impressed with the organization and training of the Israeli armed forces. The dynamism of the Israeli troops was "non pareil."[80] The Challe delegation received confirmation of Israel's new equipment needs as well as the

Israelis' requirement for a diversion operation at the moment they invaded the Sinai.

Most significantly, Challe had reported to Ely that Ben-Gurion would not engage the Israeli army unless assured of a parallel action by France. Israel also had to have, at a minimum, a guarantee that Britain would at least stay neutral.[81]

Ely and Challe took this word to Bourgès-Maunoury on October 7. The next day the defense minister issued a directive to Admiral Barjot. Barjot was to draw up an amended military plan with two options: a French intervention unilaterally in support of Israel or an Anglo-French operation in coordination with Israel.

Bourgès-Maunoury wished to move regardless of the British attitude. To Ely, he stressed the adverse effect on the French armed forces of renouncing a military intervention at this point. Ely insisted that any intervention had to include the British.[82]

Ely and Challe briefed Prime Minister Mollet on October 9. Mollet, while considering it a manifest necessity to support Israel and prevent it from being wiped off the map, had received reports that Eden was facing growing opposition back in London. Like Ely, Mollet preferred not to undertake any military operation without London's participation.

As for the Americans, French intelligence reported that the important thing for Washington was that nothing take place before the presidential elections on November 6. After that the Americans would leave the initiative to the British and the French. Nevertheless, Mollet was concerned and uncertain about the American attitude.[83]

Mollet sent Challe on to New York to brief Pineau. With the UN Security Council vote in the offing, Challe briefed Pineau privately at the Waldorf Astoria Hotel.[84] Pineau was impressed by Challe's estimate that the Israeli Defense Forces, capable of expanding their strength fivefold in an ultra-rapid mobilization, would alone be able to overwhelm the Egyptians. "We must go forward, but it remains to convince the English," he said.[85]

So the problem was now "to convince the English." Challe went back to Paris, where his prime minister, Guy Mollet, sent him on to London along with the acting foreign minister (with Pineau in New York), Albert Gazier, to brief Eden himself. The French ambassador to London, Chauvel, met the plane but he did not know where the pair went. He did not know that the man with Gazier was General Challe.[86]

Challe and Gazier had their extraordinary meeting on the afternoon of October 14. They met at Chequers, the British prime minister's country estate.[87] One other British official was there, Anthony Nutting, Lloyd's deputy at the Foreign Office.

Challe was the obvious choice to make the pitch in this secret conversation. In clandestine parlance, he had become Mollet's "case officer" for the Israeli "account." He had the military credibility, too. He could offer Eden a fresh way to solve the Suez and Egypt problem.

To Challe, Eden seemed tired and rather seriously ill. He was at logger-heads with an active Labour Party opposition, and not all the Conservatives were behind him.

"Once more," Challe remembered feeling that "a sizeable proportion of the British want to yield with finesse, that is, pull back while making speeches. It is the strange destiny of this old, solid people, this old merchant people that hopes, in giving in, to retain its markets."[88]

"I did not beat around the bush," said Challe, in reporting to Bourgès-Maunoury and Ely the next day in Paris. According to Ely's account: "[Challe] presented to [Eden] a possible plan in the hypothesis that a conflict broke out between Egypt and Israel: let the Israelis launch [an attack] on Egypt, then have the Anglo-French forces intervene without delay at the Canal to restore peace in an operation which would ostensibly be for the purpose of maintaining order."

What did Eden think of this remarkable plan? "M. Eden appeared very interested in this proposition."

Reporting to Ely in Paris, Challe admitted that when Eden reacted so positively, "he was astonished." It was not that Challe thought the plan he was presenting was unworthy. Challe was surprised, because "it seemed as though the British had not thought of this maneuver." Ely remembered: "If M. Gazier, concluded Challe artlessly, hadn't been there and hadn't had himself the same impression, I would have wondered if Eden wasn't mocking me."[89]

JERUSALEM

PHILIP ZELIKOW

WAIT AND SEE: JULY 26–SEPTEMBER 1

The Israeli government's immediate reaction to the crisis over Nasser's nationalization of the Suez Canal was to step back and not get in the way of a useful fight. The Israeli Foreign Ministry instructed its representatives around the world to "refrain from making public statements on this matter in order not to weaken the head-on collision between the Powers and Egypt by magnifying the Israel factor."[1]

Ben-Gurion was not eager for a war, at least not yet. He thought Israel would probably not be ready enough until early 1957. He worried, in particular, about air raids. Ben-Gurion had been in London for a time during the war; the German bombing of the city had made a lasting impression on him and he wondered if Israeli city dwellers could handle such attacks. He wanted to wait until Israeli air defenses were stronger.

A few days after Nasser's announcement, as Dayan came to him with possible war plans against Egypt in the Sinai and Gaza, Ben-Gurion told him, "Nasser is not coordinating his time-table with us. We cannot do anything meanwhile except sit tight and conclude the French [arms] deal quickly [described in Part One], reinforce our strength, and then, at a later stage, find the right moment to strike."[2]

When Nasser made his Suez Canal move, Shimon Peres was in Paris, working on more arms shopping. By the end of July, Peres was able to see French defense minister Bourgès-Maunoury and his assistant, Abel Thomas. They had some very important and secret information and requests.

Peres returned to Israel and conveyed the French message, in person, to Ben-Gurion. Ben-Gurion heard that the French took Nasser's decision very seriously, beyond what one could tell by reading the French press. "They view a defeat over Suez like a defeat in Algeria."

The prime minister recorded in his diary that Peres had been told, on August 1, that "the English and the French had decided in principle on a joint military action to conquer the Canal." The operation might be only a few weeks away.

According to the French, the English were insisting that Israel "not take part in this action, and would not even be informed of it at this stage (to prevent all the Arabs from uniting around Nasser)." Obviously the French were not exactly heeding the British request. The French wanted the Israelis to send a military man to Paris to discuss planning and advice and possibly "more than that."[3]

Ben-Gurion made it clear that Israel would cooperate fully with France. Ben-Gurion told Peres, "This will be our test whether we can give the French the information that is first and foremost important to them and not only the information that interests us. If we hide anything that is vital for them, we will be betraying their trust in us." If the French wanted information, including about Israeli port facilities or anything else, Ben-Gurion instructed Moshe Dayan, "We must provide it in good faith. We must treat them like brothers in everything. Their aid and assistance, as well as our partnership with them, are invaluable and we must cooperate with them totally."[4]

At the same time, though, Ben-Gurion was wary about whether any military action would really happen. He doubted the British would act without U.S. backing. As for that, he remarked, "there is no hope of that scoundrel Dulles supporting any daring action against the Arabs and the Russians."[5]

A week later, on August 9, watching the diplomacy unfold that would lead to the first London conference, Ben-Gurion confided to Dayan, "We have more time now. Nasser is busy with England."

Dayan was happy to stay out, at least for a while. The armed forces were still absorbing the new French equipment and were not ready. Dayan replied, "We should not interfere in the Suez affair."[6]

For the rest of August and on into September, the Israelis watched and waited. They offered bits of secret cooperation to the French. They worked on receiving and absorbing the still-arriving shipments of French arms. Ben-Gurion still thought "the English will apparently do nothing against [Nasser], and without force Nasser will not surrender." So he expected an eventual military confrontation with an emboldened Nasser.

The French seemed warlike enough, Ben-Gurion noted after a meeting with their ambassador, but the prime minister noted in his diary: "I do not believe that even with the assistance of France alone something can be done. U.S. agreement is needed." Israel should not carry out an operation on its own, "at the present time." Israel needed to be in "'respectable company,'" and "a solitary 'operation' on our part may well turn out to be calamitous."[7]

When the Americans took the lead in organizing a conference in London to discuss the crisis, Israel asked to participate. The request was declined; Israel was not invited. The organizers—the American, British, and French governments—preferred to keep the Arab-Israeli issues out of this crisis.

The Israelis watched as the eighteen-nation position to come out of the London conference was presented to Nasser and rejected. Dulles then organized another London conference, this one to prepare a different way of contributing an international voice in the management of the canal, a Suez Canal Users Association. As this conference was put together, the Israelis again asked to participate. Again the organizers preferred to keep Israel out of this. They did assure Israel that any international management would seek to restore Israel's right to use the canal.[8]

David Ben-Gurion publicly summed up Israel's situation to the Israeli Labour Party Convention on August 27. His message was that it was folly for Israel to contemplate preventive war against its enemies; Israel could never win a final victory. He denounced those in Israel, including the leaders of the right-wing parties, who called for such a move.[9]

THE FRENCH PROPOSE JOINT WAR PREPARATIONS
AND ISRAEL ACCEPTS: SEPTEMBER 1–28

On September 1 Ben-Gurion received an urgent message from his other Defense Ministry representative in Paris, Yosef Nahmias. French defense officials had told Nahmias that they and the British were preparing for war. The French commander intended to invite Israel to join the military operation a week after it started, on D + 7, with some story for the British about the necessity of this. The French expected Israel to accept enthusiastically and were a bit surprised that Israel's stance in the Suez crisis so far had seemed so "restrained and reserved." The French expressed confidence about British commitment and the outcome. "France's main aim is to have Nasser removed, which coincides with British interest."

Dayan flagged that this was the first time Israel had been asked to join a coming Anglo-French campaign. He recorded in his diary: "If indeed Britain and France capture the Suez Canal and restore its international status by force of arms, the political implications for us will be of the highest importance. Not only will the Canal be open (I hope) to Israeli shipping, but Britain will be engaged in a military conflict with Egypt over interests which serve us too."[10]

Ben-Gurion told Dayan and Peres that "in principle, we are willing to cooperate." Peres dispatched the reply to Nahmias: "The Old Man approves cooperation of course." Israel would send Dayan's deputy chief of staff. Ben-Gurion's and Dayan's instructions authorized cooperation, but reserved final decisions, to be taken with the cabinet, on just what the military would do.[11]

In early September, the immediate security problem for Israel was on the border with Jordan. There was more violence there from infiltrators. Earlier in the year the Jordanians had dismissed the British head of their disciplined Arab Legion and the associated British advisers, who had been a moderating force. As the year had progressed, the whole future of the Jordanian state seemed increasingly uncertain. Ben-Gurion and his colleagues had lost confidence in the UN truce supervisors, who adjudicated incidents and made statements, but could do little to check the violence. As Ben-Gurion told the chief UN supervisor, a Canadian general, "The experience of eight years has proven to us that agreements are worthless when neighbours want to uproot Israel. Without a radical change there's no value at all to the agreements."

At this point Ben-Gurion began to believe that the possible shape of war would be to stay on the defensive against Egypt while first concentrating on Jordan, focusing on the Old City of Jerusalem and the West Bank city of Hebron (the Old City and the West Bank of the Jordan were on the Jordanian side of the 1949 armistice lines). "Jordan must be hit first and forced out of the game." He believed "Jordan is the main enemy from a point of view of land, Egypt—for power. We'll break both of them, one after the other."[12]

As for Egypt, the French still seemed determined to act. Their foreign minister told the Israeli ambassador in Paris that, to France, "there was no other way out except Nasser's surrender or war." The minister, Pineau, said, "The chances of war seemed to him to be about 50%." It was true the Egyptians were being "bolstered by Russia." Yet Pineau believed "the Russians are not prepared for war and hope that the West would be deterred."[13]

Ben-Gurion still "did not believe that Eden would do something serious" about Egypt. Yet he found it "hard to accept that two governments of European powers would make laughing stocks of themselves by threatening to dispatch armies, navies and air forces" and "then submit to the Egyptian dictator."[14]

After preliminary military discussions between French and Israeli officers, Peres and Dayan traveled secretly to Paris on September 18. By this time Dayan had been involved in some emotionally wrenching supervision of more clashes on the Jordanian border. The Egyptian border was not quiet, but there the Israelis were retaliating with more low-key ambushes of infiltrators rather than with high-profile reprisal raids of the kind the Israelis were launching into Jordan.

Dayan had also done further work with his staff to refine Israeli military plans for various offensives into the Sinai Peninsula. "We have no aspirations to reach Suez and become an involved party in the dispute." But Israel did want to gain control over the Gaza Strip and the Straits of Tiran (by driving to Sharm el Sheikh at the southern tip of Sinai).[15]

The big news from the discussions in Paris was that the French were losing confidence in British readiness to proceed. The French defense minister, Bourgès-Maunoury, told Peres—who reported to Ben-Gurion—that "personally, he [the minister] thought other ways and other partners have to be found for war against Nasser." The Anglo-Saxon hesitations about working with Israel seemed "excessive," since the Arab countries would side with Egypt in any case. Both the French minister and his Israeli counterparts were leaning toward the idea of French-Israeli war against Egypt that they would initiate.

As for timing, the French knew the Israelis were in no great hurry. The Israelis could live with the "English timetable," one with more months of diplomacy. The "American timetable" would be even longer, perhaps tolerant of nationalization of the canal. But "the French timetable" was different. It required "immediate action against Nasser, bearing in mind not only the Suez situation but also developments in North Africa [mainly Algeria]."

Peres replied that "Israel prefers to choose its partners rather than the timetable." Israel would stick with France.

Ben-Gurion concurred promptly with this answer. He cabled back to Peres on September 21 the message: "It is the French timetable that is most to our liking. If they move out at a time which is convenient to them, we shall stand by them to the best of our ability."[16]

Publicly Ben-Gurion was still stressing his interest in peace. In an interview with the *Jerusalem Post* on the occasion of his seventieth birthday, he emphasized Israel's need for security and peace. "I will never make war. Never," he said. "Of course, if anybody attacks us, that is another matter. The existence, the life of Israel comes before everything. We shall fight back." Yet a few days later, on September 24, he hinted that Israel's fortunes were improving. Before long, Israel would have "a true ally."[17]

Dayan and Peres returned from France the next day, on September 25. Ben-Gurion met them just outside Tel Aviv. France, they reported, was disgusted with the latest round in the Suez diplomacy, the SCUA proposal. They and the British had just joined in calling for the matter to be referred to the UN Security Council—a prelude to a possible use of force. But the British were also giving off ever-stronger signals that they might very well opt for a diplomatic settlement with Nasser. Prime Minister Anthony Eden was eager for action but he seemed stymied by domestic opposition, even within his own party.

The French cabinet had concluded—Pineau as well as Bourgès-Maunoury—that it was time to work with Israel on planning for a joint military move against Egypt. As Ben-Gurion understood it, the plan "is also in conjunction with the English," whose only concern was that Israel must not attack Jordan—which Britain was pledged by treaty to protect against aggression. The war might begin in just a few weeks, in mid-October.[18]

Ben-Gurion, Dayan, and Peres traveled on to the capital, Jerusalem. There, after a cabinet meeting, the prime minister pulled aside a select group of a few ministers and briefed them on this French proposal. He noted the main concerns his colleagues expressed: that the Russians might send "volunteers" to fight with Egypt; that "England will betray us," and that "all the Arab nations will join in war against us."

Ben-Gurion's view was "that this is our first chance of getting an ally (and, by the way, an ally who has assisted us ever since the [1948–49] War of Independence right to this very day), and it is only due to his assistance that we are not standing helpless today." So he wanted to go ahead.

But the Israeli prime minister wanted to lay down a few clear conditions. France had to know that Israel's air and armored forces were not yet "totally ready" and would not be fully ready until early 1957. England had to back France. "The affair" had to be "carried out with the knowledge of the U.S." Finally, Israel had to come out of the war with clear access for the Straits of Tiran, allowing shipping from Eilat to reach the Red Sea.

"This summary was accepted by one and all present," Ben-Gurion noted to his diary that day. The ministers who had been brought into the planning "committed themselves to secrecy." Israel would send another secret mission back to Paris. This one would be headed by Foreign Minister Meir, joined by Dayan (and Peres) to handle the military issues, along with their chief aides. The French were demanding that the operation begin on October 15.[19]

A couple of days later Ben-Gurion put Israel's conditions into written instructions he gave to Meir before her delegation took off for Paris on September 28. Britain had to agree to Israel's inclusion. Israel would promise not to touch Jordan if Jordan (and Iraq) left Israel alone. The instructions reiterated: "We consider it necessary for the operation to be carried out with the knowledge of the United States." The United States did not need to participate; in fact it would be "desirable that it should not act." But Israel did not want to ruin its various economic ties with the United States. Israeli access to the straits needed to be assured "in practice," and Israel was prepared to see an eventual demilitarization of the entire Sinai Peninsula, although Israel wanted to retain command positions on the shore of the straits.

The delegation was empowered to make a deal, subject to "final and binding" decision after the delegation returned. In a kind of postscript, Ben-Gurion noted: "Perhaps it is also worth clarifying what will happen in the event—although this seems to me to be very far from certain—that Russia attacks us."[20]

The Meir delegation took off for France in a French bomber that had landed secretly in Israel to pick them up. That same day French prime minister Mollet told the Israeli ambassador that he was confident of the West's victory in the crisis. "Nasser's fate was sealed."[21]

SECRET PLANS . . . AND THE BRITISH
PROBLEM: SEPTEMBER 28–OCTOBER 15

Meanwhile, back in Washington, Dulles had met with the capable Israeli diplomat posted to the United States, Abba Eban. Eban complained that Israel was being excluded from the upcoming debate in the UN Security Council. Eban also raised the final success, with U.S. help, in clearing the way for Canada to sell twenty-four F-86 aircraft to Israel. Dulles then told Eban "that the transaction opened up new vistas for Israel since these planes existed in great abundance and thus there was the possibility of training pilots and obtaining major reinforcements in time of need."

Eban mulled a while over those comments about "training pilots and obtaining major reinforcements in time of need." He put it together with other things he had heard. A couple of days later he cabled Jerusalem that he had concluded that "the issue of the planes as raised in the conversation was important."

"For the first time," Eban wrote, "Israel has been told officially that there was an intention and plan to promise it an addition of force in the event it was attacked." Eban's perceptive conclusion, "based on hints and scraps of information, was that the National Security Council had, with the president's approval, adopted the principle of assistance for Israel if it was attacked. That meant that although the Americans had rejected the idea of a security pact in formal, external terms, they had accepted it from the standpoint of essential content." Eban thought this American decision should lead to a "serious review" of Israeli policy.[22]

Eban did not know that his boss, the foreign minister, was at that moment secretly in France, very far down the path toward another kind of security plan. She and her colleagues were staying in the wealthy Parisian suburb of Saint Germain-en-Laye. The "gardens were filled with Saturday strollers as sailboats glided on the Seine." Dayan paid little attention to his beautiful surroundings. He was preoccupied, his aide noted, unable to enjoy "the tranquil scene that was so rare to him. He kept turning different scenarios over in his mind."[23]

The negotiations with the French began on Sunday, September 30, on notes of uncertainty and some mutual suspicion. Pineau had a somber manner and outlined the situation in a direct, unvarnished way. To Peres, he seemed like a "deeply sad man." Meir did not like the French much. She did not like Peres either, and she was annoyed that Prime Minister Mollet did not come to the meeting. (Peres hastily arranged a separate meeting with Mollet.) The French foreign and defense ministers were there (although Pineau had to leave early), along with General Maurice Challe.

But the discussions became warmer and more direct, dominated by the defense representatives on each side. Ben-Gurion's instructions had made it clear that Meir was the head of the delegation and its members could only make proposals with her permission. Yet his written instructions stated bluntly that no one but Dayan "will discuss military matters." In private, Ben-Gurion often disagreed with Dayan. But, as Peres remembered, "In general, Ben-Gurion deeply respected Dayan. Dayan and I were like two colts galloping in the field."[24]

Both sides seemed to agree they could move only if the British went along. In the French case this was partly for practical reasons. They needed British help to use the bases in Cyprus and land their forces.

With that in mind, the French now introduced a new idea. The Israelis may have imagined the offensive moves would all be simultaneous. The French asked if the Israelis might be willing to make the first move.

Bourgès-Maunoury put it this way: "As for a pretext, which is a major issue for starting an operation, Israel's position is far more convenient."

The French also made it clear that, as part of the bargain, they expected Israel to have "demands for maximum readiness," which meant more arms supplies. If the basic concept could be agreed upon, the next step would be to send a French delegation to Israel, led by General Challe, to follow up in even more operational detail.[25]

Dayan, in turn, was candid about Israel's strengths and weaknesses. There was still not enough advanced equipment or enough trained jet pilots. "I want you to know first of all that we are a very small army . . . the Arabs have very bad armies, so in saying that our army is good, I mean in comparison with them." He added, "If we have to deal with Egyptian pilots alone, we could achieve air supremacy. If there will be [Soviet bloc 'volunteer'] Czech and Polish pilots in the sky over the Middle East, I hope there will be French ones as well."

The next day Dayan was similarly candid in talks with the French Chief of Staff General Paul Ely. "General Ely was anxious to be helpful to us but he was not disposed to talk about French plans for the Suez Canal. My efforts to get him to discuss these plans proved fruitless," Dayan wrote.

But Ely did come back to the idea of an initial move by Israel to provide a pretext for the British. Dayan stayed with the view that "obviously, the best help the French can provide the Israeli Army is a simultaneous attack against Egyptian targets to keep some of the Egyptian forces pinned down . . . the main point is simultaneous action."[26]

What about America? As instructed, Meir raised the issue. She expressed concern that critical financial aid might be cut off. Pineau doubted the Eisenhower administration would be able to impose any sanctions before the presidential elections. And, he added, "you can be sure that Dulles' instinctive reaction will be, as usual . . . not to do anything."[27]

The meetings did not reach a formal conclusion, but the planning was clearly going to advance. French officers would return to Israel with the Israelis. And throughout there was an emotional connection between the two groups that documents do not easily capture.

Peres remembered Bourgès-Maunoury, the wartime resistance leader, telling him that "there must never be another Hitler, neither great nor small." He acknowledged that "all of us are very experienced, mature people, occasionally cynical." Yet sentiments played a role. Bourgès-Maunoury said he could not describe France "without a deep feeling for the Jewish people and for Israel."

Peres was seated at dinner next to Madame Ely, the general's wife. She told him, "Look, you don't have to tell me anything. I was myself in a concentration camp with Jewish people. What more can you tell me?"

He met André Malraux, one of France's most renowned writers, who said that if he was a young man, he would want to fight with Israel. "These were the sentiments that existed in France," Peres remembered. It was like the wartime divide in France between the Resistance and the Vichy collaborators. The former Resistance supporters "completely sided with Israel."[28]

The Israeli delegation returned from France on the night of October 1 accompanied by General Challe and others to do the follow-up work. The next day Dayan told his general staff that he was conveying an "Early Warning Order" of preparation for war.

The target date was now October 20. "Tonight, at last," Dayan noted in his diary, "they were given warning of a decisive campaign."[29]

Ben-Gurion met with the delegation. He later wrote a note to record "his carefully weighed" response to what he had heard. It sounded more and more like a Franco-Israeli idea, without the British. He saw "grave problems" with such a plan.

It was, he wrote, "not at all certain that a joint action, even if successful, would bring about Nasser's removal." There could be guerrilla warfare and he doubted the French could sustain a long struggle in Egypt. The Russians might intervene.

Without the British, the French would need bases in Israel. Without the British, American opposition was more likely. Without the British, some of the pro-British Arab states were more likely to combine against Israel. All these considerations "must be stated openly and frankly to the French."[30]

Dayan, however, felt he had worked through these issues. He appears to have grasped the French idea for the "pretext" that would help bring the British in. He grasped that more French arms were likely to come in to help Israel agree to this condition.

Dayan encouraged Ben-Gurion to overcome his doubts. He advised the prime minister not to burden the French with all these worries. "It would be easy now to extinguish this tiny flame of [French] readiness to go to war against Nasser, but it will be impossible to rekindle [it]."

Ben-Gurion followed Dayan's advice. On October 3 and 4 he himself met with Challe and his chief aide, Louis Mangin. He questioned them carefully about French plans. He was not yet satisfied, but he authorized Dayan to keep working, even though "the plan was not to be implemented without Britain's approval."[31]

Dayan worked with his staff to develop an operational plan that emphasized speed above all. "We must end the campaign in the shortest possible time. The longer it lasts, the greater will be the political complications—pressure from the United States, the dispatch of 'volunteers' to aid Egypt, and so on." Speed would also take advantage of Israeli flexibility and Egyptian operational weaknesses. Sinai must be conquered in no more than two weeks. The plans were drawn up as if Israel had no foreign partners.

Dayan's staff supported the conception but worried about the feasibility of this "very ambitious" plan that "did not take into account the chance of anything going wrong." Dayan was persuaded to make modifications, including the addition of a parachute drop. The operation would be code-named Kadesh.[32]

As these plans were coming to fruition, the trouble with Jordan did not go away. The latest issue was a plan, hatched with British and American support, to send Iraqi troops into Jordan to shore up the regime of the young King Hussein. The Israelis were consulted and feared this was the long-awaited plan in which the Iraqi regime of Nuri el-Said would swallow up Jordan. In such a case, Israel planned to react. In the consultations the Israelis pressed for the Iraqi contingent to stay on the east side of the Jordan and be relatively modest. These conditions were met.[33]

A more serious issue was a sharp escalation in border violence on the Jordan border. On October 9 another group of infiltrators made their way about eight miles into Israel and killed a couple of workers, cutting off their ears, apparently to take back as proof of their accomplishment. The Israeli cabinet approved a major reprisal raid against a police fort near the Jordanian town of Qalqilya.

The operation, conducted on October 10 and 11, was difficult and costly. The Jordanians lost about seventy to ninety soldiers and police. The Israelis lost eighteen dead and sixty-eight wounded; a large fraction of their officers were among the casualties, and the situation teetered on the edge of disaster. The engagements had been so prolonged that King Hussein appealed for help from Britain, and the British were on the verge of military intervention when the fighting ended and the Israeli forces returned to their territory.

The Qalqilya episode marked another kind of turning point. The whole system of reprisal raids needed "revision," Dayan acknowledged. Dayan's view, on October 15, was that Israel had to "compel our Arab neighbors to choose between stopping the terrorism and meeting us in a full-scale war."[34]

What about the plans for a "full-scale war," at least against Egypt?

At the UN Security Council, the British and French had been tied up again in diplomatic moves that appeared to make progress toward some face-saving international management solution. From New York, Eban's October 14 comment, transmitted back to Jerusalem, was that "Britain and France undoubtedly regret the decision to bring the Suez issue before the Council."[35]

Challe and the French team had been quite impressed with their Israeli partners and with the preparations for Operation Kadesh. "Before its arrival in Israel," Dayan observed, "the French army only had a pro-Israeli *theory*; now that theory had a solid base."[36]

Franco-Israeli planning continued, including hard work on plans for French air support (including basing of French aircraft in Israel) and naval help. In the plans, the Israelis would take over the Sinai Peninsula but stay away from the Suez Canal itself; the French would concentrate their efforts on the Canal Zone. More French arms supplies were already on the move. But in the planning for war, which might be scheduled to start within a couple of weeks, still nothing had finally been decided.

The fundamental issue still revolved around the British. Challe and his colleagues could see now how to develop the ideas for an Israeli first move that would then provide the pretext for British as well as French intervention. The Israeli side could sense that the French were intrigued with this idea.

The Israeli side accepted the need for British participation. "But on one point Dayan would not budge: the two operations must be concurrent. Israel would not appear as the sole aggressor."[37]

LONDON

JILL KASTNER

INITIAL REACTION: TALK OF PEACE, PREPARE FOR WAR

On the night of July 26, the Egyptian army seized control of the Suez Canal. In London, British prime minister Anthony Eden was seated at a state dinner in Downing Street with King Feisal of Iraq and his prime minister, Nuri el-Said. When word of Nasser's move reached the dining room, the overwhelming reaction was one of shock. The voices in the room were united for a sharp move against Nasser. Labour Party leader Hugh Gaitskell encouraged Eden to act quickly. Eden's old friend Nuri counseled to "hit, hit now, and hit hard."[1]

Eden's first instinct was to follow that advice. After the dinner guests had departed, the prime minister, still in white tie, called together an emergency meeting that included French ambassador to Britain Jean Chauvel and U.S. chargé d'affaires Andrew Foster, along with four cabinet ministers (Lloyd, Salisbury, Kilmuir, and Home) and two chiefs of staff (Templer and Mountbatten). Eden was clear; Nasser must not be allowed to have "his thumb on our windpipe."[2]

Eden wanted a quick military response, perhaps by a lightly armed airborne or commando force. But Chief of the Imperial General Staff Sir Gerald Templer dashed those hopes. If Britain intended to attack Egypt, it had to do so properly. Recent austerity cuts had reduced the forces. Much of Britain's equipment was in mothballs, and some of it was inferior to the new Soviet equipment

206

now in the Egyptians' possession. Templer insisted it would take six weeks to assemble a viable invasion force. The meeting broke up at 4 a.m.[3]

Eden gathered the twenty-one ministers of his cabinet the next morning. The principle of cabinet collective responsibility meant that all ministers were required to support the cabinet vote or else resign. At this point, there was little dissension. The cabinet agreed to a two-track policy: explore diplomacy while preparing for war. Military planning and overt preparations would raise the specter of Anglo-French attack, which might force Nasser to reverse his course. But "even if we had to act alone, we could not stop short of using force to protect our position if all other means of protecting it proved unavailing." The Chiefs of Staff went off to prepare their plans.[4]

Eden sent a cable to U.S. president Dwight Eisenhower immediately after the meeting. Nasser must not be allowed to get away with it, he wrote, otherwise "our influence and yours throughout the Middle East will . . . be irretrievably undermined." He assumed the United States would stand with Britain, telling Eisenhower "we must be ready, in the last resort, to use force to bring Nasser to his senses. For our part we are prepared to do so." He proposed that tripartite talks among Britain, France, and the United States begin immediately.[5]

That same day, the cabinet created a small subcommittee, the Egypt Committee, to deal with day-to-day decision-making. Members included Eden, Foreign Secretary Selwyn Lloyd, Chancellor of the Exchequer Harold Macmillan, House of Commons leader Rab Butler, Minister of Defense Walter Monckton, Commonwealth Secretary Alec Douglas-Home, and the Lord Privy Seal, the Marquess of Salisbury. A working-level group, the Egypt (Official) Committee, would be created in late August under the supervision of Cabinet Secretary Sir Norman Brook.

For the moment, Eden believed Britain was in a strong position. Public and press reaction was loudly in favor of putting Nasser in his place. Lloyd reported that the French were comparing Nasser's move to Hitler's remilitarization of the Rhineland and were eager for action, "ready to go all the way with us." Prime Minister Guy Mollet was even prepared to put French forces under British command.[6]

The idea of Nasser as a potential Hitler or Mussolini haunted politicians, the press, and the public. The scars of war were still fresh in Britain. Almost to a man, the British government was marked by the lesson of World War II: appeasement of dictators led to more demands and, eventually, to war. This was the yardstick by which British foreign policy had been measured since the late 1930s. Eden was of that mindset, so too Macmillan and Lloyd, as well as Sir

Ivone Kirkpatrick, the government's top adviser on foreign affairs at the Foreign Office. Eden's letters to Eisenhower would be peppered with references to Hitler and Mussolini in the coming weeks.

Surveying the international mood, Eden had cause for optimism. The Israelis also wanted a strong move against Nasser. The Iraqis had given a green light. It was thought that the Soviets, despite their bravado, would probably not risk war over a vital Western interest in the Middle East. Commonwealth backing was not rock solid, but it was good enough; New Zealand and Australia were in, Canada supportive but not enthusiastic.

But with Britain's most important ally, the United States, problems began to arise almost immediately. After meeting with U.S. officials on July 28, Ambassador Sir Roger Makins reported from Washington that the United States was "weak and irresolute in the face of this crisis, and are tepid about taking any vigorous action." This seemed to be confirmed when Eisenhower sent Deputy Under Secretary of State Robert Murphy to the July 29 tripartite talks in place of Secretary of State John Foster Dulles, who was traveling in Peru. For his part, Dulles declared that as long as there was no interference in the navigation of the canal and no threats to foreign nationals in Egypt, there was no basis for military action. He ruled out the possibility of American intervention.[7]

Could it be that the Americans did not understand what was at stake for Britain and France? Both Eden and Macmillan decided to do everything possible to frighten their allies into acting more robustly. Over the next few days, they revealed to Murphy in private conversations that the British government had decided to drive Nasser out of Egypt. Military action was "necessary and inevitable." They hoped the United States would join in, but if the Americans could not, "they would understand and our friendship would be unimpaired." Both men stressed that Britain was flexible on procedures, but "whatever conferences, arrangements, public postures and maneuvers might be necessary, at the end they are determined to use force."[8]

Macmillan even invited his old friend Murphy to dinner on the night of July 30 and warned disingenuously that military action might start as early as August. "It would not take much," he asserted, until "Nasser was chased out of Egypt." Afterward he was confident of his powers of persuasion. "We went on with the good work," he wrote, and "did our best to frighten Murphy out of his life."

It worked. Murphy cabled Dulles on July 31, warning that Britain was planning to use military force to overthrow Nasser and take back the canal.[9]

Meanwhile, Eden took other steps to show resolve in the first weeks. Two days after the nationalization, the Treasury froze all Egyptian sterling balances and assets. On July 30, the British banned the export of all further war matériel to Egypt. This was followed by the call-up of 20,000 British Army reservists. Naval, air, and army reinforcements were dispatched to the Mediterranean. The world could see that Britain was serious.

To gain international control of the canal, Britain and France wanted a new Suez Canal authority created under UN auspices. Dulles countered with a plan for a conference of maritime powers based on the Constantinople Convention of 1888. While this would involve the Soviets—something Britain was trying to avoid—Eden could take solace in Dulles's promise that if the Egyptians refused to attend, or behaved unreasonably, "then the situation would be created which might call for a different approach."

To Eden's great relief, Dulles himself was dispatched to London on July 31. His presence was a victory of sorts for the British, who felt they had nudged the Americans into taking the situation more seriously.

Dulles brought with him a letter from Eisenhower. The president wrote that some kind of negotiation "must be attempted before action such as you contemplate should be undertaken. . . . Public opinion here, and I am convinced, in most of the world, would be outraged should there be a failure to make such efforts." If it did come to war, "world opinion would understand how earnestly all of us had attempted to be just, fair and considerate, but that we simply could not accept a situation that would in the long run prove disastrous to the prosperity and living standards of every nation whose economy depends directly or indirectly upon East-West shipping." From this, Eden inferred that Eisenhower would leave the military option open as long as diplomacy was first given a chance.[10]

The next day, Dulles delighted the British by saying that "a way had to be found to make Nasser disgorge what he was attempting to swallow." Eden was thrilled; he later wrote that Dulles's words "rang in my ears for months."[11]

The tripartite discussions ended with plans for a conference of maritime powers to convene in London on August 16. After Dulles's departure, Eden cabled Eisenhower that Britain had "gone to the very limits of the concessions we can make." While they agreed on the need to set up international control of the canal, Eden urged Eisenhower to recognize that Nasser was akin to Mussolini, and neither of them should forget the trauma he caused. Removing Nasser "must therefore also rank high among our objectives." If Nasser were forced to "disgorge" the canal, he might be toppled, but if he refused the conference proposals, or tried to stall, they must be prepared to go further.[12]

With just two weeks to go before the London conference, Whitehall was a flurry of activity. The chiefs of staff presented their initial plan for military action, which called for an attack on Port Said, at the northern end of the canal on the Mediterranean Sea. This would achieve security for British shipping and oil but might have little effect on getting rid of Nasser. Shortly afterward, Eden received a quiet visit from Churchill bearing a memo, dictated in the car and typed in a lay-by on the way to Chequers, arguing that toppling Nasser would require taking Cairo. With backing from Macmillan and the newly appointed task force commanders, the plan was reworked. On August 10, the Egypt Committee accepted a final version, Musketeer, that called for a joint Anglo-French assault on Alexandria beginning on September 15 (D-Day), followed by an attack on Cairo.[13]

Details of Musketeer were put on a restricted circulation list, code-named Terrapin. This effectively cut off most of the members of each ministry and reduced knowledge and planning to a small core of people. Most knew nothing, and those who knew didn't know the whole story.[14]

Macmillan, meanwhile, broached the idea of using the Israelis, asking Churchill to intervene once again with Eden. When Eden learned of this, he was incensed. He blocked circulation of Macmillan's paper on the topic and instructed Lloyd to tell the Israelis to keep "right out" of the Suez situation for the moment.[15]

Unfortunately, just as military preparations were beginning, the British public began losing its appetite for military adventure, especially with an international conference planned to deal with the crisis. To boost public support, Eden delivered a televised address on August 8. Oil was a matter of life and death for Britain and Europe, he warned, and Nasser was a liar who broke all his promises. The Egyptian's "act of plunder" could not be allowed to succeed.

The public's reaction was one of bewilderment. Why was Eden so belligerent when he had just invited Nasser to a conference in London? There were grumblings about the absence of an approach to the UN. By August 14, it was also clear the Opposition in the House had withdrawn its support for settling the dispute by force.[16]

MAKING PROGRESS: THE FIRST LONDON CONFERENCE

Representatives from twenty-two nations gathered in London on August 16 for the conference of maritime powers. Egypt, along with Greece, refused to attend. Eden felt optimistic, writing to Churchill that "the Americans seem very firmly lined up with us on internationalization." The conference ended with eighteen of the twenty-two nations adopting Dulles's plan to create a multinational Suez Canal Board on which Egypt would be guaranteed a seat. A delegation led by Australian prime minister Robert Menzies was chosen to deliver the proposals to Cairo and elicit a response from Nasser.[17]

As the conference was under way, Lloyd approached Dulles privately to ask if British officials could share their military plans with their American counterparts.

Dulles replied that "it would be an embarrassment to the United States Government if they were given this information."

An incredulous Lloyd suspected Dulles had not told the president or the State Department of this discussion. "Do you think it possible," he cabled Makins, "to find out without upsetting Mr. Dulles whether the President himself is aware of what Mr. Dulles said on this matter in London?"

On August 27, Lloyd reported to the Egypt Committee that, despite requests from the U.S. military attaché in London, "[Dulles] . . . would prefer that such information should not be imparted to their military authorities." The Americans had signaled that they did not want to know the details of British military preparations. British officials assumed this was intended to save face should awkward questions arise during the American election campaign.[18]

By the time the conference ended on August 23, sharp divisions had developed in the cabinet. The Egypt Committee had become very secretive, and ministers were worried by the lack of information. Rumors proliferated that Britain was planning military action. Minister of Housing Duncan Sandys begged Eden to better inform the entire cabinet "before it was too late," while Conservative hard-liners and the members of the old Suez Group grumbled that Britain wasn't moving fast enough.[19]

The situation came to a head at the Egypt Committee meeting on August 24, when Minister of Defense Walter Monckton let fly a tirade against the idea that military action was a foregone conclusion. It was clear to all, he said, that the political timetable was being manipulated to facilitate military action. The existing plan required a quick, negative response from Nasser by August 30 to prepare for war by September 10, yet the Menzies mission would not even reach Cairo before September 1. Such time pressure made a farce of any diplomatic procedures.

The Chiefs of Staff and Admiral Mountbatten, the First Sea Lord, were in Monckton's corner. House leader Rab Butler was not happy, and many younger cabinet members were indecisive. Commonwealth Secretary Alec Douglas-

Home reported "a definite wavering in the attitude of some of our colleagues toward the use of force."[20]

Cabinet Secretary Norman Brook also warned Eden that if he wanted cabinet support, he must wait until they had just cause. "It would be a mistake to put the Cabinet at the final fence too soon," he told the prime minister. "At least until we have Nasser's reply I would not ask them to take the final decision."[21]

On August 27, Eden wrote again to Eisenhower. The Russians were using Nasser to further their own plans, he warned, and he must not be allowed to get away with it. "We have many friends in the Middle East and in Africa and others who are shrewd enough to know where the plans of a Nasser or a Mossadegh will lead them," he wrote. "The firmer the front we show together, the greater the chance that Nasser will give way without the need for any resort to force. That is why we were grateful for your policy . . . and why we have to continue our military preparations in conjunction with our French Allies."[22]

Eden's reference to Mossadegh was apt, for the month of August was busy with clandestine planning. The prime minister was paying increasing attention to the secret services, who bolstered his belief that Nasser was an agent of communist revolution throughout the Middle East. The Lucky Break material from MI6, although of dubious origin, continued to wield influence. A ministerial culture of deference and subordination helped stoke Eden's tendency to bypass approved communication channels. Instead of the Foreign Office advising and influencing the prime minister, Eden began using first Kirkpatrick and then Patrick Dean to promote his own agenda.[23]

The intense secrecy was also prompted by the need to protect a sensitive intelligence source. In the spring of 1956, MI5 and Government Communications Headquarters (GCHQ) had planted a listening device in the cipher room of the Egyptian embassy in London. The British were effectively reading the Egyptian ciphers throughout the crisis. Eden's interpretation of Nasser's motives stemmed, in part, from a source he could not even discuss with most of his colleagues.[24]

Plotting against Nasser proceeded apace. While Foreign Office officials continued to coordinate plans with the Americans for isolating Nasser through political and economic measures, their MI6 counterparts secretly explored various schemes for Nasser's overthrow. On August 27, Julian Amery, former intelligence operative, MP, and son-in-law of Harold Macmillan, accompanied two MI6 officers to a meeting in France with Egyptian military contacts. They discussed plans for the assassination of Nasser and his entourage and the restoration of General Naguib as president. There was also a scheme to pump nerve gas into Nasser's headquarters.[25]

With his increasing reliance on private communications and privileged information, Eden's leadership was becoming more informal and impromptu. Information sharing was piecemeal. He spoke directly with Patrick Dean about the covert plans, bypassing Kirkpatrick, Dean's superior at the Foreign Office, and even Lloyd. Between Eden's secret channels, the increasing restriction on information from the Egypt Committee, and the government's public pronouncements about diplomacy, it seemed as if Britain had several foreign policies going on at once.[26]

UN OR SCUA?

Eden planned to approach the UN as soon as Nasser rejected the eighteen-nation proposals, hopefully by early September. At this point, speed was essential. Given the rigid nature of Musketeer, procedures at the UN had to finish quickly to avoid bombs falling "out of the blue" during the UN debate. Lloyd informed Dulles of this on August 28. The same day, Eden was told that the Menzies mission would not arrive in Cairo until September 3. "Oh! These delays!" he cried, his head in his hands.[27]

D-Day would have to be postponed. To add to Eden's frustration, Nasser's intelligence services rounded up most of the MI6 assets in Cairo at the end of August. And just as Menzies and his group finally arrived in the Egyptian capital on September 3, Eden received a devastating letter from Eisenhower warning that he and the American public flatly rejected the use of force.[28]

An irritated Eden wrote back that "we have worked in the closest cooperation with you about this business" to get a peaceful settlement, and "there has never been any question of our suddenly . . . resorting to arms while these processes were at work." He had it on good advice that if Nasser were not stopped, it was only "a matter of months" before revolution would engulf the entire Middle East. The British foresaw a domino-like collapse of Western positions throughout the region, and although Eisenhower might want to wait until Nasser revealed his hand, "this was the argument which prevailed in 1936 and which we both rejected in 1948." Dealing with Nasser now would be far less traumatic than waiting until he held the entire continent.[29]

Eisenhower's letter was leaked to the press. Eden was forced to comment on it publicly the next day. The president's public reticence for military action made the British mobilization efforts look suspiciously like bluff.

Then the British received news from Dulles. In place of an approach to the UN, he now suggested the creation of a users' association (later known as the

Suez Canal Users Association, or SCUA) that would oversee shipping through the canal by means of ships stationed at either end. The shipping dues formerly paid to the Suez Canal Company would now be paid to the users' association. Supposedly this would deprive Nasser of revenues and force the Egyptians to an eventual compromise.

Eden and Lloyd were wary, but they liked the idea. The plan could involve the Americans, provoke Nasser, and achieve international control of the canal. It might give them cause for action and drag the Americans in as well. It was worth a shot.[30]

On September 9, Nasser rejected the earlier Menzies proposals. Britain now had its freedom to approach the UN. The public and most of Parliament expected nothing less. But to Eden's irritation, Dulles seemed to backpedal on his new SCUA proposal. In his public statements he implied that canal users had no legal right to refuse payment to the Egyptian authority. From Eden's perspective, this would not do at all.[31]

The clock was ticking. Eden had recalled Parliament for an emergency session on September 12. All the world was expecting him to announce a move to the UN. Now he had to decide whether to go for the SCUA option instead.

The day before the parliamentary debate, Eden and Lloyd met with Mollet and French foreign minister Christian Pineau at 10 Downing Street. The French were convinced Dulles was using SCUA as a stalling tactic. Dulles had agreed that Egyptian interference with SCUA would return each signatory power's "liberty of action," but he had given no blanket endorsement for retaliatory measures by Britain and France.

Pineau, a renowned Resistance fighter and survivor of Buchenwald, insisted, "We are really wasting our time talking to the Americans . . . they will never authorize any action likely to provoke the fall of Nasser, at any rate until after the American elections . . . our two countries should now go firmly ahead on our chosen path."

Eden, too, was concerned about delaying tactics, but he still believed that endorsing SCUA would provide diplomatic gains vis-à-vis the Americans. The meeting adjourned with a decision to back SCUA provided the United States accepted equal responsibility for it. Failing that, they would go to the UN.[32]

Eden's presentation of the SCUA plan the next day sparked pandemonium in Parliament. MPs suspected Eden was not revealing his true plans, and they demanded clarification. There were reports of British troop deployments to the Mediterranean. Was Britain preparing for war?

Eden denied this, but he implied that if Egypt interfered with the users' association, Britain would be free to take forceful steps against it. "You are talking about war!" shouted Opposition ministers. "Deliberate provocation!" "Resign!"[33]

Eden's hint at military action was a misstep. Ambassador Makins had warned that Eisenhower and Dulles would not countenance the use of force, and it was "vitally important" that Eden's statement reflect this. Instead, Eden's words "embarrassed" Dulles and forced him to announce the next day that the United States did not intend to "shoot our way through" the canal.[34]

For Eden, this was maximum betrayal. He had taken the risk of presenting an unpopular plan to Parliament in deference to Dulles only to have Dulles publicly neuter it. The SCUA proposal passed the House of Commons vote, but only just. It began to look as though some Conservatives might side with the Opposition and throw the government into the minority.

Still smarting from his battering in Parliament, Eden now had to grapple with the military planners. Musketeer was in tatters. D-Day had already been postponed twice, and the reservists were demanding to be released back to their civilian lives. After October 6, encroaching winter weather would mean the plan would have to be reworked. General Keightley raised concerns, but Eden told him tartly to "mind his own business." Yet he was forced to accept Keightley's demand that Britain find a military plan that could be held in readiness almost indefinitely.[35]

The result was Musketeer Revise. An attack would kick off with a sustained Anglo-French bombing campaign (the original Musketeer had called for an amphibious landing at the outset). The eventual landing would now take place again at Port Said, not Alexandria.

Revise relied heavily on the assumption that the Egyptians would not fight. This belief was pervasive throughout the British political establishment. Eden and his ministers believed Nasser would quickly be overthrown and the Egyptians would give up. This information came from both MI6 and their old friend Nuri, who told Eden it would be "in the Egyptian character" for Nasser to resign as soon as he was attacked.[36]

But the task force commanders believed otherwise. A bombing campaign was politically impossible, and they were convinced the Egyptian army or armed civilians would not be so easily intimidated. In retrospect, Air Marshal Barnett was blunt: "The plan for Musketeer (Revise) was dictated to the Force Commanders as a result of political limitations and was never considered by them to be a sound military operation."[37]

Meanwhile, Britain continued to seek ways to provoke the Egyptians into making a false move. The Western pilots in the Canal Zone were scheduled to depart in early September. If traffic through the canal fell apart under Egyptian control, Britain and France would have their trigger. Eden solicited a plan from Transportation Secretary Harold Watkinson to deliberately hamper canal traffic, allowing Britain to move in to clear the jam caused by Egyptian "bungling." The cabinet approved the plan on September 10, but both Eden and Watkinson ignored warnings that the Egyptians were perfectly capable of running the canal. When Western pilots departed on September 15, the canal continued to operate smoothly despite the obvious and embarrassing swarm of British ships demanding passage that day.[38]

ALLIES DIVERGE

A second conference convened in London on September 19. Discussions swiftly turned to the details of SCUA. Dulles managed to smooth away the sinister tinge, so much so that participating countries began commenting on how cooperative the association would be with Egypt.

This caused heavy hearts in Whitehall. It seemed as if Dulles was constantly pulling the rug out from under SCUA. To make matters worse, Dulles told Lloyd after the conference ended that Britain and France should set up a new political warfare group that would aim for Nasser's removal in six months. An exasperated Lloyd countered that British and other public opinion was clamoring for a session of the UN Security Council, and SCUA would suffer if the UN was ignored.

Eden decided it was time to move without the Americans. With Dulles heading back to Washington, he now instructed Lloyd to put together a hasty request for a Security Council meeting, a necessary step before Britain could go to war against Egypt. Lloyd confirmed French agreement and sent the message to the Security Council in New York while Dulles's plane was still over the Atlantic.[39]

Eden knew what Dulles's reaction would be, and he tried to soften the blow. He sent a cable as Dulles was still en route, asserting that the Russians were on the verge of making the same move themselves. For Britain to be taken to the Security Council as defendants would be a diplomatic defeat. Not only that, the French were upset by the outcome of the conference, and "it is our duty to the French Government to help them."[40]

Dulles wasn't buying it. Once on the ground in Washington, he informed Ambassador Makins frostily that U.S. intelligence sources had found no evidence to support Eden's claim that the Russians would approach the UN. He was doubly concerned because he had no idea what Britain and France intended to ask the Security Council to do.[41]

As Britain prepared to go to the UN, with the possibility of war to follow, Macmillan drew Eden's attention to the United Kingdom's worsening financial situation. If the canal were cut off or permanently closed, it would be disastrous for sterling and the guarantee of oil supplies. Foreign Office mandarins believed it was an existential crisis. "If Middle Eastern oil is denied to us for a year or two, our gold reserves will disappear," warned Kirkpatrick. "If our gold reserves disappear, the sterling area disintegrates. If the sterling area disintegrates and we have no reserves, we shall not be able to maintain a force in Germany, or indeed, anywhere else. I doubt whether we shall be able to pay for the bare minimum necessary for our defence. And a country that cannot provide for its defence is finished."[42]

Macmillan was right to raise a warning flag. By the end of September, the economic problems most feared by British officials were beginning to become acute. Sterling's status as a reserve currency was under threat, particularly since the biggest sterling holders were Arab states and oil-related corporations. Dulles offered a loan from the U.S. Export-Import Bank to cover potential shortages, but British officials were hesitant to take on more debt.[43]

Military action would result in ruptured pipelines, sabotage, and oil shortages from the Middle East. Britain did not have sufficient dollar reserves to buy oil from American sources for very long. Yet the Middle East Emergency Committee set up in Washington at the end of July had continued to meet during August and September. As a result, Macmillan believed American financial support was solid. A lengthy crisis would have more damaging effects on the British economy than a quick military action; the early use of force was construed as one way to protect the economy.[44]

After the second London conference to approve the SCUA plan ended on September 21, Macmillan traveled to Washington for meetings with IMF and Treasury officials. On the morning of September 25, he slipped through a side door at the White House for a thirty-five-minute meeting with Eisenhower. Their conversation barely touched on Suez.

Then Macmillan went to the State Department. Dulles "vented his spleen" about Britain's move to the Security Council. He wanted a return to the plan to isolate Nasser in the Arab world. Privately, he told Macmillan that the United States would proceed with its political and economic efforts against Nasser after the November 6 election and warned that the U.S. government would not support a "showdown" with Nasser before then. Robert Murphy repeated this message in later talks. If the British government held off until after the election, "Between us, we should be able to encompass [Nasser's] downfall within a few months," he said. "It was high time that Nasser's pretensions and those of the Arab states were deflated."[45]

Macmillan reported to Eden that, with the upcoming election, Eisenhower would not, or could not, object if Britain and France moved against Nasser. This was a deliberate gloss on Eisenhower's mood. Eisenhower himself had not actually said any such thing to Macmillan.

Dulles had tried to focus Macmillan on the economic dangers of Nasser's reaction, which might include closing the canal. Macmillan dodged the issue. "I did not think it necessary to argue this point," he wrote, "for I did not wish to be drawn into a discussion of what our British reaction would be if Nasser refused passage to our ships. I thought this had better be left until it happened."[46]

As Chancellor of the Exchequer, Macmillan bore ultimate responsibility for ensuring that Britain was financially secure in the face of her planned assault against Egypt. The numbers did not look good. But British Treasury officials and the Foreign Office believed Macmillan's assertions that they could count on active American help or at least American passivity. Macmillan made no protective moves, such as drawing on British reserves with the IMF. His reassuring cables to Eden reinforced the prime minister's perception that America would stand behind her ally. Macmillan may have been hoping that covert plans against Nasser would come to fruition before an economic reckoning was necessary.[47]

While Macmillan was in Washington, Eden and Lloyd were also trying to placate the French. On September 24, Pineau again brought up the idea of Israeli participation in Musketeer. Eden and Lloyd flatly rejected it. Two days later, a stormy meeting in Paris led Eden to conclude that the French "are in the mood to blame everyone, including us, if military action is not taken before the end of October."[48]

To plan strategy for the UN move and beyond, the Egypt Committee met on October 1. Eden suggested they frame the argument in Cold War terms. He had sent a cable to Eisenhower along those lines, urging him to recognize the threat of Soviet influence in the Middle East and the dangers of another Munich if Nasser remained. He added that "there is no doubt in our minds that Nasser, whether he likes it or not, is now effectively in Russian hands, just as Mussolini was in Hitler's. It would be as ineffective to show weakness to Nasser now in order to placate him, as it was to show weakness to Mussolini."[49]

The next day, Dulles again made a public statement that infuriated Eden. Discussing SCUA before a group of journalists, he claimed "there is talk about the teeth being pulled out of it. There were no teeth in it." To make matters worse, he admitted that the United States, France, and Britain were treaty allies in some parts of the world, but not all. When it came to issues of "so-called colonialism . . . the United States play a somewhat independent role."[50]

The British public went wild with indignation. The Americans were naïve, unfaithful, inept. A wave of anti-Americanism swept the country.

For Eden, it was in some ways the final blow. Despite Dulles's attempts at apology, the prime minister was angry and shocked, appalled that Dulles could think Eden's determination for international control of the canal stemmed from a latent colonialism. "It was I who ended the 'so-called colonialism,'" he sputtered. "We have leaned over backwards to go along with him. And now look. How on earth can you work with people like that? It leaves us in a quite impossible position. We can't go on like this."[51]

LAST CHANCE AT THE UN

The UN debate opened in New York on October 5. Lloyd and Pineau had a series of frank talks with Dulles before the beginning of the proceedings. Lloyd, more dovish than his prime minister, insisted to Dulles that Britain was approaching the UN in a genuine effort at resolution, and the group agreed to a week of discussions with the Egyptians; some secret, some public. If they could get the Egyptians to agree to negotiations based on the eighteen-nation proposals, there might be room for a settlement. In the Security Council chamber, Britain and France presented their case. Then the council adjourned for the weekend.

That evening in London, Eden went to visit his wife, who was at that moment an inpatient at University College Hospital. There he was suddenly struck with a severe attack of cholangitis, a potentially life-threatening infection of the bile duct. He went into rigor, shaking uncontrollably; his fever spiked to 106 degrees. This was a dangerous moment. Eden had suffered a similar, less severe attack on August 20, during the first London conference. At that time, after an excruciating night, he had been given pethidine, an opioid painkiller, and his daily dose of the amphetamine Drynamil had been increased. Now he was confined in the hospital for the weekend, to be released only on the evening of Monday, October 8.[52]

His illness did not prevent him from weighing in on events in New York.

He was now totally disillusioned with Dulles's stalling. "I think we must never forget," he wrote Lloyd from his hospital bed, "that Dulles's purpose is different from ours. The Canal is in no sense vital to the United States and his game is to string us along at least until Polling Day."[53]

When further reports from Lloyd indicated that possibilities for compromise might develop, Eden was leery. "When I read the record of your conversation with Dulles and Pineau on October 5 it made me fear more than ever that our position is being eroded," he cabled. "We have been misled so often by Dulles's ideas that we cannot afford to risk another misunderstanding."[54]

Eden could not afford a diplomatic solution to the crisis if it did not get rid of Nasser as well. He ordered Lloyd to stick with the French, no matter what, as the private meetings continued in New York.

Lloyd struggled to comply, finding the French "utterly unreasonable" in the initial days of the talks. He complained that Pineau "came late, went early, made difficulties about long meetings and spent considerable time . . . arguing about some obviously false point." He cabled to Eden, "I doubt whether Pineau really believes that a peaceful settlement is possible and I am not entirely convinced that he wants one."

Lloyd was correct. When Lloyd suggested compromise on international control of the canal, Pineau urged Eden to rein in his foreign minister.[55]

Even as he awaited news of the debate in New York, Eden had new fires to extinguish in Jordan. After bloody Israeli-Jordanian border clashes in September, King Hussein had hinted he might need to invoke the defense treaty with Britain. Publicly, Eden had supported Hussein. Privately, he indicated it would be delicate for Britain to come to Jordan's aid at this time.

Hussein had promptly approached Nasser instead. So Eden frantically cabled his ally, Nuri, in Iraq to secure the offer of an Iraqi division for Jordan. Jordan and Iraq had begun talks, with British mediation, in late September. But the Israelis viewed the arrival of the Iraqi troops as a threat. If Israel took military action to prevent the deployment, Britain would, in turn, be obligated by treaty to attack Israel. But Israel was close to France, whom Britain needed to solve the Suez problem.

Eden managed to get the Israelis to accept some Iraqi troops in Jordan. On October 7 Nuri called again for Israel to withdraw back to the original partition boundaries of 1947. Foreign Minister Golda Meir promptly withdrew her assent to the Iraqi troops.

The torment of simultaneous British preparations for war against both Egypt and Israel was becoming intolerable. Britain would have to choose between Musketeer and the fulfillment of its commitment to Jordan. On October 10, General Templer warned that "we could either go to the aid of Jordan against Israel or we could launch Musketeer, we could not do both." The situation worsened during the night of October 10–11, when Israeli commando units launched a ferocious attack on a police fort near Qalqilya in Jordan, leaving 100 dead.

For Eden, the situation was spiraling out of control. It seemed Nasser might get away with it, after all. The negotiations at the UN were going all too well. The Egyptians were being reasonable. The forces to attack Egypt had been held in readiness for far too long. On October 12, the Chiefs of Staff requested further changes to Musketeer, this time in the form of a winter plan that would release the increasingly restive reservists and make a beach landing impossible between November 15 and the spring of 1957. And, of course, Nasser was still alive and well in Cairo.

As the private negotiations continued at the UN, the annual Conservative Party Conference gathered at Llandudno, on the rocky northern coast of Wales. Eden had recovered well enough from his breakdown the previous weekend to make the long journey to Wales. Once there, he was pressured by more hawkish ministers to publicly deny the apparent softening of the British approach. Either Egypt must agree to the eighteen-nation plan or Britain must fight.

At the traditional closing speech on October 13, Eden carefully defended the role of the UN while also defending the military preparations he had undertaken. Britain had shown restraint, but he would stand by his principle that the canal could not be under the control of a single nation. His words soothed his audience, and he finished to great applause.

Just before his speech, Eden had received a call from his aide, Anthony Nutting, who was still at the prime minister's country home, Chequers. Mollet wanted him to meet two French emissaries, whom he would send over the next day. Eden agreed.

Upon his return to Chequers that evening, Eden learned from Nutting that the French had secretly delivered seventy-five of their latest Mystère fighter jets to Israel without clearance with the United Kingdom and the United States, as required under the Tripartite Agreement. Eden wondered aloud if the French were bolstering the Israelis to attack Jordan. The Foreign Office experts thought this might be a possibility.[56]

At the UN, Britain and France felt increasingly cornered. Dulles told Lloyd that, even with SCUA, 90 percent of the revenue of the canal would be given to the Egyptians. Now SCUA really seemed completely useless for British purposes. Lloyd was stunned. "I cannot believe that it is what you really intend," he wrote to Dulles. "But we must face the fact that revelation of so grave a divergence between us on the purposes of SCUA would have serious repercussions in Britain."[57]

TURNING POINT: MEETING AT CHEQUERS

Hours after the heated exchange between Dulles and Lloyd, Eden took a fateful step. Mollet's emissaries arrived at Chequers. They turned out to be General Maurice Challe, deputy chief of staff of the French air force, and the French acting foreign minister, Albert Gazier. They began by telling Eden the Israelis were nervous about the pending arrival of the Iraqi troops in Jordan; Eden agreed to postpone their deployment by 48 hours.

Then the French asked if Britain would come to Egypt's aid under the Tripartite Agreement if Israel were to attack Egypt. Eden replied that he could hardly see himself fighting for Colonel Nasser. Britain would come to Jordan's aid if it were attacked, but certainly would not help Egypt.

Nutting then asked why the French believed the Israelis would attack Egypt. There was a long pause. Eden instructed his private secretary to stop taking notes.

Challe now proposed a plan: Israel would invade the Sinai Peninsula and move toward the Suez Canal Zone. British and French forces would pose to the world as peacekeepers, seizing the canal from Port Said to Suez in order to separate the combatants.[58]

Exhausted, irritable, and increasingly ill, Eden reached for a lifeline.

Observations on Part Two

PHILIP ZELIKOW

As in Part One, we have tried to restrict the viewpoints to the knowledge, beliefs, and actions the leaders would have known about at the time, reserving commentary on them. Here, though, are a few observations about the developments in Part Two, again organized around the three kinds of judgments that form an appreciation of a situation.

VALUE JUDGMENTS

In this stage, the six capitals still see their problems in very different ways. In all the capitals but Cairo, the new ingredient is to consider how much they really care about Cairo's nationalization of the canal.

In different ways, neither Jerusalem nor Moscow cares much about canal issues per se. The Israelis are not being allowed to use the canal anyway, and the Soviets do not rely much on it. The issue is instrumental to other things they do care about.

Paris cares a good deal more about the canal, but French leaders are similarly instrumental about the matter, practically from the start. For them, Nasser has overreached, and there is now a good chance to deal with him.

Other than Egypt, the country most concerned about the canal issue itself is Britain. The chapter on the view from London gives a good sense of what is weighing on Eden and his colleagues in government.

Politics and personalities aside, two particularly substantive issues stand out: British stature in the region and the security of vital oil supplies. Since Eden, at least, has also come to share the French view of Nasser as a sort of new Mussolini, this brings basic values into play—shadowed by memories of the 1930s and the 1940s—about how to deal with a dictator whose aggressive moves should be stopped sooner rather than later. Some of his colleagues agree strongly with this sort of view, but others do not.

The American attitude would have been the hardest to predict beforehand. In the first days after Nasser's announcement, American evaluations seem to fluctuate, from person to person or one day to the next. After about a week, though, Eisenhower's measured assessment—visible from the start—hardens into firm guidance.

By this time Dulles is already in London working on the next diplomatic steps with his usual skill. Dulles's own uncertain compass bearings seem strongly influenced by the British and French magnetic pull while he is there planning with them.

Yet he gets clear settings from the president once he returns home a few days later, still in early August. The basic U.S. value judgment remains constant for the next two months, as described throughout Part Two, which is that the Egyptian takeover of the canal is fundamentally tolerable and that a way should be found for all to tolerate it.

But the main action of Part Two is a complicated interplay of diplomatic and military plans. Each of these is a compound of various "reality" and "action" judgments. These expressed themselves through crucial choices in policy design.

POLICY DESIGNS

By the middle of August, when Dulles returns to London for the big conference, he is already devising strategies to tolerate Nasser's move and avoid war. While there, however, he drifts along with the tough proposal for full international control of the canal. This was the basic design, of French and British origin, he had gone along with weeks earlier. But back then it was expected Nasser would refuse, thus opening the way to war. The design no longer meshed well if the strategy was to avoid a conflict.

During the conference Dulles deflects two opportunities to make a major change of course toward diplomatic compromise. First, while Dulles was in London, Eisenhower suggests that the United States seek an international advisory approach rather than insist on direct international management. Eisenhower may not have known that such an approach would line up with what the

Soviets and Indians were pushing. He certainly could not have known that just such a diplomatic approach would finally be hammered out about two months later at the UN.

But Dulles pushes back against his president's suggestion on such a specific matter, not wanting to go back to his British and French colleagues and retract the stance he had already associated himself with in public. Far from the negotiations, Eisenhower defers to his man on the spot.

Second, Dulles declines the informal suggestion—put forward by Macmillan, for example—that Dulles himself should go to Cairo with the London conference proposal with real authority to hammer out a deal with Nasser. Dulles does not want to be on the spot in that way. So Menzies goes, but he cannot be much more than a messenger.

When Nasser rejected the London demands, Dulles then displays persistent ingenuity in trying scheme after scheme that might win general acceptance, right up through the October negotiations at the UN. At this point his diplomacy is certainly in line with what Eisenhower wanted, as Dulles keeps trying to string the allies along, sure that delay will reduce the odds for a war. He is right about that, almost.

At the end of Part Two he and Eisenhower believe they have succeeded.

The Cairo and Moscow positions in Part Two are relatively straightforward: resist. Moscow is somewhat distracted.

What is remarkable is how risky Cairo's position is and how much it depends on attitudes in Washington. Cairo's dependence on Washington seems all the more ironic since, it will be remembered, Washington's hostility to Nasser is supposed to have precipitated the crisis in the first place, with the brusque Aswan Dam move.

Nasser is getting some reassuring information from his American contacts, so his assessment of American opposition to a war is not baseless. But he is fortunate that the original military operation against him, planned for September, was delayed for reasons that have little to do with Cairo.

The first critical pause in the British and French invasion plans occurs at the end of August and in early September, mainly because of British hesitancy. The reasons are primarily political, reckoning with the strength and implications of Eisenhower's opposition.

But the delay is also partly military, because these particular military plans are elaborate and cautious, perhaps unnecessarily so. The crisis caught Britain without useful contingency plans and in relatively poor readiness for action in

Egypt. Britain's military chief, Lord Mountbatten, may be risk-averse, or perhaps is not really on board with the plan, looking for reasons to stall.

Once the invasion fleet launches it will require a voyage of about a week from Malta, and sufficient forces have not yet been pre-positioned closer to Egypt under the cover of exercises. The British overestimate Egyptian military strength and worry (mistakenly) that Soviet bloc soldiers may be manning Egyptian tanks. Then the military plans are profoundly overhauled in September, as Musketeer becomes Musketeer Revise. More delay.

By the middle of September it is Paris that becomes the main driver of the moves toward war. Note the assessment failure in Washington, Cairo, and even in Moscow. All underestimate France. Even as they might very dimly sense the growing cooperation between France and Israel, they do not grasp what plans could logically follow from it.

They do not reckon with how energetically France might compose an anti-Egypt coalition. The failure is not just in underestimating French political determination; that they understand better. They underestimate French military capability. The French move quickly. And if the French military can get there, with nearby bases for air operations or parachute drops or amphibious support, its forces are motivated and capable.

As energetic as the American diplomacy has been during September and the first half of October, it is the French efforts that—for better or worse—are more creative in their policy designs. Note how the French have developed ideas that thoroughly understand and try to address Israel's problem, as Jerusalem sees it.

Then Paris also devises an approach tailored to Eden's problem, as seen from London. And Eden, fluent in French, is always closer—culturally as well as geographically—to his French counterparts than he is to his American ones.

In contrast, the American diplomacy, for all its energy, had not quite reckoned with other ways to solve Eden's problem. The face-saving side, the aspect of British stature, was being addressed in the various international management, then advisory, schemes.

But if the Americans had come in with a strong international advisory position in mid-August, along with Eisenhower's opposition to a war, the British might have had a chance to calculate where things could end up. They might have accepted such a plan then, lacking a more appealing alternative. By October it was more of a humiliation for Eden to accept the international advisory plan, since it was such a long climb down from the August demands.

Washington does not appear to have moved creatively to address another key issue for London, the security of British oil supplies. There was a bureaucratic process for cooperation in an emergency, which the British would have cause to remember in Part Three. But the Americans did not develop a positive position that Eden could have presented as a reason why he could accept Nasser's "chokehold" on a waterway so vital to Britain's economy.

As Part Two ends, much of Britain and even some of Eden's government are now ready to accept a diplomatic settlement along the lines worked out in the UN. At that moment it is the French who throw Eden a lifeline of political and military possibility. Eden grabs for it, joining in a maneuver that none of his colleagues in London have foreseen. It is also a plan that, at that point, the Israeli prime minister stoutly opposes. It is the French who must somehow bring them all together.

PART THREE

What to Do about the War

OCTOBER 15 TO NOVEMBER 6, 1956

TIMELINE OF PUBLIC EVENTS

OCTOBER 28   Israeli forces strike deep into Egypt's Sinai desert.

OCTOBER 30   Britain and France deliver ultimatum to Egypt and Israel demanding that they stop fighting and withdraw their forces from the area near the Suez Canal.

OCTOBER 30   Britain and France veto UN Security Council action on Suez.

OCTOBER 31   Britain and France begin air attacks on Egyptian targets. The Israeli advance continues.

OCTOBER 31   The Suez issue is transferred to the UN General Assembly.

NOVEMBER 1   Hungarian leader Nagy announces Hungary's withdrawal from the Soviet bloc. Soviets and allies prepare a military assault against Budapest.

NOVEMBER 3   The Syrian president visits Moscow and receives a public pledge of assistance.

NOVEMBER 4   The UN General Assembly passes resolutions demanding a cease-fire and UN peacekeeping force.

NOVEMBER 4   Massive Soviet-led invasion of Hungary begins.

NOVEMBER 5   French and British paratroopers land in the Canal Zone and begin fighting.

NOVEMBER 5   Soviets request the United States join them in intervention in the Suez war. Eisenhower issues a public statement warning the Soviets not to intervene.

NOVEMBER 6   Election Day in the United States. Eisenhower is reelected.

NOVEMBER 6   British and French amphibious forces begin going ashore into Egypt. Khrushchev sends threatening letters to Israeli, British, and French leaders.

PART THREE

JERUSALEM

PHILIP ZELIKOW

THE FRENCH PERSUASION: OCTOBER 15–24

On October 15 the Israeli leadership found itself juggling a public crisis involving Jordan and a private crisis over what to do about Egypt. The public was still debating the aftermath of the Qalqilya reprisal raid into Jordan that had been so difficult and costly. That debate included the danger that, had the fighting in Jordan continued, Britain would have intervened militarily on Jordan's side—probably with damaging air attacks—under the terms of Britain's defense treaty with Jordan.

On top of all that there were still scares about possible movement of Iraqi troops into Jordan, supposedly to help Jordan stand up to Israel. Some Israelis feared the Iraqis, perhaps with British connivance, might be thinking of trying to take over Jordan, as the culmination of a year of political crisis and instability in that weakened monarchy.

On October 15 Ben-Gurion addressed the Knesset. His speech, initiating two days of parliamentary debate, concentrated on the Jordan crisis, defended the Qalqilya raid, attacked the British interference, and made it clear that Israel would take some sort of action if the Iraqis intervened in Jordan in force. He said Israel wanted to avoid a war.

The sharpest criticism came from the right. Menachem Begin, the leader of the Herut party, who was in favor of a preventive war that would give Israel safer borders, condemned what he characterized as the half-measures of the

231

Labour coalition government. After the debate closed, Ben-Gurion congratulated himself (in his diary) that every party except Begin's and the Communists had "accepted the Government position," a degree of consensus he believed had never been seen before in the Knesset.[1]

While that public argument was going on, Ben-Gurion was privately grappling with the problem of what to do about Egypt. Secret Israeli military plans for Operation Kadesh, the Sinai offensive against Egypt, were now well advanced. These plans had been put together, on the Israeli side, in the expectation of a joint offensive, launched concurrently along with the French. The offensive would involve direct French air and naval support as well as the simultaneous offensive that the French (and, it was hoped, the British) would be launching against the Canal Zone.

The Israelis heard firsthand how disgusted the French were with the outcome of the UN Security Council debate in New York. While still in New York and about to return to Paris, France's foreign minister, Pineau, told a secret Israeli visitor, the chief of military intelligence, that he and his government favored going ahead with the war plan. Pineau told his visitor, Ben-Gurion noted in his diary, that "he had not let the British into the picture with the actual joint plan of Israel and France, but he estimates that they suspect something. It will be difficult to hide the preparations for war. Pineau does not see the possibility of a combined British-French operation except at a later stage."[2]

On October 13, the French began dispatching to Israel three cargo ships loaded with hundreds of tanks, half-tracks, trucks, and a wealth of other equipment. They would start arriving and begin being unloaded on October 20. In his parliamentary address Ben-Gurion had alluded vaguely to fresh supplies of arms (which many in the army and air force would have known about), but he gave no details.

On October 15, as Ben-Gurion was kicking off the Knesset debate, French defense officials—including General Challe—briefed Israel's representative about their remarkable discussions at Chequers the previous day with British prime minister Eden. The French made clear, as gently as they could, that the idea developed with Eden was that Israel would start the war. Then, days later, the British and French would intervene under the pretext of protecting the canal. Although the plan was really a French scheme, with Challe as chief scriptwriter, it came across to the Israelis as something cooked up with or even by the British.

So when Peres presented this new version of the plan to Ben-Gurion on

October 16, the prime minister was furious. It seemed like the "best of British hypocrisy," in that it showed the British were really out to hurt Israel more than to get at Nasser. His initial impulse was to just shut down the whole military plan right then.

Ben-Gurion conferred with a few key ministers (Foreign Minister Meir, Finance Minister Levi Eshkol, and Dayan). Dayan was in favor of going along with this plan (which he may have already suspected was being considered). "If indeed it is the pretext that will make the British co-operate with us, we must be willing to pay the price required."

Dayan wanted to take the idea even further. If the British were to join in the war planning, he sought a broader agreement with them, "destroying Nasser and partitioning Jordan between us and Iraq," Ben-Gurion recorded.

Ben-Gurion did not think much of this idea, either that the British would agree or that Israel should wish to rule more Arabs. He thought the whole thing was "an English plot to get us entangled with Nasser and in the meantime to bring about Jordan's takeover by Iraq." But Ben-Gurion finally wrote back a reply to the French that Israel was still open to a joint action with the British and French, or just with the French, but that he was opposed to this new plan.

The French had also invited Ben-Gurion himself to come to Paris to work on the next steps. Ben-Gurion was willing to journey to Paris on October 21 if Mollet still wanted him to come. But he opposed "the British proposal."[3]

Meanwhile, following up on the Chequers talks, Eden had traveled to Paris and met secretly with Mollet. On October 17, the French debriefed the Israelis about those meetings too. The Israeli officials in Paris relayed the news back home that Eden had agreed on the plan for intervention with France after the "ultimatum to withdraw from the Canal" pretext. Also, the British would stay out of the Israeli fight with Egypt or with Jordan. The British foreign secretary, Lloyd, "was not easy" with all this, "but Eden's opinion was decisive."

What about the United States? Pineau thought the Americans would be angry but would do nothing before their presidential election on November 6. As for Russia, Pineau thought the Russians would not intervene. Mollet looked forward to welcoming Ben-Gurion in Paris.

Ben-Gurion had a lot to consider. With time to think about an agenda for a possible, unprecedented, summit of British, French, and Israeli leaders, Ben-Gurion wondered about larger ideas for restructuring the Middle East, if Britain would cooperate. It was a heady moment for the leader of the new state, who had never before felt that he had any real partners among the major powers. Visions of sugar plums danced in his head.

He now told the French ambassador that the objectives should be to oust Nasser, partition Jordan with Iraq (with the West Bank going to Israel), and make peace with Iraq, which would help resettle Arab refugees. The borders of Lebanon might also be restructured, but he was unclear about what should be done with Syria.[4]

Ben-Gurion arrived secretly in France on October 21. He told Challe, who had come to Israel to escort him on the trip, that he still had no use for "the British proposal." If that was all that was on the table, then "the only advantage of my trip to France will be that I get to make the acquaintance of your Prime Minister."[5]

Meanwhile, in public, Israel continued to make a fuss over possible Iraqi moves into Jordan. At this time Ben-Gurion and Dayan genuinely believed that, as Dayan put it in a conversation with the French, "The truth is that Jordan is falling apart and the English have reached the conclusion that Jordan should be written off as an independent country, and Iraq should take its place."

But the worry about Iraqi moves into Jordan also became partly theatrical, perhaps as a diversion. Ben-Gurion ostentatiously called home the Israeli ambassadors to the United States, Britain, France, and the USSR for consultations on the Jordan border issue and wrote to Eisenhower on October 20 asking for help with this problem.[6]

In Paris, Ben-Gurion was accompanied only by members of his own staff, plus Dayan and a few other defense and military aides. The meeting was to be kept secret, even from the Israeli cabinet. The venue was a villa in Sèvres, a suburb about six miles southwest of the center of Paris. Since his appearance was so recognizable, Ben-Gurion did not set foot outside the villa during the days he was there. Dayan, staying in a hotel, took off his eye patch when he left the villa and wore sunglasses. The villa was owned by a family with deep ties to the French Resistance movement during the war. Someday, one of the French aides mentioned, he hoped that the Sèvres conference would be famous; he just hoped it would not be famous the way "Yalta" or "Munich" were famous.[7]

The first meeting, on October 22, was just between the Israeli and French leadership. Ben-Gurion outlined what he himself called his "fantastic" plan to reorder the Middle East. He wanted the participants to think big. But his plans also imagined a deliberate campaign after more weeks of preparation. He also still wanted to formulate a plan "that Eisenhower would not oppose or would at least tacitly accept by remaining silent."

The French could not tolerate such delay. Mollet said Ben-Gurion's plan was not "fantastic" and he was willing to accept it.

But "time was pressing." Mollet and his colleagues focused attention back to the plan that was on the table for immediate action. Ben-Gurion still opposed "the British proposal" in which Israel would start the war on its own. The French defended it as the only way to bring the British along. It "took us a long time," Pineau said, "to move Great Britain from a total lack of comprehension to a partial grasp of the issue." All agreed that Britain also had to ensure that, if Jordan jumped into the war, Britain would not help Jordan if Israel counterattacked.

Finally, Ben-Gurion at least allowed Dayan to offer a formula for starting a campaign in Sinai, one that would look more like a large-scale retaliatory raid, plus a parachute drop at the Mitla Pass near Suez. Dayan's formulation was close to what the French wanted to hear.[8]

That evening, British foreign secretary Lloyd, and one aide, joined the discussions. To Dayan, Lloyd "may generally be warm, pleasant, and sociable. If so, he did a good job of hiding it. A more antagonistic exhibition than his is hardly possible. His entire manner conveyed disgust—disgust of the place, of the company, and of the substance of the matter he was compelled to deal with."

Lloyd seemed satisfied with the diplomatic elements that had been worked out in New York for handling the canal issue. But then Lloyd acknowledged that "since Her Majesty's Government considered that Nasser had to go, it was prepared to undertake military action in accordance with the latest version of the Anglo-French plan." And Britain would not protect Jordan.

Ben-Gurion and Lloyd argued about whether Israel should play the role of aggressor. Ben-Gurion then allowed Dayan to reiterate his somewhat more limited idea, for a smaller-scale initial Israeli military move to be the "pretext."

Dayan's suggestion came close to what the British had also been hoping for. Lloyd merely asked that Israeli military action be a "real act of war," so that Britain would not seem like an aggressor.

This was a turning point in the discussion. The talks then descended into a prolonged discussion of how much of a time interval could elapse between the initial Israeli attack and the British and French intervention. Ben-Gurion was anxious about exposing Israeli cities to Egyptian air attack in the interval before Israel could get aid from French air defense. Lloyd had no authorization to allow French aircraft to provide air cover over Israel from British bases in Cyprus, although he could not object to French use of Israeli bases.[9]

Since the two sides seemed stalemated on this point about timing, Lloyd planned to return to London to report the failure to reach agreement. Pineau, not so discouraged, decided to journey to London the next day to work on the issue directly with Eden.

The next day, while awaiting the outcome of the discussions in London, the French and Israelis further refined their common understanding of how the operation might unfold. The French were also busy with a parliamentary debate over an extraordinary operation their government had just carried out, the capture of Algerian rebel leaders by French diversion of a Moroccan government aircraft that had been carrying the rebels to a meeting. But the defense minister was able to secure the French president's formal approval, as required by the French constitution, for France to carry through on the commitments it was making to Israel.

All this Franco-Israeli cooperative work was partly aimed at Ben-Gurion, to reconcile him to the emerging plan. Dayan was doing the same thing internally, explaining further refinements to his operational plans. "As was his wont," one participant remembered, "Ben-Gurion asked many questions and played devil's advocate; but it was obvious that Dayan's plan helped him overcome some of his hesitations." Meanwhile Pineau was using these most recent plans as ammunition for his meeting with Eden in London.[10]

The next morning, October 24, looking "like someone who had recovered from a long and painful illness" but now rose "clad with strength and zeal," Ben-Gurion told the other Israelis he had made his decision. "If measures to protect us from aerial attacks are taken on the first day or two, until the French and the English bomb the Egyptian airfields—it seems to me that the operation must be carried out. This is the only chance that two not-so-small powers will try to destroy Nasser, and we shall not stand alone while he grows stronger and conquers all the Arab world." Ben-Gurion then wrote out lists of questions for further interrogation of "our friends" and "for ourselves."[11]

Ben-Gurion was moved by a series of factors. Among them were surely regard for the new relationship with France; Dayan's operational innovations; British reassurance about Jordan; and the idea of acting in concert with major powers. But under them all "was one fundamental assumption that Ben-Gurion shared with most of the Israeli leadership in 1956: the inevitability of a confrontation between Israel and Nasser's Egypt."[12]

In the afternoon Pineau returned to the talks. Now he was joined by two British officials (Donald Logan, who had been Lloyd's aide on October 22, and Patrick Dean, a senior Foreign Office and intelligence official). They reported success. After some further discussion, a written protocol was prepared. The operation was set to begin with Israeli action at 5 p.m., Israeli time, only five days later, on October 29.

Another agreement was signed that day and ratified shortly afterward by the French cabinet. This agreement, between just the French and Israelis, was to advance French-Israeli nuclear cooperation. The two countries had long had a friendly scientific relationship in the development of nuclear energy. France itself was on the verge of making large decisions about its nuclear future, including whether to build nuclear weapons. This was a topic on which Peres had been playing a key role, working with Ben-Gurion.

At Sèvres, officials from the two countries agreed that the two countries would advance their mutual cooperation. As part of that, France would help Israel build a nuclear reactor in the Negev, at a site called Dimona.[13]

On the flight back to Israel, having already sent orders to put preparations in motion, Dayan rested. He doodled on a piece of paper. He drew a little cartoon in which a gentleman with a top hat labeled "England" and an elegantly dressed lady labeled "France" were making way for a little boy with an Israeli "sabra" hat standing in front of an outline of "Egypt." The gentleman and lady—arms out—gesture toward the boy, with a caption (written in English): "After you."[14]

OPERATION KADESH: OCTOBER 25–NOVEMBER 6

When Dayan arrived back in Israel, he was greeted by news that, after talks in Jordan's capital, Amman, the Egyptians had announced that the heads of the Egyptian, Jordanian, and Syrian militaries had signed an agreement that set up a joint command for all of their armies, under the Egyptian army's chief of staff. The joint command would be activated in the event of war. A few days later, just before war broke out, Israeli aircraft intercepted and shot down an aircraft carrying some of the Egyptian officers who had negotiated this joint command, missing the aircraft that was carrying the Egyptian chief of staff back to Cairo.[15]

By the time Dayan returned to Israel from the secret trip to France, the mobilization of Israeli reserve forces had begun. Israel's regular armed forces were small, but much of the military-age population was prepared for service in the reserves.

Dayan set to work adjusting the operational plans to meet all the political requirements that had secretly been set in place. For example, ordinarily an offensive would begin with air strikes against enemy air power. Instead, in this case, the air role would be limited at the start to a more defensive role. Heavy armored attacks would be held back until the Anglo-French intervention was beginning. And secrecy was paramount.

By Friday, October 26, the call-ups were unmistakable. "The chauffeurs from the foreign embassies were mobilized; the hotels were emptied of employees . . . hundreds of Israelis with . . . backpacks could be seen every morning . . . rushing to their units' assembly points." Out of sight, French military personnel were also arriving at Israeli bases to support their air, naval, and coordinating activities. The initial suppositions mainly were about another flare-up of hostilities against Jordan. Eisenhower sent a message to Ben-Gurion the next day, October 27, pleading that Israel not take any military initiatives.[16]

Meanwhile Ben-Gurion had begun the process of briefing individual ministers and party leaders in his coalition government, in preparation for a full cabinet discussion and decision on whether to go to war. That cabinet meeting occurred on Sunday, October 28. There were sixteen ministers, nine from Ben-Gurion's Mapai party and the remainder from four other small parties. The cabinet ultimately approved the decision by a vote of fourteen to two, although the opponents—both from the Mapam (Israel Workers) party—agreed to stay in the government and share in its collective decision. The discussion was extensive and intense.[17]

Ben-Gurion delivered a thorough initial presentation of the reasons for war, with particular emphasis on the closing of the Straits of Tiran and the *fedayeen* raids. He disclosed the basic elements of the Sèvres agreement with the French and British, and he hoped that, as a result of the British and French actions, Nasser would be overthrown.

He reviewed the pros and cons of taking advantage of what he called "a unique historical opportunity that may never return." He thought the United States would not get involved so close to a presidential election and in opposition to its European allies. He expected that if America stayed out, so would Russia, but "I do not guarantee this." He and his allies insisted that Israel was acting in self-defense and that "I shall not use the term preventive war. We should not have such thoughts."

Ben-Gurion's allies emphasized the European friends. Meir said, "I am standing in awe; I cannot fathom what happened there, that suddenly we the meek, the small and humble became a focal point." While she trusted France, she admitted it was practically a good deed (a "mitzvah') "to suspect Britain." But Britain "cannot betray us without betraying France."

Ben-Gurion admitted that Israel would not have gone to war on its own.

If the French had not pressed to move, "it would not have come from me, because I wanted to get more arms." He might have preferred to wait another six months, but "the date was chosen by them."

The Russian and American issues both were discussed. The opponents believed the Russians would not be so distracted by Hungary that they would not intervene. There was even more discussion of the danger of U.S. opposition.

Ben-Gurion conceded that "most of all I am worried about America. America will force us to withdraw. America does not need to send military forces. America can say that she is breaking diplomatic relations, stopping Israeli fund raising, loan guarantees and more, she will consider what's more important to her—we or the Arabs."

Ben-Gurion and most of the cabinet felt the country was under siege. The siege had to be broken, even if the ultimate outcome was uncertain. "We know how we start, but there is no guarantee how it will end." But perhaps the war might give Israel a quiet period of five to eight years to concentrate on domestic concerns, building up the new country.[18]

On October 29, D-Day for Operation Kadesh, Ben-Gurion formally responded to Eisenhower's letter of the 27th, even as the American ambassador was about to deliver another Eisenhower letter (dispatched on October 28) that began to add warnings. Ben-Gurion blamed Nasser for the "ring of steel" around Israel and asked for understanding if Israel took "all necessary measures to ensure that the declared Arab aim of eliminating Israel by force should not come about."[19]

As planned, at 5 p.m. on October 29, the first contingent of IDF paratroopers dropped near the Mitla Pass, in the central part of the Sinai Peninsula, and quickly secured both ends of the pass after a difficult battle. The Israeli military operations unfolded generally according to plan and with initial success. The French and British had immediately issued their ultimatum on the night of October 29, and their air operations began early on October 31. At the same time, Israeli forces were encountering the most challenging Egyptian opposition near the coast road leading into Gaza.

Nasser had kept much of his force in the Canal Zone area, worried about British and French attack. The Egyptians had been surprised by the Israeli attack—as the Israelis had hoped and expected. Egyptian forces had moved to meet the Israeli threat.

Early on October 31, now fearing that imminent Anglo-French intervention would trap his forces in Sinai fighting the Israelis, Nasser ordered all his forces to withdraw east, over the canal, back toward the Nile Delta and Cairo. This decision then broke up the Egyptian fighting front against the Israelis. Since the Israelis also already controlled, by air or ground, the main transportation routes out of Sinai, the Egyptian forces in Sinai disintegrated as they tried to retreat under fire, and their retreat became a rout.

Having encountered some initially fierce opposition, the British delayed most of their air operations against Egyptian airfields during October 31, which caused Ben-Gurion—who had fallen ill—to practically explode with anger. Dayan helped calm him down and the British and French raids, which were quite effective, began later in the day and continued into the next. Some of these raids were conducted by the French from their Israeli bases. Israeli aircraft studiously avoided any air operations west of the Suez Canal.[20]

By the end of the day on October 31, the Israeli military campaign was on the road to complete victory. All of its objectives in the Sinai Peninsula would be attained. The fighting in Sinai had subsided by the end of the day on Friday, November 2, and the main front for engagement had become political and diplomatic.

The Eisenhower administration's reaction to Israel's moves was immediate and negative. Israel's ambassador to the United States (and the UN), Abba Eban, had been kept in the dark about the planned operations. On October 29, as the war began, he reported that Eisenhower felt "a deep crisis of confidence with Israel." His trust in Ben-Gurion was undermined and he was deeply offended that his last-minute messages had been disregarded. America's commitment to defend any nation against aggression under the Tripartite Declaration, mentioned in April with Israel in mind, might now be turned against Israel. American Jewish leaders, Eban reported, also felt "considerable embarrassment" and did not understand the reasons for the war.

In another channel, Eban's deputy—and a former chief of Israeli foreign intelligence—said that a White House confidant (unnamed) had also stressed that the president was angry that Israel had tried to pull the wool over his eyes and exploit the delicate election situation. On the other hand, this person said there were hopes that Nasser might be dealt a painful blow. It was assumed the Israelis were working with France. Nasser had to be dealt a "lightning blow" because, if the crisis continued, this person predicted that the administration would adopt an anti-Israel line.[21]

By October 30, Eisenhower—who cut off direct contact with the Israeli embassy—chose to communicate to Ben-Gurion through the head of the Zionist Organization of America, Abba Hillel Silver. His message was that Israel should promptly withdraw.

Israel might think its interests momentarily converged with Britain and France. But in the long run "Israel's strength and future are connected rather with the United States."

Ben-Gurion replied that Israeli forces would withdraw when Egypt was ready to address the various issues, which he listed, that had prompted Israel's actions.[22]

By October 31 Eban's battlefield was the UN. Britain and France had vetoed action in the UN Security Council. The United States moved the offensive to the full UN General Assembly. Without a formal announcement, the United States suspended all economic assistance to Israel through official channels.

Meanwhile Eban was beginning to work with Dulles on ideas for possible guarantees to Israel, for instance on freedom of navigation, if Israel did withdraw. Eban cabled back that if military operations could quickly be concluded successfully, he thought the United States might move closer to the British and French positions.[23]

By November 2, having accomplished their own military objectives, the Israelis were waiting impatiently for the British and French to begin their ground operations against Egypt in the Canal Zone. Pressured by the UN to at least accept a cease-fire, the Israeli government decided on November 3 that it was willing to yield to UN pressure and accept a cease-fire, should other countries agree. This angered the British and French, who had not yet landed their ground forces in Egypt. The French defense minister wanted to know, "Does Israel know that in principle this step has changed the whole situation?" Ben-Gurion then hastily tried to retract Israel's cease-fire announcement and make it conditional.[24]

The UN initiatives then went further. Picking up on the British and French pretext of separating the combatants, the United States and UN secretary-general Hammarskjöld supported a resolution (sponsored by Canada) to create a UN Emergency Force that would move into Sinai. On November 3 Britain, France, and Israel began coming around to acceptance of this force, believing their own troops might help make up that force until others could be found and deployed.

Hammarskjöld and his staff developed and submitted their UN Emergency Force plan on November 5. It would not use any British, French, or Israeli forces. The UN Emergency Force plan was immediately adopted by the UN General Assembly.

That same day, with British and French beginning their landings in Egypt (beginning with a parachute drop that day), Eban was authorized to accept an unconditional cease-fire. Britain and France were also promising that their forces would help ensure an Israeli withdrawal from Sinai.

Eban saw indications that the United States might not only withhold its own aid to Israel but also interfere with Israeli private fundraising, Eban warned that "this will be a very difficult battle" and "that preparations should be made for it in all seriousness." Eban was instructed to resist the idea of a UN Emergency Force taking over Sinai.[25]

On November 5, the Soviet Union turned its full attention to Israel for the first time. A letter arrived from the Soviet premier to Ben-Gurion. The Soviet government accused Israel of "playing in an irresponsible and criminal manner" with the fate of the world and its own fate, too. The Soviet government warned that Israel was "placing its very existence in jeopardy."

On the night of November 5–6, the Soviets called for a Security Council resolution that would deliver an ultimatum to the countries engaged in "hostile acts against Egypt." If they did not promptly withdraw, the United States and the Soviet Union would be authorized to go to Egypt with military forces. The Soviet move was voted down by a majority of the council.[26]

With the Soviet threats still not quite absorbed by Israeli leaders or the Israeli public, the mood in the country by the end of the day on November 6 was exultant. Israeli soldiers, making their way through difficult desert conditions, had captured Sharm el Sheikh, at the very southern tip of Sinai, overlooking the Straits of Tiran. The Egyptian guns there were destroyed.

Israelis were still tallying the thousands of Egyptian dead and even more thousands of prisoners, while 172 Israeli soldiers had lost their lives. "At first," Ben-Gurion wrote, "the matter looked like a daydream; then like a legend; finally, like a series of miracles."[27]

CAIRO

JON B. ALTERMAN

When the negotiations at the UN concluded in the middle of October, Egyptian diplomats believed they had won a victory of sorts. The Egyptian strategy since the beginning had been to try to draw out negotiations. Abdel Nasser believed that each passing week made war less likely.

Also, both the Americans and the Soviets had assured the Egyptians that they opposed a military solution. The American support for negotiations helped Egypt avoid being portrayed as a Soviet puppet. It also implied that America's allies would respect their patron's wishes. It wasn't according to plan, but it was perhaps as good an outcome as could be expected. Egypt still had a challenge on its hands, but it didn't have a war on its hands. Nor was the canal being taken away by some international consortium.

UN secretary-general Dag Hammarskjöld had hoped that negotiations between the French, British, and Egyptians would continue in Geneva at the end of October to flesh out a Suez Canal agreement based on the principles that had been agreed upon at the UN Security Council in New York. The Geneva meetings never materialized. The Egyptians believed the British and French wished to abandon any progress that had been made and start over from square one.[1] The French and British continued to spar with the Egyptians over what the goal of negotiations should be. Hammarskjöld did not press for keeping to his original timetable, and the matter hung unresolved.

On October 5, a Turkish official approached the Egyptian military attaché in Ankara at an Italian embassy party and told him the British and French were preparing to attack Egypt in mid-November. The attaché reported this information to Egyptian military intelligence in a cable the next day, but his cable was not treated seriously. He sent subsequent cables. He even traveled to Cairo demanding to meet with Abdel Nasser himself. He was unable to gain an appointment and returned to Ankara on October 29.[2]

That same month, the Egyptian military attaché in Paris, Tharwat Okasha, also heard disturbing reports. These were about secret meetings between Israeli and French government officials and of French military moves that appeared to indicate a mobilization of French forces. He passed the news on to Cairo.[3]

Okasha's reports were also dismissed as unlikely. As mentioned, Egypt's leaders were reassured by their knowledge that both superpowers opposed a military solution. Further, Soviet foreign minister Dmitri Shepilov stopped off in Paris on October 19 after the UN debate and met with Pineau. According to a report of that meeting received in Cairo, Shepilov had stressed to Pineau the importance of multilateral negotiations predicated on Hammarskjöld's six principles, and Pineau had seemed receptive. Shepilov reported that there appeared to be little thought in Paris of invasion.

Charles de Gaulle told the Egyptian ambassador in Paris that there was great opposition to an invasion, and the British press and the Labour Party were increasingly opposed. Indeed, the whole world seemed increasingly hostile to Anglo-French military action.[4]

While growing European public opposition to war was visible, intelligence was coming in that suggested the opposite. Information from Ankara and Cyprus suggesting possible Anglo-French military activity arrived in Cairo on October 21.[5]

That same day, a French source told Okasha of a secret agreement signed on October 22 between Britain and France to invade Egypt. The source explained that the plan had metamorphosed into one in which British and French forces would intervene on the pretense of staying an Israeli attack.

Okasha resolved to send an urgent message to Cairo but he was terrified his message would be intercepted or not arrive at all. He decided to rely on an oral message via the embassy's press attaché, sending him off with the warning "The future of Egypt rests on the quality of your memory." The emissary reached Abdel Nasser just hours before the Israelis invaded on October 29, and he delivered both the oral message and a handwritten message Okasha had sent to vouch for the veracity of the oral one.[6]

The Israeli military action on the night of October 29 caused massive confusion among the Egyptian General Staff. Egyptian military leaders thought the Israeli incursions into Egypt might, in fact, be a feint before the main Israeli move, which they thought might be an invasion of Jordan. Especially confusing to the Egyptians was the lack of Israeli air cover for their land operations.[7] As the attack unfolded, Egyptian ground forces were overwhelmed by Israeli superiority in both infantry and artillery.[8]

The Egyptian air force was caught unprepared and was, essentially, grounded the first day of the Israeli campaign. The fuel for the warplanes was being stored at a site remote from the planes themselves.[9] Egyptian troops stationed outside of Cairo to protect against an expected Anglo-French attack on Alexandria rushed to Sinai to confront the Israeli attack.

In Washington, the Egyptian ambassador in Washington, Ahmed Hussein, complained stridently. Receiving the protest, Assistant Secretary of State for Near Eastern, South Asian and African Affairs William Rountree promised a prompt approach to the UN Security Council. The Egyptian ambassador blamed the major powers: "Egypt and the Arab countries do not regard Israel as a country which stands independently. It lives with the support and aid of the larger nations which back it up. In addition, they will view its criminal attack as a result of the encouragement or at least lack of opposition of those countries."

Hussein stressed that the United States possessed "the leading role and the primary responsibility" in the current crisis.[10]

The next morning, the British ambassador went to the Egyptian Foreign Ministry and delivered a message saying that his government regretted the Israeli action and would warn Israel to withdraw.[11] Later that day, the British and French issued a joint ultimatum demanding that Israeli and Egyptian troops withdraw to points ten miles to either side of the Suez Canal. At the time the ultimatum was delivered, the foremost Israeli troops were forty miles to the east of the canal, meaning that the ultimatum allowed them to advance another thirty miles.[12]

As the Egyptian leadership made their way to a meeting with Nasser, their cars slowed by the blackout in Cairo because of the fighting that had begun against Israel, they were surprised to learn of the British-French ultimatum. It was apparent to all that Britain and France might now be preparing to join the war. But their move had not been expected.

Nasser read the ultimatum. Few of his aides spoke up. One minister then asked, "Are we prepared to face them? . . . And I have a further question: if we fight, do we have sufficient arms or shall we throw bricks at them?"[13]

As was expected, the Egyptian leadership refused the ultimatum.

In Washington, Rountree called in Ambassador Hussein. He told him about American activities in the UN to solve the crisis. He said the American delegate had refused a British and French request the afternoon of October 30 to delay consideration of the complaint against the invading Israeli forces.

Rountree also told Hussein that the first the American government had heard of the British and French ultimatum was when it was reported by the wire services. He assured Hussein that President Eisenhower had immediately sent letters to the governments of Britain and France "imploring them to give the United Nations an opportunity to settle the differences by peaceful means rather than by weakness and strength."[14]

The Egyptian government was making more concrete requests from their Soviet partners. A close aide to Nasser, Ali Sabri, went to the Soviet embassy in Cairo. His message was urgent. "With every hour the situation gets worse and is becoming very dangerous." Egypt "unofficially" wanted military assistance.

What kind of assistance did Egypt want, the Soviet ambassador asked, given that "the situation might provoke a third world war."

Sabri had prepared his response, asking for the deployment of Soviet naval vessels close to Egypt's shores and help from Soviet air power, manned by "volunteers" and, especially, pilots. Nasser separately added a direct request in a letter to Khrushchev: "We desperately need air support for our troops." Soviet volunteers could fly MiG aircraft with Egyptian markings. "We will prepare air bases and let you know regarding their location." A similar request was relayed directly to Khrushchev through Abdel Nasser's ally, the Syrian president, who—by coincidence—was in Moscow on October 30 for a state visit.[15]

At that point, Khrushchev ignored these requests. The Egyptians could guess that he might be preoccupied with his own ongoing crisis in Hungary.

At about the same time, on the afternoon of October 31, Abdel Nasser called in the U.S. ambassador and asked America to provide military assistance. "Some people might have expected [the] Egyptian government to turn to [the Soviet Union] for such aid," Abdel Nasser told him. But his government "had thought the matter over carefully" and decided to appeal to Washington. He claimed he had not even discussed turning to the Russians for such help.[16]

At 7 p.m. on October 31, British warplanes attacked Cairo. In addition, more French-made Mystère jets than the Israelis possessed were attacking Egyptian troops in Sinai, leading the Egyptians to understand that the French were cooperating in those raids. According to one participant in the meetings of the Egyptian leadership:

It became clear to us that the British and French goal in having Israel participate with them was to drive our army into Sinai. Then, in the interests of protecting the Canal and guaranteeing free passage through it, the two countries would intervene and drop their forces in the Canal Zone. Our army would be cut off in the Sinai desert to the east of the canal. The British and French forces would then move to annihilate it.[17]

At 10:20 p.m., the Egyptian cabinet decided to withdraw all Egyptian troops from the Sinai Peninsula, where they had been fighting the Israelis, to the western bank of the Suez Canal.[18]

At 11 p.m., rumors began to circulate that British paratroopers had landed in the Cairo suburb where the armed forces were headquartered. Flares illuminated the night sky, revealing possible targets and landing areas. The Egyptian leadership began to make plans to go underground and fight a guerrilla war against occupying troops.[19]

Adding to the confusion of the time, planes dropped leaflets on Cairo encouraging revolution. The British and French forces destroyed Egyptian broadcast facilities and replaced Egyptian broadcasts with pro-British broadcasts on the same frequencies.[20]

Although Anglo-French forces never landed in Cairo, the air raids continued from October 31 through November 4. Anglo-French operations drew protests from around the world. The Soviet Union, China, and India made their deep displeasure known. In the Middle East, the Saudis pressed the Americans to stop the invasion, and ARAMCO halted all oil shipments to Britain and France.[21]

On November 1 an unnamed American source told the Egyptian embassy in Washington:

The British had confirmed to the American government that their military operations will settle the situation quickly solely within Egypt's borders, and that the situation will remain quiet in the Arab countries and the Middle East. This may have some effect on the position of the American government to change from its strong condemnation of the attack to a position closer to passivity, on the basis of the British assurance of the imminent end of the government of President Gamal Abdel Nasser.

The American source confided that the American government might go from passivity back to condemnation—if the Arab countries rallied around Egypt in its conflict, threatening Middle East oil fields and military bases.[22]

On November 2 the American ambassador saw Abdel Nasser again, to deliver Eisenhower's response to Nasser's October 31 request for American military aid. The ambassador relayed the message that Eisenhower hoped to end the fighting by working through the UN. The Egyptian president said he appreciated this. He and his people, he said, were "resolved to fight to [the] end to maintain their honor."

Abdel Nasser admitted to the American diplomat that the Egyptians "had never really believed [the Americans] when we had indicated [the] possibility that British and French might embark on an independent policy which did not have [American] approval. Now he recognized he had been wrong."[23]

On November 2 Abdel Nasser addressed his nation in a speech delivered during Friday prayers at the Azhar Mosque in Cairo. He described the battles with the Israelis in Sinai as a plot to lure Egyptian forces out of position and make the areas west of the canal vulnerable to an Anglo-French attack.

He braced his countrymen for a possible invasion. He told the gathered crowd:

Life and death are in the hand of God. One can never determine his life. We shall fight. I am here with you in Cairo and shall fight with you. I am here in Cairo. My children are here with you in Cairo. I have not sent them away, and I shall not send them away. I also will stay with you in Cairo. As I said yesterday, we shall fight to the last drop of blood. We shall never surrender. We are building our country, our history, and our future.[24]

One of Nasser's ministers recalled how "most people were overwhelmed by the feeling that nothing was more important than the great campaign which was Egypt's true war of independence."

But despite these "ardent patriotic feelings," there "was no preparedness, no planning, no training nor anything else." The military disaster, which the country did not yet grasp, was compounded by a humanitarian effort to shelter and support the thousands of civilians and scattered soldiers streaming westward from the Sinai and the Canal Zone.[25]

Leading figures from the substantial dissident movement in Egypt now made their move to use the war as the occasion to unseat Abdel Nasser. They suggested to the military chief, Field Marshal Abdel Hakim 'Amr, that the imprisoned former president who had led the initial revolution in 1952, General Naguib, should be restored to power for the good of the country. The idea was that such a new government might settle on appropriate terms with the invading forces.[26]

Shortly after Nasser's defiant speech on November 2, Abdel Hakim 'Amr, the Egyptian chief of staff, approached Abdel Nasser to propose a quite different approach from inside Nasser's government. He wanted the leadership to consider requesting a cease-fire.

Field Marshal 'Amr told the small meeting: "Continuing the fighting will bring about the destruction of the country and the death of many civilians. The people will hate the regime and those who uphold it. It is better to avoid this destruction and ask for a ceasefire."[27]

Another top member of the Revolutionary Command Council, Salah Salem, voiced a similar opinion. He said, "We need to spare the country from the calamities of destruction and devastation." He suggested to Abdel Nasser that he address the people and inform them that the national interest lay in avoiding destruction and devastation. He asked for a cease-fire and a surrender. Apparently the majority of the Revolutionary Command Council was in favor of ceding power.[28]

Baghdadi recalled that he was shocked by such talk and had immediately retorted, "I think it is more honorable for me to commit suicide before doing anything like that."

In what one observer recalled as a "state of near hysteria," Abdel Nasser added, "It is better that we commit suicide together here before we take such an action." He then asked an aide to bring some bottles of potassium cyanide sufficient for the use of all present should the need arise. He added, "I'm serious about what I said."

Salem withdrew his suggestion to surrender.[29]

On November 3, the Egyptian government got a bit of encouragement. Ambassador Hussein, in Washington, heard that President Eisenhower was "personally indignant with the governments of Israel, Britain, and France for the way in which they have dealt with him in the current crisis."[30]

In Egypt, President Abdel Nasser was indignant, too. But his complaint was that, although he was the leader of the country and had military experience, he felt cut off from military decisions. He had no accurate understanding of what the situation was on the ground. Further, Salah Salem (whose official post was as a newspaper editor) appeared to be in command of the army rather

than Abdel Nasser's designated chief of staff, Abdel Hakim 'Amr. As a consequence, Salem was sent off to defend Suez and 'Amr agreed to maintain close
military contact with the president.[31]

On the night of November 4–5, Abdel Nasser decided to travel to Port Said.
He hoped his visit would boost morale among the Egyptian troops who were
going to fight the Anglo-French landing force.

Along the road to Ismailiya, where he would spend the night, Nasser saw
countless destroyed military vehicles and tanks strewn on the sides of the road.
This was but a portion of the debacle that had overtaken much of the military equipment that Egypt had purchased from the Soviet Union and its allies.
Abdel Nasser became despondent and said, "103 million [Egyptian] pounds
was lost here." And then he added in English, "I was defeated by my army."[32]

On the morning of November 5, foreign paratroopers dropped onto Port
Said. Abdel Nasser decided not to continue on to the embattled city. He re-
turned to Cairo. That night, the Soviet government issued stern threats to
Israel, Britain, and France.

As military operations and diplomatic maneuvers unfolded during the day
on November 6, Egypt had no concrete plans or preparations to receive or use
large-scale Soviet military help. What Nasser could do was wait on the development of the Anglo-French invasion of his country, prepare what resistance he
could, and hope that something would turn up.

MOSCOW

CAROL R. SAIVETZ

As illustrated in the previous Soviet cases, the USSR demonstrated its support for Cairo and what it called "anti-imperialism" through arms transfers and rhetorical backing for Egyptian opposition to the Baghdad Pact. And when President Nasser nationalized the Suez Canal, Moscow—although it had not been informed ahead of time—ultimately backed the Egyptian position. At the London conference, Foreign Minister Dmitri Shepilov maneuvered to protect Egypt. When the question of the nationalization went before the UN Security Council, the USSR exercised its veto.

During the second half of October, the Soviet government was entirely preoccupied with other matters. As Khrushchev's son would later write, "For father, affairs in the Mediterranean were put on the back burner. Practically on the same day [October 16] the situation in Poland and Hungary acquired a dramatic coloration."[1]

CRISIS IN EASTERN EUROPE

As discussed in the Moscow chapter in Part One, Khrushchev's formal speech at the Twentieth Congress of the Communist Party of the Soviet Union (CPSU) signaled a new worldview and increasing Soviet involvement in the Third World. Khrushchev, at the same congress, delivered arguably an even more important speech in which he denounced the excesses of Stalinism.

251

The so-called "secret speech" had seemed to invite dissident socialists and others who had long resented Stalinism to challenge the old conditions of Soviet dominance—political, economic, and military (a new Soviet-led military alliance of the satellite states, called the Warsaw Pact, had been created the previous year). During the summer of 1956 this unrest began to grow into a potentially revolutionary force, especially in Poland and in Hungary.

In Poland, riots broke out in Poznan in June 1956. The rebellion was put down by Polish forces, but events reinforced both the local push for reform and Moscow's need to ensure pro-Soviet stability in Warsaw. When the reformist Socialist leader Władysław Gomułka was restored to the party leadership, the Kremlin at first seemed confident that the new leadership would both maintain control and follow a moderately reformist program consistent with the new Soviet party line. But the hopes of the Soviet leaders dissipated, and they began preparing for a possible Soviet invasion of Poland.[2]

The summer of turmoil culminated on October 19, when an uninvited Soviet delegation, led by Khrushchev himself, arrived in Warsaw. The ostensible reason for their unwanted arrival was to prevent Poland's new leaders from purging pro-Moscow leaders from the party hierarchy.

Simultaneously, Soviet troops stationed in Poland began moving toward the capital city. Two battle divisions rolled into place about ten miles from Warsaw.

Gomułka, understanding that Soviet forces might well be used, attempted to placate Khrushchev. It was a close call. Despite Soviet hopes massive pro-Gomułka demonstrations had spread across several Polish cities. The Soviet leadership, meeting on October 21, chose patience, and the nearby Soviet troops were taken off alert.[3] There were no easy options.

In the Polish case, the Soviet Politburo opted for compromise and reform, and many expected the same pattern to be followed when trouble erupted in Hungary. If anything, the sequence of events in Poland seemed to have emboldened the opposition in Hungary.

In July, Moscow had made the concession of forcing the removal of Hungary's hard-liner party boss, but the new man, Ernö Gerö, did not seem to know what to do. In early October there were huge demonstrations, some on the occasion of the reburial of the remains of a Hungarian who had been executed in an earlier communist purge.

On October 22, student demonstrators in Hungary published a long list of demands, including the withdrawal of Soviet troops and the promotion of Imre Nagy to the top job. Just as Gomułka was seen as a Socialist "reformer" for Poland, so Nagy was seen as a would-be Socialist reformer in Hungary. The next day, when students again took to the streets and tore down a statue of Stalin, police fired on the crowd. Gerö asked for Soviet military intervention— under pressure to do so from Yuri Andropov, who was then the Soviet ambassador to Budapest.

At a CPSU Politburo meeting on the evening of October 23, the leadership decided to send a limited number of Soviet troops from Ukraine into Hungary. In addition, they agreed to send two political emissaries to Budapest: Anastas Mikoyan (who had opposed intervention in Poland and also opposed intervention in Hungary) and Mikhail Suslov.[4]

Between October 24 and 28, Soviet forces battled Hungarian demonstrators and street fighters. Suslov reported back that thousands of Hungarians had been hurt, with at least 600 dead. Soviet losses also were mounting into the hundreds. Gerö resigned; Nagy took his place.

Worse still, from the Soviet perspective, the introduction of military force provoked increasingly anti-Soviet popular sentiment. It could also be argued that the number of troops was insufficient to put down the uprising once and for all. Nagy could not keep ahead of the crowd; indeed, one could say he was "captured" by growing popular demands for dramatic change, including the abolition of the one-party system. Nagy called for a cease-fire.[5]

Meeting on October 28, the Soviet leadership chose caution and decided to pull their troops out of the city of Budapest.[6] The tone of the Politburo meeting of October 28 was pessimistic. One member called what was happening in Hungary a "counterrevolution."

Nonetheless, the Politburo, as evidenced in the meeting notes, was still undecided how to proceed. Would the Hungarian government under the leadership of Nagy and János Kádár be resolute enough to restore order? Would the Soviet leadership have to act to install a new government?

Perhaps the tenor of the discussion was best summed up by the former foreign minister, Molotov, who said:

We acted properly when we sent in troops. The initial messages from [Comrades] Mikoyan and Suslov were reassuring about their view of the government. The influence of the party on the masses is weak. With regard to the new government, we should support it. But regarding friendship with the USSR, they're talking about the withdrawal of troops. We must act cautiously.[7]

In the end, the Politburo decided to support the new Hungarian government. It approved the withdrawal of Soviet forces from Budapest.

Then, almost as an afterthought, Khrushchev added: "The English and the French are in a real mess in Egypt. We shouldn't get caught in the same company. But we must not foster illusions. We are saving face."[8]

The next day, October 29, news arrived that Israel had begun some sort of large-scale attack on Egyptian territory in the Sinai Desert. The day after, October 30, came word of a British and French ultimatum that seemed to be a prelude to their own possible attack on Egypt.

In an additional effort to forestall further unrest within their East European satellites, on October 30 the Soviet leaders had issued a declaration, "On Relations among Socialist States," in which Moscow acknowledged the sovereignty and equality of the members of the Warsaw Pact. In the words of one Politburo member, the declaration should be issued in the spirit of "self-criticism." Khrushchev and his Politburo colleagues appear to have hoped such a declaration would make it easier for the new governments to cement their ties to Moscow.

That same day, October 30, Nasser's ally, the president of Syria, arrived in Moscow for a state visit. Soviet documents preparing for the visit show no sign the Soviets had anticipated the outbreak of war in the Middle East. A couple of weeks earlier, the Egyptians themselves had let Soviet representatives believe that the war danger seemed to have passed. After the diplomacy in New York, "It is in large measure settled," Egypt's ambassador to Moscow had said.[9]

All this complacency was being shattered in Hungary and in Egypt. From Hungary came news that Nagy was calling for multiparty elections and preparing to pull Hungary out of the Soviet military alliance, the Warsaw Pact.

Egypt, the Soviet Union's new partner in the Middle East, was already under attack from Israel and desperately pleading for arms. Now it seemed that Britain and France might join the assault against Nasser.

HUNGARY FIRST: OCTOBER 31–NOVEMBER 4

On October 31, only a day after the release of the public statement about equal relations among Warsaw Pact members, Khrushchev's Politburo decided to invade Hungary. The Politburo was determined to put down the "counterrevolution." Prime Minister Bulganin told his colleagues that "if we fail to take measures now, we will lose Hungary."[10]

To Khrushchev, the convergence of the two crises was a jolt toward decisive action: "If we leave Hungary, that would encourage the American, British, and French imperialists. They would understand this as our weakness and would be on the offensive. Our party wouldn't understand us. Besides Egypt, we would add Hungary."[11]

What Khrushchev seems to have feared was not only the disintegration of the Soviet bloc but also the appearance of looking weak—both in Hungary and in Egypt. What ensued would be the largest combat operation in Europe since the end of World War II, this one aimed primarily at Hungarian civilians.

Khrushchev flew to the Polish-Soviet border to brief the Polish leader, then on to Romania and to Bulgaria. Moscow began preparing a replacement government for Hungary. The second Soviet assault on Budapest began on November 4 and led to about 20,000 Hungarians killed or wounded. One of the dead was Nagy himself, who fled to the Yugoslav embassy but was then turned over to the Soviets, who executed him.

Clearly, in the heated days of late October 1956, Hungary was the top priority of the Soviet regime. For several days, Egypt was put to one side. There were pro forma statements on October 30 that the USSR was "gravely concerned" about the Israeli invasion and that the leadership thought the matter should be referred to the UN. Little more.[12]

Once the Israelis attacked Egypt, Nasser looked to the USSR for support. The Soviet ambassador in Cairo reported urgent requests for military assistance. The Egyptians specifically asked for Soviet naval deployments that might ward off invaders and for Soviet air power. Egypt wanted "volunteers" and, especially, trained pilots to fly Soviet-supplied aircraft with Egyptian markings.[13]

A similar request was relayed directly to Khrushchev through Nasser's ally, the Syrian president, who—by coincidence—was in Moscow on October 30 for a state visit. When the Syrian leader questioned what the Soviet Union was prepared to do to help Egypt, Khrushchev reportedly responded: "We'll see what we can do. At present we don't know how to help Egypt, but we are having continuous meetings to discuss the problem."[14]

From Cairo, Ambassador Kiselev urged Moscow to support the Egyptians. He worried that if the Soviet Union was not resolute in its support of Cairo, public opinion in the Arab world would be convinced that, because of Poland and Hungary, the USSR was "no longer as interested in the Middle East."[15]

Again, on November 2, Khrushchev reiterated the Soviet Union's inability to help the Egyptians. At a diplomatic reception in Moscow, Khrushchev is reported to have told the Egyptian ambassador: "We are full of admiration for the way in which you are resisting aggression . . . but unfortunately there is no way in which we can help you militarily. But we are going to mobilize world public opinion."[16] This was perhaps the first hint of exactly what the Soviet leadership was contemplating.

Khrushchev did discuss Suez—at least indirectly—with the Yugoslav leader, Tito. While explaining to Tito why the Politburo had decided to intervene again in Hungary, Khrushchev reportedly told him that the British and French pressure on Egypt "provided a favorable moment for a further intervention by Soviet troops. It would help the Russians." He added: "They are bogged down there, and we are stuck in Hungary."[17]

It was only on November 4, after the military situation in Budapest seemed to be under control, that the Politburo began to turn its attention to the Middle East. Indeed, the third item on the agenda for the November 4 meeting read: "actively take part in help for Egypt . . . to think up a series of measures." And in parentheses it was noted: "a demonstration at British embassy in Moscow and wide newspaper coverage."[18]

THREATENING LETTERS

On November 5, after the uprising in Budapest had been crushed and the mopping up operations were under way, Moscow felt ready to make a major move on behalf of Egypt. Sent for the government by Premier Bulganin (Khrushchev was the head of the Soviet Communist Party, not the formal head of state), letters were cabled to President Eisenhower, to British prime minister Eden, to French prime minister Mollet, and to Israeli prime minister Ben-Gurion.

All the messages were brusque and ominous.

To Eden:

> The Soviet government considers it necessary to call your attention to the fact that the aggressive war launched by Britain and France against the Egyptian state, in which Israel played the role of instigator, is fraught with extremely dangerous consequences for general peace. . . .
>
> What kind of position would Britain be in if she had been attacked by stronger powers with all kinds of modern offensive weapons at their disposal? Yet at the present time such countries would not even need to send their naval and air forces to British shores, but could use other means, such as rockets. If rocket weapons were used against Britain and France, you would doubtless call that a barbarous act.[19]

To Mollet:

What kind of position would France be in if she were subjected to an attack by other states possessing terrible modern devices of destruction? . . .

We hope that at this critical moment the French government will show soberness in its assessment of the situation that has arisen and will draw the appropriate conclusions.[20]

To Ben-Gurion:

The government of Israel, acting as an instrument of foreign imperialist forces, is continuing its reckless venture and is thus challenging all peoples of the East. . . .

It is sowing hatred for the state of Israel among the peoples of the East; this cannot fail to have an effect on the future of Israel and jeopardize its very existence as a state. . . .

We hope that the government of Israel will understand and properly appraise this warning.[21]

What was behind these threats? Was the Soviet Union really contemplating a new world war?

Khrushchev's son later wrote that the USSR did not want to get involved in the war. It just wanted to frighten the "aggressors." His father figured: "It wouldn't be so bad to threaten Eden and Guy Mollet with rockets about which [Khrushchev] had regaled them the previous spring in London . . . Father knew well that not only did we not have the rockets, deployed in position, but they really didn't exist in the numbers [we implied]. . . . Neither the French nor the British knew how many we had."[22]

Foreign Minister Shepilov later said he was relying on Western fears about Khrushchev's unstable character. He claims that, from the beginning, he was opposed to the USSR becoming involved militarily. "There was a firm decision not to bring the matter to the point of an armed conflict."

"However," he went on, "I devised some measures of a psychological nature and carried them out. Let's say, I summoned the French, British, and Israeli ambassadors at night. Just think of it: it's night-time, their eyes are red because they're having a sleepless night, the situation is very unusual." The threats would be predicated both on the calculation that the United States would not risk superpower war and on perceptions of Khrushchev's unpredictability. "There were grounds for believing that the USSR would be ready to interfere because of the apparently unbalanced personality of Khrushchev and a seeming lack of responsibility for every single word that he said."[23]

In the message to Eisenhower, the threat was presented in a different way. It was to say that it was time for the two superpowers to intervene together to "guarantee peace" and "condemn aggression." The "situation in Egypt requires immediate and most decisive action on part of UN." Only their two governments had "all contemporary forms of armaments, including atom and hydrogen weapons. On us lies special responsibility to put stop to war, and to restore peace and tranquility to area of Near and Middle East." This message to the United States was then coupled with a message to the president of the UN Security Council arguing that it was vital that member states, especially the United States and the USSR, render military assistance to Egypt if the fighting didn't cease.

The U.S. ambassador to Moscow asked Shepilov if he really expected the United States to take up arms against Britain and France. His answer was that that would not be necessary "if the US and the USSR would make plain their 'determination' to see that the fighting come to a halt in the Middle East."[24]

The Egyptian ambassador to Moscow was called to the Soviet Ministry of Foreign Affairs on November 6. In Shepilov's office he was handed copies of the notes to Eden and Mollet. Shepilov reportedly said: "We have taken a very firm position, Mr. Ambassador . . . and we shall stand beside you to defeat aggression."[25] A similar scene was then repeated by Khrushchev, personally. He told the ambassador that, when he had earlier pushed aside pleas for help, he had intentionally deceived him because the USSR believed Egyptian codes used to send messages to Cairo had been broken.

In Khrushchev's own telling, his intent was to expose as a lie the U.S. claim to be a fighter for peace and justice. He detailed consultations with Molotov in which he laid out the proposed scenario.

Molotov replied that Eisenhower would never agree to joint action.

Khrushchev said he responded, "Of course he won't, but by putting him in the position of having to refuse, we'll expose the hypocrisy of his public statement condemning the attack against Egypt."[26]

PART THREE

PARIS

CHARLES G. COGAN

A NEW WAR PLAN

On the surface, the atmosphere of the crisis did not suddenly change from negotiation to belligerence with the meeting at Chequers between British prime
minister Eden and French general Challe on the afternoon of October 14. To
the outside world, Hammarskjöld was still pursuing a negotiated solution to
follow up on the progress that had been made on the canal issue at the UN in
New York.

But from the moment of the Eden-Challe meeting, the inner dynamic of
the situation changed. In fact, it would not be too much to describe Challe as
the sorcerer's apprentice in the Suez affair.

As conceived, the Challe plan was brazenly hypocritical, with its pretense of
Anglo-French "separation" of Egyptian and Israeli combatants. The plan could
be reconciled with language in the Anglo-Egyptian agreement of 1954 under
which the British forces had just completed their withdrawal from Egypt. Article 4 of that accord provided: "In the event of a possible armed attack by a
foreign power, Egypt will be required to accord to the United Kingdom such
facilities as would be necessary to put the [Suez Canal] base on a war footing
and use it efficiently." Of course, at the time of that agreement neither the
Egyptians nor the British had supposed the provision would be used as a way
to attack Egypt.[1]

Yet this clause was surely remembered by British (and also French) policymakers as the Suez crisis unfolded. And the "separation of forces" idea presented by Challe seemingly fitted nicely into this framework.

After Challe left Chequers on October 14, Eden immediately recalled his foreign minister from the UN. Together the two of them, Eden and Lloyd, journeyed to Paris to meet with the French leadership on the afternoon of October 16.

As for the French leadership, they were finished with trying to resolve the Suez Canal dispute peacefully. The Soviets had vetoed the preferred Anglo-French resolution in the UN Security Council. The French needed the British to be at least neutral, though Prime Minister Mollet and his chief of staff of the armed forces, Paul Ely, believed that active British participation was essential.

Apart from the political benefit of the British special relationship with the Americans, there was an operational need for London's participation. The Israelis needed French fighter support, partly to defend their cities against possible Egyptian air attacks. The British bases in Cyprus were useful, unless the French based out of Israel (which they planned to do, in part). But even then the French could not provide the long-range bomber support considered necessary to neutralize the Egyptian Air Force on the ground. The British, with their Canberra bombers, could help with this task.

Eden and Mollet met on October 16 at the office of the prime minister at the Hôtel Matignon before they went on to a larger dinner. Only four men were there: Eden, Lloyd, Pineau, and Mollet. The French took the lead. They argued that Israel was likely to attack Egypt before long. Both sides agreed that if this were to take place before the American elections, it was unlikely that Congress would be reconvened, and it was also unlikely that the UN Security Council would reach an agreement on action to be taken.[2]

Mollet then suggested it might be possible to intervene to stop fighting in the area of the canal. He left Eden with two questions:

In the event of an Israeli attack upon Egypt would the United Kingdom regard themselves as bound to intervene [on Egypt's side] under the Tripartite Declaration?

In the event of the likelihood of hostilities in the vicinity of the Canal, would the United Kingdom Government intervene to stop them?[3]

Eden and Lloyd had returned to London on the evening of October 16 supposedly to obtain cabinet approval for these answers to be given Mollet. On the next day, October 17, the British answers came back. They were what the French had hoped to hear. As recorded by Lloyd:

> In the event of an Israeli attack upon Egypt, the British Government would not regard themselves as bound to take action under the Tripartite Declaration, and secondly, that if it appeared likely that hostilities were going to develop in the Canal area, we considered that we might have to intervene in some manner to prevent that happening.[4]

The French passed the good news on to the Israeli Defense Ministry's representative in Paris. He had already been briefed by Challe about the secret Chequers meeting with Eden.[5]

The French and Israelis promptly arranged to get together in Paris to work on the details of their agreed-on plan. They then worked on getting the British to join this secret meeting.[6]

The fevered week between the Paris summit (October 16) and the British-French-Israeli meeting at Sèvres, outside Paris (October 22–24), saw two events that further impelled the French to bring the plan against Nasser to closure. The first was the seizure of a yacht called the *Athos* on the sixteenth. It had been sailing from Alexandria to Nador, Morocco, with a cargo of 100 tons of arms destined for the Algerian rebels. In France, "it was taken as proof positive that Nasser was behind the rebellion and that he would have to go."[7]

On October 22, just as the Sèvres talks were beginning, the second incident occurred. The French captured Ahmed Ben Bella and four other leaders of the rebel movement, the French Front de Libération Nationale (FLN). The method was shockingly unorthodox: the French crew of a Moroccan plane was compelled by French air traffic controllers at Algiers to land there in Algiers instead of continuing their flight to Tunis, where the FLN leaders had been planning to meet up with Sultan Mohammed V, traveling in the sultan's own plane. Algiers authorities had promised the French flight crew that their families would be spirited out of Morocco to a place of safety.

It was unclear who at the political level in Paris had been informed about this operation beforehand, though it appears to have been a subcabinet official in the Defense Ministry. Mollet was surprised and furious yet, giving way to public opinion, the French interned Ben Bella and his companions for the rest of the war.[8]

The *Athos* and Ben Bella incidents heated up French public opinion and made Mollet and his colleagues even more eager to engage the "Israeli option" without delay. Mollet had persuaded Ben-Gurion to come to Paris. The Israeli prime minister had seemed reluctant to play the heavy in the Challe "separation of forces" plan, but he finally went along.

Sèvres was an interesting venue for the secret talks, with a special resonance for these French leaders since the villa had been a safe house for the Resistance during the war.[9] The talks lasted from October 22 to 24. Initially the French and the Israelis met alone. Selwyn Lloyd, accompanied by his private secretary, Donald Logan, joined the talks in the afternoon of October 22, and discussions continued well into the evening. Near midnight on October 22, Lloyd and Logan left by plane for London to consult with Eden.

Apparently not trusting Lloyd, whose enthusiasm for a secret deal with Israel was anything but total, the other parties decided that Pineau should also go to London to put Eden in the picture. Pineau left the next day, October 23.[10]

In his meeting that same day with Eden and Lloyd, Pineau was told the British would insist on the separation of forces plan. That way the Anglo-French forces would not appear as a concerned party in the Arab-Israeli conflict. Therefore, the Israelis must not cross the canal. Furthermore, the British wanted assurances that Israel would not attack Jordan.[11] Pineau appears to have received assurances from Eden and Lloyd that the time between the Israeli attack and the RAF entering into action against Egyptian airfields would be reduced to reassure the Israelis their cities would be safeguarded from Egyptian bombers. Lloyd had been pressed the previous day at Sèvres to reduce this interval to thirty-six hours.[12]

Some of the discussions were more theatrical. Lloyd left the meeting early but dispatched a letter back to Pineau, delicately making a record: "I think I should make clear, after what was said yesterday, that the Government of the United Kingdom has not asked the Israeli Government to undertake an action of any kind." The British government, he wrote, had only been "asked what would be our reactions if certain things were to happen."[13]

Then there was the problem of finding a suitable pretext. The Israelis certainly had their grievances against Egypt. But what was the "precipitate" event to trigger an Israeli attack? Here the ever-helpful (but politically unsophisticated) Challe came up with an idea at Sèvres "that Israel might 'stage' an Egyptian bombing raid on Beersheba as a pretext" to declare war on Egypt, thereby triggering the desired Franco-British intervention against Egypt. Ben-Gurion rejected this idea vehemently. He would not "lie to the world in order to make things more convenient for England!"[14]

The British insisted that the Israeli military action would have to be a "real act of war" that would pose a threat to the canal; otherwise the British would not act. Israeli chief of staff Dayan assured all that there would be an attack at the Mitla Pass in Sinai, fairly close to the canal, so this issue was resolved.[15]

As the conference was wrapping up, the French (a British participant remembered) "produced a document in three identical copies which had just been typed in French in a neighboring room. We were asked to sign each copy of the document. This was the first time any mention had been made of setting down what had been discussed." All signed, retaining a copy.[16]

Eden was taken aback to learn of a document, not having expected that such a matter would have been committed to writing. He tried unsuccessfully to have all the copies destroyed. The French and Israelis did not comply.[17]

The protocol read:

The results of the conversations which took place at Sèvres from October 22–24 1956 between the representatives of the Governments of the United Kingdom, of the State of Israel, and of France are the following:

1. The Israeli forces launch in the evening of October 29, 1956 a large-scale attack on the Egyptian forces, with the aim of reaching the Canal Zone the following day.

2. On being apprised of these events, the British and French Governments during the day of October 30 respectively and simultaneously make two appeals to the Egyptian and Israeli Governments on the following lines:

   a. To the Egyptian Government:
      i. Halt all acts of war.
      ii. Withdraw all its troops ten miles from the Canal.
      iii. Accept temporary occupation of key positions on the Canal by Anglo-French forces to guarantee freedom of passage through the Canal by vessels of all nations until a final settlement.
   b. To the Israeli Government
      i. Halt all acts of war
      ii. Withdraw all its troops ten miles to the east of the Canal.
         In addition, the Israeli Government will be notified that the French and British Governments have demanded of the

Egyptian Government to accept temporary occupation of key positions along the Canal by the Anglo-French forces.

It is agreed that if one of the two Governments refused, or did not give its consent within twelve hours, the Anglo-French forces would intervene with the means necessary to ensure that their demands are accepted.

c. The representatives of the three governments agree that the Israeli Government will not be required to meet the conditions in the appeal addressed to it, in the event that the Egyptian Government does not accept those in the appeal addressed for their part.

3. In the event that the Egyptian Government should fail to agree within the stipulated time to the conditions of the appeal addressed to it, the Anglo-French forces will launch military operations against the Egyptian forces in the early hours of the morning of October 31.

4. The Israeli Government will send forces to occupy the western shore of the Gulf of Akaba and the group of islands Tirane and Sanafir to ensure freedom of navigation in the Gulf of Akaba.

5. Israel undertakes not to attack Jordan during the period of operations against Egypt. But in the event that during the same period Jordan should attack Israel, the British Government undertakes not to come to the aid of Jordan.

6. The arrangements of the present protocol must remain strictly secret.

7. They will enter into force after the agreements of the three Governments.[18]

One reason Ben-Gurion finally accepted the role of the "heavy" in this plan was because the French-Israeli partnership further blossomed at Sèvres. The two governments signed a separate protocol agreeing on French air defense and maritime support to Israel during the upcoming Sinai offensive. The French agreed to station squadrons of their combat aircraft in Israel and French naval ships would visit Israeli ports. French aircraft based in Cyprus (then still a British colony) would help with air resupply of the Israeli columns advancing through Sinai.[19]

"For one and a half days, the Israeli cities ran the risk of being bombed, but otherwise, the Israelis had every reason to be satisfied [with the Sèvres decisions]," one French observer wrote. "There was satisfaction also in the French camp. The scheme constructed with and around the Israelis had brought about the adherence of the British. Without that, the operation against Egypt would have been dead."[20]

Yet another aspect of the French-Israeli alliance forged at Sèvres was French agreement to assist in the Israeli nuclear energy program. The French would help build an Israeli nuclear reactor at Dimona, in the Negev desert. (This program would eventually allow Israel to develop nuclear weapons.)[21]

As of October 25, the "Rubicon had been crossed," according to the French chief of staff, General Ely. The phase of military action in the crisis was now engaged. However, the timing of the Anglo-French ground assault on the canal was not settled.[22]

Although the Anglo-French attack was specified in the protocol as beginning on October 31, this really meant the air phase. Nothing specific was stated in the document as to the start of a ground phase: the only commitment in the protocol was that, in the early hours of the morning of October 31, the British and French would launch military operations against the Egyptian forces.

Reflecting the new activism set in motion by all the decisions on the new war plan, the military staffs began preparing for action under the Musketeer Revise operations plan, aimed at the Canal Zone (rather than at Alexandria, as under the original Musketeer). The more direct plan against Egypt's key centers of commerce and government "would have been acceptable," Ely believed, "if it could have been launched in July, immediately after Nasser's coup de force. But time having passed and the crisis having become bogged down in the slowness of international procedures, it became preferable to direct the action on the Canal . . . and the campaign would be limited to a sort of police operation."[23]

French support to Israel was bilateral and not hampered by having to coordinate it with the British. French aircraft and air defense troops soon began landing secretly in Israel and by October 29 all were in place. The insignia of the planes were changed from the tricolor cocarde to the Israeli Star of David and the French pilots were given Israeli identity cards in Hebrew.[24]

THE OUTBREAK OF WAR

During the early evening of Sunday, October 29, Israel launched its war against Egyptian forces in the Sinai.

Although the French government was not yet publicly involved, French support to this offensive in the Sinai was significant from the start. For example, on the night of October 30–31, French transport planes from Cyprus dropped twenty-six tons of supplies to the Israeli 202nd Brigade, which had been isolated for twenty-eight hours at the approach to the Mitla Pass, located to the east of the southern end of the Suez Canal. The following night (October 31–November 1), another drop of supplies was made by more French aircraft from Cyprus.

One of the Egyptian counterattacks, including a regiment of Soviet-supplied tanks, was surprised and broken up by air strikes by French F-84F aircraft flying out of a base in Israel. French warships used naval gunfire to aid Israeli assaults near the Mediterranean coast and helped defeat and capture an Egyptian warship that attempted to bombard the Israeli city of Haifa.[25]

On the afternoon of October 30, the prearranged Anglo-French plan went forward: separate ultimatums were delivered to the Israeli and Egyptian embassies in London. Similar actions took place in Paris. On the same afternoon of October 30, the French ambassador in Washington, Hervé Alphand, met with Secretary of State John Foster Dulles to give him a note for President Eisenhower, informing the U.S. government of the Anglo-French ultimatum.

Alphand reported that Dulles received this news with "intense emotion. After having rapidly read the text that I gave him, he declared to me that we were now experiencing the gravest hours of Anglo-French-American relations."

"'At no moment,' [Dulles] declared, 'were we informed of the military-type initiative,'" the British and French were announcing. "'However, for three weeks I have had suspicions about what has just happened today.'" Dulles went on to "compare the expected Anglo-French intervention with the methods of Soviet totalitarianism in Hungary."

Alphand protested. Dulles acknowledged an emotional outburst. But, he said he did not see "how there can be a remedy to the blow which the confidence among our three governments has just suffered."[26]

On the evening of October 30, Prime Minister Mollet obtained the approval for his actions from France's National Assembly. A large majority supported him.

As scripted, the Israelis accepted the Anglo-French ultimatum on condition that the Egyptians do likewise. As expected, the Egyptians refused.

The UN Security Council, called into session quickly on October 30 through the initiative of the United States, was unable to pass an American resolution calling for an end to the intervention and a return to the armistice lines of 1949, due to a French and British veto. The vote had been seven to two, with two abstentions.

The French and British air attacks on Egypt had been scheduled to begin when the twelve-hour interval in the ultimatum expired on the morning of October 31. The attacks were delayed and finally began on the afternoon of the 31st, beginning with a strike on an Egyptian airfield by British Canberra bombers based in Cyprus. For the next forty-eight hours, 240 French and British planes carried out attacks against four air bases in the Nile Delta area and eight in the Cairo region. By noon on November 2, the Egyptian air force was considered neutralized. According to General Ely, "The only [Egyptian] planes which escaped were those which were removed to Saudi Arabia, Jordan and Syria." With the start of the air attacks, "the affair seemed, this time, irremediably launched."[27]

At the United Nations, the French and British were being backed into a more difficult position. On the night of October 31, the Security Council voted to transfer the Suez issue to the General Assembly. Such a vote could not be vetoed. In the General Assembly all the member nations could vote, and the permanent members of the Security Council had no veto power. Neither Paris nor London wanted to be in the position of defying a resolution that had actually been adopted by the UN, an organization then only eleven years old and still greatly respected as an authoritative voice of world opinion and international law.

"THE NECESSITY TO MOVE QUICKLY"

The tempo of maneuver at the UN, led by an energized United States, worried French leaders. The British and French ground forces had not yet landed and established their position. As General Ely put it, "The danger of too great a delay between the Israeli offensive and the landing at Port Said was obvious. The necessity to move quickly became more and more imperative."[28]

Foreign Minister Pineau saw the problem, too. By November 1 he was urging Ely to get some troops landed by November 2 or 3, before the UN General Assembly could meet for a vote on the Suez issue.

Ely had tried. That same day, November 1, he had asked Admiral Barjot, the senior French officer in the Suez operation, to try to put together "a light and very rapid operation" that could get on the ground "within 24 hours."[29]

The next day, November 2, Ely flew to London to lobby personally for immediate action. Accompanied by General Challe, Ely attended a meeting of the British Chiefs. The positions put forward varied, with Lord Mountbatten, the First Sea Lord, being opposed to any military operation. The British Chiefs as a whole were not responsive to French proposals for exploiting the rapidity of the Israeli advance.

On the same afternoon, Ely met with British prime minister Eden. To his dismay, Ely "found M. Eden rather preoccupied, disoriented even. He received me stretched out on a sofa, with that air always so distinguished but a little nonchalant which was characteristic of him."

With both men speaking in French, Eden heard out Ely's idea for immediate parachute drops on the east bank of the canal, where the troops could then join up with the advancing Israelis. To Eden, "this formula was clearly satisfactory." Yet Ely was frustrated by the reluctance of the British military commanders. It seemed to Ely that the British military leaders were "very anti-Israeli" and they "in no way wanted to give the impression that [Britain] was tied in with Israel."[30]

Later that afternoon (still November 2), Pineau also went to London to see Eden. They seemed to agree "that the landing at Port Said be speeded up so that as deep a penetration as possible could be made into Egyptian territory."

The civilian leaders seemed to get the military to start making adjustments, but the adjustments were relatively modest. The amphibious landing was advanced by only two days, to begin on November 6. The paratroop landing would not take place along the east bank of the canal but at the entryway to it, and even that would not occur until dawn on November 5.

Meanwhile, as expected, the UN General Assembly began its debate on the intervention in Egypt on the evening of November 1 and continued through the night. By this time there was a new matter to consider—initially in the Security Council: the Soviet invasion of Hungary.

On November 3 and 4 a series of resolutions were debated and voted on in the General Assembly. Canada played an important role as a lead sponsor of two resolutions, with support from the United States. One resolution was devoted to the conflict between Egypt and Israel and called for creation of a new and enlarged international peacekeeping force to police the borders between the two (returning to the 1949 armistice lines). The other was on the Suez Canal. It effectively accepted Egyptian control of the canal and called for international cooperation in efforts to reopen it, since the Egyptians had sunk dozens of ships in the waterway to make its use impossible. These resolutions passed easily (fifty-seven for, none against, nineteen abstentions).

Yet the British and the French did not halt their intervention. They were intent on gaining a "bargaining chip" by establishing a military presence along the canal. The first parachute drop took place on Egyptian soil at 7:45 a.m. on November 5. A half-regiment of French colonial troops landed south of Port Said, near the northern entryway to the canal. British paratroopers landed on an airfield in northern Egypt between Damietta and Alexandria. That afternoon, French paratroopers landed at Port Fouad on the eastern end of the Mediterranean entrance to the canal.[31]

The Soviet government reacted sharply to the Anglo-French military action. In Moscow, the French ambassador was called in during the early morning hours of November 6 to see Soviet foreign minister Shepilov. Shepilov told the ambassador that the French action was "like a thunderclap in a calm sky" and threatened France with Soviet action that might use its own terrible means of modern destruction to stop this aggression. Shepilov did not detail just what the Soviet government might do but referred generally to energetic measures, such as the sending of military units, volunteers, and arms.[32]

Absorbing this threat during the day on November 6, Mollet and Pineau happened to see the West German chancellor, Konrad Adenauer, in a previously scheduled meeting. Mollet mused with Adenauer on how to evaluate the Soviet threat to "crush the aggressors."[33]

Adenauer was contemptuous of such Soviet "vulgar threats." He stressed the Soviet outreach to Eisenhower. It was a crude offer for those two powers to act together. The Soviets must assume such an offer might be accepted. Thus, to Adenauer, this Soviet move reinforced an old suspicion going back to the Geneva summit meeting of 1954. He thought the Americans might imagine they could just get a deal directly with the Russians to assure peace. The wartime and postwar U.S. interest in Europe was diminishing. It followed that the Europeans must unite under one form or another.[34]

To test his suspicion, Adenauer said he thought it would be useful if the French asked Eisenhower whether the United States would intervene if France and Great Britain were attacked by the Russians. He inquired whether this had been done.

Said Mollet: "We did not do it because we thought it went without saying. The suggestion is a good one." Later that day, Pineau cabled to Washington and asked his ambassador to learn from Eisenhower whether the American government would confirm "in an unequivocal manner that the clauses of the [North] Atlantic Treaty would come into play immediately in the case of a Soviet attack on the allies of the United States."[35]

Mollet and his government colleagues were still determined to proceed with their ongoing military operations for at least some further period of time. The international pressure on them was intense. But the French public still appeared to be behind them and they hoped to establish a strong position and then see what was possible. As the meeting with Adenauer was coming to an end, an aide quietly interrupted to let Mollet know that Prime Minister Eden was calling. Mollet left the meeting to take the call.

WASHINGTON

EDWARD MERTA

On Sunday, October 14, the Eisenhower administration had every reason to believe the Suez crisis was receding. The secretary of state called the president that afternoon to wish him a happy birthday and to tell him that the UN talks among Britain, France, and Egypt "had gone fairly well." The basic framework for a settlement was in place. The concerned countries, including Egypt, had arranged to meet for another round of negotiations at the end of the month, in Geneva.[1]

Other conflicts were flaring up in the Middle East. Jordan's tenuously pro-Western government seemed on the verge of disintegration, with Nasserist factions maneuvering for power in advance of parliamentary elections scheduled for October 21. The Nasserites and other anti-Western forces had the upper hand.[2]

As Jordan threatened to unravel, border skirmishes in September and early October had drawn fierce Israeli counterstrikes under Ben-Gurion's reprisal policy. The biggest raid yet came on the night of October 10, when up to three battalions of Israeli troops, backed for the first time by tanks, air cover, and artillery bombardment, assaulted the West Bank town of Qalqilya. They obliterated a police station and a school, damaging numerous homes and leaving scores killed and wounded.

The Israelis appeared poised for an outright invasion of Jordan, threatening a potential war with Britain if Eden invoked the U.K.-Jordan mutual defense pact. The State Department continued to pressure the Israelis to allow a planned deployment of Iraqi troops to the eastern bank of the Jordan River to bolster the fragile regime of King Hussein. On October 15, Eisenhower dictated a lengthy memorandum for the record on the situation in Jordan.[3]

North of Jordan, in Syria, the CIA had joined with the British Secret Service, MI6, in a plot to support Syrians who planned a coup that they hoped would overthrow the pro-Nasser regime in Damascus. This coup was scheduled to take place at the end of October.[4]

In the United States, most political attention was focused on the U.S. presidential election, in which President Eisenhower was running for reelection against the Democratic Party's candidate, Illinois governor Adlai Stevenson. The election would be on November 6.

RUMORS OF WAR: OCTOBER 15–29

British and French actions soon cast doubt on whether their commitment to a Suez settlement was genuine. In the ten days after the October 12 agreement on a framework for UN talks at the end of the month, Britain and France demanded Egypt essentially agree to give up canal revenue as a precondition for negotiations. Egypt accused the allies of sabotaging the talks that Hammarskjöld said were now in doubt. In discussions with Dulles, British and French envoys reverted to their former evasiveness about whether they saw negotiations as a path to a settlement or a means to pressure Nasser.[5]

They seemed more interested in pressure. They suggested steps like a coup against Nasser (like the one already planned in Syria) or provoking him into violating the 1954 agreement under which British troops had withdrawn from the Canal Zone.[6]

U-2 flights, meanwhile, confirmed the French had secretly sent sixty Mystère fighter-bombers to Israel rather than the twenty-four officially reported. British and French naval forces remained poised for potential action in the eastern Mediterranean.[7]

Eisenhower and Dulles realized Anglo-French military action in Suez remained a real possibility. They concluded it likely wouldn't happen until after the U.S. election, and they considered inviting Eden and Mollet to a Washington summit on Suez after the election, conditioned on no military action taking place before then.[8]

They never followed through because of distraction and confusion created by other events. Despite tensions over Suez, the State Department worked with the British in pushing Iraq to deploy troops into Jordan. Nuri's government delayed, worried about provoking the Israelis or a countermove by Egypt or Syria.

With an Israeli invasion of Jordan threatening, King Hussein's regime seemed on the verge of collapse. Elections on October 21 brought a new anti-Western coalition to power in the Jordanian parliament. Hussein apparently decided to stop relying on the Iraqis and British for defense. He instead signed a new military alliance with Egypt and Syria on October 24. An Arab-Israeli war over Jordan apparently loomed just as the countdown was under way to a British- and U.S.-backed coup in Syria, scheduled for October 29.[9]

Meanwhile, Middle East events were overshadowed by a new, potentially even more dangerous conflict in Eastern Europe. Long-simmering anti-Soviet street protests in Poland provoked sympathy demonstrations in Hungary. On the night of October 23, 200,000 marched in the streets of Budapest demanding democracy and an end to Soviet occupation. The next day, the hard-line Hungarian government reacted by appointing a new, reformist-minded prime minister, Imre Nagy.

As he took office, Soviet troops entered the city and fired on demonstrators. Chaotic fighting broke out between Soviet forces and Hungarian resistance fighters, quickly spreading across the country in the ensuing days as Hungarian police and military sided with their countrymen against the occupation.[10]

In Washington, Eisenhower's top advisers viewed the Hungarian explosion as potentially heralding the collapse of the decade-old Soviet empire in Eastern Europe, which would represent a pivotal Western victory in the Cold War. Eisenhower, though, feared that disintegrating Soviet power could drive Kremlin leaders to reckless foreign aggression, just as the collapse of Germany had spurred Hitler not toward surrender but, instead, to military suicide. Hungary, the president told the NSC on October 26, raised the specter of global war. He ordered Dulles to work with the British and French to bring the Hungary situation to the UN Security Council.[11]

The fighting in Hungary, the Jordan crisis, and the impending Syria coup kept Eisenhower's administration preoccupied by matters other than Suez as October drew to a close.[12] So their attention was elsewhere over the crucial weekend of October 27–28, when U.S. intelligence reported a major Israeli military mobilization under way. Israel's forces, the intelligence community concluded, were apparently preparing to retaliate against Egypt for recent minor border incursions in the Sinai.[13]

At first, the president and the secretary of state thought the target would be Jordan, given the crisis there and the possibility the Israelis might have learned of the planned coup in Damascus. The Israelis might be moving to exploit internal disorder that would keep the Syrians from interfering in Jordan. After fixating on Jordan for several weeks, Eisenhower and Dulles were slow to connect Israel's preparations to new reports that same weekend of major Anglo-French air and naval reinforcements arriving in Cyprus just as radio traffic surged between Tel Aviv and Paris. Presidential campaign events and the urgency of marshaling a Western response in Hungary also distracted from the ominous Middle East reports.[14]

By the end of the weekend, though, the picture had come into focus amid simultaneous stonewalling from Israel, Britain, and France as Israeli forces moved toward the Sinai. Eisenhower and Dulles realized, in at least a general way, that the Israeli mobilization was probably coordinated somehow with that of France and possibly Britain as well, with Egypt as the target.

The State Department sent a war warning to U.S. missions in the Middle East on Sunday, October 28. The same evening, the president issued a public statement revealing the Israeli mobilization, calling on Israel to exercise restraint and announcing the evacuation of nonessential U.S. government personnel from Israel, Jordan, Egypt, and Syria. Unlike the earlier war scares during the Suez crisis, this one left Eisenhower with too little time, and too many distractions, to stop the war from coming at last.[15]

WAR—AND EISENHOWER SETS THE U.S.
POLICY RESPONSE: OCTOBER 29–30

The morning of Monday, October 29, brought an announcement by the Nagy government in Hungary that Soviet forces had begun to withdraw from Budapest, amid ongoing talks with Moscow. Eisenhower and Dulles thought the good news from Eastern Europe and the fact that Israel didn't take military action overnight meant that, as Dulles put it, "we have gained 24 hours."[16]

The reprieve in the Middle East turned out to be much shorter than that. That afternoon, reports poured into Washington of major attacks by Israeli ground forces against Egypt, with heavy fighting under way. Deputy Under Secretary of State Loy Henderson later recalled that John Foster Dulles seemed devastated. "I have never seen him more affected by any development," Henderson said. "For a time he was really a broken man."[17]

For three months Dulles had pushed himself to the limit, physically and emotionally, in an epic attempt to restrain America's allies from war while keeping the alliance intact. During the previous week, on October 24, Dulles had confided to Eisenhower that the breakneck pace of travel and international conferences was wearing him down. He noted he had told his president, "I said I did not think I could go on at the pace I had been going and that it would be necessary for me to have as Under Secretary someone that would be more or less understood to be prepared to take over and who with that prestige would be able to lighten my load." Now his diplomatic efforts seemed to have failed, and his health was beginning to fail, also, as exhaustion set in.[18]

The secretary of state set out as best he could to find out what was happening and what could be done to contain the damage. He met again with British and French representatives in Washington, seeking their support for some sort of joint action against Israel under the Tripartite Declaration of 1950. They said they would have to get instructions from their governments. But given Egypt's hostility toward Britain and France, and toward the declaration, they predicted that action to defend Nasser would be "impossible."[19]

U.S. intelligence, meanwhile, reported Israeli paratroops landing near the Suez Canal and heavy Israeli forces crossing the Sinai border to advance at least seventy-five miles inside Egypt. Radio traffic between Paris and Tel Aviv had increased even further in the twenty-four hours before Israel attacked. Analysts expected new strikes and demonstrations in Arab countries, on top of those already erupting in North Africa to protest the recent French abduction of Algerian rebel leaders.[20]

The president of the United States learned of the Israeli invasion that afternoon while returning from a campaign trip to Florida.[21] He arrived at the White House at about 7:10 p.m., for a meeting with top advisers, including both Dulles brothers, JCS Chairman Radford, Defense Secretary Charles Wilson, Sherman Adams, and others from the State Department and White House.

Eisenhower was seething with anger. The president later recalled issuing an edict to his secretary of state laced with fury, on what the U.S. response to the Israelis would be: "Foster, you tell 'em, Goddamnit, that we're going to apply sanctions, we're going to the United Nations, we're going to do everything that there is to so we can stop this thing."[22]

During this initial session with his advisers at the outbreak of war, the president decreed his basic course for the remainder of the Suez crisis. He would compel Israel to withdraw from Egypt, even if that meant defending Gamal Abdel Nasser—the man U.S. policy had tried for months to contain and undermine—and even if it meant confronting British and French allies who had apparently cooperated with Israel's invasion in some fashion.

With deadly intensity Eisenhower repeated over and over that the United States would "redeem its pledge" under the 1950 Tripartite Declaration to aid the victims of armed aggression in the Middle East. If Britain and France would not cooperate, the president rumbled, then "in these circumstances perhaps we cannot be bound by our traditional alliances." In that case, they would find out that "nothing justifies double crossing us."

Dulles thought it likely that Egypt would now block Suez Canal traffic. Oil pipelines through Syria would be sabotaged, thus justifying direct British and French military intervention, over and above that of Israel. In taking such action, the allies might calculate that "whatever we may think of what they have done—we have to go along with them." To disabuse them of such notions, Eisenhower planned to warn Eden directly that U.S. opposition to the use of force had not changed.

He also ordered the State Department to seek an emergency meeting of the UN Security Council the next morning. A U.S.-backed resolution demanding reversal of Israel's action, Eisenhower and advisers hoped, would prevent the Soviets from pushing for military intervention on the side of Egypt, whether unilateral or sanctioned by the UN.[23]

Shortly after concluding the meeting that set this course, Eisenhower and his secretary of state confronted the British minister in Washington, John Coulson, at the White House. The president wanted the British diplomat to tell Eden directly that Eisenhower expected Britain to honor its commitment under the 1950 Tripartite Declaration. Eisenhower went so far as to hint at American military action against Israel, warning that he would "call the Congress if necessary in order to redeem our pledge." Coulson had little to say.[24] That same evening, Press Secretary Jim Hagerty publicly repeated Eisenhower's determination to honor the 1950 pact, support "victims of aggression," and bring the matter to the UN Security Council, stating that the president would evaluate whether to call a special session of Congress "in the light of the unfolding situation."[25]

Ben-Gurion sent a message to Eisenhower overnight. He justified his country's military action against Egypt as a war "to ensure that the declared Arab aim of eliminating Israel by force should not come about."[26]

By the next morning, October 30, U.S. officials were seeing more and more evidence of French, and possibly British, support for or involvement in the Israeli attack. Ambassador Henry Cabot Lodge reported to Dulles that when he'd approached Britain's UN ambassador about supporting a Security Council resolution calling for Israeli withdrawal from Egypt, the ambassador virtually snarled with derision. "Don't be silly and moralistic," Sir Pierson Dixon spat. "We have got to be practical." Throughout the day, British and French diplomats at the UN were "white faced and hostile" to American overtures, with American ambassadors reporting similar attitudes in London and Paris. [27]

At a morning meeting with Dulles, his aides, and White House officials, Eisenhower authorized a presidential cable to Eden laying out American knowledge of French complicity in Israel's invasion of Egypt, including increased radio traffic and the French shipment of Mystère aircraft. Eisenhower wrote that he was "astonished" to find that Britain's UN envoy now seemed to regard the Tripartite Declaration as "ancient history and without current validity." Eisenhower said his own government "had no thought of repudiating that statement and we have none now."

Eisenhower warned Eden against British and French involvement with Israel in "a general Arab war." That could lead to a UN resolution condemning Israeli aggression, legitimizing Soviet military assistance to help defend Egypt, "and then the Mid East fat would really be in the fire." It was time for the United States, Britain, and France to make clear their intentions. [28]

Just after this message went to London, a cable arrived from Eden. The prime minister asserted that UN Security Council action was "unlikely to be either rapid or effective," hinting that Britain would soon take "decisive action" of its own. Eden claimed he had at least secured an Israeli promise not to attack Jordan, "but we feel under no obligation to come to the aid of Egypt."[29]

Eisenhower drafted a reply to this, then decided not to send it, discouraged by what was starting to become, as he put it to Dulles, "a sort of trans-Atlantic essay contest."[30] He was now going to answer the Israeli, French, and British moves with actions.

When advisers suggested the British were counting on American oil shipments when Egypt blocked the canal and Syria sabotaged pipelines from Saudi Arabia, Eisenhower's reply was cold. "The President said he did not see much value in an unworthy and unreliable ally and that the necessity to support them might not be as great as they believed."[31]

Eden went before his Parliament that day. The prime minister declared that Britain and France were acting to restore a dangerous breach of peace in the Middle East and protect the Suez Canal. Eden said he had consulted with the United States, falsely implying Washington knew in advance about what he announced next.

Eden gave Egypt and Israel twelve hours to cease hostilities and withdraw their forces at least ten miles from the Suez Canal. Egypt was to accept British and French occupation troops at Port Said, Ismailia, and Suez, to secure free passage for shipping through the canal. Failure by either Egypt or Israel to comply with these demands would result in Anglo-French military action. The deadline for Egyptian and Israeli compliance was 11:30 p.m., Washington time. Mollet delivered the same message to the French National Assembly.[32]

Egypt promptly rejected the demands. Israel promptly accepted.

Upon hearing of Eden's ultimatum, Eisenhower reportedly erupted in a profanity-laden tirade. For Eisenhower and Dulles, it was a breaking point. Dulles no longer doubted the British and French were "more or less conniving in an attack against Egypt" by arranging the Israeli invasion as a pretext. In a phone call with the president, the secretary called the ultimatum "about as crude and brutal as anything he has ever seen." Dulles added that "of course by tomorrow they will be in."

Eisenhower "agreed that it was pretty rough." He thought the British and French "would expect the Russians to be in on this," because otherwise "where is Egypt going to turn?" Eisenhower ordered the secretary to ignore objections from Britain and France and start the UN Security Council debate that afternoon on a U.S.-backed resolution calling for suspension of economic and military aid to Israel until a cease-fire and Israeli withdrawal from Sinai took effect.[33]

Eisenhower's administration took a series of steps that day to separate the United States from the Anglo-French action. The White House issued a statement denying any U.S. foreknowledge of the ultimatum and calling on all parties to accept a peaceful UN settlement of the crisis. Eisenhower publicly released terse notes to Eden and Mollet along similar lines.

The two prime ministers later sent messages to Eisenhower depicting their ultimatum as an exercise in disinterested, benevolent military intervention to restore peace in the Middle East. Dulles ridiculed that rationale as transparently idiotic in confrontational meetings with British and French envoys in Washington, openly accusing their governments of collusion with Israel. The secretary's verbal beating implied that allied support for military aggression put the existence of NATO itself at risk. "We are facing the destruction of our trust in each other," he warned.[34]

Secretary Dulles and his brother, the CIA director, also reluctantly agreed to end any further American cooperation with the British for a coup in Syria. The Damascus conspirators had already abandoned the operation, planned for October 29, when they got word of Israel's attack on Egypt. The Syrian government soon arrested most of them, apparently having known of the plot the whole time.[35]

Eisenhower turned his threatening language about oil supplies into action. After only two days of fighting, as the evening debate of the UN Security

Council got under way on October 30, the president met with Arthur Flemming, director of the Office of Defense Mobilization. Eisenhower ordered Flemming not to implement plans drawn up prior to hostilities for emergency oil shipments for Britain and France.

"The president said," according to minutes of the meeting, "he was inclined to think that those who began this operation should be left to work out their own oil problems—to boil in their own oil, so to speak. They would be needing oil from Venezuela, and around the Cape, and before long they would be short of dollars to finance these operations and would be calling for help. They may be planning to present us with a fait accompli, then expecting us to foot the bill." That, the president of the United States made clear, wasn't going to happen. "You'll be under pressure by some of your colleagues in the capital to move," Eisenhower told Flemming. "Don't pay any attention to them until you hear from me."[36] Eisenhower did not publicize these oil moves, but they would be apparent to their targets soon enough.

While the president's economic coercion unfolded in the shadows, Ambassador Lodge introduced a resolution in the Security Council calling for an immediate cease-fire in Egypt, a withdrawal of Israeli forces from Egyptian territory, and the end of economic, financial, and military aid to Israel until it complied. UN member states were to refrain from any use of force or threat of such use in violation of the UN Charter.

Britain and France voted no, casting their first-ever vetoes in the UN Security Council. The rupture in NATO was fully revealed for all the world to see. The Soviet Union voted with the United States.[37]

The Soviets, though, appeared disengaged from Suez and fixated on Hungary. On October 30 and 31, the CIA confirmed that Soviet troops were leaving Budapest. Negotiations between the USSR and the Nagy government for a full withdrawal from Hungary were apparently under way. After suddenly halting its violent crackdown, the Kremlin issued a new policy of noninterference in the satellite states. Nagy announced that free elections were to be held.[38]

John Foster Dulles told Vice President Nixon the news from Hungary meant "the beginning of the collapse of the Soviet Empire." Allen Dulles hailed the Hungarian revolt as "a miracle" and Moscow's declaration of noninterference in the satellite nations "one the most significant statements to come out of the USSR in the last decade."[39]

CIA analysts concluded that the abrupt turnabout in Soviet policy hinted at confusion reigning in the Kremlin, with Soviet leaders perhaps concluding their repressive policy came at too great a risk of provoking further nationalist uprisings in Eastern Europe. Preoccupied behind the Iron Curtain, the Soviets appeared unlikely to do more in the Middle East than spew propaganda and issue empty threats. "There is no indication," the CIA said, "that the USSR will make any further commitment at this time."[40]

PRESSURING THE ATTACKERS, DEVELOPING A NEW PEACEKEEPING PLAN: OCTOBER 31–NOVEMBER 4

British and French air strikes on Egypt commenced on the afternoon of October 31, Washington time, hitting Egyptian airbases around Cairo, Port Said, and the Canal Zone. Eisenhower and Dulles had expected a ground invasion, as well, but for the moment it didn't materialize.

Egypt retaliated for the attacks by sinking a 320-foot freighter in the Suez Canal, blocking it. It was the first of thirty-two ships that would litter the floor of the canal in days to come. Tankers delivering oil from the Persian Gulf to Western Europe would now have to travel around the southern tip of Africa, making shortages in Britain, France, and the other NATO countries inevitable—just as an American president determined to exploit his economic leverage had foreseen.[41]

That evening, Eisenhower addressed the nation on the crisis in a televised speech from the Oval Office. "The United States," he said of the Anglo-French attack on Egypt, "was not consulted in any way about any phase of these actions. Nor were we informed of them in advance." The president acknowledged that Egypt had begun the crisis with its reckless seizure of the canal, and he vowed to preserve the Western alliance despite the rupture between Washington and its allies over their use of force. But he pledged to seek action at the UN General Assembly to restore peace, following the British and French veto at the Security Council. "There will be," said the president, "no United States involvement in the present hostilities." America's NATO allies were on their own.[42]

Eisenhower's stance brought an outpouring of praise from the developing world, opposition politicians in the British Parliament, and most NATO governments. Radio Cairo continued to accuse Washington of conspiring with the Zionists and European colonialists, but Nasser privately asked the U.S. ambassador for U.S. military intervention on Egypt's behalf (the ambassador replied that UN action would have to suffice). Moscow continued to denounce the Americans as part of a Suez conspiracy.[43]

Foster Dulles and White House chief of staff Sherman Adams hoped the president's address to the nation would preserve his image as a strong leader heading into the election. The president's break with Britain and France had provoked a firestorm of controversy at home.

While much of the commentary from journalists and politicians saw the Anglo-French action as an ill-advised return to naked colonialism, Eisenhower, nevertheless, suffered withering condemnation from opponents who accused him of putting the existence of NATO at risk. Adlai Stevenson, the Democratic presidential nominee, charged that the administration's policy "would aid the long-held plans of Communist Russia to split the free world." James Reston of the *New York Times* wrote that Eisenhower "has lost control of events."[44]

Rumblings of dissent stirred even within the president's own administration. A November 1 meeting of the NSC devolved into a near-shouting match between Dulles and Harold Stassen, the president's adviser on disarmament. Stassen favored abandoning U.S. opposition to allied military action in Egypt and instead supporting it, or at least doing nothing to stop it. He viewed preserving NATO unity as outweighing loss of support in the developing world.

Dulles argued that siding with Eden and Mollet's brutal reassertion of colonialism would cement Soviet influence over developing states, with all their strategic resources and assets, for generations to come. NATO unity would be preserved at the cost of catastrophic defeat in the Cold War. Other NSC members weren't as adamant as Stassen but expressed varying degrees of disquiet with Secretary Dulles's jeremiad against Britain and France.

Eisenhower bridged the divide. He made clear that allowing the Atlantic alliance to fall apart was "unthinkable." Soviet intervention in the war remained possible, in his mind. If it happened, he said, "the fat would really be in the fire." At that point, U.S. support for its NATO allies would be imperative.

But the president still sided with Dulles in viewing Anglo-French-Israeli aggression as unacceptable. He ordered UN General Assembly action to proceed.[45]

To contain the political backlash, Eisenhower kept other forms of pressure hidden from the press and public. The administration made no public announcement of the oil moves against Britain and France. It said nothing publicly about the suspension of aid to Israel. In the Mediterranean, the U.S. Navy actively harassed British and French warships bound for Egypt, repeatedly buzzing them with aircraft or sending American vessels knifing across their path. The details of such tensions would only come to light years later.[46]

Foster Dulles expected the quiet economic coercion strategy to be effective. Immediately after the fractious NSC meeting, the secretary told his brother the CIA director that "there would be a strain on the Br[itish] and Fr[ench] and it will be economic and [come] quickly—the oil problem will be acute pretty soon."[47]

His prediction began to come true the next day. His ambassador in London reported that British officials were "distressed" upon hearing that U.S. government meetings to organize emergency oil shipments had been canceled.[48] The *New York Times* reported the cancellation but buried the news on page 22.[49]

The French also showed signs of panic. Attempting to deflect American pressure, French officials claimed to have intelligence of imminent Soviet deployment of combat aircraft to Syria. JCS Chairman Radford scoffed at this assertion, saying such action was likely beyond Soviet logistical capabilities (an assessment the administration would reconsider a few days later).[50]

In a November 1 conversation with Douglas Dillon, Christian Pineau sought to curry American favor by divulging at length the details of the Anglo-French conspiracy with Israel to attack Egypt and deceive the Eisenhower administration in doing so. Here at last was the "smoking gun" Eisenhower and Dulles had sought, providing firsthand evidence of the Suez collusion. Pineau apparently hoped that coming clean would prompt Washington to relax its opposition, by demonstrating the depth of allied feeling that led to such drastic action.[51]

Only hours after Pineau's confession, John Foster Dulles delivered a ferocious denunciation of America's allies before the UN General Assembly. Their actions, he said, threatened a future of international anarchy leading to a new global war that would, unlike the last one, end human civilization.

The General Assembly passed the U.S.-sponsored resolution by an overwhelming margin of sixty-four to five, with six abstentions. It called for a ceasefire in Egypt, suspension of new movement of military forces and aid into the Middle East, a withdrawal of forces to prewar lines, restoration of free transit through the Suez Canal, and recommendations by the secretary-general on further steps to end the crisis. The debate stretched on until long after midnight, and Dulles arrived back at his hotel room in New York at 5:00 a.m., utterly exhausted.[52]

Over the weekend of Friday, November 2, to Sunday, November 4, the Eisenhower administration worried about an escalation of the Middle East conflict as the war in Egypt raged on. Waves of British and French bombing raids were close to knocking out the Egyptian air force while Israeli armies inflicted a crushing defeat on the ground. U-2 overflights showed a fleet of over 100 British and French ships approaching Egypt.[53]

But Allen and Foster Dulles believed the expected Anglo-French ground invasion might not finish Nasser off. It could lead, instead, to an extended guerrilla war against British and French occupation troops in the Suez Canal Zone. The secretary of state worried that such a quagmire would inspire additional conflicts in North Africa and even in the Persian Gulf.[54]

The day after the Dulles brothers shared these worries, Nasser told the U.S. ambassador in Egypt that he was preparing for exactly that scenario. He vowed to wage a "people's war" against the imminent Anglo-French assault, withdrawing his remaining armies from Sinai to draw the European invaders into bloody house-to-house guerrilla fighting along the canal.[55]

With that prospect in mind, ambassadors from Iraq, Saudi Arabia, Lebanon, and Tunisia pleaded with State Department officials for stronger American action to stop the fighting. Their governments, they said, were barely able to contain the anger building up in restive populations. "There was danger of revolutions all over the Arab world," the Iraqi ambassador warned—from a country whose government detested Nasser.[56]

Portents of a wider war continued to emerge that weekend. Syria placed its armed forces under Egyptian command, publicly vowing to come to Nasser's defense under the recent triple military pact with Jordan and Egypt. Israeli foreign minister Golda Meir told U.S. officials that Israel regarded the Syrian announcement as, in effect, a declaration of hostilities. She claimed to have intelligence reporting both Syrian and Iraqi forces moving into Jordan. U.S. ambassador Lawson in Israel reported "IDF tanks in considerable numbers moving south and east to Jordan-Syrian frontier."[57]

On November 3, the Syrian president, in Moscow, received a public pledge from the Soviet government of "necessary assistance to overcome as rapidly as possible the vestiges of colonialism and reinforce [Syria's] independence." U.S. ambassador Chip Bohlen in Moscow thought the Soviet talks with the Syrians had a "strong smell of some military deal," apparently against Israel. The same day, the U.S. embassy in Damascus reported that, as feared, saboteurs in Syria had blown up pumping stations along the pipeline owned by the Iraq Petroleum Company, putting it out of action indefinitely.[58]

With that pipeline down and the Suez Canal closed, the oil situation in Europe was about to become critical. A CIA intelligence summary estimated that 86 percent of Western Europe's oil supply was affected. Only the Trans-Arabia pipeline from Saudi Arabia through Syria and Jordan remained operational, and it could be sabotaged just as easily.[59]

The British government was preparing to ration fuel supplies. Eisenhower's oil planners recommended keeping the quiet U.S. oil restrictions in place, because doing so would help "bring the British and French to take a constructive position" in Egypt.[60]

While Eisenhower kept the economic screws tightened on his NATO allies, the news from Hungary, which a few days earlier had seemed to indicate a break in the crisis, again became much worse. On November 1 the new Hungarian leader, Imre Nagy, declared Hungary's withdrawal from the Warsaw Pact, drawing vicious denunciations from Moscow. CIA sources on November 2 and 3 reported that Soviet forces were deploying around Budapest for a major assault on the city.[61]

As the first week of war was coming to a close on Friday, November 2, Eisenhower was leading his administration in brainstorming a major new policy move. The initial push had been twofold: One—in public, the United States had already taken a leading role to mount overwhelming international pressure against Israel, Britain, and France to desist, including UN sanctions against assistance to Israel. Two—in private, the United States had made policy decisions that would put very great economic pressure on Britain and France, constraining the availability of oil and dollars. The objective of these moves was to get the attackers to stop, but neither offered a constructive alternative to keep the peace between Egypt and Israel, the bomb that had been ticking for the last year.

In a long letter on November 2 to a close friend and confidant, Eisenhower found time to reflect on the roots of the crisis. The Suez Canal issue was, he thought, "not the real heart of the matter."

> The real point is that Britain, France and Israel had come to believe—probably correctly—that Nasser was their worst enemy in the Mid East and that until he was removed or deflated, they would have no peace. I do not quarrel with the idea that there is justification for such fears, but I have insisted long and earnestly that you cannot resort to force in international relationships because of your fear of what might happen in the future. In short, I think the British and French seized upon a very poor vehicle to use in bringing Nasser to terms.
>
> Of course, nothing in the region would be so difficult to solve except for the underlying cause of the unrest and dissension that exists there— that is, the Arab-Israel quarrel.[62]

That day, November 2, Eisenhower turned his full attention to that "underlying cause," seeking some extraordinary move to address the Arab-Israeli dispute. The American success in the UN had spurred him to envision the next steps after a possible cease-fire. Earlier in the year he and Dulles had tried secret diplomatic mediation. That had failed. Now he wanted something more public, to which he was willing to stake whatever prestige he had in the world—maybe joined by the statesman whose stature he regarded as comparably great, especially among "neutral" countries—India's prime minister, Jawaharlal Nehru.

By the end of the day, Eisenhower had zeroed in on "the idea of a neutral strip around Israel" that would require an ambitious vision for a much larger UN peacekeeping force. A smaller version of this had been part of the U.S. strategy in the spring and summer of 1956, working with Hammarskjöld to mitigate a possible war. Now Eisenhower seems to have imagined a much more ambitious UN presence, less of a border monitor, more of a force that might use thousands of troops patrolling a wide demilitarized zone.[63]

Eisenhower pushed for immediate action on this idea, while also working over the weekend of November 2 through 4 to form a UN peacekeeping force for Suez that could deploy before an Anglo-French ground invasion could begin. One part of this strategy was to work with Nehru for a significant commitment of Indian troops to help make up the new UN peacekeeping force in the Canal Zone—a proposal to which Nehru agreed. UN troops on Egyptian soil with Nasser's approval, Eisenhower and Dulles calculated, would force Eden to call off the landing rather than risk the diplomatic catastrophe of a direct military clash with the United Nations. The State Department worked feverishly to line up diplomatic support for a General Assembly resolution establishing the peacekeeping force and endorsed by the government of Egypt.[64]

Then, in the midst of all this work, Eisenhower's diplomatic architect was struck down. Dulles's health finally collapsed. After midnight on Saturday, November 3, John Foster Dulles woke up with crippling abdominal pain. An ambulance took him to Walter Reed Hospital for emergency surgery. Before going under the knife, the secretary ordered his deputy, Under Secretary Herbert Hoover Jr., to take over as acting secretary of state during what promised to be a lengthy recovery—except on any matter related to Suez. Dulles himself would continue to manage the crisis from his hospital bed. Then surgeons removed a cancerous tumor from his colon.[65]

The State Department's diplomats succeeded in bending the UN General Assembly to Eisenhower's will, orchestrating General Assembly passage of a fresh resolution, sponsored by Canada, after midnight on November 4. It directed Secretary-General Hammarskjöld to set up a UN Emergency Force within forty-eight hours. Egypt accepted it. At Eisenhower's insistence, the secretary-general was given sole authority over this task, without a committee to slow him down.

A second UN General Assembly resolution renewed the UN demand for a cease-fire. The resolution set a twelve-hour deadline for compliance and authorized Hammarskjöld to negotiate it.[66] Israeli ambassador Abba Eban stunned the delegates by agreeing to a cease-fire in the middle of the debate, provided Egypt did so, as well.[67]

As the General Assembly moved to adjourn at 3:00 a.m. on Sunday, November 4, news of another war reached New York and Washington, this one in Hungary. Imre Nagy had gone on the radio to report a massive Soviet military assault on Budapest. CIA sources would eventually report at least 200,000 Soviet troops and 4,600 tanks engaged. Paratroops, tanks, artillery, and air strikes tore the Hungarian armed forces to shreds, bombed towns and cities across the country, indiscriminately leveled buildings, and butchered civilians moving in the streets. Reports of such atrocities flooded resistance radio broadcasts and Western news media reports coming out of Hungary. They worsened the air of tension gripping official Washington as the Suez war raged.[68]

Hammarskjöld and the State Department raced to avert an Anglo-French landing in Egypt. They secured pledges of troops for a peacekeeping force from several nations and passage of a November 4 General Assembly resolution setting up a military command structure, all with Egyptian backing.[69]

TO THE PRECIPICE: NOVEMBER 5–6

Just after midnight Eastern Time on Monday, November 5, British and French paratroopers landed at Port Said, Egypt, at the northern end of the Suez Canal along the Mediterranean coast. At first, they met little resistance and arranged a fragile truce with local Egyptian authorities. Later in the day heavy house-to-house fighting erupted in Port Said and allied air strikes throughout the Canal Zone continued.[70]

In two overnight cables to Eisenhower, Eden tried to reconcile his move with what had just happened in the UN. He said the British and French would hold the Canal Zone with ground forces until the eventual arrival of a UN force would allow them to "hand over responsibility." Once the fighting was over, talks on international control of the canal could begin.[71]

Britain's UN delegation used arguments about the UN force as a way to buy time. They conditioned acceptance of a cease-fire on guarantees that a UN force would be effective enough to keep the peace and to assure free transit of the Suez Canal. Israel, meanwhile, confirmed that its forces had already accepted a cease-fire.[72]

Eden's cables and news of the allied landing at Port Said did not change Eisenhower's course. In a morning meeting at the White House he told Vice President Richard Nixon, Hoover, State Department aides, and his principal national security staffer, Colonel Andrew Goodpaster, that "we should stick with the plan as developed thus far, in spite of the UK and French landings." Work to organize a UN emergency force would continue, to be deployed once a full cease-fire went into effect.

Stopping the fighting seemed to now be even more important, given new intelligence that the British and French might widen their land war beyond the Canal Zone, thus risking a protracted conflict. Hoover also worried about possible Soviet deployment of warplanes to Syria, given reports that Moscow was preparing to back the Syrians against Israel.

To avert such dangers, Eisenhower said, denial of oil shipments to Britain and France would continue, despite Hoover's concern that NATO military readiness would suffer. "The President felt," said the minutes of the meeting, "that the purposes of peace and stability would be served by not being too quick in attempting to render extraordinary assistance." He allowed military and civilian oil transport ships to be readied for use, but for the time being they would not sail for Western Europe.[73]

Eisenhower's choice came at a cost. No other country in Western Europe besides Britain and France had the necessary harbor and storage facilities to receive massive shipments of overseas oil. Any delivery of oil, anywhere on the continent, had to go through British and French ports first, so the U.S. restrictions on emergency supplies effectively denied oil to all of Europe. The State Department expected formal NATO appeals for emergency shipments at any time, with serious shortages expected to develop within a month.[74] If the United States gave into these pleas, JCS chairman Radford expected the Saudis to retaliate by ending oil production. He thus wanted to prepare for the contingency of a possible U.S. military intervention in Saudi Arabia to keep the oil flowing in such a case.[75]

The sum of all the fears haunting the White House throughout the crisis began to unfold on the afternoon of November 5. The U.S. embassy in Moscow cabled a message from Soviet prime minister Nikolai Bulganin to Eisenhower. It proposed joint U.S.-Soviet military intervention in Egypt to uphold the resolutions of the UN General Assembly. The message said that the two superpowers were uniquely suited for this task by their possession of "atom and hydrogen weapons." The attack on Egypt, Bulganin stated, was a war to impose colonial rule that was opposed by the entire world. "If this war is not stopped," the message warned, "it is fraught with danger and can grow into [a] third world war."[76]

Bulganin sent another message to Hammarskjöld, calling French and British actions in Egypt acts of aggression and warning that "the responsibility for all the possible consequences of those actions rests with the Governments of the United Kingdom and France." Soviet foreign minister Dimitri Shepilov cabled the president of the UN Security Council demanding an immediate meeting to consider a draft Soviet resolution providing for the use of military force by UN members to defend Egypt unless Britain, France, and Israel ceased all hostilities within twelve hours and withdrew their forces within three days. The Soviet Union, said Shepilov, "for its part declares that it is ready to contribute to the cause of curbing the aggressors, of defending the victims of aggression, and of restoring peace, by sending to Egypt the air and naval forces necessary for the achievement of this purpose."[77]

Bulganin sent additional messages directly to Eden, Mollet, and Ben-Gurion, infused with menace. Bulganin declared: "We are fully determined to crush the aggressors by the use of force and to restore peace in the East."[78]

The Soviet threats of November 5 altered American calculations. For three months leading up to the Suez war, the USSR had remained in the background of the Middle East crisis, content with obstructionist diplomacy at the August conference in London plus endless propaganda denouncing Western imperialism and colonialism. As Eisenhower had always feared might happen, the Soviets had now gone much further.

From Moscow, the U.S. ambassador there, Charles "Chip" Bohlen, one of the most seasoned Soviet-watchers in the U.S. government, immediately discounted Bulganin's proposal for joint U.S.-Soviet intervention as unserious. He interpreted the Kremlin's sudden interest in Suez as partly a move to distract the world from Hungary.

But he also said that the extreme violence of the Hungary repression might indicate a greater Soviet willingness to run risks in international affairs generally. While the Soviets were not likely to start World War III directly, Bohlen didn't rule out some form of lesser intervention in the Middle East. He cited Moscow's pledge of assistance to Syria over the weekend as a possible example. Bulganin's pledge to intervene in Egypt could be another. "It would be imprudent," in Bohlen's view, "to dismiss this merely as an empty propaganda gesture."[79]

In a later afternoon meeting with State Department and White House officials, the president agreed with Bohlen's assessment. He repeated an analogy he had made a week and a half earlier, at the October 26 NSC meeting, when he had compared Hitler's suicidal irrationality during the destruction of the Third Reich to Soviet paranoia amid revolt in Moscow's East European buffer zone. "The President said," according to the record, "his concern is that the Soviets, seeing their position and their policy failing so badly in the satellites, are ready to take any wild adventure . . . The Soviets are scared and furious, and there is nothing more dangerous than a dictatorship in this state of mind."

Following this grim assessment, Eisenhower chose to issue a firm, clear threat to deter any Soviet military move into the Middle East. He ordered that a public statement be issued immediately that would draw a clear line for the Kremlin leadership, warning them against any unilateral military action in the Middle East outside the framework of UN resolutions.[80]

The White House statement went out that evening, replying directly to Bulganin's message to Eisenhower in full view of the world, without going through the diplomatic nicety of privately sending it to the Soviet government first. The statement laid down Eisenhower's warning: "Neither Soviet nor any other military forces should now enter the Middle East area except under United Nations mandate . . . The introduction of new forces under these circumstances would violate the United Nations Charter, and it would be the duty of all United Nations members, including the United States, to oppose any such effort." According to news outlets, diplomats around the world understood the American warning to be a direct threat to use military force.[81]

The next day, Tuesday, November 6, was Election Day in the United States. As the country went to the polls, the news was crowded with stories of British and French amphibious landings at Port Said. A National Intelligence Estimate prepared since the previous day's Soviet threats downplayed, as Bohlen had, the danger that the Soviets might start a nuclear war. It also pointed out that Soviet air operations in the Middle East would be difficult, with few nearby bases. If the Soviets did intervene, it could take the form of small-scale air and submarine attacks on British and French forces in the Mediterranean.

The Soviets could also send military equipment to Syria along with "volunteer" military forces, referring to Soviet troops masquerading as independent contingents. The estimate concluded with a warning that nothing was certain. "The flow of events," it said, "will be drastically affected by day to day decision and action of the main participants, including in particular the USA, and the estimate the Soviet Union reaches as to the probable course of action of the USA, the UK, and France."[82]

The president and the CIA director received other disquieting intelligence that morning. Early in the fighting, U.S. intelligence indicated the Soviets had withdrawn personnel and equipment from Egypt recently arrived under the 1955 arms deal.[83] Now, however, Allen Dulles reported evidence of the Soviet government informing Egypt that it would "do something" in the Middle East. Eisenhower and Dulles worried that this might mean Soviet deployment of aircraft into Egypt or Syria.

The president ordered U-2 flights specifically over Israel and Syria to look for Soviet aircraft. Despite the logistical challenges of such Soviet air operations, Eisenhower believed he couldn't rule out the possibility, because he couldn't know Soviet intentions for certain.

"If the Soviets attack the French and British directly, we would be in war," he said, "and we would be justified in taking military action even if Congress were not in session." If the U-2 flights found Soviet aircraft in Syria, Eisenhower added, "there would be reason for the British and French to destroy them."[84]

After Eisenhower left Washington early that Election Day morning to vote near his home in Gettysburg, Pennsylvania, new Middle East developments continued to unfold, piling on the stress. The Egyptian ambassador in Washington pleaded for U.S. military aid or direct intervention in support of his country.[85] The French ambassador virtually begged for American solidarity with NATO allies against Moscow's threats, reacting with alarm when Acting Secretary Hoover implied that NATO support was contingent on an Anglo-French withdrawal from Egypt.[86]

While Eisenhower was in Gettysburg on election morning, Bohlen sent another cable from Moscow directly to the president. Bohlen was troubled by the Soviet notes to Eden, Mollet, and Ben-Gurion. They came "as close to [an] ultimatum as possible without so stating," as did the menacing three-day deadline for withdrawal of hostile forces in Shepilov's proposed Security Council resolution. This ultimatum, along with warlike rhetoric suddenly filling the USSR's state-controlled press, suggested ominous intent.

Perhaps, Bohlen argued, Moscow might have crushed opposition in Hungary to stabilize its frontier and prepare for intervention in the Middle East. The possibility of the Suez war spreading beyond Egypt (as tensions between Israel and Syria illustrated) had apparently prompted Moscow to move to end the fighting before Soviet interests were placed at even greater risk.

It was essential, Bohlen recommended, to convince the Soviets that the United States would resist military intervention by force of arms. To remove any pretext for that intervention, Bohlen urged "some official communication from U.S. Government as to when all hostilities would cease against Egypt."[87]

Bohlen's telegram sent more shockwaves through the ranks of Eisenhower's top advisers. It came after several days of intelligence about possible Israeli or Soviet intervention in Syria. Its significance seemed bolstered by new reports of unidentified aircraft over Turkey and Soviet troops massing on the Turkish border, or readying for deployment to Egypt, or arriving already with rumored "special weapons." The latest U-2 photographs showed no signs of Soviet forces in Syria, but the roughly twenty-four-hour lag in getting U-2 intelligence to Washington meant that such intelligence was literally yesterday's news.[88]

At midday Eisenhower met with his top White House aides and the senior leadership of the State Department, Department of Defense, and CIA, as well as the entire Joint Chiefs of Staff. Eisenhower ordered a phone call placed to Prime Minister Eden, using a transatlantic telephone line that had only recently been installed.

In response to the Soviet threat to the Middle East, and to back up Eisenhower's public statements, the Joint Chiefs proposed a series of steps to increase readiness of American military forces not just in the Mediterranean area but around the world. Eisenhower approved JCS recommendations to put air defenses in North America on alert; deploy two additional aircraft carriers and other surface combat vessels to the Azores in readiness to reinforce the Sixth Fleet; order additional ships and submarines of the Atlantic and Pacific fleets to put to sea; and put troop transport aircraft on alert.

Eisenhower put aside JCS proposals to put U.S. strategic nuclear forces on alert and recall personnel on leave. His intent was to make a show of force that the Kremlin would notice, without being excessively provocative. He ordered the JCS plan implemented beginning the following day.[89]

In the middle of the White House discussion of military preparations, and only a day after British ground troops had finally hit the ground in Egypt, Anthony Eden returned Eisenhower's phone call from across the Atlantic. Eisenhower had received word that the British might quit stalling and would accept a cease-fire. He opened the conversation by welcoming this news and tried to urge Eden not to attach conditions, such as allowing British and French troops to remain to clear the canal.

Eden seemed to agree, grudgingly.

Eisenhower also preemptively suggested that no troops from the permanent members of the UN Security Council be included in any peacekeeping force. In other words—no British and French troops (or American or Soviet ones, either).

Eden was, again, reluctant. "May I think that one over?" was his response.

Eisenhower, though, had made it clear that neither clearing the canal nor participating in the UN force would allow British and French troops to remain in Egypt.[90]

That afternoon Eisenhower sent a telegram to follow up, "to emphasize my urgent view a) that the UN resolution on ceasefire and entry of a UN force be accepted without condition so as not to give Egypt with Soviet backing an opportunity to quibble or start negotiations; items such as use of technical troops to clear the canal can be handled later; b) that it is vital no excuse be given for Soviet participation in UN force, therefore all big five [UN Security Council permanent members] should be excluded from force as UN proposes."

Eden had to agree immediately, "otherwise there might be invitation to developments of greatest gravity." Eisenhower wanted Eden to agree within hours, so that later that night, when Hammarskjöld convened another UN meeting in New York, this basic issue would be settled.[91]

LONDON

JILL KASTNER

THE BRITISH GOVERNMENT CHOOSES WAR

On Saturday, October 14, Anthony Eden wrapped up his remarkable meeting with his French guests at the prime ministerial country house, Chequers. The two Frenchmen departed for their flight back to Paris.

The only other official at the meeting had been the acting foreign secretary, Anthony Nutting, who was standing in for Selwyn Lloyd while the latter completed diplomatic talks at the UN in New York. Nutting could see that the Challe plan had made a powerful and positive impression on his chief. But he urged caution. Surely, he pleaded, they should sleep on the French proposal before making any decisions. Lloyd was due back from New York by mid-week. He should be consulted before London replied to the French.

Eden would have none of it. He was feeling pressure from many quarters. The French offer posed a way out. Although he and Lloyd had steadily rejected collaborating with the Israelis, he had now changed his mind.

Eden picked up the phone and summoned Lloyd home from New York immediately. Then he instructed Nutting to tell the British ambassador in Jordan that Britain would not "treat [Israeli] raids as an act of war and intervene." The Jordanians could look for no help from Britain in the event of another raid like Qalqilya. The Iraqi troop move into Jordan was postponed.[1]

Secrecy was suddenly paramount. Nutting confided the details of the French proposal to only two Foreign Office advisers, Permanent Under Secretary Sir

Ivone Kirkpatrick and Assistant Under Secretary Archibald Ross. When Nutting suggested that he inform Sir Gerald Fitzmaurice, the Foreign Office legal adviser, Eden barked, "Fitz is the last person I want consulted. The lawyers are always against our doing anything. For God's sake, keep them out of it. This is a political affair."[2]

The normally pugnacious Kirkpatrick did not like the plan at all. He and Ross wrote a paper for Eden on October 16 warning that it would undo the work at the UN, nullify the Tripartite Declaration, and enrage world opinion. Oil installations would also be threatened.[3]

Eden ignored the report. He was never one to follow advice he did not like, particularly from the Foreign Office. But mindful of his country's system of cabinet government, he sought to steer the cabinet into making the collective decision he desired. He arranged an "informal" meeting where he presented the French plan to members of the subset of the cabinet that had been empowered to work on the Suez crisis, the Egypt Committee. In this group, Nutting and Minister of Defense Walter Monckton were skeptical; others were more receptive. Lloyd arrived from New York and joined them as the meeting was in progress. When it ended, Eden and Lloyd departed secretly for Paris.[4]

At the Quai D'Orsay, French prime minister Guy Mollet and foreign minister Christian Pineau did not mince words. Britain and France had been "double-crossed by Mr. Dulles." His SCUA proposals and shifting positions on payments to Egypt were clearly stalling tactics.

Eden, echoing Macmillan's reports from late September, suggested that if Israel acted before November 6, the U.S. Congress would not be able to convene in time to give authority for U.S. intervention. The others agreed. Nonmilitary actions or economic sanctions were not discussed.[5]

Mollet then posed two questions. First, if the Israelis attacked Egypt, would Britain come to Egypt's aid under the Tripartite Declaration? And second, would Britain intervene to stop hostilities near the canal? Eden said he thought the answers were no and yes, respectively, but he would confirm after his return to London.

The talks ended around 1:30 a.m. Eden left behind two notes for the French to deliver to the Israelis. One stipulated that if there was fighting near the canal, Britain and France would call on both sides to halt and withdraw from the area. If one or both sides refused, Anglo-French forces would intervene. The other confirmed that if Israel attacked Egypt, Britain would not come to Egypt's defense.[6]

The next day, Eden met again with the Egypt Committee to report on the

Paris talks. Despite reservations from Lloyd and another member, the notes he had left with the French were approved.[7]

Lloyd had explained his absence from the Foreign Office by saying he was home sick with a cold. When confronted by Nutting upon his return, he sheepishly revealed that Eden had accepted the plan and coordinated arrangements with the Israelis. Lloyd admitted he was to return to Paris the following week for further discussions. Nutting threatened to resign if the plan went through.[8]

The next day, October 18, Eden made a careful presentation on the situation to the full cabinet of nearly twenty ministers. First, he listed the positive outcomes from the UN negotiations. Believing a diplomatic settlement in the works, ministers agreed to request Egyptian proposals for the implementation of the Six Principles agreed to in New York.

Next, the prime minister revealed that he and Lloyd had visited Paris to discuss further steps to settle the dispute with their French allies. Here his candor receded. There were signs the Israelis were preparing for a military move, he said, but he "had reason to believe" it might now be against Egypt instead of Jordan. He had "thought it right to make it known to the Israelis, through the French," that if Egypt and Israel came to blows, Britain would render no aid to Egypt. The cabinet should be aware that diplomatic efforts to settle the dispute were still ongoing, but "it was possible that the issue might be brought more rapidly to a head as a result of military action by Israel against Egypt."[9]

Shortly afterward, instructions went out from the navy ordering the forces of Operation Cordage, designated to deal with an Israeli attack against Jordan, brought to seventy-two-hours ready status. All three of Britain's aircraft carriers in the Mediterranean were off Malta by October 24–25, ostensibly for these Jordanian defense plans. But those plans also happened to fit the needs of Musketeer, the operation against Egypt. As of October 20, British commanders in the Mediterranean still did not know whether they were planning to attack Arabs or Israelis.[10]

Over the following weekend of October 21–22, Eden gathered Lloyd, Macmillan, and other Egypt Committee members at Chequers. During their Sunday discussions, news arrived from the French. Israeli prime minister David Ben-Gurion, General Moshe Dayan, and Director-General of the Israeli Defense Ministry Shimon Peres would be in Paris the next day. They wanted to meet with a British leader. The group at Chequers decided Lloyd should go.

Accompanied by his private secretary, Donald Logan, Lloyd arrived next morning at Villacoublay military airfield near Paris. From there he was taken

to a villa in the elegant Parisian suburb of Sèvres. Mollet, French defense minister Maurice Bourgès-Maunoury, and the Israeli delegation had already begun
talks. The two Englishmen joined them.

Lloyd, stern-faced and somber, told the group that progress in New York
meant they could probably reach a settlement with Egypt within seven days
if they desired. But, he acknowledged, such an agreement would strengthen
Nasser's position. British forces were mobilized and ready, but they couldn't
stay that way much longer. And "since Her Majesty's Government considered
that Nasser had to go, it was prepared to undertake military action in accordance with the latest version of the Anglo-French plan." This plan called for
an Israeli invasion of the Sinai, followed by an Anglo-French response within
forty-eight hours.[11]

The Israelis balked at such a long interval. Forty-eight hours would give the
Egyptians too much opportunity to bomb Israeli cities, and there was a danger
that Soviet and Czech "volunteers" would be dispatched to bolster the Egyptian
Air Force. They insisted on a much shorter timeline. The participants argued
back and forth without agreement.

Lloyd departed, promising to consult the cabinet and reply the next day.
With such disagreement about the time frame, he had the impression that the
plan was off.[12]

Eden, too, believed the project had stalled. The next day, Tuesday, October
23, he admitted to the cabinet that from "secret conversations" with the Israeli
government in Paris, "it now seemed unlikely" that Israel would attack Egypt.
He also told Allied Commander-in-Chief Sir Charles Keightley "the 'hot' news
had gone cold." The forces were given the code word Relax, allowing them to
stand down after weeks of living on the edge.[13]

At the same time, Eden privately dispatched Logan back to Paris with assurances that Britain would do its part to destroy the Egyptian Air Force in
the event of hostilities. On his arrival, Logan discovered that Pineau, worried
by Lloyd's dour attitude, was just departing for London to confer with Eden.

Once in Downing Street, Pineau told Eden that the Israelis had accepted
a thirty-six-hour delay between their attack and the onset of Anglo-French
bombing. This would give the British enough time to give the appearance of
deliberation without giving the Egyptians time to mount a counterattack. The
Americans should not be informed, "owing to their pre-occupation with the
election campaign, and the generally unsatisfactory nature of our exchanges
with Mr. Dulles about US action of any character."[14]

With this new development, Eden now called another cabinet meeting. The

French, he told them, were no longer willing to negotiate about Suez at the UN. They were furious, having just intercepted a large arms shipment from Cairo to anti-French rebels in Algeria.

Meanwhile, British troops had been held in readiness for too long; the reservists were getting restless. The military chiefs wanted to adopt a new plan after the end of October that still sought control over the Suez Canal and the "downfall of Colonel Nasser's regime in Egypt." But if the crisis lingered on unresolved, the military wanted to release the reservists and unload equipment from the merchant ships. This would give the impression that military precautions had relaxed, weakening Britain's bargaining position with Egypt.

There was good news, however. It was now known that if there were an Anglo-French intervention, "Israel would make a full-scale attack against Egypt; and this might have the effect of reducing the period of preliminary air bombardment."

Ministers worried that such an operation would unite the Arab world behind Egypt. But here Eden's private information from MI6 sources may have come into play. The greater risk, he told them, was Nasser's growing prestige in the region. It was known that Nasser was already plotting against other Arab regimes. Time was crucial, for "we should never have a better pretext for intervention against him."

Eden placed great store on his belief that Nasser must be swiftly toppled. "If . . . a military operation were undertaken against Egypt," he told the cabinet, "its effect in other Arab countries would be serious *unless* it led to the early collapse of Colonel Nasser's regime. For this reason and because of undoubted international pressure, the operation must be quick and successful."[15]

The cabinet now had a choice. If they chose to negotiate further, they could "frame their demands in such a way as to make it impossible for the Egyptians to accept them," thus paving the way for military action. If they sought a genuine negotiated settlement, they would have to abandon their objective of overthrowing Nasser. The cabinet decided further discussions with the French were needed before making a final decision.[16]

Eden, ill and exhausted, retired to his bed.

Later that day, Eden summoned Patrick Dean to his side. Dean was both a senior Foreign Office official and the head of the Cabinet Office's Joint Intelligence Committee, a principal source of intelligence assessments for the government. He was one of the few advisers aware of the secret planning on Egypt and for an MI6-supported coup in Syria.

Someone had to go back to Paris immediately to resume talks with the French and Israelis. Lloyd could not go; he was due to address the House of Commons that day. Eden had chosen Dean for the mission, accompanied by Lloyd's aide, Donald Logan.

Arriving back at the villa in Sèvres, Dean and Logan engaged in lengthy discussions with their French and Israeli counterparts, and the three parties came to an agreement. This was summarized in a written protocol, typed in French. There was to be a "large-scale" Israeli attack on Egyptian forces five days later, on October 29. The Israelis would aim to reach the Canal Zone on October 30. That same day, Britain and France would consult and issue the planned ultimatums to the Egyptian and Israeli governments. Britain agreed that if Jordan were to attack Israel it would not come to Jordan's aid.[17]

Dean had misgivings about signing the document, but he and Logan acknowledged that the protocol was an accurate summary of the agreement. Had he refused to sign, he would have heightened French and Israeli suspicions. Dean, therefore, signed the protocol, subject to the approval of his government. He and Logan then returned to London, arriving late that night at 10 Downing Street, where Eden and a small group of ministers were waiting.

Eden was mortified by the existence of the protocol. He dispatched both men immediately back to Paris to retrieve and destroy all copies. After a lengthy wait at the Quai d'Orsay, the British envoys were informed that the French would not comply. The Israelis were already back in Tel Aviv with their own copy, and the French saw no reason to destroy the one they held.

Eden reconvened the Cabinet again at 10 a.m. the next morning, October 25. He revealed that the Israelis would attack after all. "They evidently felt that the ambitions of Colonel Nasser's Government threatened their continued existence as an independent State," he told the gathered ministers. The Israelis could not risk waiting for others to act.

If Israel attacked, Eden proposed that Britain and France deliver two ultimatums—the same ones secretly agreed to at Sèvres. Eden admitted they would probably be accused of "collusion" with Israel. But this would likely happen anyway, because if Britain and France moved against Egypt, Israel would no doubt attack as well. Far better to be seen holding the combatants apart than acquiescing in an Israeli attack.

Some members of the cabinet were hesitant. The Americans would surely protest. Claiming to hold the balance "evenly" between Egypt and Israel was obviously a charade, since the Egyptians would be asked to withdraw further into their own territory while the Israelis remained well outside of theirs. The plan clearly breached the Tripartite Declaration. But despite these misgivings, ministers, unaware of the full extent of the agreement with the Israelis, gave their endorsement.[18]

Cabinet ministers were not the only ones with reservations. Britain's military leaders, the Chiefs of Staff, reported that reoccupying the entire Canal Zone and possibly installing a new government in Cairo would require three to four divisions and a support staff for civil affairs. One infantry division would have to be withdrawn from Germany, and the U.K. Strategic Reserve would need to be allocated to the project. Allied Commander-in-Chief Sir Charles Keightley questioned if Britain would be better off afterward. Eden told him tartly to mind his own business.[19]

ACTION AT LAST

By October 29, Eden had excluded from decision-making anyone unsympathetic to the Anglo-French-Israeli plan. The head of the political section of MI6 found himself cut off from some cable traffic. William Clark, Eden's personal secretary, had difficulty accessing his prime minister. Only a few souls in the Foreign Office were aware of British plans, and Foreign Office channels were not used for communication with the French. After October 14, there was not much to say to U.S. officials, and what little was said was deceptive. On October 28, the day before the Israeli attack began, Lloyd went so far as to tell the U.S. ambassador in London that he "was unwilling to believe the Israelis would launch a full-scale attack on Egypt."[20]

As for Eden, the pressure continued to take a toll on his health. As October 29 approached, both Nutting and Monckton worried privately about his transformation from the brilliant diplomat they had once known. Eden had become "a very sick man." Always temperamental, he now seemed "on the verge of a breakdown."[21]

And with only three days to go, Britain was already hemorrhaging money. Traders had been selling off sterling since the beginning of September, but Macmillan now told the cabinet that gold and dollar losses for November were expected to be as much as $300 million. To keep from devaluing the British pound sterling, substantial dollar loans would be needed from the United States. The situation was so serious that it might eventually be necessary to move to a floating exchange rate, an act that would destroy the sterling trade area, Britain's way of preserving a Commonwealth version of an older imperial trading system.

Then there was the oil problem. As Macmillan put it, "If we lose the Middle East, we lose the oil. If we lose the oil, we cannot live."[22]

Despite this, Macmillan made no effort to bolster Britain's dollar reserves in the days before war broke out. Perhaps he still believed Nasser would be quickly overthrown. Perhaps he still counted on American financial support. Even as late as October 31, he told the governor of the Bank of England that he thought it unlikely there would be a real run on sterling. The bank put no measures in place to prevent foreign holders of sterling from selling.

As the clock counted down, Eden's top priority was to preserve the secrecy of the Sèvres plan. The Chiefs of Staff were told only that the Israelis would probably attack Egypt. Keightley was given October 29 as the probable date. Lieutenant General Sir Hugh Stockwell also received the October 29 date from his French staff colleagues while on a stopover at Malta. Admiral "Lofty" Power, alerted by Stockwell, was horrified. "The Government must have gone raving mad. If we are in any way mixed up with Israeli action, we shall upset the whole Muslim world and I think we shan't have the rest of world opinion behind us either. It's daft."[23]

The military chiefs did their best to get some of their forces into position. The commanding admiral's flagship and the aircraft carriers could be positioned ahead of time under cover of an exercise. But the rest of the force remained at Malta, 936 miles from Port Said, waiting for word to swing into action.

Late in the day on October 29, the Israelis attacked. In New York, an angry Dulles met his French and British counterparts with a draft resolution condemning Israel. He proposed that they go to the UN Security Council that very evening. In London, Lloyd invited U.S. ambassador Winthrop Aldrich to the Foreign Office to discuss the situation. He conceded that the issue of the Israeli attack should go to the Security Council, but he insisted it was politically impossible for Britain to take military action against Israel, which had acted in self-defense. Aldrich could not agree; there was no sympathy in the United States for Israel's actions.[24]

The British and French ultimatums were to go out later that day, October 30. Alarmed by his conversation with the American ambassador, Lloyd suggested postponing the secretly planned British military action by twenty-four hours to get more time to cultivate U.S. support. His proposal would have broken the deal that had been so carefully negotiated a week earlier with the Israelis. Lloyd knew that.

Other ministers, not so well informed about what had happened in Sèvres, liked Lloyd's idea, particularly Macmillan. Gold and dollar reserves were plummeting. Britain might be forced to ask for American economic aid and the cabinet believed "we could not afford to alienate the United States Government more than was absolutely necessary."[25]

Eden and Lloyd then went to "consult" with Mollet and Pineau, who had arrived from Paris as planned. The ultimatums were duly issued to the Israeli and Egyptian governments. At 4:30 p.m., Eden presented them to the House of Commons. Opposition leaders demanded that he take no military action without consulting them. The House then adjourned until 8 p.m. to consider the ultimatums.[26]

As Eden addressed the ministers, a telegram arrived from Eisenhower. The president asked for Eden's help "in clearing up my understanding as to exactly what is happening . . . between us, the French and yourselves." The United States knew of troop movements to Cyprus and communications between Paris and Tel Aviv. Eisenhower had been "astonished" to find that Britain's UN ambassador had opposed UN action against Israel. The president asked that the United States and the United Kingdom "quickly and clearly" lay out their views and intentions to avoid misunderstanding.[27]

Eisenhower's message had crossed with one Eden had already dispatched. Eden had explained that Britain would not come to Egypt's defense under the Tripartite Declaration because "Nasser and his press have relieved us of any such obligation by their attitude." Egypt, he asserted, had brought the situation upon herself, and in light of the threat to shipping and the canal, "decisive action should be taken at once to stop hostilities." It was fine to approach the UN, but processes there were neither rapid nor effective. He promised to write again as soon as he had consulted with the French.[28]

Eisenhower promptly wrote back a polite but terse message indicating that the United States would abide by the Tripartite Agreement. If Egypt asked for assistance, the United States might go to its aid.[29]

Meanwhile, Eden had written another letter to the president presenting the ultimatums as if they had been devised during the course of the day. Israel had a case for self-defense, he argued, even though Britain "would not wish to support or even condone" the Israeli attack. He agreed that the matter should go before the UN Security Council; Britain and France were merely acting as "trustees to protect the general interest." He asked for Eisenhower's support and promised that any action was "not part of a harking back to the old colonial and occupational concepts."[30]

At 8 p.m., the House of Commons reconvened to debate the British ultimatums to Egypt and Israel. After a vicious exchange, a confidence vote barely returned in the government's favor, 270–218.

At the UN, the United States proposed a resolution against Israel. It called for an Israeli cease-fire and withdrawal and the suspension of all military, economic, and financial aid until Israel complied. The Americans demanded an immediate vote. Britain and France vetoed it. A weaker Russian proposal was also vetoed. It was the first time Britain had used its veto on the Security Council.

That night, as the British had hoped, Nasser rejected the Anglo-French ultimatum.

Back in Washington, Dulles confronted Britain's diplomatic representative. The ultimatum, he said, was "a pretty brutal affair." The United States knew the French had been plotting with the Israelis. They were also aware of the buildup of British forces in Cyprus. It now seemed fairly obvious that Britain "had some special reason for doing this." The plan could only have been devised so quickly if it had been "concocted with the French Government before the Israeli action."[31]

On instructions, the British embassy in Washington asked the State Department to initiate procedures for the Middle East Emergency Committee (MEEC). This body had been created at the beginning of the Suez crisis, at the end of July, to coordinate oil supplies in an emergency. The British had participated in MEEC meetings through August and September, and they assumed it would function in the event of a crisis.

Now the embassy cabled back to London that the MEEC meeting scheduled for November 1 had been cancelled. The British representative reported that the Americans were deeply angry. "What rankles most," he wrote, "is what they believe to be deliberate concealment on our part, if not an actual plot with the French and the Israelis."[32]

Eden had miscalculated the magnitude of American rage. It now became doubly important to preserve the fiction of surprise at the Israeli attack. Eden had not gone along with Lloyd's proposal to stall military action for a full twenty-four hours (which Lloyd may have meant as a first step that might later end with a cabinet decision to cancel the operation altogether and abandon the Israelis). But for political and operational reasons, the British and French did delay their air assaults until late in the day on October 31.[33]

As British bombers finally headed for Egypt, Parliament resumed its debate. Eden defended himself, declaring that he and Mollet intended to protect the canal and secure a permanent settlement of the issues.

Opposition leader Hugh Gaitskell accused the government of blatantly attempting to seize the canal in collusion with France and Israel. To roars of approval, he announced that the Labour Party would oppose the British action by every constitutional means at their disposal, starting with a motion of censure.

News arrived in the chamber that Britain had begun bombing Egyptian targets. Ministers howled and shouted in protest.

Lloyd, who all along had preferred a diplomatic solution, was forced to justify the speed and surprise of the British move. "In an emergency, which this was, it is not practicable to have prior agreement," he insisted. Addressing accusations over the uncanny timing of the Israeli attack, Lloyd lied to Parliament, insisting "it is quite wrong to state that Israel was incited to this action by HMG. There was no prior agreement between us about it."[34]

PRESSURE MOUNTS: NOVEMBER 1–3

The first few days of military action offered no relief for Eden. The British Secret Service, MI6, had hoped to foment a military coup in Egypt as well as in Syria. With the beginning of the war these plans fell apart. In Syria, the coup plotters scattered or fled. In Egypt, the conspirators were waiting for the army to overthrow Nasser, but the young officers opposed to Nasser were too timid to make a move. Caches of weapons left for the coup remained untouched. Nasser's prestige was boosted by the attack, and he exhorted Egyptians to resort to guerrilla warfare if necessary.[35]

Things were no better for British commanders. Bombing operations were limited to a narrow set of military targets. Targeting against oil installations, communications systems, and railroads was ruled out because of potential civilian casualties and the threat of retaliation against British interests in other Arab countries. The amphibious landing forces were slow in making their way to reach Port Said. In the theater of war, blatant French military collaboration with the Israelis threatened to expose the full extent of the collusion among the partners. Eden sent an urgent personal message to Mollet telling him bluntly to rein in his forces (with no evident effect).[36]

As predicted, oil supplies were immediately disrupted. British bombers failed to destroy Nasser's blockships, and on November 1, the Egyptian blockship *Akka* was deployed in the middle of the canal at Ismailia, followed by many

more ships over the next few days. Britain now faced oil rationing and the prospect of purchasing oil from the Western Hemisphere in ever-scarcer dollars.
The Egypt Committee learned that oil consumption would have to be cut by
10 percent the following week; further rationing was imminent. Over the next
weekend, the pumping stations on the oil pipeline crossing Syria from Iraq to
Lebanon were sabotaged by Syrian army units. Making matters worse, Saudi
Arabia embargoed oil shipments to Britain and France.

In the House of Commons, Gaitskell demanded that the United States cite
Britain and France along with Israel in a UN resolution calling for the removal
of forces from Egypt. Debate reached fever pitch. Was the country at war or
not? Iverach McDonald, editor of *The Times*, described it as "quite the most
shattering experience I've ever sat through—the divisions, the uproar, the emotion were much worse than at the time of Munich . . . at each word the whole
of the Labour benches rose like a wall. No longer shouting, they were howling
with anger and real anguish. . . . It really was a most terrible spectacle."[37]

Eden, addressing the benches after a break in the session, finally admitted
that Britain was "neither at war nor at peace." However, if the UN were willing to take over the job of maintaining peace, "no one would be better pleased
than we."[38]

At the UN, deliberations were moved from the Security Council, where
Britain and France had veto power, to the General Assembly, where they did
not. At 2:30 a.m. on November 2, an American resolution demanding a cease-
fire was carried by sixty-four votes to five. Moments later, the delegates learned
of the Soviet invasion of Hungary. Hungarian prime minister Imre Nagy had
repudiated the Warsaw Pact and called on the United Nations for help. Later
that night, Dulles was stricken with pain and taken to the hospital, where he
underwent immediate surgery for cancer.

Eden had other problems. The assault convoy still had not reached Port
Said. The canal was unusable. World opinion seemed universally against him.
Even members of the Baghdad Pact, the Middle East security pact that was a
symbol of British influence in the region, were demanding to know whether
Britain had plotted with Israel against Egypt. Libya barred British operations
from its bases.[39]

By the afternoon of November 2, the crisis in oil supplies became acute. Lloyd
informed the cabinet that if sanctions were imposed, Britain might be forced to
use troops and warships to occupy Kuwait and Qatar, Britain's only suppliers of
oil who were not members of the UN. Such a move would irretrievably damage
relations with all other Arab states. Syria had already broken off relations with

the United Kingdom, and it was possible that Iraq, Jordan, and Libya would follow. In Iraq, Nuri would fall and the king might be overthrown.[40]

There remained the problem of how Britain was to reply to the General Assembly resolutions. One option was to ignore UN condemnation and push ahead to take up positions at strategic points along the canal. These positions could then be handed over to the new UN Emergency Force being created to keep the peace between Egypt and Israel. To mollify U.S. opinion, Eden suggested that a further note should be sent to the Israelis, who were now only twelve miles from the canal, warning them to keep a twenty-mile distance.

Meanwhile the French were pushing hard to speed up the timetable for military action and get troops on the ground. On November 2, Pineau had returned to London to press the case in person. The French wanted an immediate invasion. Anglo-French planners had devised an operation that called for a paratroop occupation of Port Said by November 3. The troops could then link up with Israeli troops advancing to the eastern bank of the canal. The British were "outraged" at the idea, which would expose their collusion. Eden's idea of calling for a further separation of Israeli and Egyptian forces further from the canal was, of course, irreconcilable with this idea.

At a subsequent meeting that evening, cabinet members became still more divided and quarrelsome. Some objected to the hypocrisy of launching an assault while offering to transfer the police action to the UN. There would be charges that the offer had been made in bad faith; government support in the House of Commons would crumble.

But, others argued, there were also good reasons to keep going. The British might finally remove Nasser from power. Eden's government would maintain the support of hard-liners who viewed an approach to the UN as an excuse for abandoning the attack.

At noon on November 3, Eden rose in the House of Commons and delivered Britain's response to the UN resolutions. Britain would agree to an Anglo-French cease-fire. But only on three conditions:

1. Egypt and Israel must both accept a UN force.

2. The UN force must stay until both the Palestine and Suez settlements had been reached.

3. Both Egypt and Israel must accept Anglo-French troops to separate the combatants until the UN force could be created and put in place.

Cries of "Murderers!" rang out in the House. As Eden left the chamber the entire Labour front bench rose and shouted for his resignation.[41]

Still there was no invasion. Photographic reconnaissance and intelligence reports indicated the Egyptians were building up defenses around Port Said, requiring further bombardment of the city before landing. Eden approved the bombing.[42]

FIGHT OR GIVE IN? NOVEMBER 4–6

The General Assembly's final resolutions were adopted by an overwhelming majority early in the day on November 4. They demanded British acceptance of a cease-fire by 8 p.m. (GMT). The five nations with permanent seats on the Security Council would be barred from participation in a UN Emergency Force. This would effectively force Britain and France to withdraw.

The Egypt Committee met at 12:30 p.m., just hours after the General Assembly had broken up. The French were still pushing for immediate invasion. But there had been a bombshell in New York. Israeli delegate Abba Eban had announced that if Egypt accepted a cease-fire, so would Israel. Britain's pretext for an invasion seemed to have vanished. British and French officials scrambled to get the Israelis to retract this offer.

With less than eight hours before the UN deadline, the Egypt Committee decided Britain should offer to accept the UN Emergency Force. But there would be no cease-fire; military operations would continue under the guise that the "increasing disorder" in the canal area required Britain and France to "carry through the initial stages of the police action which was now imperative." The committee approved an Anglo-French paratroop assault on Port Said and Port Fuad for the next morning, November 5.[43]

During a second meeting that afternoon, with only a few hours left, Britain's UN ambassador, Pierson Dixon, phoned Lloyd from New York. "Unless I have your authority for a cease-fire," he said, "a sanctions resolution will be carried against Britain and France." This would include withholding oil supplies. Upon hearing this, Macmillan threw his hands in the air and exclaimed, "Oil sanctions! That finishes it!"[44]

The Egypt Committee now moved to a full cabinet meeting, which began at 6:30 p.m. Ministers could hear commotion in the streets as 30,000 protestors gathered in Trafalgar Square and marched along Whitehall to the gates of Downing Street. Clashes erupted between police and demonstrators. Chants of "Eden must go" reached the cabinet room as the ministers debated whether to invade. Twelve wanted to proceed. Four, including possibly Macmillan, wanted to delay for twenty-four hours. Three wanted an indefinite deferral. Even the three military service ministers were divided.

With such stalemate, Eden spoke privately with Macmillan and his two chief parliamentary leaders—Rab Butler (in the House of Commons) and Lord Salisbury (in the House of Lords). He told them that if the cabinet would not agree to launch the attack he must resign. The three implored him to stay. Eden then cabled Keightley and asked if a twenty-four-hour delay was possible. Keightley said yes, but such a delay would crush morale, fortify the Egyptians, and "horrify" the French.[45]

Suddenly, with less than an hour to go before the deadline, word came that the Israelis had retracted their offer and now refused to go along with a cease-fire. With a few exceptions, "everybody [in the cabinet room] laughed and banged on the table." The attack could go ahead.[46]

At the UN, the General Assembly was scheduled to discuss the UN Emergency Force late on November 4. Britain's ambassador asked for a delay. UN secretary-general Hammarskjöld simply extended the deadline for the Anglo-French cease-fire to the early hours of November 5, 5 a.m. GMT.

In the dawn of November 5, fifteen minutes after the UN deadline expired, British and French paratroopers began drifting to the ground in northern Egypt. They quickly seized an airfield and bridges across the canal near Port Said.

Hours later, in the House of Commons, Lloyd read out Britain's reply to the UN resolutions. He welcomed the Canadian proposal for the creation of UN Emergency Force but emphasized that neither Israel nor Egypt had accepted it. An international force was needed immediately to "secure the speedy withdrawal of the Israeli forces."[47]

The Opposition were scornful. One Labour minister read out the text he had obtained of a British propaganda broadcast against Nasser. "We have here not a military action to separate Israeli and Egyptian troops," he declared. "We have a declaration of war against the Egyptian Government in the most brutal terms . . . Will the Government stop lying to the House of Commons?"[48]

As Lloyd tried to answer, Eden leapt to his feet with news from General Keightley that the Egyptians had asked for a cease-fire. Delighted Tory MPs cheered their leader. Summoning his Chiefs of Staff to No. 10 Downing Street, Eden exclaimed, "Oh my dear Chiefs, how grateful I am to you! You have been magnificent! It's all worked out perfectly!"[49]

But the cease-fire news was premature. The local Egyptian commander at Port Said may have been trying to limit further bloodshed, but Nasser quickly reversed the order. London quickly instructed the Anglo-French force to continue preparations for the amphibious landing the next morning.

Eden wrote once more to Eisenhower. Without the Anglo-French action, the situation "would have gone from bad to worse," he wrote to the president. Now that "police action" had started, it must be finished. They would be delighted to hand over the UN Emergency Force when it was ready. Eden acknowledged there had been a breach in the Anglo-American relationship, but he pleaded for reconciliation, praising Eisenhower as "a man of big enough heart and vision to take up things again on the basis of fact."[50]

As the British ground assault was getting under way, the Soviet government began its own intervention into the crisis. The Soviets, who had been busy savagely crushing the rebellion in Hungary, suddenly turned their attention back to the Middle East.

At 2:00 a.m. on November 6, Eden was awakened and handed a chilling note from Soviet premier Bulganin, versions of which were also sent to France and Israel. Bulganin was blunt. How would Britain feel if "rocket weapons" were used against Britain and France? It would be called a "barbarous action." The attack on "defenseless" Egypt was the same. "We are fully determined to crush the aggressors by the use of force and to restore peace in the East," he warned. A Soviet note to Eisenhower proposed a UN resolution "calling for general cease-fire and use of combined armed forces in the event of noncompliance."[51]

Communications intercepted from the Egyptian embassy in London convinced the Joint Intelligence Committee that the Soviets were serious. One message reported that the Soviets were preparing to mobilize their aircraft for a possible confrontation with Britain.[52]

Eden and Lloyd viewed the Soviet letters with deep concern. They knew that CIA estimates did not consider Soviet nuclear capabilities a threat at the moment. But there was fear that, if the fighting continued, the Soviets would find a way to intervene on Egypt's behalf. Perhaps they might send "volunteers" or move combat aircraft to bases in Syria. Reports were already circulating through the NATO network of Soviet overflights of Turkey in the direction of Syria.[53]

The communications from the Egyptian embassy may have been a case of disinformation (there was evidence the tap may have been discovered). But the Joint Intelligence Committee took notice. A message went out from

Anglo-French headquarters to the task force leaders warning that "Russia may intervene in the Middle East with force." Aircraft were dispersed for their protection. Airfields were prepared to withstand an attack.[54]

Finally, at 6:15 a.m. on November 6, British and French troops began the amphibious landing near Port Said. Moving to join up with the paratroopers who were already on the ground, these British and French forces began the bloody task of taking the town, unaware that their political masters were wavering. Contrary to British assumptions, the Egyptians fought back, hard. In some areas, the fighting was house-to-house and room-to-room.

On the morning of November 6, the cabinet met at 9:45 in Eden's room in the House of Commons. Messages had arrived in the night from Hammarskjöld. Israel had, indeed, now definitely accepted the cease-fire. So had Egypt. The UN General Assembly resolution had created a UN Command for the UN Emergency Force. Would Britain now agree to a cease-fire?

Eden was by this point utterly exhausted. He warned the cabinet that the government had reason to worry that the Russian notes were a cover for a military move, possibly into Syria, and in the worst-case scenario against Britain in Egypt. Ministers worried that if the Anglo-French attack continued their forces might find themselves fighting Soviet troops in the canal area.[55]

Macmillan now took the opportunity to sound the alarm about Britain's finances. He told the cabinet that Britain's dollar reserves had fallen by $280 million over the previous week, or one-eighth of total reserves. This number would later prove to be incorrect (the actual figure was closer to $85 million), but the effect of his announcement on his colleagues in the meeting was devastating.

Macmillan had also spent hours on the phone to Washington during the night, at one point calling an ailing Dulles at Walter Reed Army Medical Center. Dulles had been blunt. The United States would only help rescue sterling if Britain agreed to a cease-fire. Macmillan announced that he had to admit that "in view of the financial and economic pressures, we must stop."[56]

This was a 180-degree turn for Macmillan. At the beginning of the crisis he had displayed a "bellicosity beyond description." Now he became "the leader of the bolters." Along with the party's two parliamentary leaders, Butler and Salisbury, Macmillan argued for a cease-fire. The queen was due in the House of Lords at 11:00 a.m. to deliver her traditional speech at the opening of the new parliamentary session. The ministers were expected. Time had run out. The cabinet voted, subject to French agreement, to stop the assault.[57]

Eden phoned Mollet to tell him of the decision. Mollet was meeting with

West German chancellor Konrad Adenauer at the time, but he stepped out to take the call from Eden.

"I don't think we can go on," Eden told him. "The pressure on sterling is becoming unbearable. The English can take a lot of things, but I do not think they would be willing to accept the failure of sterling, which would have considerable consequences for the Commonwealth. And the pressure is getting worse from day to day."

Mollet pleaded for time. "Could we not wait two or three days?"

"No," replied Eden, "I cannot hold out any longer."[58]

Eden called the U.S. ambassador to his office at the House of Commons and handed him the message that he was about to send to Hammarskjöld at the UN. Britain would accept the UN cease-fire resolution. Eden was anxious that Eisenhower be informed immediately and said that he was available any time if the American president wanted to call him on the phone.[59]

Eisenhower did just that. It was Election Day in the United States and, after casting his vote in Pennsylvania, he returned to the White House and placed a call to Eden. He told the prime minister "how pleased we are that you found it possible to accept the cease-fire." Eisenhower sought confirmation that the acceptance was unconditional. Eden replied, "We cease firing tonight at midnight provided we are not attacked."

After a brief further discussion of how Eden might relay Eisenhower's views to Parliament, Eisenhower invited Eden to call him anytime. Eden knew what lay in store for him in the coming minutes. "If I survive here tonight, I will call you tomorrow," he said.[60]

At 6:04 p.m., Eden entered the House of Commons to announce that Britain would cease hostilities at midnight. He declared that Anglo-French forces would stay behind and help clear the canal of obstructions. Turning to the new danger presented by Bulganin's threatening letter, which had been made public, Eden cited Anglo-French acceptance of the UN Emergency Force as proof that Bulganin's accusation of "waging war against the national independence of the countries of the Near and Middle East" was baseless. Casualties in Egypt, he said, were nothing compared to the Soviet brutality in Hungary.

What Eden could not say was that the threat of Soviet intervention had spooked the cabinet. Or that political pressure and the run on the pound had stopped Britain in its tracks. Or that the closing of the canal and the stoppage of oil from the Middle East had threatened to cripple the British economy. Or that American fury and Commonwealth hostility had made further action impossible.

Eden also could not reveal that he was a man on the verge of collapse. As he made his long and moving address to the chamber, his future biographer, Robert Rhodes James, saw that "he looked aged and ill, defeated and broken." Sir Gerald Templer feared that "his health would collapse unless the matter could be brought to an early solution." Eden ended the day in bed at 10 Downing Street, his Chiefs of Staff by his side, his wife holding his hand, "a broken man."[61]

Final Observations: No End of Lessons

PHILIP ZELIKOW

A FEW OBSERVATIONS ON PART THREE

As Part Three closes toward the end of the day on November 6, Eden has decided to accept an unconditional cease-fire. This predictably cascaded very quickly into French acceptance of a cease-fire as well, along with the Israelis, and then a process of withdrawal. In the case of the Israelis, that withdrawal was a prolonged process that did not conclude until March 1957. So this is a good point to turn the page and offer a few of the many observations that can be made about this very rich set of histories and perspectives.

In Part Three, Washington's views eventually become the decisive factor. This more and more amounted to the viewpoint of Eisenhower. On the morning of November 3, Dulles had to go to the hospital for emergency surgery, and he would remain in the hospital until November 15. Though not in very good health himself, Eisenhower was more directly in charge than ever, working through Hoover at State and with Lodge at the UN.

Everyone seems to have misjudged the strength, speed, and depth of Washington's opposition to the Israeli-French-British assault on Egypt. In the negotiations recounted in Part Two, Ben-Gurion had, for good reason, insisted that the Americans had to go along with any assault on Egypt. He finally dropped that condition, but, as his discussion with the cabinet on October 28 showed, he was far from easy about the American factor.

Nasser shared in the misjudgments about the United States. After all,

312

Nasser had no particular right to expect Eisenhower would exert himself so energetically on his behalf. Yet the United States rescued Nasser from a gamble that could have turned out as catastrophically for him personally as it had for his army and air force, or for the thousands of Egyptians already lying dead on the various battlefields.

Of course, Eisenhower was not doing it for Nasser. While the cases portray a complicated range of views about Nasser among the important American officials, there was no great personal sympathy for the Egyptian ruler. During Part Three what is driving Eisenhower, above all, is the way he relates this crisis to the global Cold War struggle with the Soviet bloc.

If that global perspective is supreme for Eisenhower, part of the failure of assessment in London and Paris is that those other countries did not work through why the United States might then feel the need to work so fast. None had felt sure the Americans would approve of their move. Their analysis had rested on the assumption that the American reaction would be relatively slow.

Why the American haste? Eisenhower's initial anger provided some fuel for the fire; but his anger soon turned to rapid calculation. Not a man normally inclined to hasty action, Eisenhower concluded that the United States had to rush to get ahead of and channel the widespread anger about the invasion in a relatively constructive way or else the Soviets would lead that anger into more destructive directions. In their failed assessments the other capitals, especially London, did not work through the possibility that the United States would oppose them so vigorously precisely because the United States was allied with Britain and France.

Eisenhower was moving fast because the Soviet moves he feared might include the danger of a possible Soviet intervention that could pull the United States into a far more dangerous war. Again, in this sense, Eisenhower believed he was actually trying to limit damage to his allies, whom he did intend to defend, as well as the danger to his own country. This is another reason he and his team used every economic instrument they had, especially aimed at the British, who were the weakest link in the coalition. But they chose to use these instruments out of the public eye.

Soviet behavior in Part Three seems to bear out some of Eisenhower's concerns. The Hungary crisis may have delayed Moscow's reaction, which was probably too late and too rhetorical to have stopped the Israeli-French-British moves on the ground. But Moscow's sense of delay and distraction may, perhaps, have caused Khrushchev to compensate by making his move, when he did make it, even blunter and more strident.

All the capitals might have discounted Moscow's extreme threats as bluff, which the chapter suggests it was. But the others could not discount the threats altogether, and the Americans, British, and French were getting some troubling intelligence reports.

The rush to develop constructive alternatives actually produced the most creative policy move that occurred in Part Three. This was the impromptu creation of a "UN police force," what would become the UN Emergency Force. There was no significant precedent in history for such a thing on this scale, with its thousands of troops.

The UN Emergency Force seems to have emerged out of nowhere. It was, in fact, the conjuncture of four sets of creative insights. First, there was Eisenhower's immediate recognition, taking shape on November 1 and 2, that the war could be the occasion to revisit the underlying Egyptian-Israeli peace and border problem, including Eisenhower's idea of enlarged "neutral strips" of territory.

Second, at the same time, there was a suggestion of a UN police force from Canadian foreign minister Lester Pearson. Pearson, like Eisenhower, was actually trying to rescue his British friends, using his idea to deflect worse ones. At first Pearson himself was unclear about whether this was just a "Canal" measure or a broader idea that would extend to the 1949 armistice lines. It quickly became both.

Third, Eisenhower had the insight, at the height of the crisis, to recognize and treat India's Nehru as a figure of great importance. This was a genuine regard. He sought to engage Nehru as a fellow statesman in the peacemaking work. Nehru felt quite ready to play such a part. Thus it was Indian troops, and Indian commanders, who joined Canadian soldiers and officers in providing a quick, ready core for the new UN Emergency Force.

Fourth, UN secretary-general Hammarskjöld and his talented team immediately grasped the larger possibilities in such a force. Rather than posing all the easily foreseeable objections, they moved practically overnight to put flesh on these ideas and make them seem practical.[1]

In the midst of the war, on the hectic day of November 2, while so much was still uncertain, Eisenhower found time to pen a letter to his longtime friend and constant confidant, a former naval officer named Swede Hazlett. Ike often used his old friend as a sounding board for the way he was analyzing events. Even on November 2, Eisenhower was already doing a post-mortem on the crisis.

He had belatedly realized the significance of the French role. "France was perfectly cold-blooded about the matter. She has a war on her hands in Algeria, and she was anxious to get someone else fighting the Arabs on her Eastern flank so she was ready to do anything to get England and Israel in that affair." Those two countries, Ike thought, "have hurt themselves immeasurably." This saddened him because "Britain not only has been, but must be, our best friend in the world."

But Eisenhower already judged, as a professional, that "the plan, when actually put into effect, was not well coordinated." Even then he had already noticed the delay in following up the Israeli moves. He did not know that those delays were—at that moment—driving French officials and generals practically mad with frustration.

A few weeks later, after the crisis had subsided, Eisenhower made these same points to the retired Churchill, in a top-secret message. Eisenhower acknowledged that Nasser might be "a tool, possibly unwittingly, of the Soviets." He might be seeing himself as "an Egyptian Mussolini" and that would require some coordinated effort to see "that he did not grow to be a danger to our welfare." But the canal business was the wrong vehicle for action. The problem was that "not only [were the British actions] in violation of the basic principles by which this great combination of nations can be held together, but that even by the doctrine of expediency the invasion could not be judged as soundly conceived and skillfully executed."[2]

It is not terribly difficult, with access to the records, to unpack the "value" and the "reality" judgments that were driving Eden and his allies in their desire to damage Nasser's prestige and restore their own. As usual, it is the "action" judgments that are the hardest to deconstruct.

Of these, perhaps the most important was the basic impulse that there must be some vivid action. This was true above all for Eden, belying his outward diffidence and frequent bouts of illness. One of Eden's more discerning and judgmental Foreign Office subordinates during the war years had noticed back then that "when something had to be done, Anthony longed to do it. That quality was perhaps carried to a fault; but on the whole it was a good fault for a Foreign Secretary." He was a man who "always wanted to do something."[3]

Yet on October 14, at that fateful Chequers conference when Eden grabbed the lifeline that Challe threw to him, Eden had disabled much of the system for high-quality policy staffwork that had so often been a strength of British policymaking. Most of the Foreign Office was no longer plugged into serious work about next moves. Those officials were reconciling themselves to the diplomatic solution that had just emerged out of the tough talks at the UN. Hardly any were brought into the loop on the very secret new idea for military action, and at least one of those officials was determined to resign over it as soon as he could.

The British military officials had also not developed plans that were well tied in with realistic political objectives or timing. There, too, crucial officials—the defense minister and the head of the armed forces—were unsympathetic to the prime minister's plans. Few adjustments were made to the already delayed and revised Musketeer, an inflexibility that can be sharply contrasted to the kinds of rapid adjustments that Dayan was making to the Israeli plans.

Even with these adjustments, there were few serious analyses, in strategic theory or in blueprints for action, of how the Anglo-French military plans hoped to topple Nasser. If that objective was discarded, a more realistic objective might have been to reoccupy the Canal Zone. Perhaps, if that had rapidly been accomplished in the first days of November, such a fait accompli might have changed the situation at the UN, although even that is problematic.

Another noteworthy observation, then, is to notice how much influence the UN was able to exert on the outcome of the crisis. Once the issue was moved, with U.S. help, from the Security Council to the General Assembly, the warmakers were faced directly with a judgment on their actions by the assembled nations of the world. It turned out that such a verdict also carried real power.

The power was noticeable, though perhaps it was not alone overwhelming, in the case of Paris and Jerusalem. But the power was very great, indeed, on British opinion at every level. The reasons for this were historical and complex, but such an impact was also foreseeable.

The UN was a source of power for the Egyptians. The UN Emergency Force then became a shield, for Egypt and for Israel. More than ten years later, in May and June of 1967, Nasser decided to cast that UN shield aside.

AFTERMATH

After the cease-fires of November 1956 the British and French withdrew all their forces in little more than a month. The Israelis did not evacuate all of Sinai and the Gaza Strip until March 1957. But the situation did not just rewind back to the prewar status quo ante. The war did change the region.

The two countries that did the best out of the war were, oddly enough, Egypt and Israel. Nasser's army and air force were a wreck, but could be rebuilt (with more Soviet help). A veteran of Egyptian military intelligence told an interviewer, "In truth, the victory which Egypt won in 1956 was popular and political more than military."[4]

Nasser's political influence soared. His defiance had triumphed. He had led his country to withstand the "Tripartite Aggression." He consolidated his rule at home and became the Arab world's unquestioned leader. He inspired far-flung revolutions and attracted adoring throngs when he traveled. After centuries of Arab humiliation at the hands of the Ottomans, the British, the French, and others, Abdel Nasser was a proven winner and, for that reason, a hero. Egypt had not had one of those for a long time.[5]

As Nasserism rose and British influence waned in the Levant, one of the first victims was Nuri el-Said in Iraq, overthrown and murdered in 1958. Iraq's ruling monarch (and his son and much of their family) were murdered too, their corpses dragged through the streets. The Arab cold war entered a very different phase, a competition as varieties of Arab socialism or fascism put increasing pressure on more traditional or pluralistic governments in Lebanon, Jordan, or the Persian Gulf.

In 1958 Egypt and Syria formed a United Arab Republic under Nasser's leadership. Part of Yemen was affiliated with it, too. The various states soon returned to a more independent course (although Egypt fought a lengthy and inconclusive war in Yemen), but Nasser's influence remained enormous.

In 1967, after booting out the UN Emergency Force and reestablishing a blockade of Israel in the Straits of Tiran, Nasser spoke of history. "I have read every word written about the 1956 events," he said. Then, Egypt had not had a proper chance to fight Israel. Now he invited "the Jews" to "test their forces against ours and to see that what they wrote about the 1956 battle and the occupation of Sinai was all a lot of nonsense." Israel was ready to accept that invitation.[6]

On October 28, justifying the decision for war to his cabinet, Ben-Gurion said he hoped that, even if the war did not go as planned, perhaps the war might at least give Israel a quiet period of five to eight years to concentrate on domestic concerns, building up the new country. It did. He and his country got that and more, more than ten years of relative peace and safe borders. As Shimon Peres later put it, "The country enjoyed quiet along its borders and remarkable economic growth and political success."[7]

The quiet was in large part a tribute to the postwar diplomacy between December 1956 and March 1957. Under intense pressure from the United States, Israel had very grudgingly withdrawn from Sinai, from the Straits of Tiran, and from the Gaza Strip. The negotiations over Gaza were especially intricate. Dulles handled them skillfully, as did the UN's American mediator, Ralph

Bunche. The French also played a valuable part in bridging the differences and reassuring Israel.[8]

The UN Emergency Force usually numbered about 5,000 troops, more or less. It was a force Israel had criticized and belittled. Yet it turned out to be highly effective in patrolling the 1949 armistice lines, the de facto border, and thus in managing the "routine security" problem that had been the great source of constant stress since Israel's birth. Israel regained its right of way for its shipping through the Straits of Tiran.

But the UN Emergency Force was there on Egyptian sufferance. In 1967 the Egyptian government kicked it out. That move led promptly to another major war.

More than ten years before that date, on March 1, 1957, Ben-Gurion had justified Israel's withdrawal from Sinai to his military men by saying it was best for the country to get on with its life. "Perhaps we will need to fight again," he told them. "But when we do, while the whole UN may not stand at our side, some states will, the sort of states that will enable us to do so with a calmer heart." The "Old Man" was proved right about that.[9]

In Moscow, Khrushchev had set in motion a process to recruit volunteers to serve in Egypt, but the process petered out along with the crisis. The Yugoslav ambassador in Moscow recalled Khrushchev telling him, on November 12, that "they had finally threatened the West with a statement about sending volunteers, but he didn't think it would come to that. He said in conclusion that the Soviet Union was not thinking of going to war, but that the Soviet Union's latest threats of war had been necessary and correct."[10]

Khrushchev repeatedly took credit for ending the Suez crisis. In several statements and in his memoirs, he claimed that Soviet policy had forced Britain and France to back down. Other Soviet leaders seemed to agree in public. Yet at the time they chose to depose Khrushchev in 1964, they privately attacked Khrushchev's risky behavior during the Suez crisis, one of the counts in the internal indictment to explain why he should step down.[11]

Soviet-Egyptian relations remained close but guarded. This could be glimpsed in a public airing of their two interpretations of the crisis. In 1959 Nasser gave a speech in which he said that, when the "triple aggression" happened, Egyptians had to rely only on Allah and themselves. Khrushchev angrily disagreed, reiterating his claim of credit.

Nasser replied that the Soviet ultimatum had come rather late. "Of what use would the ultimatum have been that day, Mr. Chairman, if we had come to an end and fallen?"

To this Khrushchev wrote: "Knowing your impulsiveness we feared that our unlimited support of your belligerent sentiments might have prompted you to take military action which we have always regarded as undesirable."[12]

Khrushchev may have remembered his nuclear threats during the Suez crisis with some satisfaction. The French and the Israelis remembered them, too.

During the year after the crisis, those two countries made the fateful decision, in consultation with each other, that they needed to build nuclear weapons of their own. In the autumn of 1957 the French government, headed briefly by Bourgès-Maunoury, and the Israeli government, still headed by Ben-Gurion, appear to have given the decisive go-ahead.[13]

For the French government, the secret nuclear weapons program decisions were only one aspect of their bitter reflections on the way the Suez crisis had turned out. As their foreign ministry officials in the Quai d'Orsay had summed it up by November 10, it seemed obvious that "the balance-sheet of the Egyptian operation is a painful one to present."

For France, the costs included the fact that "we have compromised for a long time our relations with all the Arab states and have abandoned economic and cultural positions there which doubtless we will not recover entirely." Further, "We have not facilitated the solution of the problems in North Africa in general and of Algeria in particular."

For this, the officials mainly blamed Britain and the United States. The British had been "hesitant in action, maladroit in execution, and lacking in strong words when it came to the test." The Americans had repeatedly "left its principal partners in doubt as to its solidarity and its friendship. It chose in the present crisis to make us fail."[14]

Among the lessons France drew was that its defenses needed to be as independent as possible, including nuclear weapons. What kept Mollet and his team going after the Suez debacle was that they considered Europe their top priority and all the more important to put in place after their failure in Egypt.

"Europe will be your revenge," Konrad Adenauer is reported to have told Mollet and Pineau on November 6.[15] Suez hastened the creation of the European Economic Community; the Treaty of Rome was signed on March 25, 1957.

Only a few alternative points of view were heard in France amid the madding throng of anti-Arab and anti-Islamic voices. One was *France Observateur*, a weekly started in 1950 under the theme of a rejection of both NATO and Stalinism and that became a strong opponent of French colonial policy in Algeria. One of its editors, Gilles Martinet, concluded an article titled "Munich Is Not on the Nile," dated August 2, 1956, with the following words: "We see the people responsible for the Indochina disaster, the saboteurs of French-Maghrebian friendship, trying to create a political climate which apparently evokes, among certain valiant souls, the memory of the days of the Marne and Verdun but which, in reality, resembles terribly that ridiculous and unhealthy atmosphere which prevailed in Mussolini's Rome on the [1935] eve of the 'grandiose' enterprise of Abyssinia!"[16]

The reaction to the Suez crisis among some of those "valiant souls," especially on the nationalist right and in the seasoned and wounded ranks of the French army, was more ominous. As British and French resolve seemed to have bogged down, on October 13, Charles de Gaulle wrote a note to his son, saying: "From what has taken place in the Suez affair, it will soon be apparent that no one will be able to make people believe that action is compatible with this regime. . . . The whole ensemble—Algeria, Suez, etc.—is stirring in rather broad circles an emotion and a reaction such as I haven't seen for ten years. It is particularly the case in the Army (especially in North Africa). One will see. I will see."[17]

He did. In 1958 a military revolt overthrew France's Fourth Republic and its constitution. A new republic was created, the Fifth, that would install a powerful president, Charles de Gaulle. A leader in that military movement was General Maurice Challe. Challe would later join another revolt to save French Algeria, this time against de Gaulle, in 1961. That revolt failed, and Challe went to prison (he was pardoned and released five years later).

Eden resigned his office before the end of the year. Macmillan took over and worked hard to patch up relations with the United States. For Britons, the crisis was a searing period, a horrible argument that had divided friends and family with, afterward, many awkward silences. All could remember it, of course. But if one wished to be polite, friends did not reopen the old wounds.

It is an exaggeration to say that British influence suddenly collapsed, even in the Middle East. British influence remained important in the Persian Gulf region, for example, and in relation to its traditional oil suppliers. But the tide of empire, already well past flood, was now steadily going out. By 1957 Britain began dramatically reducing its army (abolishing conscription) and scaling back its commitments. London's sway rapidly evaporated in the Levant. The United States would have to take more of the lead in sorting out problems that involved Iraq, Syria, Lebanon, Jordan, or Israel.

In January 1957, as it was also still painstakingly negotiating the Israeli withdrawal from Egyptian territory, the U.S. president announced an "American Doctrine" (later, of course, called the "Eisenhower Doctrine") that promised U.S. aid to Middle Eastern countries fearing Soviet-sponsored aggression, which could be interpreted as "Nasserite" aggression, as well. That doctrine received a light test with support to Jordan in 1957. It was more severely tested, threateningly but inconclusively, in a serious set of crises in 1958 centered on the toppling of the government and the leader at the center of the Baghdad Pact, Iraq's Nuri el-Said, and also involving Syria and Lebanon and Jordan (again, with the U.S. flying in British troops) as well. U.S. relations with Israel also slowly began to improve again.

After the 1958 crises, the Americans eased up on the intensity of their involvement in the Middle East. The danger of Arab-Israeli war was greatly mitigated by the UN Emergency Force, and the Americans were preoccupied with more serious Soviet threats in the heart of Europe, over Berlin, and over Chinese threats over Taiwan, and then Vietnam.

The Americans also became more inclined to reduce their direct military involvement and try, as best they could, to let Arab nationalism run its course. Through the 1960s this usually meant American partnerships, in addition to that with Iran, keyed significantly toward Saudi Arabia and even trying to improve relations with Nasser's Egypt, too. Within the Arab world, the divide between oil-haves and oil-have-nots became more important than their Cold War alignments.[18]

A STRANGE CRISIS

It is easy, after the fact, to construct a logic that makes sense of what happened in the Suez crisis. One value of deconstructing the Suez crisis is to notice that, before they happened, the events actually did not make much sense at all.

Consider the crisis of Part One. There the crisis is mainly being driven by the Soviet-Czech arms deal with Egypt. There are alarms. Some attempt a diplomatic deal. The Israelis consider preventive war, then despondently reject it. Everyone tries to figure out Nasser.

By July 1956, as Part One ends, that crisis seems resolved. The Israelis have scored their secret arms deal and alliance with France, which is meant to unfold for some months to come. The Egyptian danger has taken on less panicked proportions. The danger of an Egypt-Israel war has receded, probably at least until 1957. Meanwhile the Americans are well along in planning to prevent or mitigate such a conflict. Troubles with Jordan loom.

The new crisis, the one that dominates Part Two, was not foreseen at all. Hardly anyone, including most Egyptian officials, had foreseen Nasser's move to nationalize the Suez Canal. But this is Nasser's effort to get more revenue, to better afford his national development and defense plans in some way he has not yet worked out. Perhaps, even more, Nasser was looking for a way to strike back at the "imperialists," especially the arrogant Americans. Remarkably, then, the Americans soon start trying to mitigate this crisis, too.

The French and Israeli positions in Part Two are most predictable. But what of the British? The source of British anger is an extraordinarily harsh assessment of Nasser. But that dark portrait was not really there in 1954 when Eden had successfully negotiated the withdrawal of British forces from the canal; it was not even fully developed in 1955.

So just what happened to London's views in 1956? Part of this is about Eden himself, his personal history, some of the influences on him, and his political situation. Clearly part of it also has to do with the peculiar influence that British intelligence exerted in that year and not in a helpful way.

Yet at the end of Part Two, that crisis also seems well on the way to resolution. The momentum for war is visibly dissipating in London; the momentum toward a settlement has visibly picked up in New York. Yet at this point, quite secretly, the entire crisis switches direction again.

One can comment on the role of France and Israel, yet somehow the observer would be confused or misled by poring over just the views of leaders like Mollet or Ben-Gurion. Recall how opposed Ben-Gurion himself was to the kind of ideas being cooked up by others, ideas he would scornfully deride as "the British proposal" (which it most definitely was not).

Even well-informed insiders in Paris or Jerusalem would have had difficulty assessing or replicating the extraordinarily ingenious and energetic work being done by a handful of defense and military officials in those two countries. These men had joined together in a kind of transnational coalition, cutting across their governments, uniting to persuade their respective leaders. And even fewer outsiders would have sensed and pondered the depth of Ben-Gurion's affection and wary respect for his "two colts," Dayan and Peres.

The peculiarity of the political and military developments in Part Three also would have been hard to predict. Beforehand, if given the scenario, perhaps even American analysts who knew Eisenhower would have had trouble accurately forecasting the course of events. Nor is it likely they would have grasped, as even Eisenhower was slow to grasp, how well the whole episode might turn out not only for Nasser's Egypt but also for Ben-Gurion's Israel. That the crisis might prompt France and Israel to decide to build nuclear weapons was yet one more unexpected outcome.

The Suez crisis, deconstructed into its parts and viewpoints, was one strange chapter after another. It has this in common with many other great turning points in history. The closer one looks, the stranger they get. In this crisis, assessments, pleasingly plausible, were often wrong. Policy designs, seemingly well considered, were not. Creativity married to thorough analysis was all too rare. The study of Suez is instructive because it is so humbling.

About the Contributors

PHILIP ZELIKOW is the White Burkett Miller Professor of History at the University of Virginia. He taught at Harvard University during most of the 1990s. He has also done policy work in each of the five administrations from Reagan through Obama, working in various capacities at the State Department, White House, and the Defense Department. He was also the executive director of the 9/11 Commission.

ERNEST R. MAY was the Charles Warren Professor of History at Harvard University, where he also directed the Charles Warren Center for Studies in American History. A U.S. Navy veteran, he taught international history for more than fifty years before his death in 2009.

JON B. ALTERMAN is Senior Vice President of the Center for Strategic and International Studies, where he holds the Zbigniew Brzezinski Chair in Global Security and is the director of the Middle East Program. He received his doctorate in history from Harvard University and taught there and at Johns Hopkins SAIS. He was a foreign policy aide to Senator Daniel Moynihan and a member of the State Department's Policy Planning Staff before he joined CSIS.

CHARLES G. COGAN was an associate of the International Security Program at Harvard University's Belfer Center. A U.S. Army veteran, he served for forty years as a CIA officer, including as the chief of station in Paris and as chief of the agency's Near East and South Asia Division. He received his doctorate from Harvard University and was a prize-winning scholar on French diplomacy. He passed away at the end of 2017.

JILL KASTNER is an independent writer and researcher based in London. She was a television journalist in Washington before obtaining her doctorate in history from Harvard University. Her previous research focused on German-American relations during the Cold War.

DAVID NICKLES, who contributed to the Part One case on London, is a historian for the U.S. Department of State. He obtained his doctorate in history from Harvard University.

EDWARD MERTA is an environmental attorney working in local government in New Mexico. He received his master's degree in history from Harvard University before serving as a policy analyst for a national laboratory and moving into legal work, retaining an interest in history.

CAROL R. SAIVETZ is a senior adviser with the Security Studies Program, MIT, and a research associate of Harvard University's Davis Center for Russian and Eurasian Studies and the Harvard Ukrainian Institute. She lectures in political science at MIT and has authored numerous books and articles on Russian and Soviet foreign policy.

Notes

Commonly Used Abbreviations in the Notes

BG Diary Ben-Gurion diary

CDSP *Current Digest of the Soviet Press*

CIA FOIA U.S. Central Intelligence Agency, Freedom of Information Act Electronic Reading Room

CPSU Communist Party of the Soviet Union

DDEP Louis Galambos and Daun Van Ee, eds., *The Papers of Dwight David Eisenhower* (Johns Hopkins University Press, 1996), cited by volume number and pages.

DDF Documents diplomatiques français, cited by volume number and pages. The volumes most often cited were published between 1988 and 1990 under the general direction of Jean-Baptiste Duroselle.

DFPI Documents on the Foreign Policy of Israel, cited by volume number and document number. The volumes cited were published in 2008 and 2009, edited by Baruch Gilead and Nana Sagi.

ENA Egypt National Archives

FRUS *Foreign Relations of the United States*, cited by volume number and document number. The volumes most often cited were published in 1989 and 1990 and edited by Carl Raether and Nina Noring.

NA U.S. National Archives; RG indicates the Record Group

PREM U.K. Prime Minister's office

CAB U.K. Cabinet Office

FO U.K. Foreign Office

SNIE U.S. Special National Intelligence Estimate

TNA The National Archives (United Kingdom)

Introduction

1. Geoffrey Vickers, *The Art of Judgment: A Study of Policy Making* (Thousand Oaks: Sage, 1995 [orig. 1965]). Vickers sets his argument entirely in the context of judgments made in business or in domestic public policy. But his theoretical argument about "appreciative systems" is equally valid for statecraft. For an earlier introduction of some of these ideas, see Ernest R. May and Philip Zelikow, "Introduction: Seven Tenets," in May, Zelikow, Kirsten Lundberg, and Robert Johnson, eds., *Dealing with Dictators: Dilemmas of Diplomacy and Intelligence Analysis, 1945–1990* (MIT Press, 2006), pp. 4–6. A famously successful investment manager, Bridgewater's Ray Dalio, also starts with a three-part cognitive framework of breaking down "what you want," "what is true," and "what you should do," in *Principles* (New York: Simon & Schuster, 2017), p. xi.

2. A more elaborate template, with seven steps, was first laid out in Philip Zelikow, "Foreign Policy Engineering: From Theory to Practice and Back Again," *International Security* 18, no. 4 (Spring 1994): 143–71.

3. The following passage draws a bit from Philip Zelikow, "The Nature of History's Lessons," in Hal Brands and Jeremi Suri, eds., *The Power of the Past: History and Statecraft* (Brookings Institution Press, 2016), pp. 290–91.

4. See, for example, the chapter "Regime Strategic Intent," in DCI Special Advisor on Iraq's WMD (Charles Duelfer), *Comprehensive Report*, September 30, 2004 (www.cia.gov/library/reports/general-reports-1/iraq_wmd_2004/chap1.html).

The World of 1956

1. James Salter, *All That Is* (New York: Knopf, 2013), p. 91. In this novel Salter drew occasionally on his experiences as a U.S. Air Force pilot who served throughout Western Europe during the 1950s.

2. See generally Michael J. Cohen, *Strategy and Politics in the Middle East, 1954–1960: Defending the Northern Tier* (London: Frank Cass, 2005). In the mid-1950s the principal deterrent weapon was the B-47 jet bomber, of which the United States had deployed about a thousand. Large numbers of these would occasionally deploy temporarily to bases on the European and African side of the Atlantic.

3. Quoted in Peter Hahn, *Caught in the Middle East: U.S. Policy toward the Arab-Israeli Conflict, 1945–1961* (University of North Carolina Press, 2005), p. 150.

4. George Kahin, *The Asian-African Conference* (Cornell University Press, 1956), pp. 46–47.

5. Geoffrey Barraclough and Rachel Wall, *Survey of International Affairs 1955–1956* (Oxford University Press, 1960), p. 177.

6. For an Iraqi perspective on this history, see Majid Khadduri, "Towards an Arab Union: The League of Arab States," *American Political Science Review* 40, no. 1 (February 1946): 90–100 (written when Khadduri was working for the Iraqi government); and Khadduri, *Independent Iraq, 1932–1958: A Study in Iraqi Politics*, 2d ed. (Oxford University Press, 1960).

7. Elie Podeh, *The Quest for Hegemony in the Arab World: The Struggle over the Baghdad Pact* (Leiden: E. J. Brill, 1995), p. 125.

8. A review of the British and American disagreements about the Baghdad Pact in 1954 and 1955 is a main strength of Steven Freiberger, *Dawn over Suez: The Rise of American Power in the Middle East, 1953–1957* (Chicago: Ivan Dee, 1992), pp. 83–106.

9. For a careful treatment of this complicated story, mainly from the British perspective, see William Roger Louis, "Musaddiq, Oil, and the Dilemmas of British Imperialism," in his collection, *Ends of British Imperialism: The Scramble for Empire, Suez and Decolonization* (London: I. B. Tauris, 2006), pp. 727–87.

10. Gamal Abdel Nasser, *Egypt's Liberation: The Philosophy of the Revolution* (Washington, D.C.: Public Affairs Press, 1955), pp. 87–88. See generally P. J. Vatikiotis, *Nasser and His Generation* (London: Croom Helm, 1978).

11. The seven states were Egypt, Iraq, Lebanon (much of it made up of Christian Arabs), Syria, Jordan (also called Transjordan at the time), Saudi Arabia, and Yemen.

12. See Uriel Dann, *King Hussein and the Challenge of Arab Radicalism: Jordan 1955–1967* (Oxford University Press, 1989).

13. David Tal, "The Making, Operation, and Failure of the May 1950 Tripartite Declaration on Middle East Security," *British Journal of Middle Eastern Studies* 36, no. 2 (August 2009): 177–93.

14. A succinct summary in English on the "infiltration/retaliation" issue during the early 1950s, detailing the high-level internal Israeli debates and very critical of Israeli addiction to the strategy of military retaliation, is Avi Shlaim, *The Iron Wall: Israel and the Arab World* (New York: Norton, 2000), pp. 81–129. The standard account is Benny Morris, *Israel's Border Wars, 1949–1956*, rev. ed. (Oxford: Clarendon Press, 1997).

15. On project Alpha and the various U.S. initiatives for Arab-Israeli settlement in 1955, including the Israeli debates about a security pact, see Uri Bialer, *Between East and West: Israel's Foreign Policy Orientation, 1948–1956* (Cambridge University Press, 1990), pp. 264–71; Hahn, *Caught in the Middle East*, pp. 170–86; and Zach Levey, *Israel and the Western Powers, 1952–1960* (University of North Carolina Press, 1997), pp. 7–34.

16. On the "war scare" of 1955–56 and options being considered, see Hahn, *Caught in the Middle East*, pp. 186–90. This is discussed in more detail in the Part One chapter "Jerusalem."

Part One: Moscow

1. As cited in James G. Richter, *Khrushchev's Double Bind* (Johns Hopkins University Press, 1994), p. 42.

2. In reality, the post of Secretary of the Communist Party of the Soviet Union was the most influential position; it was from this position that Stalin had managed to consolidate his hold on power after Lenin's death. The premiership was the lesser position. Why Malenkov abandoned this position of party secretary is open to speculation. One possible explanation is that Stalin, in the later years of his reign, used the title "premier" rather than "party secretary."

3. *Pravda*, March 12, 1953, as cited in Vladislav Zubok and Constantine Pleshakov, *Inside the Kremlin's Cold War* (Harvard University Press, 1996), p. 155.

4. *Pravda*, March 13, 1954, cited in Zubok and Pleshakov, *Inside the Kremlin's Cold War*, p. 166.

5. This argument follows Richter's analysis of Malenkov's foreign policy.

6. William Taubman, *Khrushchev: The Man and His Era* (New York: W. W. Norton, 2003), p. 261.

7. Ibid., pp. 259–67.

8. Richter, *Khrushchev's Double Bind* (New York: Praeger, 1974), p. 71.

9. Adam B. Ulam, *Expansion and Coexistence*, p. 566.

10. Nikita Sergeevitch Khrushchev, *Khrushchev Remembers* (Boston: Little, Brown, 1970), p. 400.

11. See the discussion in Richter, *Khrushchev's Double Bind*, and Ulam, *Expansion and Coexistence*.

12. Aleksandr Fursenko and Timothy Naftali, *Khrushchev's Cold War* (New York: W. W. Norton, 2006), p. 57.

13. Khrushchev's "open" speech at the Twentieth Party Congress, February 1956, as translated in *Current Digest of the Soviet Press* [hereinafter referred to as *CDSP*], vol. 8, no. 4 (March 7, 1956), pp. 3–12. Quotations are from pp. 7 and 9.

14. Ibid., p. 6.

15. See the discussion in Richter, *Khrushchev's Double Bind*, p. 72.

16. Molotov's speech to the Twentieth Party Congress, *Pravda*, February 20, 1956, pp. 2–3, as translated in *CDSP*, vol. 8, no. 9 (April 11, 1965), pp. 17, 18.

17. "Speech by Comrade D. T. Shepilov," *Pravda*, February 17, 1956, pp. 3–5, as translated in *CDSP*, vol. 8, no. 7 (March 28, 1956), p. 20.

18. *Bol'shaia Sovetskaia entsiklopediia* (Moscow: Gosudarstvennoe nauchnoe izdatel'stvo, 1952), p. 460.

19. "Information from the department of the countries of the Near and Middle East of the USSR Ministry of Foreign Affairs prepared for the trip of Comrade Shepilov, D. T. to Egypt," June 18, 1955, in V. V. Naumkin, ed., *Russia in the Twentieth Century: The Middle East Conflict, 1947–1956* (Moscow: Materik, 2003), doc. 184.

20. See the chronology offered in Yaacov Ro'i, *From Encroachment to Involvement: A Documentary Study of Soviet Policy in the Middle East, 1945–1973* (New Brunswick, N.J.: Transaction Books, 1974), p. 136; and the discussion in Guy Laron, *Origins of the Suez Crisis* (Washington, D.C.: Woodrow Wilson Center Press, 2013), pp. 98–100.

21. "Documents on International Affairs," 1955, as cited in Ro'i, *From Encroachment to Involvement*.

22. For a detailed analysis of changing Soviet views of the Third World, see Carol R. Saivetz and Sylvia Woodby, *Soviet–Third World Relations* (Boulder, Colo.: Westview Press, 1985).

23. Khrushchev's "open" speech, p. 12.

24. Fursenko and Naftali, *Khrushchev's Cold War*, pp. 59, 63–64; see also Alexei Vassiliev, *Russian Policy in the Middle East: From Messianism to Pragmatism* (Reading, N.Y.: Ithaca Press, 1993), p. 33.

25. Mohamed Heikal, *The Sphinx and the Commissar* (New York: Harper and Row, 1978) p. 58.

26. See Laron, *Origins of the Suez Crisis*, pp. 116–20; and the intelligence report sent to Secretary of State Dulles from the CIA Acting Director Cabell, August 25, 1955, in *Foreign Relations of the United States, 1955–1957*, vol. 14, no. 221 (Washington, D.C.: U.S. Government Printing Office, 1989).[hereinafter cited as *FRUS* with the volume and document number (common to both print and electronic editions)].

27. Vassiliev, *Russian Policy in the Middle East*, p. 38; Fursenko and Naftali, *Khrushchev's Cold War*, pp. 67–68 ("we had doubts"); and, on the Egyptian communists, Heikal, *Sphinx and the Commissar*, p. 58.

28. See the intelligence report to Dulles from Cabell, *FRUS*, vol. 14, no. 221; memcon, Dulles-Eisenhower, September 23, 1955, ibid., no. 303.

29. *Pravda*, September 29, 1955, p. 3. Note that the USSR is not mentioned. Arms deals were never discussed in the Soviet media.

30. TASS (Telegraphic Agency of the Soviet Union), October 1, 1955, as cited in Ro'i, *From Encroachment to Involvement, Pravda and Izvestiia*, October 2, 1955, p. 2.

31. "Transcript of conversation of the Ambassador of the USSR in Egypt, D. C. Solod, with the Prime Minister of Egypt, G. Nasser," September 29, 1955, in Naumkin, *Russia in the Twentieth Century*, Document 206.

32. Fursenko and Naftali, *Khrushchev's Cold War*, pp. 75–76.

33. Sergei Khrushchev and Nikita Khrushchev, *Krizisy i rakety* (Moscow: Novosti, 1994), p. 215.

34. Khrushchev, *Khrushchev Remembers*, p. 433.

35. Dulles memorandum of conversation (memcon) of his Geneva meeting with Molotov, October 31, 1955, in *FRUS*, vol. 14, no. 375.

36. On the Foreign Ministry position, see "Beseda nasera i tovarisha Shepilova 18 iuniia 1965" [Memorandum of conversation between Nasser and Shepilov]; also memorandum of the Committee of Information at the Foreign Ministry of the USSR on the positions of the Western powers, Israel, and the Arab Countries on the issue of the Arab-Israeli conflict, October 5, 1956, cited in Zubok and Pleshakov, *Inside the Kremlin's Cold War*, p. 190. For Khrushchev's declaration, see *New Times* (Moscow), January 5, 1956, pp. 30–31.

37. "Soviet's Papers Play Up Mideast," *New York Times*, January 13, 1956.

38. "More Arms for Egypt," *New York Times*, May 21, 1956.

39. "Arab-Israeli Row Seen as War Trigger," *Washington Post*, July 2, 1956, p. 1.

40. Kennett Love, *Suez, the Twice Fought War* (New York: McGraw-Hill, 1969), pp. 251, 255.

41. The full text of the communiqué appeared in *Pravda*, June 23, 1956, p. 3.

42. Khrushchev and Khrushchev, *Krizisy i rakety*, p. 216.

43. See "World Bank Reassures Egypt on Dam," *Washington Post*, July 24, 1956, p. 7, and details of conflicting reports in "Nasser in Bitter Attack on US," *Washington Post*, July 25, 1956, p. 4.

44. "Shepilov Hints Russia Will Decline to Help Egyptians Build Aswan Dam," *Washington Post*, July 22, 1956, p. 1.

Part One: Jerusalem

1. During 1955 Israeli troops and police reported they had killed at least thirty-six Arab infiltrators and captured about 120 other "hostile" infiltrators. These numbers, which Morris suspects are too low, are separate from the numbers killed in military reprisal raids. Benny Morris, *Israel's Border Wars, 1949–1956*, rev. ed. (Oxford: Clarendon Press, 1997), pp. 100, 146.

2. A good summary of the buildup of these two factions during 1955 is Motti Golani, "Shall We Go to War? And If We Do, When? The Genesis of the Internal Debate in Israel on the Road to the Sinai War," *Israel Affairs* 6, nos. 3, 4 (2000): 22–42.

3. Michael Bar-Zohar, *Ben-Gurion: A Biography*, trans. Peretz Kidron (New York: Delacorte, 1978), p. 203.

4. An excellent, recent short biography of Dayan by his former staffer turned historian, Mordechai Bar-On, is *Moshe Dayan: Israel's Controversial Hero* (Yale University Press, 2012). The office description is from a memoir by one of Dayan's aides, Neora Matalon, quoted by Bar-On, p. 47.

5. Bar-Zohar, *Ben-Gurion*, p. 202.

6. See Morris, *Israel's Border Wars*, pp. 359–70; and Motti Golani, *Israel in Search of a War: The Sinai Campaign, 1955–1956* (Sussex Academic Press, 1998), pp. 8–11.

7. Moshe Sharett, *Personal Diary*, vol. 5, translated by Mordechai Bar-On (Tel Aviv: Maariv Publications, 1978), p. 1229.

8. "Earth-shattering," Bar-On, *Moshe Dayan*, p. 63; on Israeli intelligence challenges in analyzing the arms deal, see Ohad Leslau, "Israeli Intelligence and the Czech-Egyptian Arms Deal," *Intelligence and National Security* 27, no. 3 (2012): 327–48. The estimates actually became graver during the winter of 1955–56 and then, as more information came in about Egyptian activity, the estimates began to calm down in the late spring of 1956.

9. "Changed everything," Morris, *Israel's Border Wars*, p. 291; "national survival," Golani, *Israel in Search of a War*, p. 13.

10. Then-lieutenant colonel Mordechai Bar-On's 1958 remarks quoted in Golani, *Israel in Search of a War*, p. 19.

11. Eban and Harel papers, October 1955, in Mordechai Bar-On, *The Gates of Gaza: Israel's Road to Suez and Back*, trans. Ruth Rossing (New York: St. Martin's Press, 1994), pp. 4–5. Bar-On believes that Harel's and Eban's views may have been influenced by initial U.S. reactions to the news, including in the CIA. But see the portrait of U.S. attitudes in the Washington chapter for this period.

12. Bar-On, *Gates of Gaza*, p. 44.

13. "Heavy sense of dread," Bar-On, *Gates of Gaza*, p. 13; David Ben-Gurion, *Israel: A Personal History* (New York: Funk & Wagnall, 1971), pp. 446–50.

14. Quoted from Sharett's *Diary*, November 1955, in ibid., p. 52.

15. Bar-On, *Moshe Dayan*, p. 67; Michael Brecher, *Decisions in Israel's Foreign Policy* (Oxford University Press, 1974), p. 247; Sharett, *Diary*, vol. 5, p. 1239.

16. Bar-On, *Moshe Dayan*, pp. 68–69; Bar-On, *Gates of Gaza*, p. 40; see also

Moshe Dayan, *Diary of the Sinai Campaign* (London: Weidenfeld & Nicolson, 1966), pp. 13–16.

17. Baruch Gilead, "Introduction," Israel State Archives, *Documents on the Foreign Policy of Israel*, vol. 11 (Jerusalem: Government Printer, 2008) [hereinafter *DFPI*], p. xiv n. 9.

18. For background, see Michael Oren, *Origins of the Second Arab-Israel War: Egypt, Israel and the Great Powers, 1952–56* (London: Frank Cass, 1992), pp. 112–16.

19. Peres was usually assisted by a Defense Ministry procurement official, Yosef Nahmias. A recent summary of the development of Israeli-French relations in this period, mainly from the Israeli perspective and significantly updating his earlier work, is Zach Levey, "French-Israeli Relations, 1950–1956: The Strategic Dimension," in Simon Smith, ed., *Reassessing Suez 1956: New Perspectives on the Crisis and Its Aftermath* (Burlington: Ashgate, 2008), pp. 87–106.

20. Lawson to State, November 17, 1955, *FRUS*, vol. 14, no. 417. A summary of the strained relations between Britain and Israel in this period is in Zach Levey, *Israel and the Western Powers, 1952–1960* (University of North Carolina Press, 1997), pp. 35–54.

21. For more on the origins of the Anderson mission, which on the Israeli side was arranged with the help of James Angleton, the CIA liaison to the Israeli foreign intelligence service, the Mossad, and a Ben-Gurion aide, Teddy Kollek, see Bar-On, *Gates of Gaza*, p. 104; the Eisenhower letter to Ben-Gurion is summarized in Editorial Note, *FRUS*, vol. 15, no. 12.

22. Sharett-Lawson memcon sent from Jerusalem to Embassy Washington, January 24, in *DFPI*, vol. 11, no. 45.

23. Eban to Sharett, January 25 and January 26, *DFPI*, vol. 11, nos. 48, 53. The "preservation" language is from the January 25 message. But the real message from Dulles was not in that message written for "general information." The real message was in Eban's January 26 message that discussed the secret Anderson mission. Eban also met with "the brother," CIA director Allen Dulles, and got a similar message; also a similar message from the White House, gleaned from a meeting the American Zionist leader Abba Hillel Silver had with White House chief of staff Sherman Adams. Eban to MFA, January 28, in ibid., no. 58. On the U.S. side the secret Anderson mission was known as project Gamma.

24. Sharett to Eban, January 26, *DFPI*, vol. 11, no. 54. The Israeli effort to arrange direct negotiations between Israel and Egypt had been tried before, in December 1954, with some preliminary contacts that did not produce a high-level meeting. See also Sharett to Eban, January 30, in ibid., no. 61. The U.S. approach to Negev concessions did not demand as much from the Israelis as the much larger and more centrally located concessions the British would have preferred. But no Israeli leader was ready to consider any such territorial concessions in the Negev at all. See, for instance, the map in Oren, *Origins*, p. 120, and the discussion on pp. 114–25. On the identity of views between Sharett and Ben-Gurion on the issue of territorial concessions, see Zaki Shalom, *David Ben-Gurion, the State of Israel and the Arab World, 1949–1956* (Sussex Academic Press, 2002), pp. 93–94.

25. See Shiloah to MFA, March 6; Eban to Sharett, March 6; Shiloah to Sharett, March 7 and 8, in *DFPI*, vol. 11, nos. 128, 129, 130, 137, 141. The quoted State Department official was Francis Russell, meeting with Reuven Shiloah. Shiloah had been the first head of Israel's foreign intelligence service, the Mossad. In this period he was working as a senior diplomat at the Israeli embassy in Washington.

26. Herzog (MFA) to Eban and Shiloah, March 12–13, *DFPI*, vol. 11, no. 144.

27. Ben-Gurion to Eisenhower, March 16, *FRUS*, vol. 15, no. 201 (emphasis in original). Because of the Dulles meeting with Eban at the end of March, Eisenhower did not send a pro forma reply to Ben-Gurion's letter until the end of April.

28. Shiloah to Sharett, March 28; Sharett to Eban, March 30, *DFPI*, vol. 11, nos. 165, 167; Sharett, *Diary* (entry for April 1), p. 1380, Bar-On translation.

29. Eban and Shiloah to Sharett, April 2, *DFPI*, vol. 11, no. 174.

30. Shimon Peres with David Landau, *Ben-Gurion: A Political Life* (New York: Schocken, 2011), p. 163.

31. Bar-On, *Gates of Gaza*, p. 66.

32. Quoted in Golani, *Israel in Search of a War*, p. 26.

33. Shimon Peres, *David's Sling* (London: Weidenfeld & Nicolson, 1970), pp. 60–61; Sylvia Crosbie, *A Tacit Alliance: France and Israel from Suez to the Six Day War* (Princeton University Press, 1974), p. 64.

34. Ben-Gurion quoted in Golani, *Israel in Search of a War*, p. 23.

35. E. L. M. Burns, *Between Arab and Israeli* (New York: Ivan Obolensky, 1962), pp. 144ff.

36. Sharett quoted in Bar-On, *Gates of Gaza*, p. 121. On the April 1956 violence, see Morris, *Israel's Border Wars*, pp. 386–96.

37. Bar-On, *Moshe Dayan*, p. 75.

38. Bar-On, *Gates of Gaza*, p. 128; Dayan, *Diary*, p. 19.

39. Bar-Zohar, *Ben-Gurion*, p. 226.

40. The recipient of the letter shared it with Sharett, who put it in his diaries. It is quoted in Yaakov Sharett, "Moshe Sharett—Right or Wrong?" *Israel Studies* 20, no. 3 (2015): 158, 168.

41. Bar-Zohar, *Ben-Gurion*, p. 228; see also, from a more critical perspective emphasizing the domestic political benefits of Ben-Gurion's "siege mentality," Guy Laron, "The Domestic Sources of Israel's Decision to Launch the 1956 Sinai Campaign," *British Journal of Middle Eastern Studies* 42, no. 2 (2015): 200, 216.

42. Guy Ziv, "Shimon Peres and the French-Israeli Alliance, 1954–9," *Journal of Contemporary History* 45, no. 2 (2010): 406, 408.

43. Bar-On, *Moshe Dayan*, pp. 76–77.

44. Golani, *Israel in Search of a War*, pp. 27–36 (which also has a good summary of the state of French-Israeli military and intelligence cooperation against Nasser or Nasser's allies during June and July); Bar-On, *Gates of Gaza*, pp. 168–72; Bar-On, *Moshe Dayan*, pp. 78–79. These sources tend to misspell the name of the French suburb as Vermars (or Veimars) rather than Vémars, and they sometimes place it south of Paris instead of north. It is just north of the modern-day Charles de Gaulle

airport. Some sources also refer to this conference as being in Chantilly, a larger town north of Vémars.

45. On reevaluations in the spring and summer of 1956, see Leslau, "Israeli Intelligence and the Czech-Egyptian Arms Deal," pp. 336–39, 347–48; Guy Laron, "'Logic dictates that they may attack when they feel they can win': The 1955 Czech-Egyptian Arms Deal, the Egyptian Army, and Israeli Intelligence," *Middle East Journal* 63, no. 1 (2009): 69, 78–80.

46. Golani, *Israel in Search of a War*, p. 29. On tamping down reprisal raids, Bar-On, *Moshe Dayan*, p. 79, gives an example in early July when Dayan counseled against raids that even Ben-Gurion proposed.

47. Bar-On, *Moshe Dayan*, p. 79. The *Chelif* had once been the *Missouri Valley* in the U.S. Navy and had been part of the U.S. assault force at the 1945 battle of Okinawa. Paul Silverstone, *The Navy of World War II, 1922–1947* (London: Routledge, 2008), p. 226.

Part One: Paris

1. Charles de Gaulle, *Memoires de Guerre*, vol. 3, *Le Salut, 1944–1946* (Paris: Plon, 1959), p. 214.

2. Charles de Gaulle, *Discours et Messages*, vol. 3, *Avec le renouveau, Mai 1958–Juillet 1962* (Paris: Plon, 1970), p. 127.

3. Jean Raymond Tournoux, *Secrets d'Etat* (Paris: Plon, 1960), p. 197.

4. Cited in Andrew Knapp and Vincent Wright, *The Government and Politics of France*, 4th ed. (London: Routledge, 2001) pp. 202–03.

5. Technically, however, the prime minister (though not the president) could dismiss the National Assembly under the Constitution of the Fourth Republic, if the Assembly twice voted no confidence in a government by an absolute majority in an eighteen-month period. This was done by Prime Minister Edgar Faure at the end of 1955, in what was the first such action since 1877. Faure lost his gamble, for in the ensuing elections the rival Republican Front, led by Guy Mollet for the Socialists and Pierre Mendès France for the Radicals, won. Mollet became prime minister.

6. Robert Murphy, *Diplomat among Warriors* (New York: Doubleday, 1964), p. 382.

7. Stanley Hoffmann has described what he refers to as the "old, centrist Radical party" in the following words: "socially and fiscally conservative but ideologically 'Republican' and Jacobin, whose strength in rural and small-town France kept it in power almost continually between the beginning of this century and the fall of the Third Republic." *New York Review of Books*, July 13, 1995, p. 55.

8. Frédérique Schillo, "Genèse de la 'collusion': Les fondemets stratégiques de l'alliance franco-israélienne de 1956," *Revue d'histoire diplomatique* 4 (Winter 2007): 305, 307; see also Sofia Papastamkou, "Egyptian-French Relations before the Suez Crisis (1954–1956)," in Philippe Vial, Georges-Henri Soutou, Robert Frank, and

Martin Alexander, eds., *Les Occidentaux et la crise de Suez: Une relecture politico-militaire* (Paris: Publications de la Sorbonne, 2015), pp. 77–94.

9. Foreign Ministry aide-mémoire relayed in Pinay to Embassy London, January 14, 1956, *Documents diplomatiques français* [hereinafter referred to as *DDF*], 1956, vol. 1, pp. 39–41.

10. See Abel Thomas, *Comment Israel fut sauvé* (Paris: Albin, 1978), p. 61; Paul Gaujac, *Suez 1956* (Paris: Charles Lavauzele, 1986), p. 10; and the Pinay-Sharett meeting record (from the meeting on December 16) relayed to Middle Eastern embassies, December 21, 1955, *DDF*, 1955, vol. 2, p. 966.

11. Editorial note to a report from the French military attaché in Israel, January 11, 1956, *DDF*, 1956, vol. 1, p. 34, note 1.

12. Maurice Vaïsse, "France and the Suez Crisis," in Wm. Roger Louis and Roger Owen, eds., *Suez 1956: The Crisis and Its Consequences* (Oxford: Clarendon Press, 1991), p. 132.

13. Interview of Paul Gaujac with the author, July 11, 1995.

14. Ibid.

15. See Paul Ely, *Mémoires* (Paris: Plon, 1969).

16. Dayan, *Moshe Dayan: Story of My Life* (New York: William Morrow, 1976), p. 198.

17. Denis Lefebvre, *L'Affaire de Suez* (Paris: Editions Bruno Leprince, 1997), p. 79; see also the documents collected in Marc Ferro, ed., *1956: La crise de Suez* (Paris: La Documentation Française, 1986).

18. On the affinity, see Paul Marie de la Gorce, *Apogée et mort de la IVème République* (Paris: Grasset, 1979), p. 367.

19. Memcon, Mollet-Eden, March 11, 1956, *DDF*, 1956, vol. 1, pp. 379–84.

20. Interview with Jean Lacouture in 1970, in Lacouture's *Nasser* (Paris: Seuil, 1971), p. 154.

21. Editorial note to memcon, Pineau-Lloyd-Dulles, May 6, 1956, *DDF*, 1956, vol. 1, p. 713, note 1.

22. The name of this suburb is often erroneously given as Vermars. E.g., Shimon Peres, *Battling for Peace* (New York: Random House, 1995), p. 104.

23. Mordechai Bar-On, "David Ben-Gurion and the Sèvres Collusion," in Louis and Owen, eds., *Suez 1956*, p. 152; and Mordechai Bar-On, "Israeli-French Relations during the Suez Crisis," in *La France et l'opération de Suez de 1956: Actes d'une table ronde organisée sous la direction de Maurice Vaïsse*, Centre d'études d'histoire de la Défense (CEHD) (Paris: ADDIM, 1997), pp. 100–01.

24. Peres, *Battling for Peace*, p. 105.

25. Mordechai Bar-On, *The Gates of Gaza* (New York: St. Martin's Press, 1994), pp. 169–70. According to Bar-On, the seaborne equipment consisted of 120 AMX-13 tanks, 40 Super-Sherman tanks, 18 105mm mobile artillery guns, and ammunition and spare parts. The entire deal would cost Israel $80 million. In *Battling for Peace*, Peres's figures are slightly different.

26. Alistair Horne, *A Savage War of Peace* (New York: Penguin Books, 1987), p. 85.

27. De Murville to Paris, July 20, 1956, *DDF*, 1956, vol. 2, pp. 131–34.

Part One: London

1. Anthony Nutting, *No End of a Lesson: The Story of Suez* (London: Constable, 1967), pp. 21–23; Keith Kyle, *Suez: Britain's End of Empire in the Middle East* (New York: St. Martin's Press, 1991), p. 81 (quoting Ivone Kirkpatrick).

2. Michael S. Goodman, *The Official History of the Joint Intelligence Committee*, vol. 1: *From the Approach of the Second World War to the Suez Crisis* (Abingdon, Oxon: Routledge, 2014), pp. 375–76.

3. Nutting, *Lesson*, p. 23.

4. David Reynolds, "Eden the Diplomatist, 1931–56: Suicide of a Statesman," *History* 240 (1989), p. 76.

5. Hugh Thomas, *The Suez Affair* (London: Weidenfeld & Nicolson, 1967), p. 13.

6. W. Scott Lucas, *Divided We Stand: Britain, the US and the Suez Crisis* (London: Hodder & Stoughton, 1991), p. 73.

7. Alistair Horne, *Harold Macmillan*, vol. 1: *1894–1956* (New York: Viking, 1989), p. 374.

8. Evelyn Shuckburgh, *Descent to Suez, Diaries 1951–56* (New York: W. W. Norton, 1987), p. 14.

9. See Rt. Hon. Lord Owen, CH, "The Effect of Prime Minister Anthony Eden's Illness on His Decision-Making during the Suez Crisis," *QJM* 98, no. 6 (June 2005): 387–402; quotation from p. 392.

10. Shuckburgh, *Descent*, p. 278; Harold Macmillan, *Tides of Fortune: 1945–1955* (New York: Harper & Row, 1969), p. 635.

11. See Jonathan Bloch and Patrick Fitzgerald, *British Intelligence and Covert Action* (Kerry, Ireland: Brandon, 1983), p. 117; Lucas, *Divided We Stand*, pp. 52, 58, 59; Kyle, *Suez*, p. 74; and Goodman, *Official History*, pp. 375–76.

12. Dulles-Macmillan memcon, September 26, 1955, *FRUS*, vol. 14, p. 518; Shuckburgh, *Descent*, p. 281.

13. Roger Makins, *The Suez Crisis—The Makins Experience*, private memoir made available to the editors by Christopher Makins, pp. 4–5. For more on Makins and the U.S.-U.K. relationship in this period, see Richard Wevill, *Diplomacy, Roger Makins and the Anglo-American Relationship* (New York: Routledge, 2016).

14. Macmillan-Dulles memcon, New York, September 26, 1955, *FRUS*, vol. 14, p. 518.

15. Kyle, *Suez*, p. 81.

16. Makins, *Experience*, p. 5.

17. Macmillan-Dulles memcon, Department of State, October 3, 1955, *FRUS*, vol. 14, p. 550; Makins, *Experience*, p. 6; Kyle, *Suez*, p. 81.

18. Goodman, *Official History*, p. 376.

19. Anthony Eden, *Full Circle: The Memoirs of the Rt. Hon. Sir Anthony Eden, K.G., P.C., M.C.* (London: Cassell, 1960), pp. 256–57; Lucas, *Divided We Stand*, p. 66.

20. Makins, *Experience*, p. 12.

21. "Dull, Duller, Dulles" from Louis Jefferson, *The John Foster Dulles Book of Humor* (New York: St. Martin's Press, 1986), dust jacket; see Eden, *Full Circle*, pp. 63–64; "our man," in Shuckburgh, *Descent*, p. 23.

22. Macmillan, *Tides of Fortune*, p. 650; on Eden's view, Lucas, *Divided We Stand*, p. 80.

23. Shuckburgh, *Descent*, p. 293; Macmillan, *Tides of Fortune*, p. 652; Kyle, *Suez*, p. 80; Bloch and Fitzgerald, *British Intelligence*, p. 117.

24. See Kyle, *Suez*, p. 74–76; Lucas, *Divided We Stand*, p. 63.

25. Shuckburgh, *Descent*, pp. 251, 297; Nutting, *Lesson*, pp. 49, 89.

26. Macmillan, *Tides of Fortune*, p. 633; Kyle, *Suez*, p. 56; see also Memorandum of Conversation, Paris, October 26 1955, *FRUS*, vol. 14, p. 652; Lucas, *Divided We Stand*, p. 106.

27. Kyle, *Suez*, p. 82.

28. On the work with the Americans and the significance of Jordan and the Baghdad Pact to the British, see the American report from the foreign ministers meeting at Geneva, November 3, 1955, *FRUS*, vol. 14, pp. 707–10.

29. Lucas, *Divided We Stand*, pp. 75–76; on the Egyptian attitudes, see also Humphrey Trevelyan, *The Middle East in Revolution* (London: Macmillan, 1970), p. 57.

30. Shuckburgh, *Descent*, pp. 281–82.

31. Makins, *Experience*, p. 10.

32. Alex von Tunzelman, *Blood and Sand: Suez, Hungary and the Crisis That Shook the World* (London: Simon & Schuster, 2016), p. 160; Goodman, *Official History*, p. 378.

33. Ibid., p. 378.

34. See Lucas, *Divided We Stand*, p. 85; Nutting, *No End of a Lesson*, pp. 25–26; Lord Butler, *The Art of the Possible: The Memoirs of Lord Butler* (London: Hamish Hamilton, 1971), p. 183; and Lord Kilmuir, *Political Adventure: The Memoirs of the Earl of Kilmuir* (London: Weidenfeld & Nicolson, 1964), p. 256–57.

35. Selwyn Lloyd, *Suez 1956: A Personal Account* (London: Jonathan Cape, 1978), p. 4; Lucas, *Divided We Stand*, p. 81; von Tunzelman, *Blood and Sand*, p. 46.

36. Shuckburgh, *Descent*, p. 326.

37. Eden, *Full Circle*, p. 335.

38. Lucas, *Divided We Stand*, p. 90; Lloyd, *Suez 1956*, p. 42.

39. Lucas, *Divided We Stand*, p. 91.

40. Nutting, *Lesson*, pp. 28–30; Embassy London Report to State, March 9, 1956, *FRUS*, vol. 13, p. 296.

41. Nutting, *Lesson*, pp. 31–32.

42. Quoted in Diane Kunz, *The Economic Diplomacy of the Suez Crisis* (University of North Carolina Press, 1991), p. 62; Lucas, *Divided We Stand*, p. 105.

43. Shuckburgh, *Descent*, pp. 341, 345–46. Eden compared Nasser to Mussolini as early as January 1956.

44. Von Tunzelman, *Blood and Sand*, p. 160.

45. Ibid., p. 163; see Kyle, *Suez*, pp. 102–03.

46. Kunz, *Economic Diplomacy*, p. 62.

47. Robert Rhodes James, *Anthony Eden* (London: Weidenfeld & Nicholson, 1986), p. 432; Lucas, *Divided We Stand*, pp. 97–98.

48. Nutting, *Lesson*, p. 35; von Tunzelman, *Blood and Sand*, p. 1.

49. Eden to Eisenhower, London, March 15, 1956, *FRUS*, vol. 15, pp. 364–65.

50. Macmillan, *Full Circle*, p. 94.

51. Nutting, *Lesson*, p. 36; Shuckburgh, *Descent*, pp. 346–47.

52. Makins, *Experience*, pp. 16–21.

53. See Macmillan, *Full Circle*, p. 95; Kyle, *Suez*, p. 105; Lucas, *Divided We Stand*, p. 121.

54. Kyle, *Suez*, p. 128.

55. Makins, *Experience*, p. 21.

56. Lucas, *Divided We Stand*, p. 137.

57. Kunz, *Economic Diplomacy*, p. 66.

58. Nutting, *Lesson*, p. 46; Thomas, *The Suez Affair*, p. 26.

Part One: Washington

1. Dulles-Eisenhower call, September 23, 1955, *FRUS*, vol. 14, no. 303. See also David Nichols, *Eisenhower 1956* (New York: Simon & Schuster, 2011), p. 20.

2. See Clarence Lasby, *Eisenhower's Heart Attack: How Ike Beat Heart Disease and Held On to the Presidency* (University Press of Kansas, 1997).

3. Keith Kyle, *Suez* (London: Weidenfeld & Nicolson, 1991), p. 45. Kyle, whose book is the best one-volume narrative history of the Suez crisis, was part of that Washington press corps in 1956, working for *The Economist*. A well-judged overall interpretation of the Eisenhower presidency is William Hitchcock, *The Age of Eisenhower* (New York: Simon & Schuster, 2018).

4. Kyle, *Suez*, p. 46.

5. Cairo 1373, March 20, 1955, *FRUS*, vol. 12, p. 42.

6. Memcon, September 26, 1955, *FRUS*, vol. 14, no. 310.

7. Memcon, Dulles-Macmillan, October 3; memcon of 260th NSC meeting, October 6; and CIA SNIE 30–3–55, "Probable Consequences of the Egyptian Arms Deal with the Soviet Bloc," October 12, *FRUS*, vol. 14, nos. 323, 326, 335.

8. Memcon of 262d NSC, October 20, ibid., no. 345. On the CIA, Nasser, and the deal announcement, see Hugh Wilford, *America's Great Game: The CIA's Secret Arabists and the Shaping of the Modern Middle East* (New York: Basic Books, 2013), pp. 195–97.

9. Memcon of 262d NSC, October 20, *FRUS*, vol. 14, no. 345.

10. Dulles-Sharett, October 26, in section 38, ibid., no. 359.

11. The "trump card" expression was Eden's. W. Scott Lucas, *Divided We Stand: Britain, the U.S. and the Suez Crisis* (London: Hodder & Stoughton, 1991), p. 68. The British do seem to have played the key role in developing the Aswan Dam "carrot" idea. See also William Roger Louis, "Dulles, Suez, and the British," in Richard Immerman, ed., *John Foster Dulles and the Diplomacy of the Cold War* (Princeton University Press, 1990), pp. 144–45.

12. See ibid., nos. 384, 387, 391, 393, 396, 407. The Anglo-American political context in this period, the British effort to forge an "Anglo-American 'alliance' in the Middle East," is depicted in Lucas, *Divided We Stand*, pp. 67–79.

13. "Biggest single undertaking," in Hoover-Black-Makins (British ambassador to the United States) memcon, November 16, *FRUS*, vol. 14, no. 415.

14. Eisenhower to Dulles, December 5, in Louis Galambos and Daun Van Ee, eds., *The Papers of Dwight David Eisenhower*, vol. 16 (Johns Hopkins University Press, 1996), pp. 1921–22 [hereinafter *DDEP*].

15. See Wilford, *America's Great Game*, pp. 204–08; "most capable" and presidential material in Eisenhower diary, January 11, 1956, in *DDEP*, 16:1953. In late November Eisenhower had suggested his brother Milton as a possible mediator; State's Hoover had preferred to stick with Anderson, arguing that he would attract less attention. Hoover to Dulles, November 28, *FRUS*, vol. 14, no. 430.

16. Memcon, Eisenhower-Dulles (by Dulles), December 8, *FRUS*, vol. 14, no. 442. For Dulles effectively indicating a no to Israeli arms requests, see State 445 to Embassy Tel Aviv, December 29, and Dulles-Eban memcon, December 30, ibid., nos. 471, 472. "Interests of this country," Eisenhower diary, January 11, 1956, *DDEP*, 16:1953.

17. Memcon, Dulles-Sharett, November 21, ibid., no. 421; see also the paper given to the Israelis at that meeting, and memcon of the follow-up meeting, Dulles-Sharett, December 6, ibid., nos. 424, 437. For the Negev issue as a key obstacle, see the follow-up December 8 meeting between Russell and Israeli diplomat Reuven Shiloah and the Sharett letter to Dulles, December 12, ibid., nos. 446, 448.

18. For the atmosphere of those weeks, see Nichols, *Eisenhower 1956*, the specific quote is on p. 58, from an NSC meeting on January 12, 1956.

19. See, among other documents, CIA message (probably by Kim Roosevelt), January 24 (with the quote about Nuri); Anderson to State, January 27; Dulles to Anderson, January 27 (with quotes on Nasser's position); Allen Dulles to his representatives in Jerusalem and Cairo, January 29; Editorial Note (re "all out effort") on Dulles to Anderson, January 30; Anderson to State, February 3, *FRUS*, vol. 15, nos. 32, 41, 42, 48, 53, 72.

20. Eisenhower-Eden memcon, January 30, *FRUS*, vol. 12, no. 95; Dulles-Eden memcon, January 30, *FRUS*, vol. 15, no. 54.

21. On the views of Major General E. L. M. Burns, the Canadian officer who was the chief of staff of the UN truce supervision force, see, for example, Tel Aviv 772, February 2, ibid., no. 71.

22. CIA report from Cairo, February 22, ibid., no. 112.

23. On Nasser's views, see the report from Ambassador Byroade and his separate personal letter to Dulles, February 22 and 23, and the CIA report (probably from Kim Roosevelt) to CIA Director Dulles, February 22, ibid., nos. 113, 114, 115; and Special National Intelligence Estimate (SNIE) 30–56, "Critical Aspects of the Arab-Israeli Situation," February 28, in ibid., no. 137.

24. Hoover to Dulles, March 1; Dulles note on meeting with Eisenhower, March 2, ibid., nos. 141, 150.

25. Quotes are from two messages from Anderson to Dulles (then in Karachi), March 6, ibid., no. 164, 168.

26. Eden to Eisenhower, March 5, in Peter Boyle, ed., *The Eden-Eisenhower*

Correspondence, 1955–1957 (University of North Carolina Press, 2005), p. 119; Hoover to Dulles, March 5; Hoover-Eisenhower memcon, March 6, *FRUS*, vol. 15, nos. 161, 165.

27. Dulles to Hoover (and Eisenhower), March 8, ibid., no. 176; Eisenhower diary entries, March 8 and 13, *DDEP*, 16:2054, 2069.

28. Eden to Eisenhower with attached report, March 15, *FRUS*, vol. 15, no. 197; Eisenhower diary, March 19, *DDEP*, 16:2077; Allen-Kirkpatrick memcon, March 15, *FRUS*, vol. 15, no. 198; see also the detailed British indictment of Nasser passed to State on March 21, ibid., no. 208.

29. Joint Chiefs of Staff (JCS) Secretary (Phillips) to Secretary of Defense Wilson (passed to State), April 25, *FRUS*, vol. 15, no. 331. This estimate did not appear to take into account the impact of any major new Israeli purchases of arms.

30. Lucas, *Divided We Stand*, pp. 110–11.

31. There is a certain confusion in some sources about the nature of the Omega program. Some voice a general assumption that this became a U.S.-U.K. effort to weaken and overthrow Nasser, including with covert action. For instance, Peter Hahn summarized: "Under the Omega initiative of early 1956, Eisenhower canceled economic aid offers to Egypt, challenged Nasser's prestige, and contemplated covert operations to unseat him." *Caught in the Middle East*, p. 266.

On the aspects of Omega mentioned in the text, see especially Hoover to Dulles, March 16; NEA Bureau, "United States Policy in the Near East," March 28; Dulles to Eisenhower, March 28; and memcons by State's Rountree and by White House's Goodpaster of White House interagency meeting (not a formal NSC meeting, but including key State and Defense officials), March 28, *FRUS*, vol. 15, nos. 200, 222, 223, 224, 225. Goodpaster's meeting notes are most revealing. Eisenhower's brief comments on it to his diary, March 28, are in *DDEP*, 16:2096–97.

32. The quote is from the Goodpaster memcon, March 28, *FRUS*, vol. 15, no. 225. The move to the UN to support Hammarskjöld began formally on March 20. On April 4 the Soviet Union joined a unanimous UN Security Council resolution to back this work. MacArthur was the Omega coordinator. Some sources confuse this with the roles played by State Department diplomats such as Francis Russell or Raymond Hare.

33. The CIA did not plan covert action to overthrow Nasser at any time before the Suez Canal takeover in late July. After the Suez crisis broke, discussed in Part Two, Dulles and his aides began pushing at least for consideration of such covert action. Even then the CIA never favored it or started work on it. President Eisenhower did not favor it either. Foster Dulles appears to have acknowledged, on occasion, that he too was against a "CIA-type" solution.

The CIA had never quite given up on Nasser. When they first went to London to hear what the British wanted to do (in early April), the CIA was scornful, to put it mildly, about everything they heard. Partly to forestall those anti-Nasser plots, the CIA people later, in July, went along with at least exploring the situation in Syria, where some feared the leader would become a real Soviet satellite. Even in Syria, the CIA never saw this as more than an exploration until after the canal seizure; and even then it seems to have participated modestly, at most, in the British planning that later fell apart so completely during October 1956. The best account is W. Scott Lucas and Alistair Morey, "The Hidden 'Alliance': The CIA and MI6 before and after Suez," available either in David Stafford and Rhodri Jeffreys-Jones, eds., *American-British-Canadian Intelligence Relations, 1939–2000* (London: Frank Cass, 2000), pp. 95–120, or in the special issue on the same topic in *Intelligence and National Security* 15 no. 2 (Summer 2000).

The main action component of Omega was not in the CIA. It was about military-political planning to head off or manage a possible Arab-Israeli war. The Goodpaster memcon of the March 28 meeting that authorized Omega is most revealing on how important this issue was even at the start (*FRUS*, vol. 15, no. 225).

Aside from the various State political efforts, the really heavy lifts involved work with the Pentagon. Less than two weeks after Omega got under way, by April 9, the military contingency work had really picked up, as shown by the memcon of the meeting that day between Dulles, Radford, and Douglas MacArthur II (the State Department counselor and the person in charge of coordinating Omega) (*FRUS*, vol. 15, no. 259). The lines of work planning for three kinds of major military intervention, and also readying possible arms deliveries to Israel or to Egypt, become a big deal in the weeks that followed.

There was quite a bit of work that spring and summer, mainly in U.S.-U.K. military channels. Eisenhower was following it regularly. Dulles and Radford reviewed it on May 16 (*FRUS*, vol. 15, no. 35; also see note 3). These were big plans for major military interventions. The JCS official history for this period, also suggests the scope and nature of the joint planning. Kenneth Condit, *The Joint Chiefs of Staff and National Policy, 1955–1956* (Washington, D.C.: Joint Staff Historical Office, 1992), p. 173. Some of the details of this work also surface in British archives (Kyle, *Suez*, pp. 104–05).

34. See generally Lucas and Morey, "The Hidden 'Alliance'"; Wilford, *America's Great Game*, pp. 218–27 ("Bond" on p. 221, station chief Robert L. Eichelberger quoted on p. 226); Lucas, *Divided We Stand*, pp. 116–18; Kyle, *Suez*, p. 102.

35. Rountree (NEA) to Dulles, May 23 (this memo considered sending an envoy, like Anderson, back out to Egypt to see if Nasser might have changed his view); State to Middle Eastern embassies, July 9 (with the quoted passages); NEA (Allen) to Dulles, July 10 (on Egyptian peace talk and "considerable skepticism"), *FRUS*, vol. 15, nos. 360, 434, 437.

36. Black memcon, June 25, ibid., no. 410.

37. 289th NSC memcon, June 28, ibid., no. 412.

38. NEA (Allen) to Dulles, July 17, ibid., no. 467.

39. Dulles-Hussein memcon, ibid., no. 478.

40. *Time*, July 30, 1956, p. 7.

Part One: Cairo

1. Cairo to Ankara, Athens, and Belgrade, January 12, 1953; Athens to Cairo, February 1, 1953; Belgrade to Cairo, February 22, 1953, in Egypt National Archives [hereinafter ENA], Foreign Ministry Archives, Box 1550.

2. One American embassy official wrote, "Without the High Aswan Dam, the outlook for Egypt appears hopeless." Cairo to State, October 22, 1954, in U.S. National Archives [hereinafter NA], Record Group (RG) 469, Records Relating to Economic Aid to Egypt, 1952–1955, HQ Office of Deputy Director for Operations, Box 1. According to American government records, the Egyptian junta took "a definite decision to proceed with construction of the High Aswan Dam" as early as January 1954, significantly before funding had been secured. Cairo to Washington, January 11, 1954, in NA, RG 469, DD Ops/NEA Ops/NE Central Files. Egypt Project Files 1953–1958, Box 7.

3. The government of Egypt contributed an additional $15 million to the project. The pattern of joint financing was inspired by American development programs in Latin America in the 1940s called *servicios*.

4. Memcon, May 11, 1953, *FRUS*, vol. 9, pp. 4–6.

5. Ibid., p. 13.

6. The outstanding issues were (1) whether British military officials who remained in the Canal Zone during the transition period would be allowed to wear uniforms, and (2) whether Britain would be allowed to reoccupy the base without consultation with the Egyptian government in the event of an attack on a non-Arab Middle Eastern country such as Iran or Turkey.

7. Embassy Washington to Cairo on meeting with Deputy Assistant Secretary of State John D. Jernegan, January 2, 1954, ENA, Foreign Ministry Archives, Box 697.

8. See *New York Times*, December 28, 1953, p. 3, and January 5, 1954, p. 5, respectively.

9. Ali Kamal Fahmy [DCM, Egyptian Embassy, Washington] to Cairo, January 18, 1954, with memcon of meeting with Byroade, Hart, Boardman, and Burdett, ENA, Foreign Ministry Archives, Box 698.

10. Ibid.

11. Caffrey to State, July 31, 1954, *FRUS*, vol. 9, p. 2290.

12. Abdel Nasser believed Egyptian public opinion would not allow signing a treaty of alliance with a foreign power since Egypt had signed such treaties in the past from a position of weakness and subsequently been at the mercy of outside forces.

13. Hussein to Cairo, September 17, 1954, ENA, Foreign Ministry Archives, Box 1558. *FRUS* reprints several memoranda that generally confirm the accounts of former CIA officials Wilbur C. Eveland and Miles Copeland concerning negotiations that continued through the fall between Abdel Nasser and the CIA. These accounts suggest the CIA was attempting to create a situation whereby Egypt could divert economic development funds for military uses. Such efforts failed; famously, a $3 million cash bribe the CIA gave Abdel Nasser to win his fealty was used to build a large tower visible from much of Cairo. Egyptians popularly (and famously) called it "Roosevelt's erection."

14. The sourcing for this citation has been lost in the more than twenty years since it was found in the archives. From the context, it seems clearly drawn from a contemporaneous communication between Ambassador Hussein and Cairo found in the Egyptian National Archives.

15. Muhammad Hasanayn Haykal, *Milaffat al-Suways* (Cairo: Markaz al-Ahram, 1986), p. 340.

16. Mohamed H. Heikal, *Cutting the Lion's Tail* (London: A. Deutch, 1986), pp. 66–67. This author is the same as the one whose name is transliterated under more orthodox schemes as "Haykal." My usage gives it as Haykal when transliterated from the Arabic and Heikal if an English-language publication presented it that way.

17. Quoted material from Mordechai Bar-On, *The Gates of Gaza*, p. 87 (citing an April 1955 meeting with the U.S. ambassador recounted in British archives). Similarly the ambassador, Henry Byroade, did report on March–April 1955 meetings with the Egyptian foreign minister that stressed the land-link demand, which could not merely be a "corridor." Memcon of Byroade and Fawzi, March 26; Byroade to State, April 3, *FRUS*, vol. 15, nos. 58 (attachment), 62.

18. Haykal, *Milaffat al-Suways*, p. 342. No record of the meeting appears in *FRUS* except for a reference to a March 19 meeting in *FRUS*, vol. 15, n. 6, p. 122.

19. For the traditional view, see, for example, Heikal, *Cutting the Lion's Tail*, p. 69. In a discussion with another journalist, Haykal claimed Abdel Nasser raised the issue of Soviet arms with the Soviet ambassador at a party at the Sudanese embassy before he left for Bandung, and mentioned the issue to Zhou Enlai only as a follow-up. Fouad Mattar, *Bi-Siraha 'an 'Abdel Nasser* (Cairo: Dar al-Qadaya al-Fikriya, 1975) p. 83. One version of the alternate view was expressed by Hussein Fahmy, the former editor of the government-sponsored newspaper *al-Gumhuriyyah* and an old college friend of Abdel Nasser. He told this author that Soviet ambassador Daniel Solod lived in his building in the mid-1950s and made clear several months before Bandung (and before the Gaza raid) that Soviet aid was available if the Egyptians wanted it.

20. Hussein to Cairo, March 6, ENA, Foreign Ministry Archives, Box 698.

21. Hussein to Cairo, March 30, ENA, Foreign Ministry Archives, Box 397.

22. "The Economic Development of Egypt," World Bank Report #A.S. 40a, August 25, 1955, p. ii.

23. Ibid.

24. Some 695,000 acres would be converted from basin to perennial irrigation, and 1,349,400 acres would come under new cultivation.

25. Ibid., p. 12.

26. Ibid., p. 18.

27. Ibid., p. iii.

28. The agreed-on fiction was that the arms had come from Czechoslovakia. The Egyptians had continued discussion of possible military aid from the United States through the summer, but Secretary Dulles recommended against it after Khrushchev told him in July that the Soviets were not contemplating supplying Egypt with arms. Hahn, *The United States, Britain and Egypt*, p. 192.

29. Hussein to Cairo, October 18, ENA, Foreign Ministry Archives, Box 1454

(also printed in Haykal, *Milaffat al-Suways*, pp. 774–76, although mistakenly printing "Yemen" for "China"). The last paragraph is translated somewhat more liberally in Heikal, *Cutting the Lion's Tail*, p. 81.

30. Reprinted in *FRUS*, vol. 14, no. 461.

31. Hussein to Cairo, December 22, ENA, Foreign Ministry Archives, Box 397.

32. Hussein to Cairo, December 28, ENA, Foreign Ministry Archives, Box 397.

33. Byroade Eyes Only to Dulles, April 3, 1956, *FRUS*, vol. 15, no. 238.

34. There is no indication anywhere that Anderson ever linked funding for the high dam with a regional peace settlement during their discussions with the Egyptians.

35. Hussein to Cairo, March 1, 1956, ENA, Foreign Ministry Archives, Box 397.

36. Memorandum, March 17, ENA, Foreign Ministry Archives, Box 698.

37. Ibid.

38. Hussein to Cairo, March 29, ENA, Foreign Ministry Archives, Box 397.

39. Washington to Cairo, April 12, ENA, Foreign Ministry Archives, Box 373 (also reprinted in Haykal, *Milaffat al-Suways*, pp. 790–91).

40. Samih Anwar, handwritten memo, April 15, in ENA, Foreign Ministry Archives, Box 397.

41. See Barnaby Crowcroft, "Egypt's Other Nationalists and the Suez Crisis of 1956," *Historical Journal* 59, no. 1 (2016): 253, 262–63, 267–69.

42. 'Abd Allah Imaam, *Ali Sabri Yatadhakir* [Ali Sabri Remembers] (Beirut: Dar al-Wahdah, 1988), p. 20. Haykal claims that the idea came to Abdel Nasser during a sleepless night on July 20–21, after a meeting with Indian prime minister Jawaharlal Nehru. *Milaffat al-Suways*, p. 455.

43. Haykal, *Milaffat al-Suways*, p. 459. For a good sifting of the evidence about the timing of Nasser's move, concluding that the ingredients did come together in late July, see Laura James, "When Did Nasser Expect War? The Suez Nationalization and its Aftermath in Egypt," in Simon Smith, ed., *Reassessing Suez 1956: New Perspectives on the Crisis and Its Aftermath* (Aldershot: Ashgate, 2008), pp. 149–55.

44. Ibid., p. 460. In her analysis, Laura James also noticed that Nasser appears to have downplayed the likelihood of a military response against him. "When Did Nasser Expect War?," pp. 154–56.

45. On the opposition of Field Marshal 'Amr, and the negative reaction to the announcement from him and from the defense minister, see Crowcroft, "Egypt's Other Nationalists, 1956," p. 263.

46. An Arabic version of the speech is at http://nasser.bibalex.org/Speeches/browser.aspx?SID=495&lang=en.

47. Haykal, *Milaffat al-Suways*, pp. 460–63.

Part Two: Washington

1. Embassy London to State, July 27, 1956, *FRUS*, vol. 16, no. 2. On Nasser's speech, see Editorial Note, ibid., no. 1; Embassy Cairo to State, *FRUS*, vol. 15, no. 511; Keith Kyle, *Suez: Britain's End of Empire in the Middle East* (New York: I. B.

Tauris, 1991), pp. 132–34; Donald Neff, *Warriors at Suez: Eisenhower Takes America into the Middle East* (New York: Simon & Schuster, 1981), pp. 268–72.

2. On U.S. views of the strategic importance of the canal, implications of Egyptian nationalization, and Anglo-French views on these subjects, see *FRUS*, vol. 16, nos. 3, 14, 19, 30, 40, 42; Neff, *Warriors at Suez*, pp. 281–82.

3. Eden to Eisenhower, July 27, 1956, *FRUS*, vol. 16, no. 5. On British and French determination to reverse Nasser's takeover by any means, including force, see ibid., nos., 4, 7, 17, 18, 38.

4. Memcon with Eisenhower, July 27, 1956, ibid., no. 6.

5. Memcon, Eisenhower-Dulles, July 29, 1956, ibid., no. 23.

6. On U.S. views of legal and political support for Nasser's action and the risks of using force before trying diplomacy, see ibid., nos. 8, 9, 14, 15, 23, 40.

˙ 7. On Murphy's talks with the British and French, see ibid., nos. 21, 24, 25, 26, 27, 28, 32, 36, 37.

8. Murphy to State, July 31, 1956, ibid., no. 33.

9. Memcon with Eisenhower, July 31, 1956, ibid., no. 34. U.S. officials viewed Nasser as a volatile, ambitious personality but also as sensitive to international opinion and, because he was determined to hold on to the canal, likely to try to avoid an incident that could offer a pretext for Western military intervention. See ibid., nos. 3, 31, 40.

10. Eisenhower to Eden, July 31, 1956, ibid., no. 35. Eisenhower sent a similar letter to Mollet, July 31, 1956, ibid., no. 39.

11. On Dulles's talks with British and French officials in London, including his statements that the U.S. aim was to compel Nasser to "disgorge" the canal, see ibid., nos. 41, 42. Additional records of the talks are in ibid., nos. 43, 44, 46, 49, 53.

Some scholars view Eisenhower and Dulles as determined from the outset of the crisis to prevent British and French use of force under any circumstances. In this view, Dulles or Eisenhower, or both, deceived the British and French when they depicted an international conference as a potential prelude to the use of force. See, for example, Doran, *Ike's Gamble*, pp. 177–79; Laron, *Origins of the Suez Crisis*, p. 156; von Tunzelmann, *Blood and Sand*, pp. 62–65. We think these interpretations oversimplify the tensions and evolution in U.S. thinking during the first weeks of the crisis, including differences between Eisenhower and Dulles.

On Dulles's account of what he'd accomplished in London, see Dulles to Eisenhower, August 2, 1956, *FRUS*, vol. 16, no. 48. See also Dwight D. Eisenhower, *Waging Peace, 1956–1961: The White House Years* (Garden City, N.Y.: Doubleday, 1956), p. 42. On British and French preparations for military action up to the time of the London conference, see Embassy London to State, August 16, 1956, *FRUS*, vol. 16, no. 84.

12. Russell to Dulles (reflecting views of others at State and perhaps at CIA), "U.S. Policies toward Nasser," August 4, *FRUS*, vol. 16, no. 62.

13. Kenneth Condit, *The Joint Chiefs of Staff and National Policy*, pp. 178–81 (Radford quote on p. 179 from the NSC meeting on August 9); see also memo from Wilson to Lay, August 7, 1956, *FRUS*, vol. 16, no. 68. See also JCS papers in Boggs to NSC, August 22, 1956, ibid., no. 118.

14. Eisenhower made sure studies of military options were placed on the agenda in advance of the August 9 NSC meeting, although he agreed with Dulles that formal NSC debate or decisions on military action were premature. Telcon (notes of a telephone conversation), Dillon Anderson-Dulles, August 6, 1956, ibid., no. 65; memcon, President's Office, August 6, 1956, ibid., no. 67. For a description of JCS options to be discussed by the JCS at the August 9 meeting, see Wilson to Lay, August 7, 1956, ibid., no. 68. See also Eisenhower, *Waging Peace*, pp. 43–44. The resulting studies are summarized in Condit, *The Joint Chiefs of Staff*, pp. 180–81.

15. Memo of NSC Discussion, August 9, 1956, *FRUS*, vol. 16, no. 72. Consistent with the NSC decision on contingency studies for possible use of force, Dulles authorized the State Department in the days following the August 9 NSC meeting to sign off on Defense Department release of radios, ammunition, and aircraft parts to the British and French, for use by military forces deploying for potential action at Suez. This release of equipment was to be kept secret. Telcon, Dulles-Gray, *FRUS*, vol. 16, no. 73; Editorial Note, *FRUS*, vol. 16, no. 77. See also Kyle, *Suez*, pp. 181–82.

While he was ready to accept that force might be necessary, that did not mean Dulles wanted a war. The day after the August 9 NSC meeting, when UN Secretary General Hammarskjöld told Dulles that too much time had passed for the allies to gain international support for military action, Dulles didn't disagree. "I said," he recorded, "that I certainly thought the more delay there was the less likelihood there was it would be invoked. That was one reason why I advocated the conference." Memcon, Dulles-Hammarskjöld, August 10, 1956, *FRUS*, vol. 16, no. 76.

This remark might indicate the secretary's intent to sabotage British and French plans to use force, with no intention of ever supporting military action. See, for example, Kyle, *Suez*, p. 182. On the other hand, Dulles's private statements to Eisenhower and other U.S. officials prior to the London conference suggest awareness that force might become necessary. He certainly made no effort to obstruct contingency planning for that eventuality. Ever the lawyer, though, Dulles had a reputation for trying to find common ground with different audiences—or, less charitably, saying what he thought the client wanted to hear. On the lawyerly aspects of Dulles's approach to diplomacy, see William Roger Louis, "An American Volcano in the Middle East: John Foster Dulles and the Suez Crisis," in Louis, *The Ends of British Imperialism: The Scramble for Empire, Suez, and Decolonization* (New York: I. B. Tauris, 2006), pp. 639–64. See also von Tunzelmann, *Blood and Sand*, pp. 65–66.

16. Memcon, White House, August 12, 1956, *FRUS*, vol. 16, no. 78.

17. Hahn, *Caught in the Middle East*, pp. 195–96; Laron, *Origins of the Suez Crisis*, pp. 155–56. The intelligence community expressed views similar to Eisenhower's and Dulles's on this topic throughout the crisis; for example, Special National Intelligence Estimate (SNIE), September 5, 1956, *FRUS*, vol. 16, no. 175. British officials told the Americans they saw the same signs of a powder keg of anti-Western hostility in the Arab world. But they argued that this made military action against Nasser more imperative, not less, because otherwise he would move quickly to exploit the roiling emotions throughout the region. Kyle, *Suez*, pp. 224–25, 276–77.

18. Dulles to Eisenhower, August 16, *FRUS*, vol. 16, no. 86.

19. For the memcon of a key meeting in this process, on August 2, see ibid., no.

49. Subsequent drafting mainly reflected the choices made at this August 2 meeting, as succinctly summarized in a message from State to key embassies on August 5. Ibid., no. 63.

20. On Dulles's lobbying of non-Western governments, see ibid., nos. 63, 81, 91, 111. Contrary to the Western proposal for international control over the canal, India and the Soviet Union pushed the Egyptian government's demand for unconstrained sovereignty. Ibid., nos. 83, 89, 114. See also Laron, *Origins of the Suez Crisis*, p. 162.

On U.S. diplomacy to sideline Israel during August and September, including deferring shipment of Canadian F-86 and French Mystère combat aircraft, see *FRUS*, vol. 16, nos. 4, 13, 18, 29, 60, 75, 80, 204, 220; Hahn, *Caught in the Middle East*, p. 196. Dulles dropped opposition to the Canadian F-86 shipment in late September for reasons that aren't clear, but Dulles indicated sensitivity to "the political standpoint" and said that State wouldn't publicize the move. State to Embassy Tel Aviv, September 22, 1956, *FRUS*, vol. 16, no. 255, footnote 2. See also ibid., nos. 204, 223, 281.

21. Dulles quote is in Eisenhower-Dulles memcon, August 14, 1956, *FRUS*, vol. 16, no. 81. On British and French reluctance to accept Soviet participation, see, for example, ibid., nos. 25, 28, 36. On efforts by Dulles and the State Department to encourage a constructive Soviet role in the London negotiations, see ibid., nos. 66, 69, 85, 86, 93, 94.

22. Dulles to Eisenhower, August 18, ibid., no. 93.

23. For the exchanges, see Eisenhower to Dulles, August 19 and 20, *DDEP*, pp. 2251–54; Dulles to Eisenhower, August 18 and 20, *FRUS*, vol. 16, nos. 94, 100. In his comments on the planned U.S. proposal, Eisenhower is referring to the conference document in ibid., no. 95.

24. Ibid., nos. 59, 70, 77, 105, 111, 114, 117; Eisenhower, *Waging Peace*, p. 47. One author of a recent book on the crisis argues that the secretary of state "had come to the conference with a secret plan—to cut a backroom deal with Moscow." See Doran, *Ike's Gamble*, p. 180. Yet Dulles, in fact, took the opposite course, pushing back against Eisenhower's proposed compromise approach, which was not far from the principle Shepilov had urged Dulles to consider. Dulles undoubtedly wanted Soviet agreement, but it is hard to imagine what terms he thought could bring them along.

25. The final language is at Editorial Note, *FRUS*, vol. 16, no. 110.

26. Dulles to Eisenhower, August 23, 1956, ibid., no. 125. The British had pushed for Dulles himself to lead the delegation. Dulles declined, pleading too many commitments in the rest of his job. Eisenhower said it would be a bad idea for the secretary to lead a mission "with an anticipated probability of negative results in the end." Eisenhower to Dulles, August 20, 1956, ibid., no. 103. See also ibid., nos. 108, 109, 117.

27. Britain and France resisted efforts by Dulles to grant Menzies flexibility to negotiate with Nasser, rather than simply presenting the London proposal as a near-ultimatum. See ibid., nos. 139, 142, 145, 153.

28. Memcon, Dulles and Lloyd, August 23, 1956, ibid., no. 126. Pineau had already voiced a similar warning to Douglas Dillon, U.S. ambassador to France. Memcon, August 20, 1956, ibid., no. 107.

29. Memcon, Eden and Dulles, ibid., no. 129.

30. Eden to Eisenhower, August 27, 1956, ibid., no. 137. Eden repeated his readiness to use force in a conversation with Loy Henderson, U.S. representative on the Menzies mission. Embassy London to State, August 28, 1956, ibid., no. 142. See also note from British Minister Coulson to Dulles, ibid., no. 147; memcon, State, August 29, 1956, ibid, no. 148; memcon, Eisenhower-Dulles, August 29, 1956, ibid., no. 144; ibid., nos. 156, 160, 162, 164, 165. U.S. intelligence assessed that an Israeli attack on Egypt to take advantage of Anglo-French military action was "highly unlikely." SNIE, September 5, 1956, ibid., no. 175.

31. On Anderson's mission and U.S. attempts to encourage Saudi pressure against Nasser, see *FRUS*, vol. 16, nos. 92, 96, 121, 127, 130, 131, 132, 136, 141.

32. Earlier in the crisis, Eisenhower had observed that competent Egyptian operation of the canal would make military action to retake the canal hard to justify. Memcon, White House, August 12, 1956, ibid., no. 78; Eisenhower, *Waging Peace*, pp. 39–40. U.S. intelligence judged that Nasser was determined to run the canal competently and impartially, without offering a pretext for Western attack. See SNIE, September 19, 1956, *FRUS*, vol. 16, no. 236. On U.S. perceptions of domestic opposition to Eden's policy, see ibid., nos. 97, 99, 158. CIA briefing to NSC, September 4, 1956, CIA, Freedom of Information Act Electronic Reading Room (https://www.cia.gov/library/readingroom/) [hereinafter CIA FOIA], doc. no. CIA-RDP79R00890A000700090024–5; *FRUS*, vol. 16, nos. 185, 188, 224, 225.

33. Memo of 295th NSC Meeting, August 30, 1956, ibid., no. 149.

34. Memcon, Eisenhower-Dulles, August 30, 1956, ibid., no. 151. The intelligence community also offered a prediction of widespread Arab revolt. SNIE, September 5, 1956, ibid, no. 175.

The efforts to rally other Arab countries make up a major topic in U.S. diplomatic discussions during August 1956. To put this in the broader context of U.S. efforts to channel or work with Arab nationalists during this period, see Hahn, *Caught in the Middle East*, p. 196; Salim Yaqub, *Containing Arab Nationalism: The Eisenhower Doctrine and the Middle East* (University of North Carolina Press, 2004) p. 48; and Wilford, *America's Great Game*, pp. 245–49.

On the British covert action efforts in Syria and U.S. semidetachment from them, see Lucas and Morey, "The Hidden 'Alliance,'" pp. 95–120. The August 4 memo from Dulles's aide, Francis Russell, urging the CIA to consider covert action against Nasser is discussed in Wilford, *America's Great Game*, p. 245–46. But by late August and thereafter, neither the CIA agents, nor their CIA director, nor Eisenhower, nor, it seems, even Dulles himself wished to go down that road. Ibid., pp. 256–57; Lucas and Morey, "The Hidden 'Alliance.'"

35. On the development of the users' association idea, see *FRUS*, vol. 16, nos. 167, 168, 170, 177, 184, 185, 189, 193, 197, 209.

36. See, for example, memcon, Department of State, ibid., no. 217. As they had throughout the crisis, the British, French, and Americans also continued to discuss other economic sanctions against Egypt, such as a trade embargo and freezing Egyptian assets abroad. See, for example, ibid., nos. 62, 84, 123, 133, 207.

37. Memcon, Eisenhower-Dulles, September 7, 1956, ibid., no. 189.

38. Dulles to Hughes quote is in Emmett John Hughes, *The Ordeal of Power: A Political Memoir of the Eisenhower Years* (New York: Dell, 1963), pp. 177–78. See also memcon, Eisenhower-Dulles, September 8, 1956, *FRUS*, vol. 16, no. 191; Louis, "American Volcano," p. 654; Stephen Ambrose, *Eisenhower*, vol. 2: *The President* (New York: Simon & Schuster, 1984), p. 339; Robert R. Bowie, "Eisenhower, Dulles, and the Suez Crisis," in William Roger Louis and Roger Owen, eds., *Suez 1956: The Crisis and Its Consequences* (Oxford: Clarendon Press, 1989), p. 213; Kyle, *Suez*, pp. 223–24; and William Roger Louis, "Dulles, Suez, and the British," in Richard H. Immerman, ed., *John Foster Dulles and the Diplomacy of the Cold War* (Princeton University Press, 1990), pp. 148–49.

39. Eden's "most hazardous" quote is in Eden to Eisenhower, August 27, 1956, *FRUS*, vol. 16, no. 137. Eisenhower quotes from his reply letter are in Eisenhower to Eden, September 2, 1956, ibid., 16, no. 163.

40. Eden to Eisenhower, September 6, 1956, ibid., no. 181. Dulles called this letter "intemperate" and "not thought through." Memcon, Eisenhower-Dulles, September 7, 1956, ibid., no. 182.

41. All Eisenhower quotes are in Eisenhower to Eden, September 8, 1956, ibid., no. 192. For an annotated edition of the entire Eisenhower-Eden exchange, see Peter Boyle, ed., *The Eden-Eisenhower Correspondence, 1955–1957* (University of North Carolina Press, 2005), pp. 162–69.

42. On the outcome of the Menzies mission, see *FRUS*, vol. 16, nos. 169, 173, 178, 180, 186, 194, 195.

43. For U.S. intelligence on British and French military preparations, see Annex to Watch Committee Reports, ibid., nos. 174, 214. The latter source said, "There are strong indications that the UK and France may launch military action against Egypt in the event that their minimum objectives cannot be obtained by non-military means."

44. Quoted in Kyle, *Suez*, pp. 243–44.

45. Makins to Dulles, September 10, 1956, *FRUS*, vol. 16, no. 206.

46. Egypt's ambassador to the United States denounced the users' association as an instrument of coercion, saying "its implementation means war." Memcon, Egypt Ambassador and Dulles, *FRUS*, vol. 16, no. 216. Egypt counterproposed a diplomatic conference to discuss Soviet and Indian proposals for protecting Egyptian sovereignty over the canal. State to Certain Diplomatic Missions, ibid., no. 221. Dulles's press conference remarks are described in ibid., note 2, and Louis, "American Volcano," p. 655.

47. *FRUS*, vol. 16, nos. 197, 205, 209, 210.

48. "Screwya," from Chester L. Cooper, *The Lion's Last Roar: Suez, 1956* (New York: Harper & Row, 1978), p. 133. For the rest, see Editorial Note, *FRUS*, vol. 16, no. 235; SNIE, September 19, 1956, ibid., no. 236.

49. Annex to Watch Committee Report, September 20, 1956, ibid., no. 243; and the reports on September 27, 1956, ibid., no. 274, and October 3, 1956, ibid., no. 294.

50. On negotiations at the conference, see ibid., nos. 232, 244, 251, 252.

Diplomats considered several acronyms for the new organization before settling on "SCUA." The alternatives all had connotations in various languages that were politically objectionable, otherwise derogatory, or obscene. See Kyle, *Suez*, p. 254.

51. On U.S. assessments of Soviet intentions, and of how the allies viewed those intentions, see National Intelligence Estimate (NIE), *FRUS*, vol. 16, no. 236; Annex to Watch Committee Report, ibid., no. 243. U.S. analysts did not expect Soviet military intervention outright but were concerned by Soviet arms shipments and unconfirmed reports of Soviet advisers in Egypt. See ibid., no. 214.

52. Dulles questioned Eden's optimistic predictions of a short, decisive military campaign, to no avail. Memcon, Eden-Dulles, September 20, 1956, ibid., no. 245. Eisenhower shared Dulles's views that British military plans in Suez did not promise a quick resolution. Memcon, Eisenhower-Dulles, September 22, 1956, ibid., no. 257. Macmillan also expressed bellicose views in a conversation with U.S. ambassador to France Douglas Dillon. Macmillan hinted at military action "in about a month." Dillon to Dulles, September 19, 1956, ibid., no. 233. Dillon reported during the London conference that Mollet and his ministers were complaining about U.S. reluctance to confront Nasser and apparent weakening of British resolve as well. Dillon to Dulles, September 21, 1956, ibid., no. 248.

53. Memcon of Dulles meeting in London, September 21, 1956, ibid., no. 247; "not right" and no "CIA type work" are from a September 22 memcon quoted in von Tunzelmann, *Blood and Sand*, p. 199; see also Wilford, *America's Great Game*, p. 256–59.

54. Memcon, Department of State, September 22, 1956, *FRUS*, vol. 16, no. 254.

55. On British and French evasiveness about their motivations for action at the Security Council, see ibid., nos. 256, 259, 261, 262, 263, 276, 278, 291, 298. Dillon warned that Mollet seemed to be set on military action by late October. Embassy Paris to State, September 26, 1956, ibid., no. 269. Dillon briefly became more optimistic in late September and early October. Ibid., nos. 286, 290. While the issue of a Security Council resolution remained unresolved, the State Department tried to continue negotiations over detailed implementation of SCUA. See, for example, ibid., nos. 268, 286, 290.

56. U.S. assessments of the Israel-Jordan clashes and the proposed Iraqi troops deployment into Jordan are in ibid., nos. 240, 255, 267, 271, 273, 277, 279, 285, 288, 293, 295, 296, 318, 322, 324, 332, 333, 335. See also Kyle, *Suez*, pp. 263–66.

57. On September 5, the U.S. embassy in Tel Aviv first reported intelligence about the Mystère shipment. Memo, Assistant Secretary of State Near East to Under Secretary of State, September 20, 1956, ibid., no. 242; Memo, Secretary of State's Special Assistant to Acting Secretary of State, September 21, 1956, ibid., no. 253. The reported rise in the number of Mystères, from forty-eight to sixty, is in Memo, Acting Secretary of State to Assistant Secretary of State for Near East, October 6, 1956, ibid., no. 305. A December 1956 State Department history of the Anglo-French-Israeli collusion doesn't explain why U.S. officials were not more concerned at the time by what the history called "arms dealings which contravened both the spirit and the letter" of arrangements under the 1950 Tripartite Declaration. Memo,

Secretary of State's Special Assistant for Intelligence to Secretary of State, December 5, 1956, ibid., no. 637.

58. This paragraph and the preceding one are based on a partially declassified official CIA history, Gregory W. Pedlow and Donald E. Walzenbach, *The CIA and the U-2 Program, 1954–1974* (Washington, D.C.: CIA History Staff, Center for the Study of Intelligence, U.S. Central Intelligence Agency, 1998), pp. 112–17. The *FRUS* documents cited above indicate that initial reports of the Mystère shipment came from traditional intelligence sources on the ground, but it appears likely that the U-2 played a role in elaborating those reports. By October 15 the U-2 would definitely confirm that the size of the Mystère shipment had grown to sixty. See also Michael R. Beschloss, *Mayday: Eisenhower, Khrushchev, and the U-2* (New York: Harper & Row, 1986), pp. 136–37.

59. See *FRUS*, vol. 16, nos. 24, 43, 149, 174, 175, 201, 236, 248, 261, 300, 306, 637.

60. Memo of Discussion, 299th NSC Meeting, October 4, 1956, ibid., no. 297.

61. Laron, *Origins of the Suez Crisis*, pp. 172–73; Irwin M. Wall, *France, the United States, and the Algerian War* (University of California Press, 2001), pp. 9–66. For Dillon's quote and his grim assessment of French politics, see Embassy Paris to Dulles, October 6, 1956, *FRUS*, vol. 16, no. 306. See also CIA briefing to NSC, September 4, 1956, CIA FOIA. U.S. officials were concerned about unstable French politics and questioning of NATO prior to the Suez crisis. See, for example, NIE 22–56, "The Outlook for France," July 10, 1956, available from CIA FOIA.

62. Dulles memcon of his meeting with Eisenhower, October 2, 1956, *FRUS*, 16, no. 291.

63. Quotes from Dulles and Young are in Wilford, *America's Great Game*, pp. 257–59. See also Kyle, *Suez*, p. 275.

64. On tensions within NATO over force structure and their political implications, see Eden to Eisenhower, July 18, 1956, *FRUS*, vol. 4, no. 34; Editorial Note, ibid., no. 36; Dulles to Eisenhower, October 1, 1956, ibid., no. 37; memcon with President, October 2, 1956, ibid., no. 38; memcon, Dulles and German Ambassador, *FRUS*, vol. 26, no. 64; Laron, *Origins of the Suez Crisis*, pp. 163–75.

65. Louis, "American Volcano," p. 657; Kyle, *Suez*, p. 273.

66. State to Embassy Paris, copied to Embassy London, October 4, 1956, *FRUS*, vol. 16, no. 298. Dillon replied with worries that French politics were drifting toward a vision of European unity that was "fundamentally anti-American." Aldrich replied by saying, "I agree that the Suez problem has strained US-British relations to an extent greater than any of the issues which have disturbed our alliance during my four years here and beyond the limits of divergencies which we might regard as generally normal between allies." Embassy London to State, October 9, 1956, ibid., no. 316.

67. Memcon, Dulles Suite, Waldorf Astoria, October 5, 1956, ibid., no. 300; "make or break," Dulles to Eisenhower, October 5, 1956, ibid., no. 302. That evening, Dulles told C. D. Jackson, publisher of *Fortune* magazine and a former Eisenhower adviser on psychological warfare, that he'd been using SCUA as "a delaying action" against British and French inclinations to use force. He confessed that he "did not

know how it would all end" or even "what his next moves might be," except perhaps to improvise "further SCUAs." David Nichols, *Eisenhower 1956* (New York: Simon & Schuster, 2011), p. 174.

68. On the UN deliberations and Hammarskjöld's talks with the British, French, and Egyptians, see *FRUS*, vol. 16, nos. 303, 307, 308, 310, 313, 315, 317, 319, 321, 326, 327, 329, 330, 331, 332, 334, 336. During the talks, Dulles agreed to a request from Lloyd to postpone Israeli participation in the council debate until later in the session, to avoid complicating the issue by injection of the Arab-Israeli conflict. Ibid., no. 308. On White House ideas for presidential involvement in these talks, see ibid., nos. 310, 311, 323. Dulles convinced Eisenhower that direct talks at the UN were promising enough to keep the president himself in reserve in case things went south. Nichols, *Eisenhower 1956*, pp. 175–78.

69. Nichols, *Eisenhower 1956*, p. 179.

70. Editorial Note, *FRUS*, vol. 16, no. 337. CIA Office of Current Intelligence, "Current Intelligence Bulletin, October 13, 1956," CIA FOIA, doc. no. CIA-RDP79T00975A002700560001–0.

Part Two: Cairo

1. Letter from Nehru to Abdel Nasser, reprinted in Muhammad Hasanayn Haykal, *Milaffat al-Suways [The Suez Files]* (Cairo: Markaz al-Ahram lil-Taijamah wa-al-Nashr, 1986), pp. 797–98.

2. Heikal, *Cutting the Lion's Tail*, p. 136. Diplomatic communications between India and Egypt that the author has seen were written in English. Presumably the English version here is the authentic text, and the Arabic text in *Milaffat al-Suways* is a translation of that text.

3. Ibid., p. 137. The text of the 1888 convention can be found in J. C. Hurewitz, *Middle East Diplomacy*, vol. 2 (Princeton, N.J.: Van Nostrand, 1956), pp. 454–56.

4. Heikal, *Cutting the Lion's Tail*, p. 140.

5. Reprinted in ibid., p. 137–38.

6. Abd al-Latif al-Baghdadi, *Mudhakirat Abd al-Latif al-Baghdadi*, vol. 1 (Cairo: al-Maktab al-Misri al-Hadith, 1977), p. 331. Mahmoud Fawzi, in his memoirs, ascribed the decision to "the tone of some Cairo newspapers . . . that Egypt's attendance at the London Conference would have been both unwise and below her dignity, and that her attendance as a mere invitee or as a party to be cross-examined, was quite unacceptable." Mahmoud Fawzi, *Suez 1956: An Egyptian Perspective* (London: Shorouk, 1987), p. 50.

7. Heikal, *Cutting the Lion's Tail*, pp. 140–42.

8. Haykal, *Milaffat al-Suways*, pp. 821–22. This is probably a reference to the U.S. ambassador to Saudi Arabia, George Wadsworth. Later in August the U.S. officials sent out a special envoy to Saudi Arabia, Robert Anderson (the same Robert Anderson who had been used earlier that year as a presidential envoy to work on Israel-Egyptian peace). Traveling undercover as if he were just visiting Aramco,

Anderson did not arrive in Saudi Arabia until August 23. On Nasser discouraging Saudi attendance, Heikal, *Cutting the Lion's Tail*, p. 157.

9. Personal diary of Ambassador Ahmed Hussein (private collection of the author), entry for August 24, 1956.

10. Baghdadi, *Mudhakirat*, p. 332.

11. Henderson was a former U.S. ambassador to Iran, then serving as a deputy under secretary of state for administration.

12. Haykal, *Milaffat al-Suways*, pp. 497–98.

13. Ibid., p. 501. Heikal recounts the same conversation a different way in *Cutting the Lion's Tail*, p. 151. He states in each book that the discussions are based on unpublished memoranda of conversations, which he does not reprint.

14. From "Sayyid Mar'i's Political Papers," ed. Moshe Shemesh, in Selwyn Ilan Troen and Moshe Shemesh, eds., *The Suez-Sinai Crisis 1956: Retrospective and Reappraisal* (Columbia University Press, 1990), pp. 362–63. See also Laura James, "When Did Nasser Expect War? The Suez Nationalization and Its Aftermath in Egypt," in Smith, ed., *Reassessing Suez 1956*, pp. 158–60.

15. Nasser's request through the KGB chief in Cairo on October 7 was documented by Soviet archivists whose records are used in Fursenko and Naftali, *Khrushchev's Cold War*, pp. 111–12.

16. Diary of Ahmed Hussein, entry for September 14, 1956.

17. Baghdadi, *Mudhakirat*, p. 330.

18. Hussein to Cairo, September 27, reprinted in Haykal, *Milaffat al-Suways*, pp. 824–25.

19. Hussein to Cairo, September 29, reprinted in ibid., pp. 825–26.

20. Roosevelt's October 9 report from Cairo on his meeting with Ali Sabri and Muhammad Haykal is discussed in Fursenko and Naftali, *Khrushchev's Cold War*, p. 112.

21. Haykal, *Milaffat al-Suways*, p. 829. Inexplicably, Haykal cites the same passage from the same cable in *Cutting the Lion's Tail* thus: "Shepilov went on to ask Fawzi's opinion about a rumour that a body called the 'Committee of the Nile' was about to be set up. Fawzi replied that he knew little more than the Russians about the idea, which was but one of many rumours—mostly originated by Egypt's enemies in the hope of spreading confusion—then circulating in the UN. (In any event, the Committee of the Nile never materialized and the rumour was quickly forgotten)." Heikal, *Cutting the Lion's Tail*, p. 162.

22. Abdel Nasser to Fawzi, in Haykal, *Milaffat al-Suways*, pp. 830–31.

23. Egyptian UN Mission to Abdel Nasser, October 5, in ibid., p. 834.

24. Egyptian UN Mission to Abdel Nasser, October 6, in ibid., pp. 835–36.

25. Heikal, *Cutting the Lion's Tail*, p. 208.

26. King Saud to Abdel Nasser, October 7, reprinted in Haykal, *Milaffat al-Suways*, p. 858.

27. Egyptian UN Mission to Abdel Nasser, October 10, in ibid., p. 840.

28. Egyptian UN Mission to Abdel Nasser, October 12, in ibid., p. 847. In *Cutting the Lion's Tail*, p. 171, Heikal writes that the telegram concluded with Fawzi

writing, "It seems to me that Dulles may know more than he is prepared to tell me." This quotation appears nowhere in the Arabic text.

29. Egyptian UN Mission to Abdel Nasser, October 12, reprinted in Haykal, *Milaffat al-Suways*, p. 847.

30. Ibid., pp. 848–49. Lloyd wrote of his supposed ally shortly thereafter that Pineau "behaved in a rather extraordinary manner. In the first three days of the private talks he appeared utterly unreasonable. He came late, went early, made difficulties about long meetings and spent considerable time at the beginning of some of the meeting arguing about some obviously false point." Quoted in Keith Kyle, *Suez* (London: I. B. Tauris, 1991), p. 282.

31. Fawzi, *Suez 1956*, p. 70. Fawzi asserts that the principles were a British draft rather than the work of Hammarskjöld.

Part Two: Moscow

1. Heikal, *The Sphinx and the Commissar*, p. 68.

2. Khrushchev and Khrushchev, *Krizisy i rakety*, p. 217.

3. Transcript of Conversation Between the USSR Minister of Foreign Affairs, D. T. Shepilov with the Egyptian Ambassador to the USSR M. Al-Kuni, dated July 27, 1956, in Vitali Naumkin, ed., *Russia in the Twentieth Century: The Middle East Conflict, 1947–1956* (Moscow: Materik, 2003), Document 266.

4. In a formal directive, the Foreign Ministry outlined a multifaceted press campaign to support Egypt in the aftermath of the nationalization. See "Project of Proposed Measures by the Soviet Union to Support Egypt on the Question of the Nationalization of the Suez Canal," July 28, 1956, in Naumkin, *Russia in the Twentieth Century*, doc. 267.

5. *Pravda*, August 1, 1956 as cited in David J. Dallin, *Soviet Foreign Policy after Stalin* (New York: J. B. Lippincott, 1961), p. 401.

6. "Soviet 'Ready' for Suez Talks," *Washington Post*, July 31, 1956, p. 1.

7. Fursenko and Naftali, *Khrushchev's Cold War*, pp. 95–99.

8. Kyle, *Suez*, p. 182.

9. Bohlen to Dulles, August 7, 1956, *FRUS*, vol. 16, no. 69.

10. The statement was published in *Pravda*, August 10, 1956, p. 1. This translation is a Soviet translation: The statement was also published as a supplement to *New Times*, no. 33, 1956, pp. 3–6.

11. Dimitri Shepilov, *Suetskii vopros* (Moscow: Gozpolitizdat, 1956), pp. 28–30.

12. Dulles to Eisenhower, August 16 and August 18, *FRUS*, vol. 16, nos. 86, 94; on the substance of Shepilov's compromise idea, see memcon, Dulles-Shepilov meeting of August 18, *FRUS*, vol. 16, no. 93. On Shepilov's room for maneuver to avoid a war, see Fursenko and Naftali, *Khrushchev's Cold War*, p. 100.

Dulles told Eisenhower that the Soviet approach amounted to "some kind of an arrangement with us and perhaps join to impose it upon Egypt if on the one hand it were couched in a way which would not gravely prejudice the Soviet Union with the Arab world and if on the other hand we would more or less make it a two-party affair with some downgrading of the British and French." Dulles was not sure "Soviet agreement is worth having at that price," but said he would do what he could "short of disloyalty to the British and the French" to get Soviet agreement. Dulles to Eisenhower, August 18, *FRUS*, vol. 16, no. 94.

13. Fursenko and Naftali, *Khrushchev's Cold War*, p. 104.

14. Shepilov, *Suetskii vopros*, pp. 41–42; Dulles to Eisenhower, August 21, 1956, *FRUS*, vol. 16, no. 111.

15. Heikal, *The Sphinx and the Commissar*, p. 69, has the more colorful version; see also "Khrushchev Says Arabs Would Get Help in War," *Washington Post*, August 24, 1956, p. 1, and "Khrushchev Warns West on a Suez War," *New York Times*, August 24, 1956, pp. 1, 2.

16. Fursenko and Naftali, *Khrushchev's Cold War*, p. 106.

17. Vassiliev, *Russian Policy in the Middle East*, p. 39.

18. "Press conference of President Nasir," *Pravda*, September 4, 1956; "The Suez Question," *International Affairs*, September 1956, pp. 5–14, quote on p. 8.

19. See, for example, "West Frets as Reds Continue to Pour Weapons into Egypt," *Washington Post*, September 2, 1956, p. Al; see also Fursenko and Naftali, *Khrushchev's Cold War*, p. 108.

20. See the discussion in Fursenko and Naftali, *Khrushchev's Cold War*, pp. 107–08.

21. Cited in Love, *Suez*, p. 428.

22. Formal Soviet statement as reported in *Pravda*, September 16, 1956.

23. On the assessments, including the influence of the defected British spies Guy Burgess and Donald Maclean and the visiting Labour leader Tom Driberg (who also saw his old friends Burgess and Maclean), see Fursenko and Naftali, *Khrushchev's Cold War*, pp. 108–11.

24. See, for example, Naumkin, *Russia in the Twentieth Century*, docs. 284–89.

25. See Laurent Rucker, "The Soviet Union and the Suez Crisis," in David Tal, ed., *The 1956 War: Collusion and Rivalry in the Middle East* (London: Frank Cass, 2001), p. 74.

26. Fursenko and Naftali, *Khrushchev's Cold War*, p. 111, and note 109 on p. 562.

27. See the report in the *Washington Post*, October 9, 1956, pp. 1, 5.

28. Kyle, *Suez*, p. 281.

29. Ibid., p. 280.

30. Fursenko and Naftali, *Khrushchev's Cold War*, p. 112.

31. The "reminder" point was offered by former Soviet deputy foreign minister Sergei Tarasenko at the Ditchley conference discussing earlier drafts of the studies in this book, December 6–8, 1996.

32. On the Soviet strategy and Shepilov's satisfaction, also see Rucker, "The Soviet Union and the Suez Crisis," p. 74.

Part Two: Paris

1. Marc Ferro, ed., *1956: La crise de Suez* (Paris: La Documentation Française, 1986), p. 17.

2. Christian Pineau, *1956/Suez* (Paris: Robert Laffont, 1976), p. 71.

3. *Le Monde*, July 31, 1956, in Ferro, *1956*, p. 20.

4. The convention concluded at Constantinople on October 29, 1888, was aimed at guaranteeing the free use of the Suez Canal. Its preamble affirmed the will of the signatories (Germany, Austria-Hungary, Spain, France, Great Britain, Italy, Netherlands, Russia, and Turkey) to "establish the free usage of the Suez Canal." Chauvel (Embassy London) to Paris, July 27, 1956, *DDF*, 1956, vol. 2, p. 165.

5. Pineau, *1956/Suez*, p. 78.

6. Keith Kyle, "Britain and the Crisis, 1955–1956," in Louis and Owen, eds., *Suez 1956*, p. 112.

7. Chauvel to Paris, July 27, 1956, *DDF*, 1956, vol. 2, p. 165.

8. Ibid., pp. 165–66.

9. Ibid., p. 187.

10. Pineau's report relayed in Chauvel to Paris, July 30, 1956, ibid., pp. 187–88.

11. Paul Gaujac, *Suez 1956* (Paris: Charles-Lavauzelle, 1986), p. 28.

12. Ibid.

13. Ely, *Mémoires*, pp. 80–81.

14. Ibid., pp. 81–85.

15. Thomas, *Comment Israel fut sauvé*, pp. 144–45.

16. Peres, *Battling for Peace*, p. 106.

17. Memcon, Pineau-Dulles, August 1, 1956, *DDF*, 1956, vol. 2, pp. 208–10.

18. Pineau, *1956/Suez*, p. 175.

19. In French, the word *contrôle* means *monitoring*. It does not have the force of the same word in English.

20. Pineau report relayed in Chauvel to Paris, August 2, 1956, *DDF*, 1956, vol. 2, p. 211.

21. Ely, *Mémoires*, pp. 81–85.

22. La Documentation française, "Notes et études documentaires, documents relatifs au canal de Suez," no. 2205, August 16, 1956, p. 12.

23. Gaujac, *Suez 1956*, p. 28.

24. Ibid.

25. Ibid., p. 30.

26. Service historique de l'armée de terre (SHAT), archive 3T161, "*Rapport sur l'opération d'Egypte*," Tome I, "*La preparation*," Annex 2, p. 13 [hereinafter cited as the Beaufre Report].

27. Gaujac, *Suez 1956*, pp. 28–29. This first sketchy operation, though called Hamilcar by the British, apparently was baptized by the French as Operation 700 because of the fact that they spelled Hamilcar starting with an "A."

28. Beaufre Report, Tome I, p. 3.

29. Ibid., Tome I, Annex 2, Piece 1, p. 1.

30. Ibid. p. 2.

31. André Beaufre, *L'Expédition de Suez* (Paris: Grasset, 1967), pp. 39–40.

32. Ibid. p. 13.

33. Service historique de l'armée de l'air (SHAA), Archive C2310, Report of Brigadier General Raymond Brohon on the Composite Group No. 1 at Cyprus [hereinafter referred to as the Brohon Report], Annex 1, p. 1.

34. Louise Richardson, *When Allies Differ: Anglo-American Relations during the Suez and Falklands Crises* (New York: St. Martin's Press, 1996), p. 48.

35. Gaujac, *Suez 1956*, p. 12.

36. Ibid. The Egyptian government statement of September 10 had regretted "deployments of force directed against it" as well as attempts "to provoke defections among the technical personnel, with the object of disturbing navigation in the Suez Canal." Chayla (Cairo) to Paris, relaying the Egyptian statement, *DDF*, 1956, vol. 2, p. 355.

37. Gaujac, *Suez 1956*, p. 55.

38. Dejean (Moscow) to Paris, August 30, 1956, *DDF*, 1956, vol. 2, p. 325.

39. The reference to Pineau was to a speech the French foreign minister had made on September 2. Recalling France's "extraordinary patience" with the Egyptian authorities and evoking Hitler, Pineau stated, "Isn't it our duty to stop Nasser immediately? If we say no, what will be the situation into which our procrastination will lead us?" Dejean to Paris, September 11, 1956, *DDF*, 1956, vol. 2, p. 366.

40. Ibid.

41. Dejean to Paris, September 11, 1956 (sent a couple of hours before the previously cited message), in ibid., p. 365

42. Gaujac, *Suez 1956*, p. 37, quoting Merry and Serge Bromberger, *Les secrets de l'expédition d'Egypte* (Paris: Fils Aymon, 1957).

43. Fears that Britain would back out of concerted military action prompted the French minister for overseas territories (France d'outre-mer), Gaston Defferre, to suggest that France take unilateral covert action to divert the course of the Nile or dry up some of its tributaries to destabilize Nasser's grip on power. This far-fetched scheme was never seriously considered. Denis Lefebvre, *Les secrets de l'expédition de Suez, 1956* (Paris: Perrin, 2010), pp. 148–51.

44. Memcon of French-British discussions in London, September 11, 1956, *DDF*, 1956, vol. 2, p. 371.

45. Lefebvre, *Les secrets de l'expédition de Suez*, pp. 70–77. Lefebvre notes that Pineau, in an interview in 1989, referred to these proposals as just another of Mollet's "customary whims." Yet Lefebvre also explains that such ideas for a Franco-British union were not uncommon among French anglophiles and Europeanists in the 1950s.

46. Gaujac, *Suez 1956*, p. 95.

47. Ibid., p. 96.

48. Ibid., p. 95.

49. Beaufre, *L'Expédition de Suez*, p. 73.

50. Gaujac, *Suez 1956*, p. 91.

51. Ibid., p. 95.

52. Ibid.

53. Chauvel to Paris, September 21, 1956, *DDF*, 1956, vol. 2, p. 430.

54. Pineau report relayed in Chauvel to Paris, September 20, 1956, ibid., p. 414.

55. Pineau to Chauvel relaying aide-mémoire to be given to British, September 24, ibid., p. 443.

56. Pineau to French diplomatic missions, September 25, 1956, ibid., pp. 463–65.

57. Gaujac, *Suez 1956*, p. 95.

58. Ibid., p. 100.

59. Beaufre, *L'Expédition de Suez*, pp. 91–99.

60. Gaujac, *Suez 1956*, p. 110.

61. Ibid.

62. Ely, *Mémoires*, pp. 122–23.

63. Bar-On, *The Gates of Gaza*, p. 194.

64. Mordechai Bar-On, "Israeli-French Relations during the Suez Crisis," in *La France et l'opération de Suez de 1956: Actes d'une table ronde organisée sous la direction de Maurice Vaïsse*, Centre d'Études d'Histoire de la Défense (CEHD) (Paris: ADDIM, 1997), p. 101.

65. Dayan, *Moshe Dayan*, pp. 193–96. Abel Thomas's account (*Comment Israel fut sauvé*) generally squares with that of Dayan as regards Pineau's remarks.

66. Ely, *Mémoires*, pp. 124–25.

67. *"Air actualités,"* June 1996, p. 30.

68. Bar-On, *The Gates of Gaza*, p. 225.

69. Kyle, *Suez*, pp. 260–62.

70. Chauvel to Paris, October 1, 1956, *DDF*, 1956, vol. 2, p. 482–83.

71. Ibid., p. 483; French government secretariat note, October 2, 1956, ibid., p. 502.

72. Alphand (Washington) to Paris reporting transcript of Dulles remarks, October 2, 1956, ibid., p. 492–93.

73. Chauvel to Pineau, October 5, 1956, ibid., p. 514.

74. Cornut-Gentille (United Nations) to Paris, October 5, 1956, ibid., p. 520.

75. Ibid., pp. 522–23.

76. Cornut-Gentille to Paris, October 12, 1956, ibid., p. 566.

77. Ibid., p. 567.

78. Pineau to Paris, October 13, 1956, ibid., pp. 569–70.

79. Cornut-Gentille to Paris, October 14, 1956, ibid., p. 588.

80. Ely, *Mémoires*, pp. 129–30.

81. Ibid., pp. 130–31.

82. Ibid., pp. 131–32.

83. Ibid., pp. 132–33.

84. Ibid., p. 135.

85. Maurice Challe, *Notre Révolte* (Paris: Presses de la Cité, 1968), pp. 26–27.

86. Ely, *Mémoires*, p. 136.

87. Kyle, "Britain and the Crisis, 1955–1956," pp. 124–25.

88. Challe, *Notre Révolte*, p. 27.

89. Ely, *Mémoires*, pp. 137–38.

Part Two: Jerusalem

1. Jerusalem to the Israel Missions Abroad, July 29, 1956, *DFPI*, no. 356.

2. Golani, *Israel in Search of a War*, pp. 59–65; "wait," from Ben-Gurion diary, July 29, 1956, quoted in Bar-On, *The Gates of Gaza*, p. 183, and, in a slightly different translation, in Golani, *Israel in Search of a War*, p. 65.

3. Ben-Gurion diary, August 3, from the primary material excerpted, translated, and published in "Ben-Gurion's Diary: The Suez-Sinai Campaign," ed. Selwyn Ilan Troen, in Troen and Shemesh, eds., *The Suez-Sinai Crisis 1956* [hereinafter cited as BG Diary with entry date and page from this excerpt edited by Troen], p. 292.

4. Bar-On, *Gates of Gaza*, pp. 183–84.

5. Ben-Gurion on August 2, from Michael Bar-Zohar, *Ben-Gurion: A Biography*, translated by Peretz Kidron (New York: Delacorte Press, 1978), p. 230.

6. Golani, *Israel in Search of a War*, pp. 57–58; also on Dayan's desire for more time to ready the army, see Bar-On, *Moshe Dayan*, p. 80.

7. BG Diary, entries of August 10, 13, and 22, pp. 294–95.

8. On Israeli diplomacy and the conferences, see, as the first of many efforts to see that Israeli interests were heard, Eban to Meir, August 1; Elath (London) to Jerusalem, August 3; Eban to Jerusalem, August 3; *DFPI*, vol. 11, nos. 363, 367, 368. The Israelis also offered to help ease oil deliveries, in light of the canal problems, by helping to build an oil pipeline that would run from Eilat to the Mediterranean. Thus, in theory, oil tankers could come up the Red Sea, go into the Gulf of Aqaba instead of the Gulf of Suez, and offload their product in Eilat for transshipment to a port like Haifa. The project had some technical merit, but the powers—still counting on using the canal—did not really wish to discuss it. See Jerusalem to embassies in Washington, Paris, and London, August 2; draft memo by Meir Sherman, August 23; Shiloah to Meir, September 1; Tsur to Jerusalem, September 14, *DFPI*, vol. 11, nos. 365, 397, 407, 421.

9. "BG Warns against Panic, Complacency" (excerpts from David Ben-Gurion's Address to the Mapai [Labour Party] Convention, Tel Aviv), *Jerusalem Post*, August 27, 1956.

10. Dayan, *Diary of the Sinai Campaign*, pp. 20–21.

11. Golani, *Israel in Search of a War*, pp. 72–74.

12. BG Diary (entries of September 3, 9), pp. 296–97.

13. Tsur to Jerusalem, September 3, *DFPI*, vol. 11, no. 409.

14. BG Diary (entries of September 10, quoted, and 12), pp. 297–98.

15. On the September 12 border clashes, where Dayan witnessed the near-fatal wounding of a paratrooper he greatly admired, and on preparations for Paris, see Bar-On, *Moshe Dayan*, p. 82, and Dayan, *Diary* (entry for September 17), p. 22.

16. Golani, *Israel in Search of a War*, pp. 74–75; Bar-On, *Gates of Gaza*, pp. 192–93 (with a slightly different translation of Ben-Gurion's message).

17. "Mr. Ben-Gurion Gets Talking of the Future," *Jerusalem Post*, September 21, 1956; "Israel May Soon Have 'True Ally,' B-G Says," September 24, 1956 (excerpts

from David Ben-Gurion's comments at the Mapai Central Committee meeting, Tel Aviv), *Jerusalem Post*, September 24, 1956.

18. BG Diary (entry for September 25), p. 299; Golani, *Israel in Search of a War*, pp. 75–76.

19. BG Diary (entry for September 25), pp. 299–300.

20. Ben-Gurion to Meir, September 27, *DFPI*, vol. 11, no. 442. The English translation of these instructions in the official archives differs materially from the translation in Bar-On, *Gates of Gaza*, p. 194. For more on some of the concerns about Jordan and Iraq on this day, see Dayan, *Diary* (entry for September 27), pp. 27–29.

21. Tsur to Jerusalem, September 28, *DFPI*, vol. 11, no. 448.

22. Eban to Meir and Herzog, September 28; and Eban to Jerusalem, September 30, *DFPI*, vol. 11, nos. 446, 451. The American record of the September 28 Eban-Dulles conversation (*FRUS*, vol. 16, no. 281) has the "new vistas" comment but not the rest. That record does have Dulles reiterating Eisenhower's public March 1956 pledge to aid Israel in case of aggression.

As discussed in the Washington chapter in Part One, Eban's guesstimate about American positions and plans was astonishingly close to the mark, including Eisenhower's private judgments at the White House meeting of March 28 and the subsequent, project Omega–related, U.S. work to preposition at least twenty-four F-86 aircraft for possible aid to Israel. But neither the Israelis nor the Americans had begun meaningful direct conversations with each other about these Omega contingency plans.

23. Bar-On, *Moshe Dayan*, p. 83.

24. For the instructions, Ben-Gurion to Meir, cited in note 20. Peres gives a bit of the personal flavor, including the observation about Pineau and Meir's view that "everything I did was wrong," in Peres with Landau, *Ben-Gurion*, pp. 165–66, and "two colts," p. 177.

25. The best summaries of these crucial Franco-Israeli negotiations, based largely on Bar-On's original notes of the meeting (he was there as Dayan's staffer), are, of course, Bar-On's own, in *Gates of Gaza*, pp. 195–99, but also Golani, *Israel in Search of a War*, pp. 77–87. Golani convincingly argues that the military-military discussions were pivotal. For the Bourgès-Maunoury quote, I've used the version in Golani (p. 81); a somewhat different translation is in Bar-On (p. 198).

26. Golani, *Israel in Search of a War*, p. 83 (including the quoted material); Dayan, *Diary* (entry for October 1), pp. 30–31.

27. Bar-On, *Gates of Gaza*, p. 196.

28. Shimon Peres, "The Road to Sèvres: Franco-Israeli Strategic Cooperation," in Troen and Shemesh, eds., *The Suez-Sinai Crisis 1956*, p. 144. At the time this pro-Israeli attitude also extended to Charles de Gaulle, then in a sort of retirement but also leading part of the opposition. Peres visited de Gaulle. The general "knew what we were doing, and he supported it." Peres with Landau, *Ben-Gurion*, pp. 163–64.

29. Dayan, *Diary* (entry of October 2), pp. 31–33.

30. Ben-Gurion note for the record, October 3 (just before his meetings with the French military visitors), *DFPI*, vol. 11, no. 456.

31. Bar-Zohar, *Ben-Gurion*, p. 233; Golani, *Israel in Search of a War*, pp. 88–90.

32. Dayan, *Diary* (entries of October 3, 7, 8), pp. 34–38; Bar-On, *Moshe Dayan*, p. 84.

33. See Editorial Note, *FRUS*, vol. 16, no. 296. At a late stage of the matter, see, for example, Jerusalem to Eban, October 12, *DFPI*, vol. 11, no. 481.

34. Dayan, *Diary* (entry of October 15), pp. 56–57; see also Benny Morris, *Israel's Border Wars, 1949–1956*, rev. ed. (Oxford: Clarendon Press, 1997), pp. 413–16.

35. Eban to Jerusalem, October 14, *DFPI*, vol. 11, no. 489.

36. Dayan quoted in Bar-On, *Gates of Gaza*, p. 222.

37. Golani, *Israel in Search of a War*, p. 95.

Part Two: London

1. Hugh Gaitskell, *The Diary of Hugh Gaitskell: 1945–56*, ed. Philip M. William (London: Jonathan Cape, 1983), p. 553; Lucas, *Divided We Stand*, p. 142.

2. Thomas, *The Suez Affair*, p. 31.

3. Saul Kelly and Anthony Gorst, *Whitehall and the Suez Crisis* (Abingdon, Oxon: Frank Cass, 2000), p. 34.

4. Cabinet Minutes, The National Archives of the U.K. (TNA), Cabinet Office files (CAB) 128/30. Cabinet Minutes (56) 54, 27 July 1956.

5. Eden to Eisenhower, July 27, 1956, *FRUS*, vol. 16, no. 5.

6. Lucas, *Divided We Stand*, p. 149.

7. Jonathan Pearson, *Reluctant Gamble: Anthony Eden and the Suez Crisis* (London: Palgrave Macmillan, 2003), p. 30.

8. Embassy London to State, London, July 31, 1956, *FRUS*, 16, pp. 61–62.

9. Pearson, *Gamble*, p. 32; Embassy London to State, July 31, 1956, *FRUS*, 16, no. 37.

10. Eisenhower to Eden, July 31, 1956, TNA, Prime Minister's office files (PREM) 11/1098.

11. Kyle, *Suez*, p. 160.

12. Foreign Office to Washington, No. 3568, August 5, 1956, TNA, Foreign Office files (FO) 800/726.

13. Owen, Illness, p. 391.

14. Kyle, *Suez*, pp. 170–176.

15. "Record of a Meeting at 11 Downing Street on Friday, 3 August 1956," TNA, PREM 11/1099; Harold Macmillan, *Riding the Storm: 1956–1959* (New York: Macmillan, 1971), pp. 111–12; Selwyn Lloyd, "Timetable of Events Leading Up to Suez Operation," Secret, TNA, PREM 11/1158.

16. Cabinet Meeting (56) 59th Conclusions, August 14, 1956, TNA, CAB 128/30.

17. Owen, "Illness," p. 391.

18. Foreign Office to Washington, Secret, September 1, 1956, TNA, PREM 11/1176; Extract from EC (56) 22nd Meeting, Top Secret, August 27, 1956, TNA, PREM 11/1176.

19. Eden to Sandys, PM's Personal Minute M 188/56, August 22, 1956, TNA, PREM 11/1152; Sandys to Eden, August 23, 1956, TNA, PREM 11/1152.

20. Kunz, *The Economic Diplomacy*, p. 93; see The Earl of Birkenhead, *Monckton* (London: Weidenfeld & Nicolson, 1969), p. 307; The Marquess of Salisbury to Eden, August 24, 1956, Alan Lennox-Boyd to Eden, August 24, 1956, The Earl of Home to Eden, August 25, 1956, all in TNA, PREM 11/1152.

21. Sir Norman Brook to Eden, August 25, 1956, TNA, PREM 11/1152.

22. Eden to Eisenhower, August 27, 1956, *FRUS*, vol. 16, no. 137.

23. Kelly and Gorst, *Whitehall*, p. 210.

24. David Easter, "Spying on Nasser: British Signals Intelligence in Middle East Crises and Conflicts, 1956–67," *Intelligence and National Security* 28 no. 6 (2013), p. 827.

25. Kyle, *Suez*, pp. 150–51; Pearson, *Gamble*, p. 36; Lucas and Morey, "The Hidden 'Alliance,'" p. 107.

26. Kelly and Gorst, *Whitehall*, p. 121.

27. Kyle, *Suez*, pp. 223, 212.

28. Ibid., p. 219; Eisenhower to Eden, September 2, 1956, *FRUS*, vol. 16, no. 163.

29. Eden to Eisenhower, September 6, 1956, TNA, FO 800/726.

30. Kyle, *Suez*, p. 223; Lloyd to Makins (Washington), September 6, 1956, Foreign Office to Washington, No. 4069, September 6, 1956, TNA, PREM 11/1100.

31. Foreign Office to Washington, No. 4102, September 8, 1956, TNA, PREM 11/1100.

32. Paris to Foreign Office, No. 295, September 9, 1956, TNA, PREM 11/1100; Sir Anthony Eden, *Full Circle*, pp. 484, 534.

33. Foreign Office to Washington, No. 4136, September 10, 1956, TNA, FO 371/119129; Kyle, *Suez*, p. 244.

34. Washington to Foreign Office, nos. 1892, 1896, September 13, 1956, TNA, FO 800/740; Makins, *The Suez Crisis*, p. 30. For more on Makins and the U.S.--U.K. relationship in this period, see Wevill, *Diplomacy, Roger Makins and the Anglo-American Relationship*.

35. See TNA, PREM 11 /1104, WM (56) 118, September 7, 1956. (Keightley's Note begins at f 128.) A revised version of the plan was sent to the Egypt Committee on September 17, 1956. TNA, Cabinet conclusions (WM) 120/56 ff 74–85; TNA, PREM 11/1104, "Operation Musketeer: Implications of Postponement, Memorandum by the Chiefs of Staff, September 20, 1956.

36. Kyle, *Suez*, p. 170.

37. Air Marshall Denis Barnett, "Summary of Operations during Operation *Musketeer*," TNA, Royal Air Force (AIR) 20/10746.

38. See TNA, FO 371/119129, Foreign Office to Washington, No. 4126, September 9, 1956; Washington to Foreign Office, Nos. 1844 and 1845, September 9, 1956; Foreign Office 371/119130, No. 1851, September 9, 1956; CAB 128/30,

Cabinet Meeting (56) 59th Conclusions, August 14, 1956; CAB 134/1216, Egypt Committee (56), September 9, 1956; FO 371/119128, Beeley, "Suez Canal," August 31, 1956; PREM 11/1101 Egypt Committee (56) 28th Meeting, Minute 2, September 14, 1956; CAB 128/30 Point 2, Memo by Harold Watkinson, September 10, 1956. JE 14211/1784.

39. Eden to Lloyd, September 21, 1956, TNA, FO 371/119177.

40. Eden to Dulles, No. 4389, September 22, 1956, TNA, PREM 11/1102.

41. Washington to Foreign Office, No. 1979, September 22, 1956, TNA, PREM 11/1102.

42. Macmillan, *Storm*, pp. 109–10; Kirkpatrick to Makins (Washington), September 10, 1956, TNA, FO 800/740.

43. Kunz, *Diplomacy*, p. 101.

44. Cabinet Meeting (56) 64th Conclusions, September 12, 1956, TNA, CAB 128/30.

45. Makins, *The Suez Crisis*, pp. 32–33.

46. Washington to Foreign Office, No. 2001, September 26, 1956, TNA, PREM 11/1102; Washington to Foreign Office, No. 2004, September 25; to Eden, September 26, 1956, TNA, FO 800 740; Washington to Foreign Office, Nos. 2001 and 2002, September 25, 1956, TNA, PREM 11/1102; Macmillan, "Note of a Private Talk with Mr. Dulles," September 25, 1956, TNA, PREM 11/1102.

47. Bridges to Macmillan, September 7, 1956, TNA, Treasury (T) 236/41S8; Kunz, *Diplomacy*, pp. 106–07; Lucas and Morey, "Alliance," p. 108.

48. Paris to Foreign Office, No. 337, September 27, 1956, TNA, FO 800/740.

49. Foreign Office to Washington, No. 4540, October 1, 1956, TNA, PREM 11/1102.

50. Kyle, *Suez*, p. 273.

51. Pearson, *Gamble*, p. 116.

52. Owen, "Illness," p. 393.

53. Foreign Office to New York, No. 1063, October 6, 1956, TNA, PREM 11/1102.

54. Foreign Office to New York, No. 1078, October 8, 1956, TNA, PREM 11/1102.

55. Lloyd, "M. Pineau and Mr. Dulles in New York," October 15, 1956, TNA, FO 800/728; Lloyd to Eden, T 454/56, October 11, 1956, TNA, PREM 11/1102.

56. Owen, "Illness," p. 394; Nutting, *Lesson*, p. 89.

57. Lloyd to Dulles, October 15, 1956, TNA, PREM 11/1103.

58. Kyle, *Suez*, p. 297; Nutting, *Lesson*, p. 92.

Part Three: Jerusalem

1. BG Diary, October 17, 1956. p. 302; see also "Cabinet Debates U.K. Threat to Aid Jordan," *Jerusalem Post*, October 15, 1956; Ben-Gurion's Address to the Knesset, October 15, 1956, quoted in Meron Medzini, ed., *Israel's Foreign Relations: Selected Documents. 1947–1974*, vol. 1 (Jerusalem: Ministry for Foreign Affairs, 1976), pp. 357–64; "Begin Hits 'Punishment Policy'," *Jerusalem Post*, October 16, 1956.

2. BG Diary, October 15, p. 302.

3. BG Diary, October 17, pp. 302–03; Bar-On, *The Gates of Gaza*, pp. 228–29; for "pay the price required," and more on Dayan's and Peres' work to bring along the "Old Man," Golani, *Israel in Search of a War*, pp. 111, 113.

4. BG Diary, October 18, 19, pp. 304–05; Bar-On, *Gates of Gaza*, pp. 229–31.

5. Bar-On, *Gates of Gaza*, p. 231.

6. Dayan (on October 21) quoted in Golani, *Israel in Search of a War*, p. 115; on the rest, see Abba Eban, *An Autobiography* (New York: Random House, 1977), p. 256; Ben-Gurion to Eisenhower, October 20, *FRUS*, vol. 16, no. 361.

7. Bar-On, *Moshe Dayan*, p. 88; Abel Thomas quoted by Bar-On (who was a principal note taker for the Israeli delegation), *Gates of Gaza*, p. 233.

8. Bar-On, *Gates of Gaza*, pp. 233–35; Golani, *Israel in Search of a War*, pp. 116–18; Mollet's reaction in BG Diary, October 22, p. 307. Ben-Gurion explains more about his reasoning behind his big idea, and his desire to keep the United States on board, earlier in this diary entry (p. 306).

9. Bar-On, *Gates of Gaza*, pp. 235–37; Golani, *Israel in Search of a War*, p. 118; BG Diary, October 22, pp. 308–09; Bar-On, *Moshe Dayan*, pp. 88–89.

10. "Devil's advocate," Bar-On, *Gates of Gaza*, pp. 239–40. An instructive close analysis of these negotiations, highlighting Dayan's role in the operational adjustments, working with the French, to bring Ben-Gurion along, is Golani, *Israel in Search of a War*, pp. 121–30. One idea for a pretext was to stage a fake Egyptian attack on Beersheba. Ben-Gurion rejected it, refusing to "mislead the world and stage such a thing." BG Diary, October 23, p. 311.

11. For the impression of the "recovered" Ben-Gurion, Bar-On, *Gates of Gaza*, p. 241; the rest from BG Diary, October 24, pp. 311–12.

12. Bar-On, *Gates of Gaza*, p. 247.

13. For an excellent account of this Franco-Israeli relationship, which appears to have culminated a year later in mutual decisions to go forward with nuclear weapons and help each other in that enterprise, see Binyamin Pinkus, "Atomic Power to Israel's Rescue: French-Israeli Nuclear Cooperation, 1949–1957," translated by Moshe Tlamim, *Israel Studies* 7, no. 1 (2002): 104–38.

Based on the work done by Pinkus, it would be wrong to simplify this nuclear deal as a quid pro quo for Israeli agreement to accede to the French approach on Suez. There was a long-standing cooperative relationship that was a two-way street. It had blossomed in 1955 and 1956. The intensifying defense cooperation did help, as did the enlarged influence in 1956 (and later) of Bourgès-Maunoury, who was also an important figure in the French nuclear development. But it is more appropriate to see the nuclear cooperation as part of this wider context of growing common work and interests, not just part of a deal struck only at Sèvres.

14. Bar-On, *Gates of Gaza*, p. 243. A copy of Dayan's drawing is in Selwyn Ilan Troen, "The Sinai Campaign as a 'War of No Alternative': Ben-Gurion's View of the Israel-Egyptian Conflict," in Troen and Shemesh, eds., *The Suez-Sinai Crisis*, at p. 193. For the Israeli copy of the Sèvres protocol, see Israel State Archives, *DFPI*, vol. 11, no. 500.

15. The shootdown reportedly killed ten Egyptian officers. Nasser seems to have

mistakenly believed that the British were responsible. Oren, *Origins of the Second Arab-Israel War*, p. 144 (citing an October 30 U.S. report from its embassy in Damascus).

16. Bar-On, *Gates of Gaza*, pp. 253–54; Eisenhower to Ben-Gurion, October 27, *FRUS*, 16, no. 388.

17. The detailed notes, "protocols," of the cabinet meeting seem practically verbatim and are 42 pages long. They were declassified in 2008. An excellent summary in English is Pnina Lahav, "A Small Nation Goes to War: Israel's Cabinet Authorization of the 1956 War," *Israel Studies* 15, no. 3 (2010): 61–86.

18. Quoted material is from Lahav, "A Small Nation Goes to War," pp. 65, 68, 70, 71, 74, 77. After the cabinet decision, Ben-Gurion briefed his country's president and Begin, the leader of the opposition. Editorial Note, *DFPI*, vol. 12, no. 5 (2009).

19. Ben-Gurion to Eisenhower, October 29, *FRUS*, 16, no. 414.

20. Bar-On, *Gates of Gaza*, pp. 258–62; Golani, *Israel in Search of a War*, pp. 140–47. For concise and knowledgeable appraisals of the military operations, compare Rechavam Zeevy, "Military Lessons of the Sinai Campaign: The Israeli Perspective," and Bar-On, "The Influence of Political Considerations on Operational Planning in the Sinai Campaign," both in Troen and Shemesh, eds., *The Suez-Sinai Crisis*, pp. 60–73, 196–217.

21. Eban to Ben-Gurion and Meir, October 29, and Shiloah to Herzog, October 30, *DFPI*, vol. 12, no. 10, and note 8 to that document.

22. Eban to Ben-Gurion, October 30; Herzog to Eban and Shiloah, October 31, *DFPI*, vol. 12, nos. 14, 21.

23. Eban to Meir, November 1 and 2, *DFPI*, vol. 12, no. 25, and note 1, no. 31.

24. Elath to Meir, November 4; Nahmias to Peres (with the quote), November 4, *DFPI*, vol. 12, nos. 46, 47, and note 2; see also Bar-On, *Gates of Gaza*, pp. 266–67.

25. Jerusalem to Eban, November 5; Eban to Jerusalem, November 5; Jerusalem to Eban, November 5, *DFPI*, vol. 12, nos. 53, 54, 56.

26. Bulganin to Ben-Gurion, November 5; and Editorial Note, *DFPI*, vol. 12, nos. 61, 60.

27. Bar-Zohar, *Ben-Gurion*, p. 249.

Part Three: Cairo

1. Salah Bassiouni, *Misr wa-Azmat al-Suways* [Egypt and the Suez Crisis] (Cairo: Dar al-Ma'arif bi-Misr, 1970), pp. 154–55. Bassiouni, an Egyptian diplomat, apparently consulted Egyptian Foreign Ministry files when he wrote this book.

2. Ahmed Hamrouche, *Shuhud Thawrat Yulyu* (vol. 4 of *Qissat Thawrat Yulyu* [Witnesses to the July Revolution]) (Cairo: Maktabat Madbuli, 1984), pp. 164–65. It is worth observing that the longest-lived survivors of the Suez Crisis on the Egyptian side have portrayed themselves to be the staunch heroes of the crisis. Because exceedingly little independent documentary evidence is available on the Egyptian side from the time the first shot rang out, and since considerable information has been available from the perspectives of Western governments for some time, one must

take the participants at their word while considering the possibility that some may be burnishing their own reputations.

3. Tharwat Okasha, *Mudhakirati fi al-Siyasah wa-al-Thaqafah* [My Recollections in Politics and Culture], vol. 1 (Cairo: Maktabat Madbuli, 1987), p. 209–10.

4. Bassiouni, *Misr wa-Azmat al-Suways*, pp. 193, 195–96. For more on Egypt's assumptions about a reduced or negligible danger of a war during mid-to-late October, see Laura James, "When Did Nasser Expect War? The Suez Nationalization and Its Aftermath in Egypt," in Smith, ed., *Reassessing Suez 1956*, pp. 159–61.

5. Bassiouni, *Misr wa-Azmat al-Suways*, p. 190.

6. Okasha, *Mudhakirati*, p. 212. Okasha told an interviewer that when he returned to Egypt, Abdel Nasser told him, "I did not believe the possibility of this invasion occurring despite the fact that you told me about it. All of the assessments pointed to the impossibility of the invasion occurring. However, I depended on the information when I had to quickly take the decision to withdraw my troops from Sinai." Hamrouche, *Shuhud Thawrat Yulyu*, p. 106. Okasha's written message, which was a long appraisal of Anglo-French collaboration in the near term in the Middle East, is reprinted in his memoirs, vol. 1, pp. 272–74.

7. Heikal, *Cutting the Lion's Tail*, p. 177.

8. Bassiouni, *Misr wa-Azmat al-Suways*, p. 204.

9. Abd al-Latif al-Baghdadi, *Mudhakirat 'Abd al-Latif al-Baghdadi*, vol. 1 (Cairo: al-Maktab al-Misri al-Hadith, 1977), p. 337.

10. Personal Diary of Ambassador Ahmed Hussein [collection of the author], October 29, 1956.

11. Bassiouni, *Misr wa-Azmat al-Suways*, p. 202.

12. Ibid., p. 205.

13. From "Sayyid Mar'i's Political Papers," ed. Moshe Shemesh, in Troen and Shemesh, eds., *The Suez-Sinai Crisis 1956*, p. 365.

14. Hussein diary, October 30, 1956.

15. On the Ali Sabri exchange with Soviet ambassador Kiselev on October 30 and Abdel Nasser's message, see Fursenko and Naftali, *Khrushchev's Cold War*, pp. 126–27. On the request relayed through the Syrian president (also denying the use of Kiselev as a conduit), Kennet Love's account of his interview on this topic with Nasser in *Suez, the Twice Fought War*, p. 610.

16. Hare to State, October 31 (the meeting with Abdel Nasser had been at 1:15 p.m., Cairo time), *FRUS*, vol. 16, no. 451.

17. Baghdadi, *Mudhakirat*, p. 339.

18. Ibid., p. 339. Some of these troops had been in Sinai only a matter of hours before the order for withdrawal came. Bassiouni says Abdel Nasser made the decision himself at 8 p.m., which does not necessarily contradict Baghdadi's later time for the cabinet to make the same decision. Heikal claims that Abdel Nasser "went into the operations room, took the telephone and had himself put through to all the senior officers in the Fourth Division, down to battalion level, telling them who he was and explaining to them the absolute necessity of immediate withdrawal if they were not

to be caught in the trap prepared for them. They were not to wait till morning but to start the withdrawal that instant." Bassiouni, *Misr wa-Azmat al-Suways*, p. 206; Heikal, *Cutting the Lion's Tail*, p. 181.

19. Baghdadi, *Mudhakirat*, p. 340.

20. Bassiouni, *Misr wa-Azmat al-Suways*, p. 242.

21. Ibid., p. 220

22. Hussein diary, November 1, 1956.

23. Hare to State, November 2 (recounting a meeting that morning), *FRUS*, vol. 16, no. 472.

24. Translation based on Foreign Broadcast Information Service text, November 2, 1956, p. A2. Al-Ahram printed the prepared text of the speech, but Abdel Nasser's delivery departed substantially from that text. "Bayan al-Ra'is," *al-Ahram*, November 3, 1956, p. 1. What appears to be an edited audio recording of the speech is available on cassette tape: *al-Za'im al-Khalid Gamal Abdel Nasser* [The Eternal Leader Gamal Abdel Nasser], tape 2 (Cairo: al-Sharq al-Awsat lil-Intaj al-Fanni, n.d.).

25. "Sayyid Mar'i's Political Papers," pp. 366–67.

26. See Crowcroft, "Egypt's Other Nationalists," pp. 253, 276–77.

27. Baghdadi, *Mudhakirat*, p. 344.

28. Ibid., p. 345; Crowcroft, "Egypt's Other Nationalists," p. 277.

29. Baghdadi, *Mudhakirat*, p. 345; "near hysteria" from Abdel Nasser's intelligence chief, Salah Nasr, quoted in Crowcroft, "Egypt's Other Nationalists," p. 278.

30. Hussein diary, November 3, 1956.

31. Baghdadi, *Mudhakirat*, pp. 350–51.

32. Ibid., p. 354. The sum, which reflects the cost of Egypt's aggressive rearmament program beginning in 1955, is equivalent to approximately $295 million (in 1956 dollars), or about $1.6 billion in current dollars.

Part Three: Moscow

1. Khrushchev, *Nikita Khrushchev*, p. 220.

2. Zbigniew Brzezinski, *The Soviet Bloc* (Harvard University Press, 1967), p. 246.

3. See Fursenko and Naftali, *Khrushchev's Cold War*, p. 119; and Mark Kramer, "Change and Upheaval in Eastern Europe, 1953–1956: Intra-Bloc and East-West Dimensions," in Silvio Pons, Sophie Quinn-Judge, and Norman Naimark, eds., *The Cambridge History of Communism*, vol. 2 (Cambridge University Press, forthcoming).

4. Malin's summary, "Working Notes from the Session of the CPSU Central Committee Presidium [Politburo], October 23, 1956. APRF. F. 3, Op. 12, D. 1006, L1.4–4ob.

5. Kramer, "Change and Upheaval."

6. An interesting insight into the deliberations of the Soviet leadership is provided by declassified summary notes of the Politburo meetings at which Hungary was discussed, notes taken by V. N. Malin, head of the General Department of CPSU. It is important to realize that the summaries we have deal with Hungary. There may,

indeed, have been separate meetings devoted to Suez, but there are no documents currently available.

7. "Working Notes from the Session on October 28, 1956," APRF, F. 3, Op. 12, D. 1005, LI. 54–63, translated by Mark Kramer.

8. Malin notes, October 28, 1956.

9. Ibid., p. 121.

10. Cited in Kramer, "Change and Upheaval."

11. "Working Notes of the Session of October 31, 1956," as contained in "*Kak reshalis' voprosy Vengrii*" [How the Hungarian Question Was Decided], *Istoricheskii Arkhiv.*, no. 3 (1996), p. 87.

12. Ibid., p. 131; on the statements see, for example, *Washington Post*, October 31, 1956, p. 7.

13. On the Ali Sabri exchange with Soviet ambassador Kiselev on October 30 and Abdel Nasser's message requesting help, see Fursenko and Naftali, *Khrushchev's Cold War*, pp. 126–27.

14. Heikal, *Sphinx and the Commissar*, p. 71; see also Kennet Love's account of his interview on this topic with Nasser in *Suez, the Twice Fought War*, p. 610.

15. Kiselev to Foreign Ministry, October 30, 1956, in Naumkin, *Russia in the Twentieth Century*, Document No. 313.

16. Heikal, *Sphinx and the Commissar*, p. 71.

17. Veljko Micunovic (then the Yugoslav ambassador to Moscow), *Moscow Diary* (London: Chatto and Windus, 1980), p. 134.

18. "Working Notes of the Session of 4 November 1956," *Istorickeskii Arkhiv* 3 (1996), p. 111.

19. The letters have been reprinted and extracted in many sources. They were also published in both *Pravda* and *Izvestiia* in the November 6 editions. This translation is from the *Current Digest of the Soviet Press (CDSP)*, vol. 8 (1956), no. 45, p. 23–24.

20. *Pravda* and *Izvestiia*. November 6, 1956, p. 1, *CDSP*, p. 24.

21. *Pravda* and *Izvestiia*, November 6, 1956, p. 1, *CDSP*, p. 25. Emphasis added.

22. Sergei Khrushchev, *Nikita Khrushchev*, p. 266.

23. Vassiliev, *Russian Policy in the Middle East*, p. 40.

24. Both quotations from "Telegram from Embassy in the Soviet Union to the Department of State, 6:00 PM." Cited in *FRUS*, vol. 16 (1955–1957), p. 993.

25. Heikal, *Sphinx and the Commissar*, p. 72.

26. *Khrushchev Remembers* (Boston: Little, Brown, 1970), p. 434. Khrushchev confuses the time frame of these events in his memoir. See also similar accounts of Khrushchev's desire to "expose" the United States when he explained his actions to the Yugoslavs. Micunovic, *Moscow Diary*, p. 148.

Part Three: Paris

1. La Documentation Française, *Notes et études documentaires*, "*Documents relatifs au canal de Suez*," No. 2205, August 16, 1956, p. 12.

2. TNA, Foreign Office 800/725 (Selwyn Lloyd memorandum). We have not found French records of this meeting.

3. Ibid.

4. Ibid. But British records indicate that only the first query was later put before the cabinet. Gorst and Johnman, *The Suez Crisis*, p. 91. See also the London chapter in Part Three of this volume.

5. For the slightly more elaborate version of these answers as received by the Israelis, see Bar-On, *The Gates of Gaza*, pp. 229–30.

6. For details see Dayan, *Moshe Dayan*, p. 211; Ely, *Mémoires*, p. 143.

7. Departmental note, "Sur les ingérences égyptiennes en Afrique du Nord," October 20, 1956, *DDF*, 1956, vol. 2, p. 652. This may have been one of the first such shipments from Egypt to the FLN rebels. "Proof positive," Richardson, *When Allies Differ*, p. 63.

8. See Ely, *Mémoires*, p. 149; and Denis Lefebvre, *L'Affaire de Suez* (Paris: Bruno Leprince Editeur, 1997), p. 84. The episode seemed to be an "anarchy of state," with no minister standing up to take responsibility for it. Jean Lacouture, *Pierre Mendès France* (Paris: Seuil, 1981), p. 425.

9. The venue of the secret talks at Sèvres, near Paris, was symbolic of the wartime Resistance background of the French leadership in the Suez affair. It was the villa of a friend of Defense Minister Maurice Bourgès-Maunoury, and the latter had used it as a safe house during the Resistance. This friend was Fernand Bonnier de la Chapelle, uncle of the young man (with the same name) in the "short straw" incident that preceded the assassination of Admiral Francis Darlan, the Vichy governor of North Africa notorious for his collaboration with the Germans. Darlan was assassinated in Algiers on Christmas Eve 1942, after the Americans had landed and occupied the city. It was Fernand who drew the short straw and was designated to "execute" Darlan. Fernand was put to death three days later on orders of General Henri Giraud, the American-picked successor to Darlan as governor of North Africa. Gaullists and French monarchists were variously suspected to be behind the Darlan assassination plot, but the origin of it was never established.

10. Pineau, *1956/Suez*, p. 134. Pineau's account is slightly off in recalling the dates.

11. Ibid., pp. 134–35.

12. Gorst and Johnman, *The Suez Crisis*, pp. 94, 96. On the Israeli concerns, and the agreement that the Royal Air Force's Bomber Command would intervene against Egyptian airfields within 36 hours of the Israeli attack instead of the seventy-two hours initially projected, see Gaujac, *Suez 1956*, pp. 125, 128.

13. Lefebvre, *L'Affaire de Suez*, p. 88.

14. Peres, *Battling for Peace*, p. 111.

15. Gorst and Johnman, *The Suez Crisis*, p. 98; Mordechai Bar-On, "Israeli–French Relations during the Suez Crisis," in *La France et l'opération de Suez de 1956 : Actes d'une table ronde organisée sous la direction de Maurice Vaïsse*, Centre d'Études d'Histoire de la Défense (CEHD) (Paris: ADDIM, 1997), p. 104.

16. Gorst and Johnman, *The Suez Crisis*, p. 98.

17. Ibid., p. 99; also, Kyle, "Britain and the Crisis, 1955–1956," in Louis and Owen, eds., *Suez 1956*, p. 127. An authentic copy of the three-page document, the so-called Sèvres Protocol, finally surfaced in 1996. A television company obtained a photocopy in the possession of the Israeli government. A British participant, Donald Logan, vouched for its authenticity. Guy Mollet's chief biographer, Denis Lefebvre, also found a photocopy of the first two pages of the three-page document in Mollet's papers and a poor photocopy of the third page is in Christian Pineau's papers in the French National Archives. Pineau's memoir contains an accurate paraphrasing of the seven articles, plus a commentary on them. See Denis Lefebvre, *Guy Mollet: Le mal aimé* (Paris: Plon, 1992), p. 254; *Le Nouvel Observateur*, October 17–23, 1996, p. 47; Pineau, *1956/Suez*, pp. 149–52.

18. This authenticated English translation is from Kyle, *Suez*, appendix A, pp. 565–66.

19. Lefebvre, *L'Affaire de Suez*, p. 89; Pineau, *1956/Suez*, p. 154.

20. Gaujac, *Suez 1956*, p. 128; see also Golani, *Israel in Search of a War*, pp. 148, 159.

21. Bar-On, "Israeli–French Relations during the Suez Crisis," pp. 107–08; see also Peres, *Battling for Peace*, p. 113. The Israeli recollections were confirmed by French historian Georgette Elgey, "Le gouvernement Guy Mollet et l'intervention," in *La France et l'opération de Suez de 1956*, pp. 32–33.

22. Ely, *Mémoires*, p. 152–53.

23. Ibid., pp. 104–05.

24. Details about the French deployments are drawn from Service Historique de l'Armée de l'Air (SHAA) archives, oral history of General Edmond Jouhaud; Gaujac, *Suez 1956*, pp. 142–47; and Philippe Vial, "À l'épreuve des faits: La participation de la Marine à la crise de Suez," in *La France et l'opération de Suez de 1956*, pp. 189–92.

25. Ely, *Mémoires*, p. 155; Gaujac, *Suez 1956*, pp. 146–47; Vial, "À l'épreuve des faits," pp. 189–92.

26. Alphand to Paris, October 30, 1956, *DDF*, 1956, vol. 3, pp. 93–94.

27. Ely, *Mémoires*, p. 159.

28. Ibid., p. 161.

29. Ibid., p. 163. Ely acknowledges that reports of the French intelligence service (Service de Documentation Extérieure et de Contre-espionnage [SDECE]) on a deteriorating internal situation in Egypt were exaggerated. Ibid., p. 160.

30. Ibid., pp. 165–66.

31. Editorial note to Dejean to Pineau, November 6, 1956, *DDF*, 1956, vol. 3, p. 210, note 2.

32. Dejean to Paris, November 6, 1956, ibid., p. 209.

33. Memcon, Mollet-Adenauer, November 6, 1956, ibid., p. 233.

34. Ibid., p. 235–37.

35. Ibid., pp. 238; Pineau to Alphand, November 6, ibid., p. 222. When Alphand took this message to Acting Secretary of State Herbert Hoover Jr. the same afternoon, Hoover told him the only solution was to have Britain and France accept unequivocally the UN decisions on Egypt. Alphand to Paris, November 6, 1956,

ibid., p. 223. Later, when Alphand actually met Eisenhower on November 8, the president said he considered that the moment was not particularly appropriate to send a public warning to the USSR. It was necessary to look at things calmly and not lose one's sangfroid. Alphand to Pineau, November 8, 1956, ibid., p. 252.

Part Three: Washington

1. Telcon, Eisenhower-Dulles, October 14, 1956, *FRUS*, vol.16, no. 343.

2. For background, see Lawrence Tal, *Politics, the Military, and National Security in Jordan, 1955–1967* (New York: Palgrave Macmillan, 2002), pp. 21–37; and reports from Embassy Amman on September 29 and from the Jordan desk at State, *FRUS*, vol. 13, nos. 38, 40.

3. *FRUS*, 16, nos. 332, 344, 345, 346. Eisenhower's October 15 memorandum for the record on Jordan (*FRUS*, no. 345) is also at *DDEP*, vol. 17, pp. 2328–30. On the Israeli strike against Qalqilya, see Kyle, *Suez*, pp. 293–94; Neff, *Warriors at Suez*, pp. 330–33.

4. Both the British and Americans were working with a lead coup plotter, Mikhail Ilyan. The British, however, were also working with other groups allied with their friendly government in Iraq led by Nuri el-Said. The CIA may not have been aware of this aspect of the British planning. See Lucas and Morey, "The Hidden 'Alliance,'" p. 109; and Wilford, *America's Great Game*, pp. 247–50, 260.

5. *FRUS*, vol. 16, nos. 347, 348, 349, 350, 351, 352, 353, 354, 356, 358, 363, 367, 368.

6. Memcon, Eisenhower-Dulles-Hoover, October 21, *FRUS*, vol. 16, no. 362.

7. Intelligence Advisory Committee, "Minutes of Meeting Held in IAC Conference Room," October 9, 1956, CIA FOIA, doc. no. CIA-RDP82–00400R0001 00090014–2; *FRUS*, vol. 16, nos. 344, 345, 355.

8. *FRUS*, vol. 16, nos. 357, 359, 360, 362, 364, 365, 370, 376. On the summit proposal as a road not taken toward possible resolution of the crisis, see Kyle, *Suez*, p. 339.

9. CIA Office of Current Intelligence, *Current Intelligence Bulletin* (October 25, 1956), p. 13, CIA FOIA, doc. no. CIA-RDP79T00975A002800050001–5; *FRUS*, vol. 16, nos. 344, 372; Hahn, *Caught in the Middle East*, p. 200; Kyle, *Suez*, pp. 323–24.

10. Legation Budapest to State, October 24, *FRUS*, vol. 25, no. 103; On the outbreak of fighting in Hungary on October 24, see Neff, *Warriors at Suez*, p. 189.

11. *FRUS*, vol. 25, nos. 111, 112, 113, 116, 117, 120, 121.

12. An intelligence report on October 24, the day fighting erupted in Hungary, saw little risk of imminent allied military action in Egypt. See Editorial Note, *FRUS*, vol. 16, no. 369. On the same day Israel began mobilizing, the NSC discussion of the Middle East was focused on Jordan, not Egypt. See Memo of Discussion, 301st NSC Meeting, October 26, *FRUS*, vol. 16, no. 378.

On the administration's distraction by other events, see also Hahn, *The United States, Great Britain, and Egypt, 1945–1956*, pp. 225–29. Eisenhower's health may have played a role, as well. He suffered a serious attack of intestinal pain and diarrhea on October 25 that would last for most of a month, on top of his existing irregular heartbeat, persistent respiratory infection, and abdominal cramps. See, e.g., Nichols, *Eisenhower 1956*, pp. 191–95.

Some accounts of the Suez crisis assert that Allen Dulles had, or may have had, advance knowledge of Anglo-French collusion with Israel over Suez. See Neff, *Warriors at Suez*, pp. 352–53, and von Tunzelmann, *Blood and Sand*, pp. 176–77, both of which cite (among other sources) Leonard Mosley, *Dulles: A Biography of Eleanor, Allen, and John Foster Dulles and Their Family Network* (New York: Dial Press, 1978). Similarly, Douglas Dillon claimed after the crisis to have received such advance knowledge and reported it to Washington. Kyle, *Suez*, p. 310. For differing views of Dillon's recollection, compare *FRUS*, vol. 16, no. 357, with Lucas, *Divided We Stand*, p. 253.

We do not find support for such assertions in the contemporary documentary record of the Suez crisis. See, for example, Charles G. Cogan, "From the Politics of Lying to the Farce at Suez: What the US Knew," *Intelligence and National Security* 13, no. 2 (1998); Kyle, *Suez*; Louis, "An American Volcano"; Nichols, *Eisenhower 1956*, pp. 192–97.

13. *FRUS*, vol. 16, nos. 379, 381, 382, 391.

14. On Eisenhower's and Dulles' focus on Jordan, see *FRUS*, vol. 16, no. 387. On the U.S. effort to organize a Western response in Hungary, see *FRUS*, vol. 25, nos. 123, 124, 125, 126, 127. On presidential politics as a distraction for Eisenhower and Dulles, see Neff, *Warriors at Suez*, p. 355; Nichols, *Eisenhower 1956*, p. 196; Speech by Secretary of State, October 27, 1956, *FRUS*, vol. 25, no. 128; *FRUS*, vol. 16, no. 387, footnote 4.

15. On U.S. suspicions of coordinated military preparations by Britain, France, and Israel: *FRUS*, vol. 16, nos. 386, 396, 397, 398, 399, 400, 402, 403.

On Eisenhower's warnings to Ben-Gurion over the weekend of October 27–28 to refrain from hostilities: Memcon, President and Secretary of State, October 27, *FRUS*, vol. 16, no. 387; Eisenhower to Ben-Gurion, October 27 and 28, ibid., nos. 388, 394, also at *DDEP*, vol. 17, pp. 2336–37, 2338–39; Ben-Gurion's vague reply to Eisenhower's first message is in Embassy Tel Aviv to State, October 28, *FRUS*, vol. 16, no. 401. Eisenhower's public statement is in ibid., October 28, no. 395. For the State Department's war warning to U.S. missions, State to Embassy Cairo, October 27, ibid., no. 390.

16. CIA Information Report to State et al., October 30, CIA FOIA doc. no. CIA-RDP81–00280R001300010066–6; von Tunzelmann, *Blood and Sand*, pp. 216–17; Editorial Note, *FRUS*, vol. 16, no. 402; memcon, Eisenhower-Dulles, October 29, *FRUS*, 25, no. 131.

17. Neff, *Warriors at Suez*, p. 365; Nichols, *Eisenhower 1956*, p. 201.

18. Bevan Sewell, "John Foster Dulles, Illness, Masculinity, and U.S. Foreign Relations, 1953–1961," *International History Review*, vol. 39, no. 4 (2017): 713–47 (Dulles quoted on p. 729). See also Louis, "American Volcano," p. 641; Nichols, *Eisenhower 1956*, pp. 155, 203, 221.

19. *FRUS*, vol. 16, no. 406, footnote 4; memcon, Department of State, ibid., no. 409.

20. JCS to Certain Specified and Unified Commanders, October 29, 1956, ibid., no. 415; see also discussion at evening White House meeting of intelligence reports through the day, ibid., no. 411.

21. Nichols, *Eisenhower 1956*, p. 201.

22. Jean Edward Smith, *Eisenhower in War and Peace* (New York: Random House, 2012), p. 697 (citing a 1964 interview with Eisenhower).

23. Memcon with Eisenhower, October 29, *FRUS*, vol. 16, no. 411.

24. Ibid., no. 412.

25. Ibid., no. 411, note 6.

26. Ben-Gurion to Eisenhower, October 29, ibid., no. 414.

27. Editorial Note, ibid., no. 413; Kyle, *Suez*, p. 354; Neff, *Warriors at Suez*, p. 371; Embassy London to State, October 30, *FRUS*, vol. 16, no. 416; Embassy Paris to State, October 30, ibid., no 417; Mission at UN to State, October 30, ibid., no. 423.

28. Eisenhower to Eden, October 30, ibid., no. 418, and *DDEP*, vol. 17, pp. 2340–42.

29. Eden to Eisenhower, October 30, *FRUS*, vol. 16, no. 421.

30. For the draft message and the quote from an October 30 phone call with Dulles, see *DDEP*, vol. 17, pp. 2344–45.

31. Memcon with Eisenhower, October 30, *FRUS*, vol. 16, no. 419. Some accounts of the Suez war contend that Eisenhower and Dulles were ready to accept the landing of British and French ground forces in Egypt, provided it was done quickly, perhaps thinking this would cause the collapse of Nasser's government. This interpretation cites recollections by Eisenhower to that effect years after leaving office, as well as the former president's later apparent regret that his harsh opposition to Britain's Suez adventure left Nasser in power to cause further trouble in the Middle East. Eisenhower and Dulles also marveled at various points during or just after the fighting that the British and French took so long to put ground forces in Egypt that might have inflicted a crushing military defeat and toppled Nasser from power. Some CIA officials in Washington (such as Robert Amory and perhaps Allen Dulles) also may have initially signaled that they thought Washington might tolerate a rapid Anglo-French ground invasion. For varying interpretations of some of this evidence, see, for example, Doran, *Ike's Gamble*, pp. 191–203; Hahn, *United States, Great Britain, and Egypt*, p. 236; Lucas, *Divided We Stand*, pp. 269–70, 278–88; and Lucas and Morey, "The Hidden 'Alliance,'" p. 110

The evidence indicates initial ambivalence among some at CIA headquarters. But there is little evidence, at the time, that Secretary of State Dulles shared this ambivalence and—fatigued and sick as Dulles was in those days—he was keenly sensitive to the views of his boss. And there is no evidence at all that, at the time, President Eisenhower was ready to accept a major British, French, or even just an Israeli military action, under any circumstances. His unsent letter to Eden of November 1, which never became policy, mentions a possible "temporary" allied presence on Egyptian soil, but only in the context of a subsequent withdrawal. *FRUS*, vol. 16, no. 460. From the start, Eisenhower made his views loud and clear to the circle of top officials. Eisenhower and Dulles were determined from the moment fighting broke out in Egypt to impose a cease-fire and compel a withdrawal of all foreign forces.

During the fighting or immediately afterward, Eisenhower and Dulles did make remarks criticizing the allied failure to force Nasser's overthrow via a quick land invasion, but these statements were expressing incredulity toward incompetence, mixed with their anger at having had to oppose America's allies. See, for example, von Tunzelmann, *Blood and Sand*, pp. 235–37, 249–50, 255, 281–89, 342–43 (detailing the initial Eisenhower and Dulles reactions and fragmented views within CIA); Ambrose, *Eisenhower*, pp. 358–373; Kunz, *The Economic Diplomacy of the Suez Crisis*, pp. 116–152; Kyle, *Suez*, pp. 353–476; Neff, *Warriors at Suez*, pp. 365–415; Nichols, *Eisenhower 1956*, pp. 199–257; Tore T. Petersen, *The Middle East between the Great Powers: Anglo-American Conflict and Cooperation, 1952–7* (New York: St. Martin's Press, 2000), pp. 92–104; Thomas, *Ike's Bluff*, p. 232; and Eisenhower's own account in *The White House Years: Waging Peace* (Garden City, N.Y.: Doubleday, 1965), pp. 58–99.

32. Editorial Note, *FRUS*, vol. 16, no. 420.

33. Neff, *Warriors at Suez*, p. 208; Isaac Alteras, "Eisenhower and the Sinai Campaign of 1956: The First Major Crisis in US-Israeli Relations," in David Tal, ed., *The 1956 War: Collusion and Rivalry in the Middle East* (London: Frank Cass, 2001), p. 30; memcon, Secretary of State and Senator Walter F. George, October 30, *FRUS*, vol. 16, no. 425; memcon, Secretary of State and Senator William F. Knowland, October 30, ibid., no. 426; memcon, President and Secretary of State, October 30, ibid., no. 427.

34. Memcon, Eisenhower-Dulles, October 30, ibid., no. 433; Nichols, *Eisenhower 1956*, p. 207; Kyle, *Suez*, p. 362; Eisenhower to Eden and Mollet, October 30, *FRUS*, vol. 16, no. 430; Mollet to Eisenhower, October 30, ibid., no. 432; Eden to Eisenhower, October 30, ibid., no. 434; memcons, Department of State, October 30, ibid., nos. 431, 437; the Dulles "destruction of our trust in each other" quote is in Kyle, *Suez*, p. 365.

35. Kyle, *Suez*, p. 367; Lucas and Morey, "Hidden 'Alliance,'" p. 110; Wilford, *America's Great Game*, p. 261; Yaqub, *Containing Arab Nationalism*, p. 52. According to former CIA officer Chester Cooper, who was the U.S. liaison officer in London to the British Joint Intelligence Committee, the United States moved to curtail intelligence sharing with the British during the Egypt hostilities, lifting the restrictions only after the Soviet ultimatum of November 5 calling for withdrawal of foreign forces. Cooper, *The Lion's Last Roar*, pp. 198–200.

36. Memcon with Eisenhower, October 30, *FRUS*, vol. 16, no. 435; Thomas, *Ike's Bluff*, p. 221. On the role of U.S. oil planning in the Suez Crisis, see Kunz, *Economic Diplomacy*, pp. 86–88, 102, 123–33.

37. Editorial Note, *FRUS*, vol. 16, no. 439; Kyle, *Suez*, pp. 363–65.

38. Editorial Note, *FRUS*, vol. 25, no. 141; CIA Office of Current Intelligence, Current Intelligence Weekly Summary, November 1, CIA FOIA, doc. no. CIA-RDP79–00927A001000060001–6, Part I, pp. 10–11.

39. Memcon, Vice President and Secretary of State, October 31, *FRUS*, vol. 16, no. 442; Memo of Discussion at 302d NSC, November 1, *FRUS*, 25, no. 152.

40. CIA Office of Current Intelligence, Current Intelligence Weekly Summary, Nov. 1, CIA FOIA, doc. no. CIA-RDP79–00927A001000060001–6, Part I, p. 4 of 11. See also Nichols, *Eisenhower 1956*, p. 208–209; Editorial Note, *FRUS*, vol. 25, no. 141.

41. Editorial Note, ibid., no. 452; Kyle, *Suez*, pp. 380–85; Nichols, *Eisenhower 1956*, pp. 208–13; von Tunzelmann, *Blood and Sand*, pp. 286–88, 303–04.

42. Ambrose, *Eisenhower*, p. 362; Nichols, *Eisenhower 1956*, pp. 214–15; von Tunzelmann, *Blood and Sand*, pp. 289–90.

43. Memcon, Secretary of State and Representative at UN, October 31, *FRUS*, vol. 16, no. 444; Embassy Cairo to Department of State, October 31, ibid., no. 451; Ambrose, *Eisenhower*, pp. 361–62; Kyle, *Suez*, p. 387, 401–02; Nichols, *Eisenhower 1956*, pp. 211–12.

44. Kyle, *Suez*, p. 426; Nichols, *Eisenhower 1956*, pp. 208–15 (Stevenson's remarks are on p. 213); von Tunzelmann, *Blood and Sand*, pp. 269, 286–87; memcon, Vice President and Secretary of State, *FRUS*, vol. 16, no. 442.

45. Memo of Discussion, 302d NSC, November 1, ibid., no. 455.

46. On U.S. suspension of aid to Israel, see ibid., nos. 411, 442, 454, 455, 456, 457, 458, 461, 462, 463; Ambrose, *Eisenhower*, pp. 352–53. On keeping the oil moves against Britain and France quiet, see memcon, Secretary of State and Secretary of Commerce, November 1, ibid., no. 457; Nichols, *Eisenhower 1956*, p. 221. On U.S. Navy harassment of the Anglo-French fleet in the Mediterranean, see Kyle, *Suez*, pp. 411–13; Nichols, *Eisenhower 1956*, p. 217; von Tunzelmann, *Blood and Sand*, pp. 305, 318–19. At the November 1 NSC meeting, Defense Secretary Charles Wilson seemed uncomfortable with the Sixth Fleet's deployment, suggesting that it withdraw from the zone of hostilities once the evacuation of American citizens from the region was complete. Memo of Discussion, 302d NSC, November 1, *FRUS*, vol. 16, no. 455.

47. Memcon, John Foster Dulles–Allen Dulles, November 1, ibid., no. 458.

48. Embassy London to Department of State, November 2, ibid., no. 468. British sources were also alarmed by reports that Eisenhower had withdrawn the antitrust law immunity that U.S. oil companies would require if they were to cooperate in the delivery of emergency oil aid. Three days later, the State Department cabled the U.S. representative to the North Atlantic Council saying reports of the antitrust removal were not accurate. Department of State to Representative on North Atlantic Council, November 5, ibid., no. 513.

49. Nichols, *Eisenhower 1956*, p. 223.

50. Embassy Paris to Department of State, November 1, *FRUS*, vol. 16, no. 466.

51. Ibid., nos. 453, 459.

52. Editorial Note, ibid., no. 467; von Tunzelmann, *Blood and Sand*, pp. 311–12; Kyle, *Suez*, pp. 402–04. On State Department preparations for the UN debate, see *FRUS*, vol.16, nos. 449, 450, 456, 461.

53. Ambrose, *Eisenhower*, p. 365; Kyle, *Suez*, pp. 412–13; Nichols, *Eisenhower 1956*, pp. 227, 230, 232.

54. Memcon, Secretary of State and Director CIA, November 1, *FRUS*, vol. 16, no. 458.

55. Embassy Cairo to Department of State, November 2, ibid., no. 472.

56. Memcon, Department of State, November 3, ibid., no. 478.

57. Embassy Tel Aviv to Department of State, midnight November 3/4, ibid., no. 488; Department of State to Embassy Tel Aviv, November 4, ibid., no. 490.

58. Nichols, *Eisenhower 1956*, p. 237; *FRUS*, vol. 16, no. 506, footnote 3; Embassy Damascus to Department of State, November 3, *FRUS*, vol. 13, no. 336.

59. CIA Office of Current Intelligence, Weekly Intelligence Summary, November 8, CIA FOIA, doc. no. CIA-RDP79–00927A001000070001–05, Part II, p. 7 of 17.

60. Embassy London to Department of State, November 2, *FRUS*, vol. 16, no. 468. Memcon, Executive Office Building, November 4, ibid., no. 491; Yaqub, *Containing Arab Nationalism*, pp. 52–53.

61. On the deterioration of events in Hungary from November 1 to 3, see von Tunzelmann, *Blood and Sand*, pp. 291–356; Nichols, *Eisenhower 1956*, pp. 216–37.

62. Eisenhower to "Swede" Hazlett, November 2, *FRUS*, vol. 16, no. 475, also *DDEP*, vol. 17, pp. 2353–57 (quote on p. 2355).

63. Hoover to Dulles and memcon of White House meeting, November 2, *FRUS*, vol. 16, nos. 469, 470. For a skeptical view of Eisenhower's ideas, see Nichols, *Eisenhower 1956*, pp. 228–30.

64. Ibid., nos. 471, 473, 474, 476, 477, 479, 480, 481, 482, 484, 487, 492. These sources also detail how Eisenhower directed the State Department to push for the establishment of two UN committees, one on the Suez Canal dispute and one on the Arab-Israeli conflict, to develop permanent settlements of those issues after the current fighting had ended. The president thought this might strengthen American credibility in the crisis by signaling a willingness to address its fundamental causes. See also Eisenhower to Nehru, November 6, *DDEP*, vol. 17, pp. 2368–69 (the two leaders had been corresponding throughout the crisis).

65. Von Tunzelmann, *Blood and Sand*, pp. 339–40.

66. Editorial Note, *FRUS*, vol. 16, no. 485; Nichols, *Eisenhower 1956*, pp. 235–36.

67. Kyle, *Suez*, pp. 436–38.

68. CIA Office of Current Intelligence, Current Intelligence Bulletin, November 6, CIA FOIA, doc. no. CIA-RDP79T00975A002800150001–4; Neff, *Warriors at Suez*, pp. 386–87; von Tunzelmann, *Blood and Sand*, pp. 357–62, 386–87.

69. *FRUS*, 16, nos. 492, 493, 494, 496, 497, 498.

70. Kyle, *Suez*, pp. 444–56; von Tunzelmann, *Blood and Sand*, p. 337–96.

71. Eden to Eisenhower, November 5, *FRUS*, vol. 16, no. 499.

72. Editorial Note, ibid., no. 514.

73. Memo of Conference with President, November 5, ibid., no. 500.

74. Department of State to Representative on North Atlantic Council, November 5, ibid., no. 513. The necessity of West European oil going through Britain and France was a topic of discussion at the weekly National Security Council three days later. Memo of Discussion, 303d NSC, November 8, ibid., no. 554.

75. Memcon, Department of State, November 5, ibid., no. 508.

76. Bulganin to Eisenhower, November 5, ibid., no. 505.

77. Editorial Note, ibid., no. 504.

78. Kyle, *Suez*, pp. 456–57.

79. Embassy Moscow to Department of State, November 5, *FRUS*, vol. 16, nos. 503, 506.

80. Memo of Conference with President, November 5, ibid., no. 509.

81. White House News Release, November 5, ibid., no. 512; Ambrose, *Eisenhower*, p. 368; Nichols, *Eisenhower 1956*, pp. 245–46.

82. SNIE, November 6, ibid., no. 521.

83. Hahn, *Caught in the Middle East*, p. 205.

84. Memo of Conference with President, November 6, ibid., no. 518; Eisenhower, *Waging Peace*, p. 91.

85. Memcon, Department of State, November 6, ibid., no. 523.

86. Memcon, Department of State, November 6, ibid., no. 524; Nichols, *Eisenhower 1956*, pp. 250–51.

87. Embassy Moscow to Department of State, November 6, ibid., no. 520.

88. Eisenhower, *Waging Peace*, p. 91; Nichols, *Eisenhower 1956*, pp. 252–53. On the twenty-four-hour delay getting U-2 information to Washington, see Pedlow and Walzenbach, *CIA and U-2*, p. 120.

89. Condit, *The Joint Chiefs of Staff and National Policy*, vol. 6, p. 189; Eisenhower, *Waging Peace*, p. 91; Nichols, *Eisenhower 1956*, pp. 252–54.

90. Transcript of Telcon, Eisenhower-Eden, November 6, *FRUS*, vol. 16, no. 525.

91. Eisenhower to Eden, November 6, ibid., no. 527; also in Boyle, ed., *The Eisenhower-Eden Correspondence*, pp. 184–85.

Part Three: London

1. Lucas, *Divided We Stand*, p. 237.

2. Nutting, *Lesson*, p. 95.

3. Kyle, *Suez*, p. 301. There is no existing record of this paper. Its content was related to Keith Kyle by Sir Archibald Ross.

4. Lucas, *Divided*, p. 238.

5. Lloyd memo, October 18, 1956, TNA, PREM, 11/1126; Lucas, *Divided*, p. 239; Lloyd, memo on the diplomatic exchanges and negotiations from the Egyptian nationalization of the Suez Canal Company on July 26, 1956, to the Outbreak of Hostilities between Israel and Egypt on October 29, 1956, TNA, PREM 11/1126.

6. Lucas, *Divided*, p. 240.

7. Jebb to Lloyd, October 17, 1956; Eden to Lloyd, October 19, 1956, TNA, PREM 11/1126.

8. Kyle, *Suez*, p. 302. Nutting did in fact hand in his resignation on October 31, but he agreed to postpone a public announcement until November 5.

9. Cabinet Meeting (56) 71st Conclusions, October 18, 1956, TNA, CAB, 128/30.

10. Kyle, *Suez*, pp. 309–10.

11. Dayan, *Story of My Life*, pp. 218–19.

12. Memo by Sir Donald Logan, "Suez, Meeting at Sèvres, 22–25 October 1956,"

dated October 24, 1986, given by Logan to the author, December 7, 1996; author conversation with Keith Kyle, December 7, 1996.

13. Kyle, *Suez*, p. 322. According to Kyle, Eden's admission of contacts with the Israelis appears in only one version of the cabinet minutes available at the Public Record Office. Other copies of the minutes, including that in the author's possession, read "it now seemed likely" that the Israelis would not act alone. Mention of the meeting with the Israelis has been eliminated.

14. Lloyd, Top Secret Memo, October 24, 1956, TNA, PREM 11/1126.

15. Cabinet Meeting (56) 73rd Conclusions, October 24, 1956, TNA, CAB 128/30/73 (emphasis added).

16. Cabinet Meeting (56) 73rd Conclusions, Confidential Annex, October 24, 1956, TNA, CAB 128/30.

17. Author conversation with Sir Donald Logan, December 7, 1996; English translation printed in Kyle, *Suez*, appendix A, pp. 565–66. The full text of the protocol is in the Paris chapter in Part Three of this volume.

18. Cabinet Meeting (56) 74th Conclusions, October 25, 1956, TNA, CAB 128/30.

19. Egypt Committee. "Military Implications of Mounting Operation Musketeer," Memorandum by Chiefs of Staff, Egypt Committee (56) 63rd Meeting, October 25, 1956, TNA, PREM 11/1100; Kyle, *Suez*, p. 335.

20. Lucas, *Divided*, p. 255.

21. Nutting, *Lesson*, p. 107.

22. Kyle, *Suez*, p. 335; Lucas, *Divided*, p. 251.

23. Admiral Sir Manley Power, unpublished autobiography, p. 100, Churchill College Archives, Cambridge, quoted in Kyle, *Suez*, p. 341.

24. Embassy London to State, October 30, 1956, *FRUS*, vol. 16, no. 416.

25. Cabinet Meeting (56) 75th Conclusions, October 29, 1956, TNA, CAB 128/30.

26. The delivery of the ultimatum from the Israeli embassy in London to the Israeli government began to look like a comedy of errors. The ultimatum was issued at 4:15 GMT. Five hours later a representative of the Israeli Foreign Ministry phoned the British embassy to ask where the note was. Time was crucial given the scant 12-hour period for a response. The problem was that the note had been translated into Hebrew and then encoded, then transmitted. Upon arrival in Jerusalem it needed to be deciphered, but couldn't at first be delivered due to a blackout. The Israelis were given the British embassy's copy of the ultimatum, but it took another hour to get the proper response from a Foreign Ministry staffer unaware of the Sèvres Protocol. See Kyle, *Suez*, pp. 367–68.

27. Eisenhower to Eden, October 30, 1956, *FRUS*, vol. 16, no. 418.

28. Eden to Eisenhower, October 30, 1956, TNA, FO 800/741.

29. Eisenhower to Eden, October 30, 1956, *FRUS*, vol. 16, no. 424.

30. Eden to Eisenhower, Prime Minister's Personal Telegram T485/56, October 30, 1956, TNA, PREM 11/1105.

31. Coulson to Lloyd, October 30, 1956, TNA, FO 800/741.

32. Foreign Office to Washington, No. 5052 and 5053, October 31, 1956; Washington to Foreign Office, No. 2218, October 31, 1956, TNA, FO 371/ 120832; Kunz, *Diplomacy*, p. 127; Coulson to Lloyd, October 31, 1956, TNA, PREM 11/1105.

33. Kyle, *Suez*, pp. 372–74.

34. Great Britain, House of Commons, Parliamentary Debates (Hansard), vol. 558, October 31, 1956, cols. 1441–572.

35. Lucas, *Divided*, p. 273.

36. Egypt Committee (56) 37th Meeting, Confidential Annex, Minute 4, November 1, 1956, TNA, PREM 11/1104; Eden to Mollet, November 1, 1956, TNA, FO 800/727.

37. Kyle, *Suez*, pp. 388–89.

38. Ibid., p. 389.

39. Mountbatten to Eden, November 2, 1956, TNA, PREM 11/1090.

40. Cabinet Meeting (56), 77th Conclusions, November 2, 1956, 4:30 p.m., TNA, CAB 128/30/77.

41. Foreign Office to Paris, November 3, 1956, TNA, PREM 11/1105; Lucas, *Divided*, p. 283.

42. Some Americans who sympathized with London were impatient about the delay in Britain's military operations. Robert Amory, the CIA's chief analyst as deputy director of intelligence, telephoned Chester Cooper, the CIA liaison with the Joint Intelligence Committee. "Tell your friends to comply with the God-damn ceasefire or go ahead with the God-damn invasion. Either way, we'll back them up if they do it fast. What we can't stand is their God-damn hesitation, waltzing while Hungary is burning." Lucas, *Divided*, p. 282. There is no evidence that Amory was speaking for his bosses or that Cooper actually told his "friends" anything that influenced British government thinking, but the episode is an example of how many Americans were ambivalent about the situation or were privately rooting for the British to prevail.

43. Egypt Committee (56) 38th Meeting, Confidential Annex, November 4, 1956, TNA, PREM 11/1105.

44. Kyle, *Suez*, p. 440.

45. Cabinet Meeting (56) 79th Conclusions, November 4, 1956, TNA, PREM 11/1105; Lucas, p. 286.

46. Kyle, *Suez*, p. 442; von Tunzelman, *Blood and Sand*, p. 311.

47. Kyle, *Suez*, p. 451.

48. Aneurin Bevan quoted in ibid.

49. Ibid, p. 452.

50. Eden to Eisenhower, November 5, 1956, TNA, FO 800/726.

51. Moscow to Foreign Office, November 4, 1956, TNA, PREM 11/1105; Noble Frankland (ed.), *Documents on International Affairs, 1956* (London: Royal Institute of International Affairs, 1957), pp. 288–92; von Tunzelman, *Blood and Sand*, p. 343; New York to Foreign Office, November 6, 1956, TNA, PREM 11/1105.

52. Easter, "Spying on Nasser," p. 829.

53. Kyle, *Suez*, p. 458, p. 34; SNIE, November 6, 1956, *FRUS*, vol. 16, no. 521.

54. Von Tunzelman, *Blood and Sand*, p. 337, p. 342.

55. Easter, "Spying on Nasser," p. 830.

56. Von Tunzelman, *Blood and Sand*, p. 343; Selwyn Lloyd, *Suez 1956: A Personal Account* (London: Jonathan Cape, 1978), p. 209. What the cabinet did not know was that Macmillan's figures were hugely inflated; the next day he learned that losses for the week were only $85 million. Whether Macmillan deliberately falsified the numbers to obtain the cease-fire or whether he merely panicked is unclear, but Britain desperately needed U.S. support. The sterling crisis was as good a reason as any to argue for accepting the cease-fire.

57. Cabinet Meeting (56) 80th Conclusions, November 6, 1956, TNA, CAB 128/30; Kunz, *Diplomacy*, pp. 131–33; Kyle, *Suez*, pp. 464–465; Horne, *Macmillan*, p. 440.

58. Pineau, *Suez 1956*, p. 191.

59. Embassy London to State, November 6, 1956, *FRUS*, vol. 16, no. 519.

60. The American transcript of the November 6 telephone call, *FRUS*, vol. 16, no. 525.

61. Kyle, *Suez*, pp. 467–68.

Final Observations: No End of Lessons

1. A useful early reconstruction of the decisions around the creation of the UN Emergency Force, though without access to the input that Eisenhower was giving to the process, is in Gabriella Rosner, *The United Nations Emergency Force* (Columbia University Press, 1963). In the depths of the war, on November 3, Nasser—through Heikal—indicated his readiness to accept a "UN police force to guarantee Arab-Israeli border." Hare to State, November 3, *FRUS*, vol. 16, no. 486.

2. Eisenhower to Hazlett, November 2, and Eisenhower to Churchill, November 27, *DDEP*, vol. 17, pp. 2356–57, 2412–14.

3. Alexander Cadogan quoted in James, *Anthony Eden*, pp. 246, 412.

4. Kemal Rifa'at to Ahmed Hamrouche, in Hamrouche, *Shuhud Thawrat Yulyu* (vol. 4 of *Qissat Thawrat Yulyu*) [Witnesses to the July Revolution] (Cairo: Maktabat Madbuli, 1984), p. 328.

5. See Elie Podeh, "Regaining Lost Pride: The Impact of the Suez Affair on Egypt and the Arab World," in David Tal, ed., *The 1956 War: Collusion and Rivalry in the Middle East* (London: Frank Cass, 2001), pp. 209–24.

6. Nasser quoted in Kyle, *Suez: Britain's End of Empire*, p. 574.

7. Peres with Landau, *Ben-Gurion*, p. 171.

8. A sharply analyzed account of the final bargaining is Mordechai Gazit, "The 1956 Sinai Campaign: David Ben-Gurion's Policy on Gaza, the Armistice Agreement and French Mediation," *Israel Affairs* 6, nos. 3, 4 (2000): 43–67.

9. Bar-On, *Moshe Dayan*, p. 105.

10. Micunovic, *Moscow Diary*, p. 157.

11. See *Khrushchev Remembers* (Boston: Little, Brown, 1970), p. 435; for the public praise from Anastas Mikoyan, see Zubok and Pleshakov, *Inside the Kremlin's Cold*

War, pp. 191–92; for the private condemnation, including by Mikoyan, see Fursenko and Naftali, *Khrushchev's Cold War*, p. 142 and note 15.

12. Kyle, *Suez*, p. 573 (quoting Mohamed Heikal).

13. See Pinkus, "Atomic Power to Israel's Rescue," p. 104–38.

14. *DDF*, 1956, vol. 3, pp. 271–72.

15. Pineau, *1956/Suez*, p. 191. Though Adenauer argued during the November 6 meeting in favor of a strengthened Europe, the quoted statement from Pineau is not included in the official French account of the Adenauer meeting.

16. *France Observateur*, August 2, 1956, pp. 4–5.

17. Charles de Gaulle, *Lettres, Notes et Carnets*, vol. 7 (Paris: Plon, 1985), pp. 297–98.

18. A good summary of the transition is Richard Damms, "In Search of 'Some Big, Imaginative Plan': The Eisenhower Administration and American Strategy in the Middle East after Suez," in Simon Smith, ed., *Reassessing Suez 1956: New Perspectives on the Crisis and Its Aftermath* (Aldershot: Ashgate, 2008), pp. 179–94. For more detailed surveys, compare Peter Hahn, *The United States, Great Britain, and Egypt, 1945–1956*; Yaqub, *Containing Arab Nationalism*; and Nathan Citino, *From Arab Nationalism to OPEC: Eisenhower, King Saud, and the Making of US-Saudi Relations* (Indiana University Press, 2002).

Index